A Geography of Contemporary Britain

David Flint
David Lambert and Graham Butt
Rex Walford John Whomsley

'The north/south divide seems to be based around money and class rather than actual geography ...'

Jonathan Powell, Head of Serials, BBC, talking about EastEnders.

Longman Group UK Limited,
Longman House, Burnt Mill, Harlow,
Essex CM20 2JE, England
and Associated Companies throughout the world.

© Longman Group UK Limited 1990
All rights reserved; no part of this publication
may be reproduced, stored in a retrieval system,
or transmitted in any form or by any means, electronic,
mechanical, photocopying, recording, or otherwise,
without the prior written permission of the Publishers
or a licence permitting restricted copying issued by
the copyright Licensing Agency Ltd, 33–34 Alfred
Place, London WC1E 7DP

First published 1990

Set in 10/12 point Palatino
Produced by Longman Group (FE) Limited.
Printed in Hong Kong

ISBN 0 582 33202 8

Acknowledgements
We are indebted to the Controller of Her Majesty's Stationery Office for permission to reproduce an extract from *Statement by the Secretary of State for Energy to the House of Commons* 25th February, 1988.

We are grateful to the following for permission to reproduce photographs and other copyright material:
Ace Photo Agency, plate 14; Aerofilms Ltd, plates 9, 31, 47, pages 12, 13 *below* 39, 71, 82 *above*, 87 *left*, 87 *right*, 102, 130; Architectural Press, page 192 (photo: Nicholas Sargeant); Barnaby's Picture Library, page 15; Bidwells Chartered Surveyors, Cambridge, plate 5; David Blunkett MP, page 152 *below*; British Coal, plate 41, pages 42 *above left*, 173; British Gas plc, plates 44, 45; Confederation of British Industry, page 152 *above*; British Petroleum plc, pages 179 *left*, 179 *right*; British Rail, page 201; British Telecom, plate 48, page 208; BSC Consett, pages 113, 114; Camera Press, pages 4 (photo: Victor Patterson), 5 (photo: Herbie Knott); Cameron Hall Developments Ltd, page 104 *below*; J Allan Cash, plates 19, 23, page 105; Celtic Picture Agency, page 117 (photo: M J Thomas); Central Electricity Generating Board, plate 43, page 186; Commission for the New Towns, page 110; Countryside Commission, plate 11 (photo: Jerry Brabbs), pages 65, 72 (photo: Charles Meecham); DER, page 207; Ercol Furniture Ltd, page 43 *above left*; The Commission of the European Communities, pages 214–215 *below*; Farmers Weekly, plate 10, pages 30 *below*, 32; Firestone, plate 27; Forestry Commission, pages 42 *below*, 43 *below*; Friends of the Earth Ltd, page 31 *right*; First Garden City Heritage Museum, pages 108–9, 133; GEC Transportation Projects Limited, page 205; Chas E Goad Ltd, page 103; Bryan Gould MP, page 167; Simon Gourlay, page 30 *above*; Sally & Richard Greenhill, plate 6, pages 21, 83; *The Guardian*, page 158; Guardian News Service Ltd for articles 'The boom town that turned into a loser' in *The Guardian* 12.2.86, 'Chips boost creates 1000 jobs' in *The Guardian* 6.3.84, 'Rhondda hopes to mine a seam of history' in *The Guardian* & 'Severn barrage to generate electricity' in *The Guardian*; Handford Photograph, page 138; Cartoon by Honesett, page 197; Hulton-Deutsch, pages 20, 89 *above*, 94 *above left*; International Wool Secretariat, page 140; The ISE Photo Library – London, plates 17, 29; A.F. Kersting, page 18; Lakeland Photographic, plate 2; Landscape Only, plate 16 (photo: Charlie Waite); Bob Langrish, page 42 *above right*; London Borough of Hounslow, Local Collection, Hounslow Library Centre, page 135; London Borough of Lambeth, page 85 *above*; London Dockland Development Corporation, pages 94 *above right*, 94 *below*, 97; London Transport Museum, page 86; Mid Glamorgan County Council, page 163 (Peter Gill Associates); pictures supplied by The Creative Company on behalf of Milton Keynes Development Corporation, page 193; John Murray Ltd for extracts from poems 'Middlesex' & 'The Planster's Dream' by John Betjeman from *Collected Poems*; The National Trust, Wallington Hall, plate 25 (photo: Bridgeman Art Library); Network, plates 1 (photo: John Sturrock), 4 (photo: John Sturrock), pages 185 *right* (photo: John Sturrock), 213 (photo: John Sturrock), 214–215 *above* (photo: Mike Abrahams); News (UK) Ltd for article 'Dreams borne by desolation' in *Today* newspaper 20.3.86; Northern Ireland Tourist Board, page 3; The Observer Ltd for article 'Incomer's threat to Dales' in *The Observer* 28.8.83. Ordnance Survey, Crown Copyright, reproduced by permission of the Controller of Her Majesty's Stationery Office, (c) Crown Copyright, pages 82 *below*, 87 *below*, 89 *below*; Pacemaker Press International Ltd, page 2; Picturepoint Ltd, plate 24; Railway Museum, Swindon, plate 30; Rex Features, page 215; Rover Group plc, plate 28, page 143; Royal Air Force Museum, plate 20; Ryton Gravel Company Ltd, page 53; Sealand Aerial Photography, plates 22, 32, page 204; Sefton Photo Library, plates 7, 26; Severn Trent Water, page 59; W A Sharman, plate 46; Shell UK, plate 42; Shetland Islands Council, page 179 *above*; Shotton Paper, page 43 *above right*; Spectrum Colour Library, plates 12, 18; Norman Tebbit MP, page 166; Telefocus, plate 48; Tesco, plate 21, page 104; Thorpe Park, Surrey, plate 15; William Waldegrave, Minister for Housing & Planning, page 85 *below*; Rex Walford, page 89 *centre*; The Rt Hon Peter Walker MBE MP, page 185 *left*; A C Waltham, Trent Polytechnic, Nottingham, page 13 *above*; Paul Wigens, page 31 *left*; Woodmansterne, plate 3; Yorkshire Dales National Park, page 51.
We are unable to trace the copyright holders of illustrative material on pages 6, 17, 81 and plate 13 and would appreciate receiving any information that would enable us to do so.

Contents

Part I Introduction   1

1 Britain: three worlds or four?   1
2 Britain's physical environment   10
3 Britain's population   15

Part II Britain's rural environment   26   David Flint

4 Agriculture   27
5 Forestry   42
6 Mining and quarrying   49
7 Water supply   55
8 Leisure and the countryside   64

Part III Britain's urban areas   76

9 How a conurbation grows   79
10 Shopping   100
11 Other urban areas   108
12 Urban living? Country living?   115

Part IV Britain's industry   122   David Lambert and Graham Butt

13 Traditional manufacturing industries   125
14 Twentieth-century manufacturing industries   133
15 The second industrial revolution   146
16 The role of Government   160

Part V Britain's energy and communications   170   John Whomsley

17 The case for coal   172
18 Oil and gas   176
19 Electricity, nuclear power, and the future   184
20 Transport and communications   196

Part VI Conclusion   212

21 Beyond Britain's borders   212

Index   218

Preface

Any book which seeks to provide an account of the 'geography of contemporary Britain' runs the risk of having its material made historic as it goes through the processes of production. Nevertheless the new demands of both GCSE and the National Curriculum (in which geography is a foundation subject) make it clear that a considerable knowledge of the home nation is a priority objective in the brave new world which is following the 1988 Education Act.

This book seeks to provide a basis of content to the British scene through thematic approaches supplemented by case-studies. Locally-based work, and the study and use of magazines, newspapers, radio and television will be necessary to put it in proper context.

The development of geographical skills and techniques is also encouraged through the practical exercises provided; these are largely concentrated in the database and workbase pages.

The text is punctuated by a series of 'contrasting viewpoints' contributed specially for the book by well-known public figures. The presentation of opposed opinions does not always reflect the variety and complexity of views on an issue, but it will, we hope, be a clear indication of the existence and importance of different 'attitudes and values' on important topics.

R.W.

Part I Introduction

Chapter 1
Britain: Three worlds or four?

Newspapers, radio and television often use the term **Third World**. Countries of the Third World are usually considered to have the characteristics shown in Fig. 1.1(a):

The phrase Third World assumes that there is a **First World** and a **Second World** though these terms are not used so often.

The First World is generally taken to be the countries of Western Europe and North America (sometimes also called the 'free world').

The Second World is generally taken to be the countries of Eastern Europe and the USSR (sometimes also called the 'Communist World').

The First and Second World countries differ in their forms of government but share similar characteristics which are the *opposite* of those described above. The First and Second World are often called **developed** countries, and the Third World countries **develo*ping*** or **less-developed** countries (LDCs).

In recent years, Britain's standard of living has not risen as fast as many other countries. Though its Gross National Product (GNP) is relatively high, manufacturing industries have declined and even disappeared, creating job losses and long-term unemployment. These signs have also occurred in some other European countries (e.g. Belgium and France). Countries which were the leaders in industrial development during the nineteenth century industrial revolution now suffer the handicap of 'old' industrial plant. Such countries may be the new **Fourth World**.

This book will explore some of the features of modern Britain and its prospects for the future. There are hopeful signs as well as gloomy ones.

- a low standard of living
- a high percentage of workers in domestic agriculture
- a high rate of infant deaths
- a low rate of literacy

Figure 1.1(a)

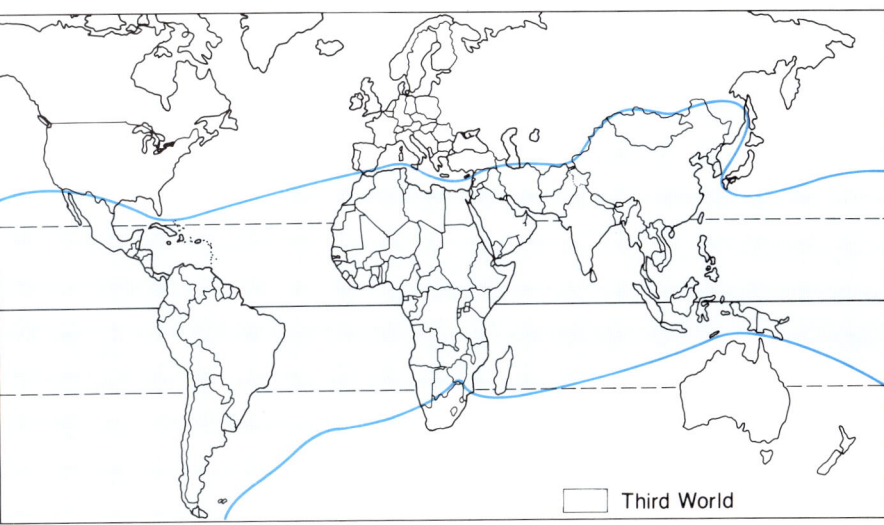

Figure 1.1(b) The tinted area represents the Third World in broad, general terms

Britain – one nation or many?

The British Isles lie on the continental shelf of Europe, separated from the mainland of the European continent by the shallow waters of the English Channel and the North Sea. The waters of the Atlantic Ocean are twenty times deeper than the English Channel.

The British Isles consist of:

- the island of Great Britain – consisting of the countries of England, Scotland and Wales;
- the island of Ireland – consisting of the countries of Northern Ireland (Ulster) and Eire (the Republic of Ireland).

There are also several smaller groups of islands around the coasts of these two major islands. Of these, the Isle of Man and the Channel Islands are separate in government in some respects; they have their own domestic Parliaments and can levy their own taxes and make their own laws.

England, Scotland, Wales and Northern Ireland form the **United Kingdom**, which is governed by the Parliament at Westminster in London.

From 1690 to 1921 all of Ireland was part of the United Kingdom, but in 1921 the south of Ireland (predominantly a Roman Catholic area) separated to form its own 'Catholic state', following a period in which there were many civil disturbances.

The House of Commons at Westminster contains MPs from England, Scotland, Wales and Northern Ireland, but the four countries remain distinct in certain ways:

- **Scotland** has a separate education system, a separate legal system and its own forms of local government;
- **Wales** has special provision in law for the maintenance of the Welsh language (e.g. railway-station names, road signs and official forms are shown in two languages);
- **Northern Ireland** has some separate laws and a distinct pattern of schooling in which most pupils go to either Protestant or Catholic church schools.

Figure 1.2 Protestants march through an area of recen[t]

How united is the United Kingdom?

Wales was united to England in 1536 when King Henry VIII assumed rule over both countries; he was himself the son of a Welshman. The union was a peaceful one. Scotland was united with England in 1603 when James I came to the throne of England by succession; he was already King James VI of Scotland. Ireland was united with England by King William III – largely through a military triumph at the Battle of the Boyne in 1690.

Since 1690 the United Kingdom has remained united, though in Scotland and Wales there have always been groups of people ('nationalists') who have campaigned for the independence of their own country. In Northern Ireland a largely Roman Catholic minority has sought to reunite their nation with Southern Ireland, since the latter became independent in 1921. The majority of people in Northern Ireland ('Loyalists' or 'Unionists') has favoured the country remaining part of the United Kingdom.

The views of nationalists vary on the amount of independence which they seek and the means by which they seek it. Some Scottish Nationalists and Welsh Nationalists (Plaid Cymru) sit in the House of Commons at Westminster and try to change things by Parliamentary means; Nationalists in Northern Ireland do not usually take up their seats at Westminster, if elected to Parliament.

Figure 1.3 The hexagonal basalt blocks of the Giant's Causeway, one of Northern Ireland's most famous tourist attractions

The Ulster question

Since 1970 there has been much unrest in Northern Ireland and the media carry news about this on most days of every week. It is as well to remember that many people lead quite normal lives in Ulster and that the dramatic reporting of 'incidents' on television and in the Press can sometimes lead to a misguided view of what life is really like in a particular place.

Northern Ireland, the old Irish province of Ulster, became part of the United Kingdom in 1921 after the southern part of Ireland had negotiated its independence. Most Roman Catholics lived in the South, though there was a minority (about one-third of the population) in Ulster. But the Protestants of Ulster strongly wanted to stay within the United Kingdom, owing allegiance to the British Crown.

At the time it suited the South to accept the division because it made it easier to create a new nation based on 'Catholic principles' – including strong disapproval of divorce, and of any form of artificial birth-control.

The actual proposals for boundaries in 1921 were subject to much political bargaining and the borders eventually agreed were a compromise. Many Catholics living in towns like Londonderry and Strabane found themselves on the 'wrong' side of the border, and vice-versa for Protestants in places like Dundalk.

This did not cause immediate problems, but as the years passed the Catholic minority in the North began to feel that there was discrimination

CONTRASTING VIEWPOINTS

'Should Ulster remain part of the United Kingdom'

John Hume, Leader of Social Democratic Labour Party of Northern Ireland.

Northern Ireland was created in an attempt to put the failures of the relationships between Britain and Ireland into one corner of these islands. In doing so it reinforced the siege mentality of the minority British (mainly Protestant) tradition in Ireland which forms Northern Unionism. It also created an Irish Catholic minority trapped inside the northern state which discriminated against them. It could not be a solution to the centuries' long British-Irish problem.

The challenge is not to confine our search for 'solutions' to the narrow grounds of Northern Ireland because this ignores the real dimensions of the problem. Rather we must provide a framework which matches the dimensions of the problem. That means a British-Irish framework as provided by the Anglo-Irish Agreement of 1985.

The two main traditions in Northern Ireland have different identities. Many countries contain differences but most have learned not to push those differences to the point of division. The essence of unity and stability is the acceptance of diversity – the realisation that difference is not a threat.

This requires full equality – that is the only basis on which reconciliation can take place. By recognising and respecting the identities of both traditions in an international agreement, the ground is laid for equality and new relationships. The task now is to break down the barriers of division in our community. Working in partnership to deal with the affairs of the community in the north is one way of building the trust and confidence, born of working together, between our different traditions, in order to replace the prejudice and distrust that have disfigured us for centuries. Out of such common effort will evolve the new relationships, not only within Northern Ireland but within Ireland and Britain, that will finally lay to rest our ancient quarrels.

against it when seeking jobs and in public life in general. Its protests reached a climax in the 1970s. A minority of Catholics in the North now actively seek to reunify Ulster with the South and some (supporters of the Irish Republican Army) are prepared to use violence to achieve this. This has led to equally extreme viewpoints and actions being taken up by 'Loyalists' in response.

Both Protestants and Catholics have strong historic and religious traditions and show these openly in the summer months by marches. Such marches are sometimes the focus for demonstrations, shouting-matches and violence. The British Army has been extensively involved in trying to 'keep the peace' in Ulster since 1974.

In 1985 the Governments of the United Kingdom and Eire attempted to improve the unsettled state of Ulster by setting up an 'Anglo-Irish' agreement and giving the Eire Government a consultative role in some aspects of Ulster politics. Though this pleased the Catholic minority, it infuriated the Protestant majority more than expected, even to the point of them openly speaking about 'Independence' from the rest of the United Kingdom, rather than the preservation of the Union.

Rev Dr Ian R K Paisley, MP, MEP
Leader of the Democratic Unionist Party (DUP) of Northern Ireland

The wide and increasing divergence between North and South in Ireland was given permanent expression with the secession of the twenty-six counties in 1921 after the rebellion of 1916. Northern Ireland naturally opted to remain within the nation of which she had been an undoubted part for centuries. Thus the Border was, and still is, the inevitable consequence of differences in natural allegiance, outlook and temperament between the two peoples in Ireland. The notion, therefore, that partition was imposed on a united, homogeneous, Ireland by the British Government against the will of a united Irish people is utterly wrong.

From the time of "The Ulster Plantation" in the early years of the 17th Century, when Scots immigrants settled in large numbers in six northern counties, the two parts of Ireland have developed along distinct and separate lines: the South clinging to its exclusively Catholic and Gaelic culture, traditions and way of life; North holding to a way of life which reflected its British and Protestant heritage.

The view that Northern Ireland today is "held" against its will within the United Kingdom by the British Government and British troops is totally and absolutely false. Despite incessant agitation from those who seek to force an all-Ireland Republic and in spite of the long campaign of IRA terrorism aimed at shaking the resolve of Northern Ireland, the Province has freely and constantly declared its unambiguous wish to remain part of the United Kingdom in every election since 1921. That determination was most clearly expressed in the Referendum in 1973 when all voters in Northern Ireland were asked whether they wished the Province to remain part of the United Kingdom or to be joined with the Irish Republic outside the United Kingdom. In this poll 591,820 or 98.9% of those voting supported the Union, only 6,463 or 1.08% voted for unity with the Republic.

Northern Ireland's constitutional status was radically altered without reference to the Ulster people when the Anglo/Irish Agreement was signed in November 1985. In effect, a form of joint authority between London and Dublin was established for the Province. Unless that Agreement is superceded by an alternative Agreement, capable of support by the majority of the Ulster people, the Ulster people will be forced to decide where their future lies. That course will never be union with the Irish Republic.

The divisions between the two Irish communities are deep and historic. Since almost all Protestants and Catholics are educated separately, the divide begins very early, and 'bridges' are difficult to build. Even areas once jointly inhabited by Protestants and Catholics have split apart in the last twenty years. Solutions which seem commonsense when devised by politicans in other parts of the British Isles have shown little sign of being realistic in the atmosphere of Ulster's divided communities.

This division and unrest has had an effect on the economy of the province. There is a reluctance to invest money in new industry or business in Ulster, despite United Kingdom Government support. Some new industries (eg the de Lorean car factory, the Lear Jet aircraft factory) have not proved lasting successes for other reasons. The major employers in Belfast are the large shipbuilders, Harland and Wolff, and the aircraft builders, Short's. Elsewhere in Ulster farming and fishing are important. But the differences in religion and politics affect the whole region.

Though Ulster has a dramatic coastline and countryside (the Giant's Causeway and the Mountains of Mourne are famous beauty spots) tourists are deterred from visiting because of the possible dangers.

Is there a regional divide?

There is another way in which people often describe the differences between places in Britain. It is to talk – sometimes seriously, sometimes jokingly – about the 'gulf between the North and the South'.

As some of the comments on this page show, it is difficult to define this supposed division with any accuracy. Geographers often describe the *physical* division of Britain by a line drawn from the River Tees in the North-East to the River Exe in the South-West; but it may be too easy to use the same line to describe a divide between the prosperous South-East and the rest of the country.

Such a line places industrial areas like the West Midlands in the 'prosperous' part of the country, when the reality is that it, too, has been having a difficult time in recent years. In any case, the actual division itself is disputed by many people.

If there is some kind of cultural difference between North and South, it is not completely reflected in economic terms:

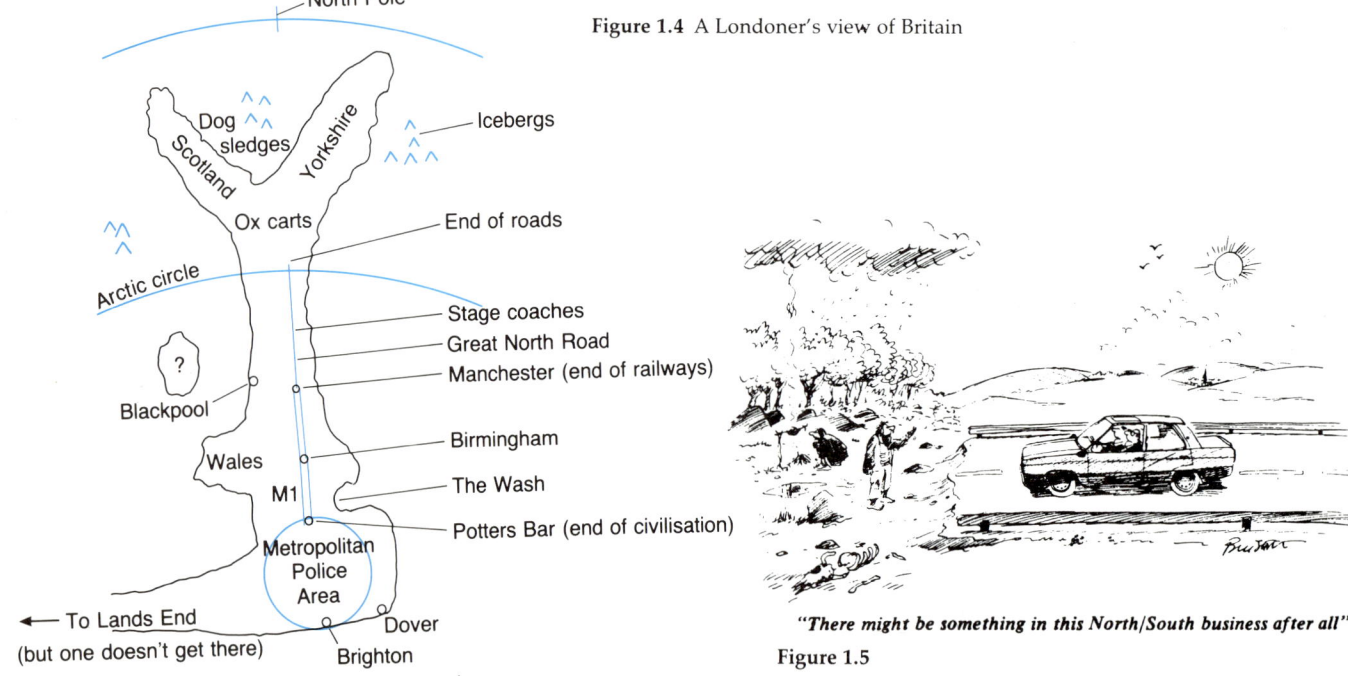

Figure 1.4 A Londoner's view of Britain

"There might be something in this North/South business after all"

Figure 1.5

> Ask where the North? – At York 'tis the Tweed:
> In Scotland at the Orcades; and there
> At Greenland, Zemla or the Lord knows where ...
>
> Alexander Pope
>
> The British are great line drawers and demarcators. A nation so homogeneous has to become adept at making fine distinctions ... in the past this art centred on class. Now, with the Marks and Spencerisation of the whole nation, that restless search for boundaries concentrates on geographical lines ... As England has shrunk, we cling to local identities more tenaciously, particularly in the North, defined as that part of the map where real people live, chip butties are eaten and brass bands play ... the boundary is the Tees.
>
> Austin Mitchell

A hundred years ago the effects of the industrial revolution were clearly changing the landscape. Towns on the coalfields were prospering, as industries powered by steam and electricity used the coal to develop mechanical processes of various kinds – spinning, weaving, traction engines, and many more.

The exploitation of the coalfields changed the face of Britain within thirty years. Factories replaced the old home 'cottage' industries because new forms of power could encourage mass-production of goods. Around the factories quickly grew row upon row of workers' houses (often literally back-to-back) for workers attracted from rural life by the lure of higher wages.

Today, some of those coalfields have reached the end of their useful life, and the industries have paid the price of early development. They are now unable to compete with better technology and cheaper modes of production in other countries. So some coalfield and coastal towns – former heartlands of engineering, shipbuilding and textile manufacture – now have to seek a new base for their activities.

But it would be wrong to see this as a simple division between North and South. There are prosperous areas in northern Britain, just as there are areas of great deprivation in southern inner-city areas. New industries are being encouraged to replace old ones, such as the giant new Nissan car factory at Washington, County Durham. The boom in oil and gas production brought at least temporary prosperity to north-east Scotland for a decade; there is a flourishing high-technology belt in central Scotland.

The diversion of central government functions to outlying cities also helps to restore balance. The DHSS offices are at Newcastle, the Driver Licensing Centre at Swansea, and there are other major offices in Dundee and Coventry.

There are good leisure opportunities, eating places and community centres in North as well as South. It is too simple to see a division between two halves of the country, on the basis of particular patches of prosperity and decline. (See Plate 40.)

Figure 1.6 *The Guardian*, 12 February 1986

The boom town that turned into a loser

Thirty pits once fuelled Workington's [in Cumbria] heavy industry economy. The last deep mine, Hay Pit, is due to close next month and the town's coal industry will then be limited to heavily mechanised open-cast mining. The steel works, which once covered half the town, have contracted. Some 3,000 jobs were lost in 1981 alone.

Alan Clarke, a steel worker for 40 years before being made redundant at 60, is among the port's new entrepreneurs, having invested some of his redundancy cheque in a small fishing boat. 'A lot of people bought boats; there's nothing else to do,' he said. He shook his head over the folly of the £14 million investment in his former works, just 18 months before it closed.

'Immediately after the war this was a boom town,' said Peter Wilson, chief housing officer for Allerdale District Council. 'But as transport patterns changed the town changed and it started to be away from the markets; that's the top and bottom of it'. As major employers closed their doors the unemployment infection spread to their local suppliers.

Financial incentives and the provision of business starter units funded by the local authority and English industrial Estates have encouraged new enterprises, but largely in the service industries, with small numbers of jobs. The foundations of recovery among the 25,000 population – including £2,500,000 in landscaping and infrastructure – have yet to materialise. 'What we never managed to do was to get in a major employer to replace a lot of those lost jobs,' said Mr Wilson....

Councillor Wilson, aged 48, has lived in Workington all his life. When he left school in 1953 there was a choice of well-paid work. 'Sadly, out here in West Cumbria now, there isn't anything for young people to look forward to,' he said.

Database: Britain and the world

Figure 1.7 Characteristics of selected world nations

	Population (in millions)	GNP per head (in US dollars)	Percentage of labour force in agriculture	Infant deaths per 100	Percentage of literate adults
Bangladesh	98.1	130	74	12.4	26
Bolivia	6.2	540	50	11.8	63
Burkina Faso	6.6	160	82	14.6	5
Ethiopia	42.2	110	80	17.2	15
Haiti	5.1	320	74	12.4	23
Japan	120.0	10,630	12	0.6	98
Kuwait	1.7	16,720	2	2.2	60
Libya	3.5	8,520	19	9.1	22
Papua New Guinea	3.4	710	82	6.9	32
Trinidad & Tobago	1.2	7,150	10	2.2	95
United Kingdom	56.4	8,570	2	1.0	99
USA	237.0	15,340	2	1.1	99
USSR	275.0	(est) 7,000	14	(est) 3.3	100
West Germany	61.2	11,130	4	1.0	99
Yugoslavia	23.0	2,120	29	2.8	85

Sources: World Bank Reports, 1981 and 1986; World Development Report, 1986.

Figure 1.8

Country	Number of MPs elected in June 1987
England	523
Scotland	72
Wales	38
Northern Ireland	17

Figure 1.9 Regional differences in Britain

	Av. gross weekly earnings Males	Females	% Unemployment	Cars per 1000	% over retiring age	Ratio of deaths
North	£167	£110	18.8	230	17.5	111
Yorks & Humberside	£167	£107	14.8	251	18.0	105
E. Midlands	£164	£106	12.5	279	17.3	98
E. Anglia	£167	£110	10.1	328	18.8	89
S. East & London	£198	£130	9.7	329	18.1	92
S. West	£166	£110	11.7	337	20.9	89
W. Midlands	£167	£110	15.7	295	16.5	102
N. West	£171	£112	16.1	259	17.9	110
England	£179	£118	12.8	297	18.1	98
Wales	£166	£111	16.8	275	18.8	104
Scotland	£179	£111	15.2	223	17.1	112
N.Ireland	£164	£112	21.0	262	14.5	110
United Kingdom	£179	£117	13.3	288	17.9	100

A standardised mortality ratio, ie adjusted (for age structure of population.)

Workbase

1. Study Fig. 1.7.
   a) Identify six members of the First and Second Worlds.
   b) Identify six members of the Third World.
   c) With the help of an atlas or a world map, classify the fifteen countries by continent.
   d) What might explain Libya's high GNP figure?
   e) Which country seems half way between Third and First Worlds?

2. Below are listed some *formerly* famous major manufacturing companies which were British in origin. Each set of three belongs to a particular industry. Can you name the industry?
   a) Smith-Corona; Imperial; Underwood.
   b) James; Matchless; Francis-Barnett.
   c) Hillman; Jowett; Lanchester.

3. What are the important 'names' which have now replaced those above in the industries concerned? In which country or countries are they based?

4. In sport there are interesting differences in the way in which the United Kingdom is represented by national teams. (For instance in cricket the four nations are represented at top international level by one team called England. A Welshman and a Scotsman have been captain of England in recent years.)
   a) Find out how the United Kingdom is usually represented in soccer, hockey, netball and rugby.
   b) Look at the sports pages of a daily newspaper and see if the United Britain plays as ONE country or four separate ones for TWO other sports.

5. Identify some other aspects of life in which Scotland, Wales and Northern Ireland are distinct from England.

6. Consider the 'Contrasting viewpoints' about Ulster on pages 4–5. Write a paragraph giving your own opinions about the present difficulties which the Province faces. What do you think is the best long-term solution?

7. Collect press-cuttings about Ulster for a period of a week and see how they reflect the different aspects of the situation described in the earlier pages.

8. Using Figure 1.9 identify:
   a) which region has the lowest average gross weekly earnings for men and women;
   b) Which region has the highest average gross weekly earnings for men and women;
   c) which regions have the highest and lowest unemployment rates.

9. In which regions, do you think the full-page colour photographs, Plates 1, 4, 5, 6, and 7 were taken? Write a paragraph relating those photographs to the data in Figure 1.9.

Chapter 2
Britain's physical environment

The first human beings in Britain probably lived about 10,000 years ago, soon after the Ice Ages were at their climax and the ice reached its most southerly extent (see Fig. 2.1). As the ice sheets and glaciers retreated and the climate became warmer, it became possible for European peoples to move northwards into the area we know now as the British Isles.

But – as Fig. 2.2 shows – the oldest rocks in Britain were formed hundreds of millions of years ago and they are very much older than our own human ancestors.

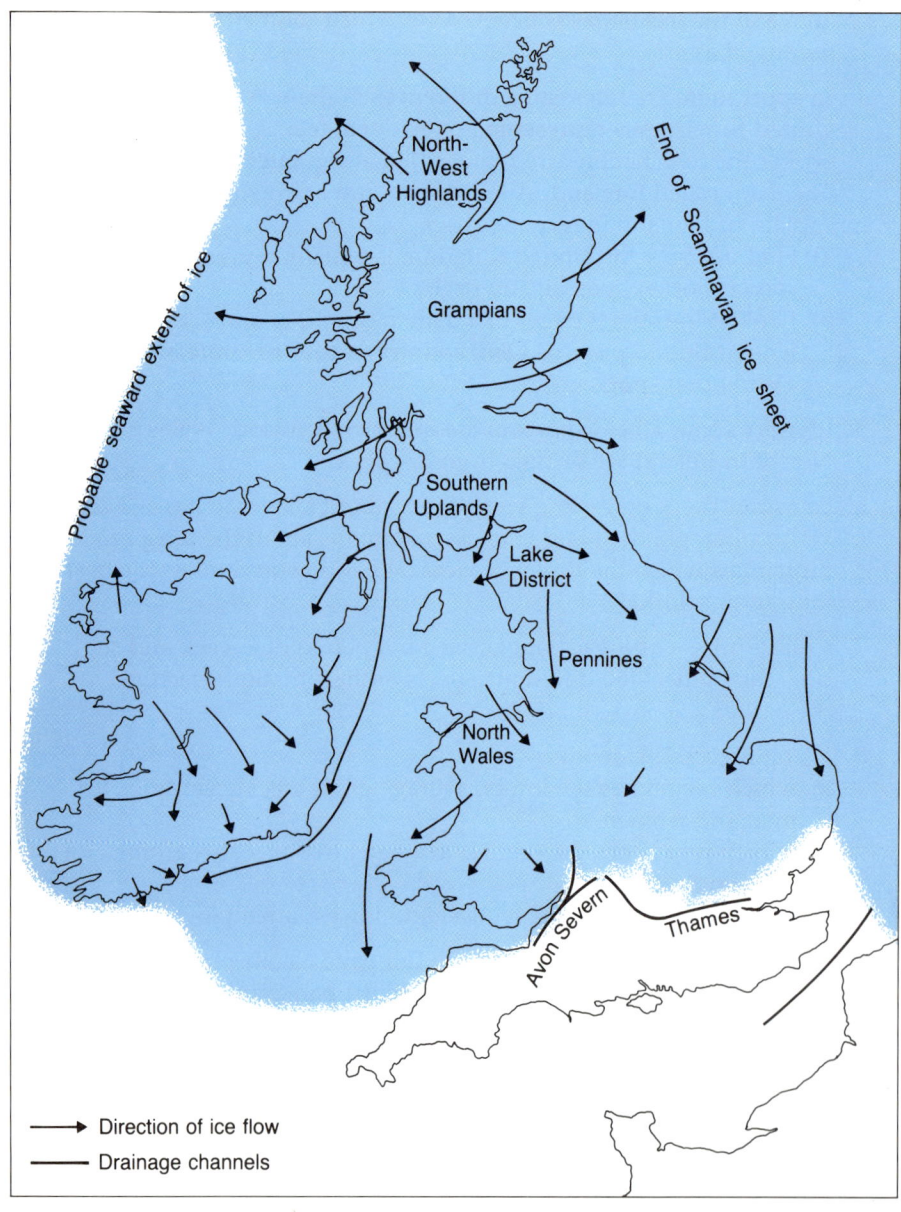

Figure 2.1 The greatest extent of the ice-sheets which have covered Britain during past eras

Some of these older rocks are **igneous** (formed by the cooling of molten lava thrust up from the centre of the earth), or **metamorphic** (changed from their original form by the reheating and reconstitution of their elements). Later rocks are mainly **sedimentary**, formed in successive layers by the deposition of materials through geological time. (See Plate 34).

The **Carboniferous** series of sedimentary rocks are an important part of Britain's physical history and geography, since they are plentiful in northern England, South Wales and central Scotland. They were formed in the period when great forests were decaying; after being compressed they were changed into what we know today as the 'Coal Measures'. The easy mining of these rocks was a significant factor in developing the coalfields on which the industrial revolution was based.

Some of our most fertile soils are formed from **alluvium**, laid down by the flood plains or rivers; these have formed in only the last few hundred thousand years.

Figure 2.2 The division of geological time

Age	Era	Period	Epoch/Duration
Age of man	Cainozoic Era	Quaternary Period (Pleistocene and Recent Epochs) about 2 million years	
Age of mammals		Tertiary	Pliocene about 5 million years
			Miocene 19 million years
			Oligocene 12 million years
			Eocene 16 million years
			Palaeocene 11.5 million years
Age of reptiles	Mesozoic Era	Cretaceous	(Upper Cretaceous 35 million years) 71 million years (Lower Cretaceous 36 million years)
		Jurassic	about 57 million years
		Triassic	about 32 million years
Age of amphibians	Palaeozoic Era	Permian	55 million years
		Carboniferous	(Upper Carboniferous 45 million years) 65 million years (Lower Carboniferous 20 million years)
Age of fish		Devonian	50 million years
		Silurian	about 40 million years
Age of invertebrates		Ordovician	about 65 million years
		Cambrian	70 million years
		Pre Cambrian	

The earliest human inhabitants of Britain used the natural environment of caves in the rocks to provide shelter. By hunting and killing animals they provided food for themselves (by meat) and clothing (using skins and furs). Their life was simple but tough: survival was the main objective.

As the climate grew warmer, the people made camps using animal skins (for tents) and gathered wild plants for food. In the time of the Middle Stone Age they settled either near the coasts or on the uplands. They avoided the highest parts of the hills and mountains because these were too exposed; they also avoided the forested lowlands, as they had neither the tools nor the labour to clear such areas. They needed to be near fresh water for drinking supplies, and they fished as well as hunted small animals.

As the ice gradually retreated, it revealed a landscape in which the effect of glaciers was clearly shown.

Figure 2.3 Glacial erosion; the Langdale Valley, Cumbria

Britain's physical environment 13

Figure 2.4 Glacial deposition; drumlins in the Eden Valley, Cumbria

Figure 2.5 A river valley 'drowned' by a rise in sea level; Salcombe, Devon

The retreat of the glaciers had another effect, from the melting of ice and the resulting rise in sea-levels.

Some valleys became drowned by the rising waters, such as the Dart and the Fal in Devon and Cornwall (see Fig. 2.5). It was at this time that the Isle of Wight was created, as low lying land in the area of the Solent was flooded and left a small area of higher land 'marooned'

The rising waters also cut off Britain from the main continent of Europe to which it had once been joined. Thus the English Channel is a quite shallow stretch of water compared with the deeper parts of the North Sea and the Atlantic Ocean, which lie to the west and east of Britain. This shallowness makes it possible to think of tunnelling under it in the 1990s.

Database and Workbase

1. Look at the relief map of Britain (Plate 33) and the geological map (Plate 34).
    a) Can you make any general comment about the relationship between relief and geology in Britain?
    b) Which rock types are the most widely found in Britain?
    c) Identify the areas where the Carboniferous rocks are found on the surface.

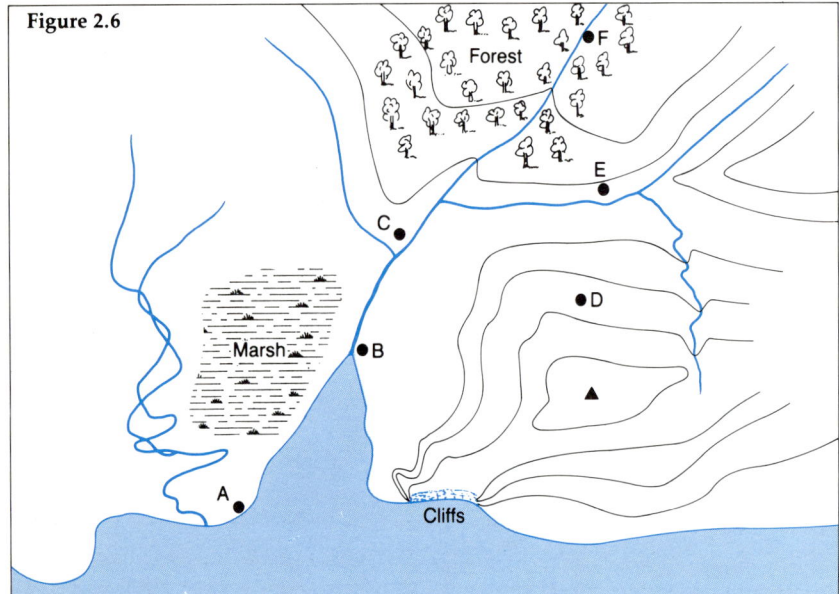

Figure 2.6

2. Imagine that you a settler of the Middle Stone Age, looking for somewhere to set up an encampment. Consider the map above and the locations (listed by the letters A-F) which are possible sites. In view of your needs and your life-style (see page 12) which site would you choose and why?

3. On pages 12–13 you will see pictures which show physical features. Identify their locations by reference to the captions and your atlas.

4. Draw a sketch of the pictures in your own notebooks, adding labels to explain how the features were created. (You may need a physical geography textbook to help you, or your teacher may explain, if you cannot work it out.)

5. What *physical* geographical features influenced the first siting of the town or city in which you live? (Or nearest to where you live?) Is there any evidence **remaining** of its original site? Local guide-books and pamphlets may help you with the answers to these questions.

Chapter 3
Britain's population

The early visitors

In the centuries following the retreat of the ice, successive generations of newcomers came to the British Isles. These waves of **immigrants** brought with them new skills and ideas, as well as different lifestyles, but they were gradually absorbed into the life of the nation.

In the **Neolithic Age**, peoples came from lands around the Mediterranean, and brought knowledge of farming techniques, originally developed in the Middle East. They knew how to grow and tend wheat, barley and cattle. They developed rough stone axes and could also make pottery. Many of them were buried in huge communal graves (**barrows**), some of which can still be seen in the landscape. It is likely that the great Druid temple of Stonehenge dates from this period.

In the **Bronze Age** (around 2000 BC) other groups came to Britain from Europe. They knew how to shape metal and were the first blacksmiths; they could make primitive **weapons** (daggers and swords), as well as implements for tilling the soil of farms more effectively. Their custom was to bury their dead singly, and so one still visible remnant in the landscape of their civilisation is the small, round barrow.

From 500 BC **Celtic** peoples came to Britain – the true ancestors of the Scots and Welsh. Many came from northern France and they introduced the **Iron Age**. They used charcoal to smelt iron for farming tools; the iron-plough, pulled by two oxen helped to extend farming from the light soils of the chalk uplands to the wetter clay areas. The Celts were also miners and traders, and weaving was a favourite occupation in Celtic encampments. Some of their hill-forts still remain, as do traces of their agricultural systems (Celtic fields).

Figure 3.1 Stonehenge, Wiltshire

Some of the Celts came to Britain as refugees from the persecution of the Roman Empire. But the **Romans** also came to Britain and forced them back to the highland areas of Britain (Scotland and Wales). Julius Caesar's attempt at an invasion of Britain (55 BC) was not successful, but 100 years later the Emperor Claudius succeeded in establishing a Roman colony in 'Albion'. For 350 years, the Romans ruled Britain as a military power.

Though the existing Britons fought to keep the Romans at bay, they were no match for the highly organised legions of the Roman Empire. The Romans established forts for their soldiers and later turned these into fortified towns (Colchester, Lancaster, Manchester) at commanding, defensive locations. They surrounded these by walls, including some civilian settlers within them. Corn was the staple food of Roman diet and so the lowland corn-growing areas formed the major areas of settlement. Roman villas were grouped on the lighter soils, each at the centre of an agricultural estate. Sometimes a Briton who had adopted Roman ways eventually came to own the villa and its lands.

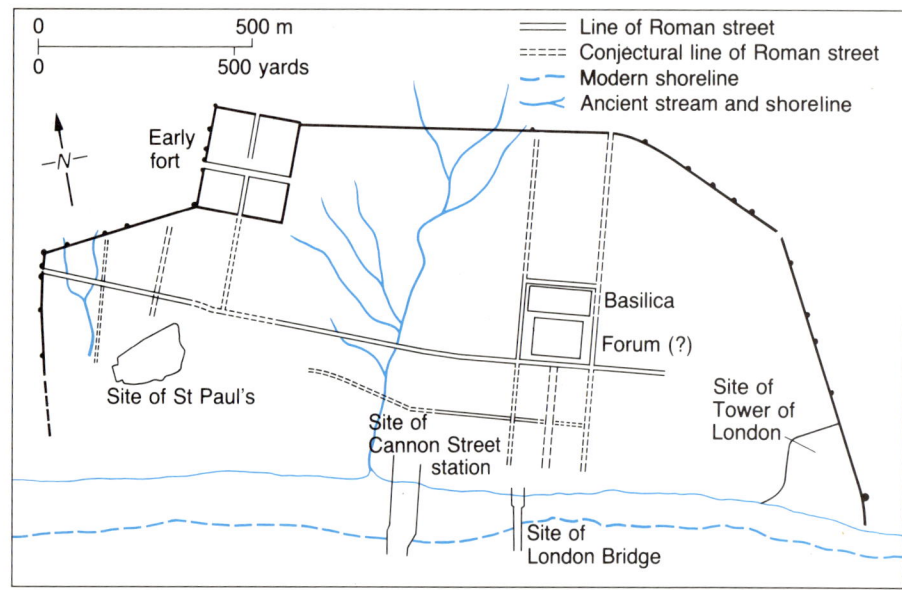

Figure 3.2 Roman London

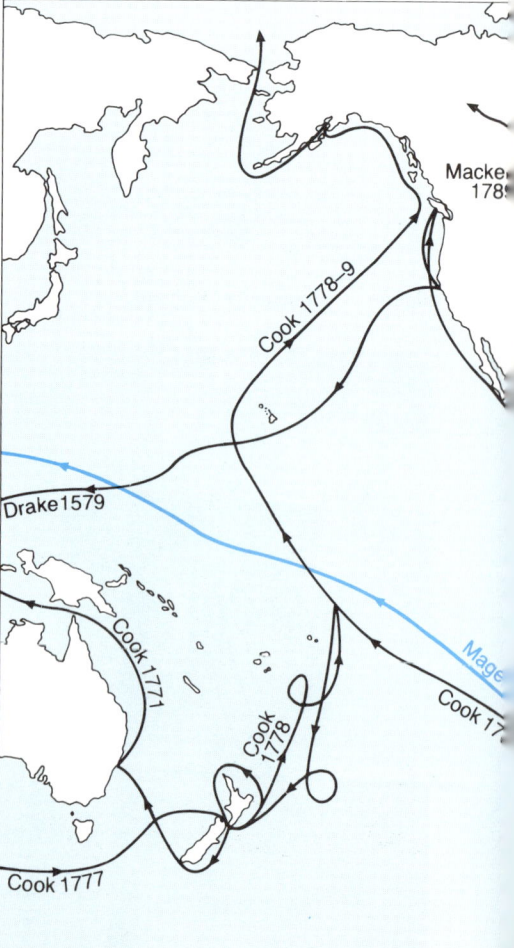

In AD 410 Roman troops were withdrawn from Britain, because of the need to defend the Empire elsewhere. The influence of the Empire in Britain declined rapidly, and there were increasing raids and settlements made by the **Angles** and the **Saxons**, both groups from northern Europe.

It was the Angles who gave the name to Eng-land as we now know it; but though many of them came to stay in the British Isles, little of their civilisation has survived. Nor did they maintain the excellent road system, town-life and cultural pattern which the Romans had established.

The Norwegian **Vikings** and their neighbours, the **Danes**, were excellent seamen and in the eighth and ninth centuries began to make an increasing number of raiding journeys on Britain. Some of the raiders stayed to settle. From their initial settlement in the north of Scotland they spread southwards, and at one time they ruled much of eastern Britain.

Saxon kings (such as Alfred the Great) sometimes fought off the Scandinavian invaders, but it was only at the Battle of Stamford Bridge in Yorkshire (1065) that Saxon rule was re-established. Within a few weeks, King Harold had to march south to face another set of challenges to Saxon power. 1066 is one of the most famous dates of British history, and the victory of Duke William of Normandy at the Battle of Hastings one of the best known events. It signalled the start of an effective settling of southern

Britain by the Normans, and gave the country orderly government, efficient law, and a time of peace and stability.

One significant Norman achievement was the Domesday Survey – the first proper inventory of the country's land and resources. Nine hundred years later many British schools helped to carry out a similar exercise – the results of which are stored on video-disc, rather than parchment.

Under Norman rule, England became preoccupied with events in Europe and particularly in the struggle for control of France. But under the reign of Tudor monarchs in the fifteenth and sixteenth centuries England asserted both her independence from the Catholic Church of Rome and from the political affairs of the European mainland. Instead the nation's mind turned towards more distant shores.

Exploration, enclosures, and two revolutions

New knowledge about navigation and the improved seaworthiness of vessels led many English sailors across the oceans in voyages of discovery in the fifteenth and sixteenth centuries. Settlement and trade followed in the wake of such 'seadogs' as Drake and Raleigh. People from Britain went out to live in the West Indies, on the coasts of Africa and in eastern North America. Government support (and the claim of territory) followed later. At home, powerful trading companies were established, such as the Merchant Adventurers of Bristol, and the East India Company.

Figure 3.3 Carrying out the first Domesday survey

Figure 3.4 European exploration of the world

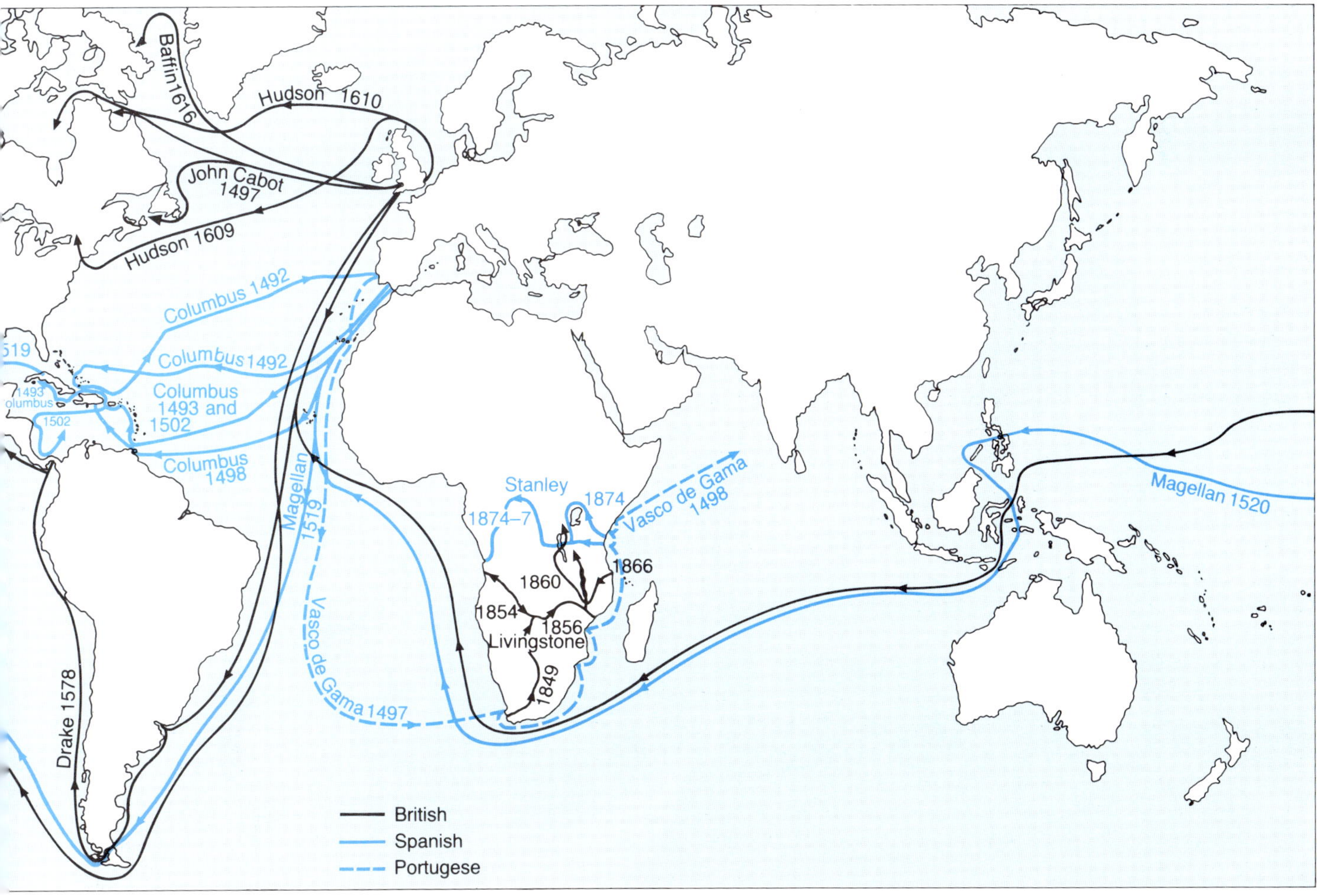

In Britain itself the population continued to increase. More land was needed for crops and livestock to feed the growing population. The traditional system of farming in Britain had grown up around 'open fields' in which each family grew their crops on narrow strips of land, and utilised wasteland or common land for the grazing of their animals. The system had grown up by custom, but was not efficient.

So in the eighteenth century, Parliament legalised the **enclosure** of fields and of new forest areas. This turned some formerly independent farmers into the tenants of large landowners and brought great changes to the British landscape. It was an **agricultural revolution**, later speeded on by the development of new farming implements and methods (such as crop rotation).

In the nineteenth century a comparable **industrial revolution** took place, as the technique for smelting iron from coal was developed and the invention of the steam-engine put to use. The use of steam-powered engines changed not only the size and scope of industry, but its most suitable locations.

Before 1800 the centre of Britain's woollen industry had been in the prosperous villages of Norfolk and Suffolk. But these areas lacked nearby supplies of coal. The centre of the industry shifted to Leeds and Bradford in Yorkshire. Other large cities, such as Sheffield (based on the making of iron and steel products, notably knives) and Manchester (based on cotton, brewing and dye-making), grew very rapidly.

Since many of the inventions and discoveries of the industrial revolution were made in Britain, the nature of its industry changed before many other countries. But this nineteenth-century advantage is a twentieth-century handicap, since other countries have learnt from Britain's experiences and yet have newer industrial plant.

Figure 3.5 Lavenham Church, Suffolk; a sign of the region's prosperity before the Industrial Revolution

The present pattern

Britain's present population pattern (see Plate 36) still reflects the major effects of the industrial revolution of the last century.

London stands out as the prime city of the nation, with a population of five million living within the Greater London area. But it is difficult to be precise about London's actual population size, since there are many ways of defining it. The built-up area of London stretches beyond the fringes of the 'Greater London Boroughs'.

There are other major population concentrations in the West Midlands, Merseyside, around Manchester, in West Yorkshire and around Newcastle. But many of the old coalfield areas are also closely populated, although now losing population to other areas.

New industries (in the 'sunrise belt' which stretches from Bristol round to Cambridge) are attracting people from other areas. The South of England in general has increased in population in the last twenty years.

In Wales the southern 'valleys' region, centre of the coalfields, still contains the great majority of the population. The mountainous central and northern areas remain only sparsely inhabited.

And though there have been some increases in the Highlands of Scotland in the last decade (partly because of industrial development and partly because of growing tourism), the numbers are small in absolute terms.

The rural-urban shift

In 1951 10.4 million people (i.e. 20 per cent of the total population of Britain) lived in rural areas. By 1971 the figures were 12.8 million people and 23 per cent of the total; in 1981 there were 14 million people and 25 per cent of the total. These figures seem to indicate that population in rural areas is increasing. But these are average figures which conceal other important trends:

- in some of the more remote rural areas more people are leaving the villages than are moving in (i.e. rural depopulation is taking place);
- retired people are moving into some rural areas looking for a quiet life and cheap housing;
- in some areas, which are accessible to towns and cities, commuters are moving out to live in the surrounding villages.

Leaving the countryside

A sample of people who had been living in the countryside were asked in a recent survey why they had decided to migrate to the towns. These are some of the answers they gave:

'I did not have a job when I left school, and there were no prospects locally, so I came to try my luck in town.'

'I used to work on a farm, but the owner bought a machine to do most of my job, so I was made redundant.'

'My boyfriend lived and worked in the town and when we decided to get married I moved to the town.'

'I used to run my own farm, but it was very small and I could not make a very good living. When I had a good offer to sell it I could not refuse.'

'My wage on the farm was so low I could not afford to pay for my daughter to go to college, so I got a better paid job in town.'

'When my children got older they had to travel 25 miles (40 kilometres) each way every day to school. They were falling asleep at 6 o'clock and could not do their work, so we moved to town.'

'My best friend came back to the village after her family had moved away, and when she said how nice it was in the town we were persuaded to move close to them.'

'The nearest hospital was over 25 miles (40 kilometres) from our house, and when Grandad became ill we could not visit him every evening. We were just too far from proper hospitals.'

'I guess I am just a born wanderer and I drift from place to place.'

'When my grandparents died they left us a bungalow in town, so we decided to move in there.'

'There was never anything to do at night – no clubs or discos, so we just got more and more bored.'

Living in rural areas

- Every year since 1945 there has been a decrease of 2–3 per cent in the size of the agricultural labour force.
- A recent survey of the nine English rural counties produced the following information:

Percentage of villages without the service

Any bus service	10
A food shop	20–30
A sub-post office	15–25
A doctor's surgery	65–70
A dispensing chemist	80–90

Figure 3.6 On Barra, Outer Hebrides, the post van also serves as a bus

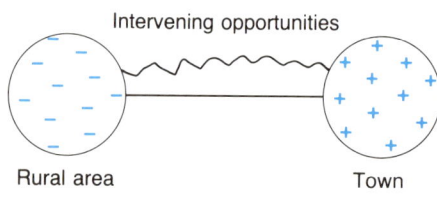

− Negative or 'push' factors
+ Positive or 'pull' factors

Figure 3.7 A model of migration

Although people living in rural areas now generally have more and better services than fifty years ago, many in small and remote villages are a long distance from a doctor's surgery, or post office or school.

If a proportion of people own cars in villages and use them to shop, this may make it unprofitable for the bus service to continue, unless it charges much higher fares. This in turn discourages passengers, unless there is some grant to help pay the extra costs. In some villages, community self-help projects have been started in which local people take it in turns to drive a minibus to nearby centres, picking up those who need it, just like a taxi service.

A great age for great age

As in many other developing countries, Britain now has a population which has a longer life-expectancy than that of its parents. More people are living into old age.

Since 1981 the number of people over seventy-five has risen by 10 per cent and the number of people over eighty-five by 14 per cent. The change has been dramatic and it has not finished yet.

Economic prosperity, better diets and improvements in health care and medical treatment are the causes of the change. They are likely to go on increasing the proportion of the population who draw the OAP (Old Age Pension).

Look at the population pyramid below. You will see how Britain's population structure begins to look top-heavy compared to a pyramid. Why do you think this is?

Our own birth-rate is quite low – with families barely producing enough children to sustain the present rate of the population. But we are undoubtedly moving into the era of the four-generation family. Your grandparents may well be around to see the birth of *your* children.

Figure 3.8 Senior citizens at the seaside

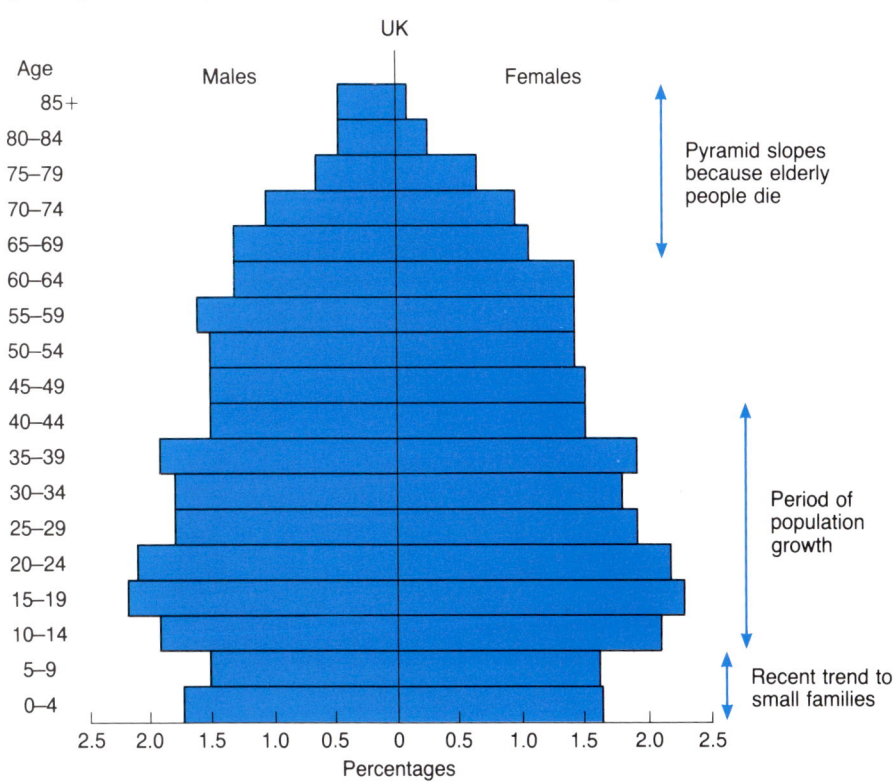

Figure 3.9 Britain's population pyramid

About 6 per cent of our total population is over seventy-five. And as the graph shows (Fig. 3.10) they are a growing number.

These days, it is possible to identify some towns which almost 'specialise' in providing retirement homes for older people. The provision of 'sheltered housing', where a warden and medical help can be on hand for those who may be getting frail, is obviously a specialist facility which is attractive for people over seventy-five.

Some former resort towns have made up for their loss of long-stay summer holiday makers by becoming 'retirement havens'. If they have lots of sun and a pleasant promenade to walk down, the attraction of living there can be very strong. Thus, in certain parts of the country, the proportion of older people rises in a very spectacular way. (See Plate 36)

Multi-cultural Britain

Britain has always received a steady number of migrants from other countries through the centuries.

Huguenot weavers, fleeing from persecution in Holland, set up their looms in southern England and East Anglia in the fifteenth century and were at the centre of a revived woollen industry which flourished in those regions until the industrial revolution.

There has been a steady trickle of migrants from Ireland, and there are now strong Irish communities in towns like Liverpool and Glasgow. In the 1930s groups of Italians migrated to Britain, finding work in the market-gardens and brickfields of the Midlands.

But most of those who have come to Britain have been citizens of the Commonwealth, the name for the grouping of independent nations once ruled by Britain as an Empire.

There was a surge of migrants from 'New Commonwealth' countries in the 1950s and 1960s, recruited to fill vacant jobs in Britain's hospital and transport services. Though many of the immigrants were black they had more reason to see themselves as 'sons and daughters' of the 'mother

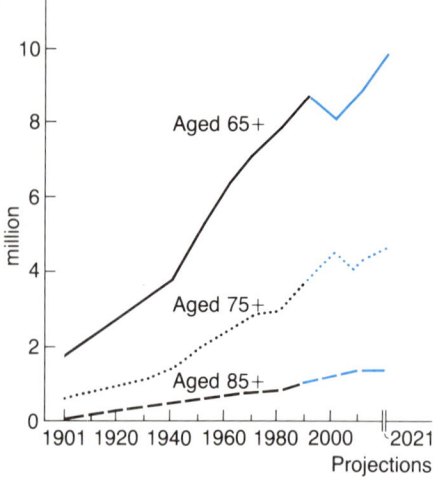

Figure 3.10 Old people in England and Wales

Figure 3.11 Population in private households: ethnic group by region of residence, selected metropolitan counties 1983–1985

	All groups	White	Total
Great Britain	54,118	50,964	2,349
North	3,057	2,984	37
Yorkshire and Humberside	4,846	4,598	174
West Yorkshire	2,035	1,873	133
East Midlands	3,833	3,620	153
East Anglia	1,912	1,859	29
South East	16,825	15,318	1,227
Greater London	6,664	5,569	965
South West	4,365	4,251	46
West Midlands	5,126	4,665	394
North West	6,321	5,998	212
Greater Manchester	2,569	2,394	124
England	46,285	43,294	2,270
Wales	2,777	2,705	37
Scotland	5,056	4,965	41

The population totals in this table relate to the estimated population in private households and are therefore lower than the mid-year population estimates used elsewhere in this volume.
Source: Office of Population Censuses and Surveys, 1983–1985 Labour Force Surveys.

Figure 3.12 Popuulation in private household: ethic group by region of residence, selected metropolitan counties 1983–1985

	Non-white								Not stated
	West Indian	Indian	Pakistani	Bangladeshi	Chinese	African	Mixed	Other (inc Arab)	
Great Britain	528	762	377	92	112	101	212	165	806
North	—	5	11	2	7	2	4	5	37
Yorkshire and Humberside	26	40	75	6	5	4	13	6	74
West Yorkshire	17	36	62	4	2	2	6	3	29
East Midlands	23	90	13	—	6	4	11	6	60
East Anglia	5	4	4	1	2	2	6	4	24
South East	352	372	88	62	60	76	110	106	281
Greater London	303	297	53	49	37	64	76	84	130
South West	11	8	4	—	6	2	9	6	68
West Midlands	79	164	97	15	6	3	20	8	68
North West	28	65	59	4	13	7	26	10	110
Greater Manchester	22	32	37	4	5	3	14	5	51
England	525	749	351	90	105	99	199	152	722
Wales	3	7	6	2	2	1	9	6	34
Scotland	—	6	20	—	5	1	3	7	50

1 The population totals in this table relate to the estimated population in private households and are therefore lower than the mid-year population estimates used elsewhere in this volume.
2 Results from the last 3 years surveys have been avgraged.
Source: Office of Population Censuses and Surveys 1983–1985 Labour Force Surveys.

country' than other groups of white-skinned immigrants who now also sought to be 'British'.

The difficulties of adjustment in some communities were not foreseen. After a while the Government introduced legislation to restrict the number of migrants who could enter the country, in order to try and stabilise the situation and work out the problems of developing communities with many different cultures and not just one. It was necessary to introduce laws to combat 'racism'.

The question of building a multi-cultural society is a sensitive one and many people have strong views on the matter. But (as pages 15–16 show) these issues are not new ones. Through history there has been a constant tide of migrants who make their contribution to the nation and change the nature and balance of 'the British'.

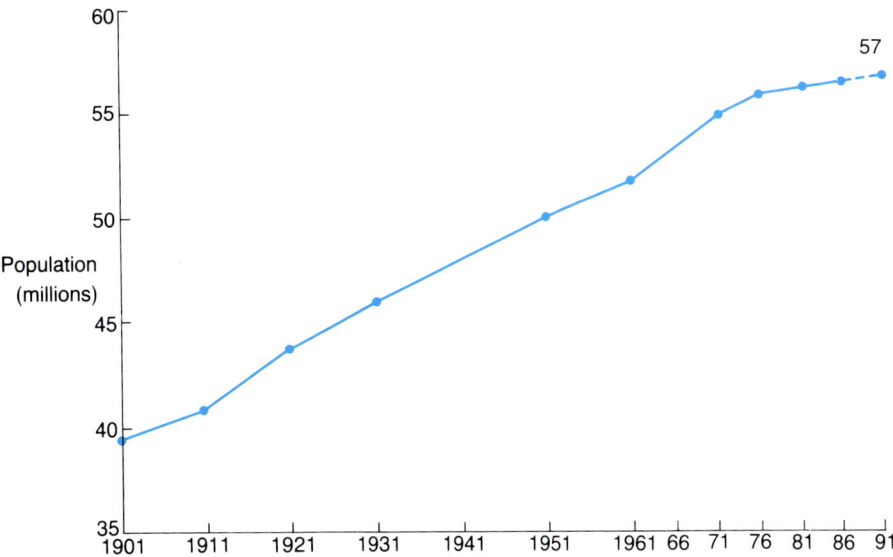

Figure 3.13 The growth of Britain's Population

Database: Britain's population

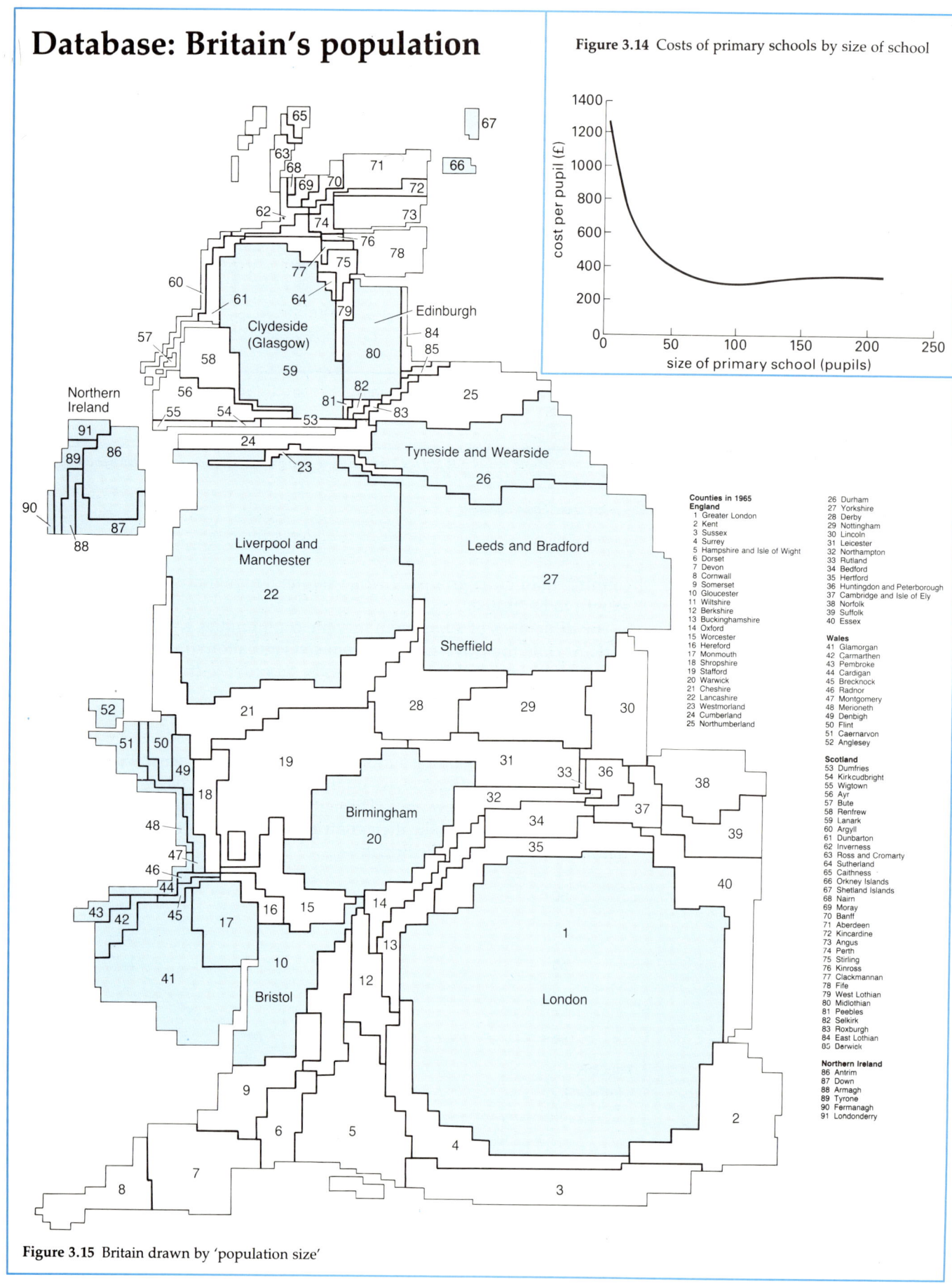

Figure 3.14 Costs of primary schools by size of school

Figure 3.15 Britain drawn by 'population size'

Workbase

The map (Fig. 3.15) on the opposite page has been drawn to reflect the population of Britain rather than merely the area. Thus one small square of the map equals a number of people rather than a number of acres or hectares. Notice the effect that this has in inflating the size of London, Glasgow and other conurbations. Regions which are large in area but which have relatively few people (e.g. Central Wales, Northern Scotland) 'shrink' accordingly.

This kind of map is called a map transformation. You can find another of 'shrinking Britain' on page 199. See if you can invent one yourself, taking another set of data from one of the tables in the book.

1. Consult an ordinary atlas and compare this map of Britain with that in the atlas. Write down the major *differences* which show up.

2. Fig. 3.14 shows the problem of keeping small schools open in remote rural areas. If you were speaking on behalf of a small school threatened with closure by a County Council, what arguments would you put forward to try and save the school?

3. Migration is a combination of 'push' and 'pull' factors – pushing people out of rural areas, pulling them towards urban ones. Make a list of things which can be counted as push and pull factors, e.g. the loss of a village bus service would be a push factor; the offer of a job in the town would be a pull factor.

4. Do you think it is best for recent migrants to live in separate communities or to try to integrate with the existing population? Put yourself in the place of a community leader of a group new to Britain. What would you advise your family and friends about finding somewhere to live?

5. Identify any recent migrant communities in your area. What links have been created with them in order to develop friendship?

Part II Britain's rural environment

Where are the rural areas of Britain and what are they like?

The map of urban-rural population (Plate 36) shows those areas which are rural and which have the following characteristics:

- few houses, factories or other buildings;
- few people living in the area;
- most of the land as field, moor, marsh or water.

some rural areas also have:

- people moving away from the area to live in towns;
- a majority of retired (over sixty-five) people;
- reliance on farming or forestry for jobs;
- remoteness from large centres of population.

There are no sharp lines dividing rural areas from towns, but a gradual change from wildscapes, through countryside areas, to urban settlements. Between 12–15 per cent of the population (seven million) live on 85 per cent of the land in Britain.

There are big differences between rural areas. Some are highland areas with steep slopes, thin soils and heavy rainfall; others are lowland, or coastal sites with deep, fertile soils.

Rural areas and rural resources

All rural areas have a variety of **resources** (things we find useful), both on land and water. These resources are in limited supply and there is much competition to make use of them. Careful management is needed to try and meet conflicting claims and to preserve the resources for the future. Some of the main pressures competing for the use of rural resources are shown in Fig. II.1.

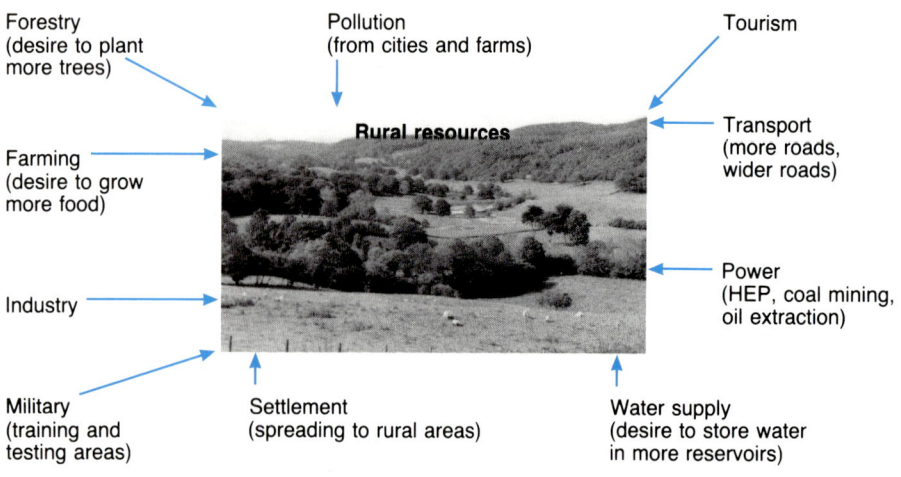

Figure II.1 Pressures on rural resources

Chapter 4
Agriculture

Agriculture is one of Britain's most important industries because:

- it is the source of much of our food (see Database on pages 40–41) and many of our raw materials. We now produce over 50 per cent of our own needs; of the remainder, half consists of products such as tea, rice and bananas which our climate does not allow us to grow;
- it generates spending in related industries: fertilisers and lime (about £450 million per year); machinery (over £600 million); machinery repairs and fuel (£200 million); food concentrates for animals (£1770 million);
- although only 3 per cent of Britain's population are farmers they manage 70 per cent of the land area.

Changes in British farming

Farming has changed dramatically since the end of the Second World War and these changes are often called the *second* agricultural revolution. (The first is usually reckoned to have taken place in the eighteenth century when new methods of breeding and of rotating crops, and new machinery were introduced – see page 18.)

Because food imports were difficult and expensive in the Second World War the Government encouraged farmers (by grants of money) to plough up more land on which to grow food. Animal numbers declined as crop production increased. Since 1945 some good farmland has been lost to city growth or new roads, but food production has continued to expand. This expansion is due to increasing yields which in turn depend on farmers using more artificial fertilisers, more pesticides, better strains of seeds and animals, and more and bigger machines.

As more machines have been introduced the number of farm-workers has declined. And as the machinery used in farming becomes more and more expensive it is only the richer and larger farmers who can afford the new machines. So this encourages farmers to buy up land from their neighbours in order to create a larger more profitable farm unit.

Not only have farms increased in size (see Fig. 4.12) but field size has also greatly increased by the removal of hedges. Hedgerows take up space which could be used for crop production, and they need looking after; they also restrict the size of farm machines which can be used, shade crops and restrict growth, and block drainage ditches with their roots. To avoid all this, over a quarter of all British hedgerows has disappeared since 1945, and in some places (like Norfolk) over half of the hedgerows has been destroyed in twenty-five years.

Removal of hedges has sometimes led to increased soil erosion as the wind blows away exposed top soil. It has also made it easier for animals to stray into crops. Hedges provided a valuable habitat for many species of wildlife, winter jobs for farm labourers, and colour and pattern in the English countryside – so their loss has not gone unchallenged.

Plate 1 He's "going South" for good he believes. Can you suggest his reasons and what his prospects are?

Plate 2 Langdale Valley in the Lake District. What evidence on the picture suggests that this valley has been glaciated?

Plate 3 Durdle Door in Dorset. Can you explain how such a coastal feature is likely to have been formed?

Plate 4 A former factory site on Teesside. What kind of industries have declined in Britain in recent years and why?

Plate 5 A new factory site in Cambridge. What kind of industries have grown in Britain in recent years and why?

Plate 6 The London Notting Hill Carnival. Which other cities in Britain have large populations of minority groups?

Plate 7 Pensioners at Torquay, Devon. Why do the populations of many towns on the south coast have *increasing* numbers of over 65's?

Plate 8 This is a Landsat 'false-colour' photograph of an area near Brighton, Sussex. It is made up of a number of images taken from a satellite orbiting about 900km above the earth's surface. Urban areas show up as blue, and growing vegetation in various shades of red and orange. Can you identify:
   i) The coastal urban area stretching from Shoreham (where the River Adur reaches the sea) towards Brighton (where two piers can be seen jutting into the sea)?
   ii) The downland areas north of Shoreham and Brighton, partly open land and partly developed with housing?
   iii) Further north still the mosaic of fields and villages which form the Low Weald?
   iv) A cement works (in square L11), Shoreham Airfield (M8) and the ribbon of the London-Brighton railway line stretching north (U 13–25)?

⑤

⑥

(7)

26
25
24
23
22
21
20
19
18
17
16
15
14
13
12
11
10
9
8
7
6
5
4
3
2
1
A B C D E F G H I J K L M N O P Q R S T U V W X

Agribusiness

The new farming has been called **agribusiness**, because it is equipped and managed like an industrial business. The emphasis is upon intensive farming, designed to give the maximum output of crops, or animals. Intensive farming often demands new farm buildings, such as machine sheds for the tractors and combine harvesters, together with grain silos and milking parlours.

Factory farming methods are now used in some areas, particularly for rearing poultry or pigs. The animals spend their whole lives inside the rearing units where their food, heating and lighting are all carefully controlled to encourage rapid growth. The animals only leave the rearing unit when they are to be slaughtered.

These factory farming methods are controversial, because some people feel animals should not be confined in small cages, or pens, and never be allowed to exercise in the open air. Other people argue that pork, bacon, eggs and chicken would be much more expensive without such methods.

Changing eating habits have been important factors in producing changes in farming. Much more food is now frozen as more and more people own refrigerators or deep freezers. As more women have gone out to work, so the consumption of 'convenience' foods has increased. There is, in addition, a rising demand for processed, dried or tinned food, together with a desire to have fresh fruit and vegetables available all year round, whilst meat consumption has also increased.

Why have farms become larger and more specialised? Because:

- it is easier for larger farms to obtain credit and loans for improvements such as buying new machinery;
- large, specialised farms can buy such things as fertiliser, seed, pesticides and other inputs in bulk and so reduce costs;
- large-scale farms can afford to store the produce, but smaller farms have to sell immediately after the harvest when prices may be low;
- specialisation of people and of machines may make production more efficient;
- large farms can make more efficient use of expensive machinery.

Farms as systems

Farming is big business and, like industry, farms can be seen as **systems** – with a set of **inputs** into the farm, **processes** which occur on the farm, and **outputs** or products which leave the farm (see Fig. 4.1).

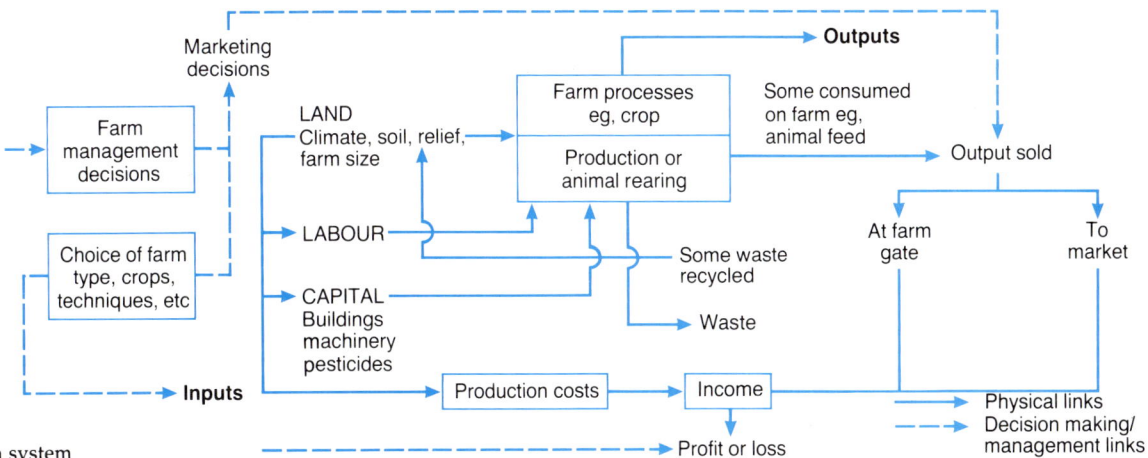

Figure 4.1 The farm system

CONTRASTING VIEWPOINTS

'Are farmers destroying the countryside?'

Sir Simon Gourlay, President of the National Farmers' Union

There is very little completely 'natural' landscape or vegetation in England and Wales. Since our prehistoric ancestors first began to clear the forest which then covered most of the land surface, using axe and fire, the countryside has become increasingly man-made.

Farmers have been much criticised for their part in changing the countryside — for removing hedges, for example. It is true that some of the hedges which were present in 1945 have been removed, but two points must be taken into account when considering this:

1. Farmers had to produce more food on behalf of everyone during the Second World War and were encouraged by the Government to do so right up to the early 1980s. Indeed, for many years, Government advisors encouraged farmers to make fields larger so that farm machinery could work more efficiently to produce the extra food. This meant removing hedges.
2. Two hundred and fifty years ago, before the Enclosure Acts, there were relatively few hedges. As a result of those Acts, many hedges were planted to enclose parcels of land and to subdivide them into fields. These hedges were created by a quirk in English History. Now that some farms no longer keep livestock, hedges have become redundant and have no agricultural use on such farms. They can, of course, be valuable for wildlife and landscape and this is why many farmers retain them even though the hedge may have no practical use and costs money to maintain.

Farmers have changed the countryside in ways that have always reflected the changing needs of the population over time. It is only in recent years that some people have sought to prevent further change because they wish to maintain the countryside in some particular form. Many farmers are willing to accept this wish, and they are prepared to co-operate. However, they cannot earn a living if they do not farm efficiently and it is necessary to compensate them when they give up part of their living in order to preserve the countryside in a specific way which other people choose.

Jonathon Porritt, Friends of the Earth

It's not so much individual farmers who are destroying the countryside, as the *system* which pays them to destroy it.

For years, people have been making it clear that they do not want the countryside turned into a factory floor covered in factory farms. Nor do they wish to go on coughing up larger and larger subsidies to produce food that is never eaten, that rots away as unwanted surpluses.

And yet the system has just carried right on. Whilst a few farmers (the notorious 'barley barons' of East Anglia) carry right on getting richer and richer, the majority are now struggling to keep their heads above water. With falling incomes and large debts, what can they do but go on trying to increase production yet further, even though that means increasing the use of costly fertilisers and dangerous pesticides, even though the produce often isn't wanted, even though the countryside goes on suffering.

The second rate land they bring into production often provides valuable wildlife habitats. Wild flower and rich hay-meadows, chalk and limestone grasslands, heath and moor, ancient woods and wetlands; many of these have been ploughed, felled and drained over the last few years.

The answer is simple: pay farmers to protect the countryside, not to destroy it. Provide incentives for environmentally-sensitive farming, for going organic, for using fewer chemicals. Reward farmers for good husbandry, rather than for simply producing more.

Most farmers want to be seen and to *act* as stewards of the land. It's the Government and the Common Agricultural Policies of the EEC that has turned them into vandals.

Figure 4.2 Marshcroft Farm. Large fields, but still some hedgerows and tree-breaks

The farmer has to decide what to produce, e.g. crops or livestock, or both, and how to manage the farm's resources to achieve this. Some resources, such as land, climate and soils, are fixed so the farmer has relatively little influence over them (though the use of lime or fertiliser may improve the soil). The farmer has also to consider what capital is required and how much labour will be needed and if it is readily available. Other decisions include what to sell and who to sell to – whether to sell direct to the public or to bodies such as the Milk Marketing Board.

The inputs of land, labour and capital are managed by the farmer to produce outputs such as crops, livestock or livestock products, eg milk. Most of the outputs go to processing plants such as freezing factories, dairies, flour mills or abattoirs. However, some outputs are consumed on the farm, eg the animals may eat some of the cereals and, in turn, animal wastes, may be recycled and fed back into the system.

Farming is clearly an important decision-making operation. The farmer has to compare the income from sales of farm products (and subsidies from the European Community (EC) or Government) with the costs of production, to assess whether the farm is making a profit or a loss. This in turn will affect decisions about what crops to grow or what animals to rear, as well as decisions about the use of new machinery, pesticides, fertiliser and other inputs.

The Government and farming

The British Government intervenes in farming in order:

- to ensure that farmers have a reasonable income;
- to ensure that the whole industry remains stable and efficient;
- to protect farmers against too much foreign competition (so that Britain does not become too dependent on imported food and raw materials).

There is also intervention by the European Economic Community (EC) of which Britain is a member. One of the most controversial parts of EC policy is the 'Common Agricultural Policy' (CAP) which provides grants to farmers and also guarantees them a price for their produce. This may help to keep some inefficient farmers in business, as well as giving help to those who genuinely need it.

The EC has erected high tariff barriers so that it is difficult to import food from outside the Community. Thus, for instance, although butter from new Zealand is produced more cheaply than butter in France, Ireland or Britain, the EC tariff pushes up its price; this allows European dairy farmers a better chance to sell their own butter. The CAP seems to have encouraged over-production in some areas; there are now 'butter mountains' and 'grain-mountains' of unsold produce which cannot be easily sold off without reducing the price of these goods in a way which would ruin the farmers – who have produced them because they were encouraged by subsidies.

Figure 4.3 British farmers demonstrate in Brussels against the CAP of the European Community

Two-thirds of the whole budget of the EC goes, as subsidies, to the eight million farmers in the Community. In 1983 201,000 British farmers received £1,688,000,000, – an average of £8,400 to each farmer. These subsidies were paid to keep prices stable, encourage more investment in farming and prevent some farmers from going out of business.

The British Government also gives subsidies to its own farmers and intervenes in a number of other ways:

- by setting production quotas to prevent the over-production of particular commodities (over-production would force the price *down* for farmers);
- by advertising campaigns (e.g. to encourage people to drink more milk);
- by grants for the consolidation of land (to encourage efficient farm units);
- by grants to encourage the control of pollution in the environment.

Types of farming in Britain

The main types of farming can be grouped as follows:

- **subsistence farming** – most of the produce is grown for consumption on the farm. In Britain this is rare and only **crofting** in parts of northern Scotland and western Ireland comes close to it (but here farmers often have other money-making occupations, like making cloth or selling souvenirs to tourists);
- **commercial farming** – most of the produce is for sale. Most British farming is of this type and can be further divided in type:
- **hill farming** (with sheep and cattle) is found in areas with poorer soils and rougher pastures. The land is 'marginal' in terms of profitability;
- **arable farming** emphasises crop production and occurs on the more fertile soils;
- **dairy farming** rears cattle primarily for milk production;
- **stock farming** rears livestock primarily for meat (e.g. beef, lamb);
- **mixed farming** has elements of cattle-rearing and crop-growing and is found in most areas of rural Britain;
- **market gardening** is the growing of vegetables and fruit which can be rapidly transported to market while fresh. It is often found near large urban areas which provide the market for such goods as lettuce, tomatoes and strawberries. Much market gardening is done 'under glass', and with the aid of artificial heat and light, to protect the crops and ripen them more quickly.

Case study : a typical Scottish hill farm

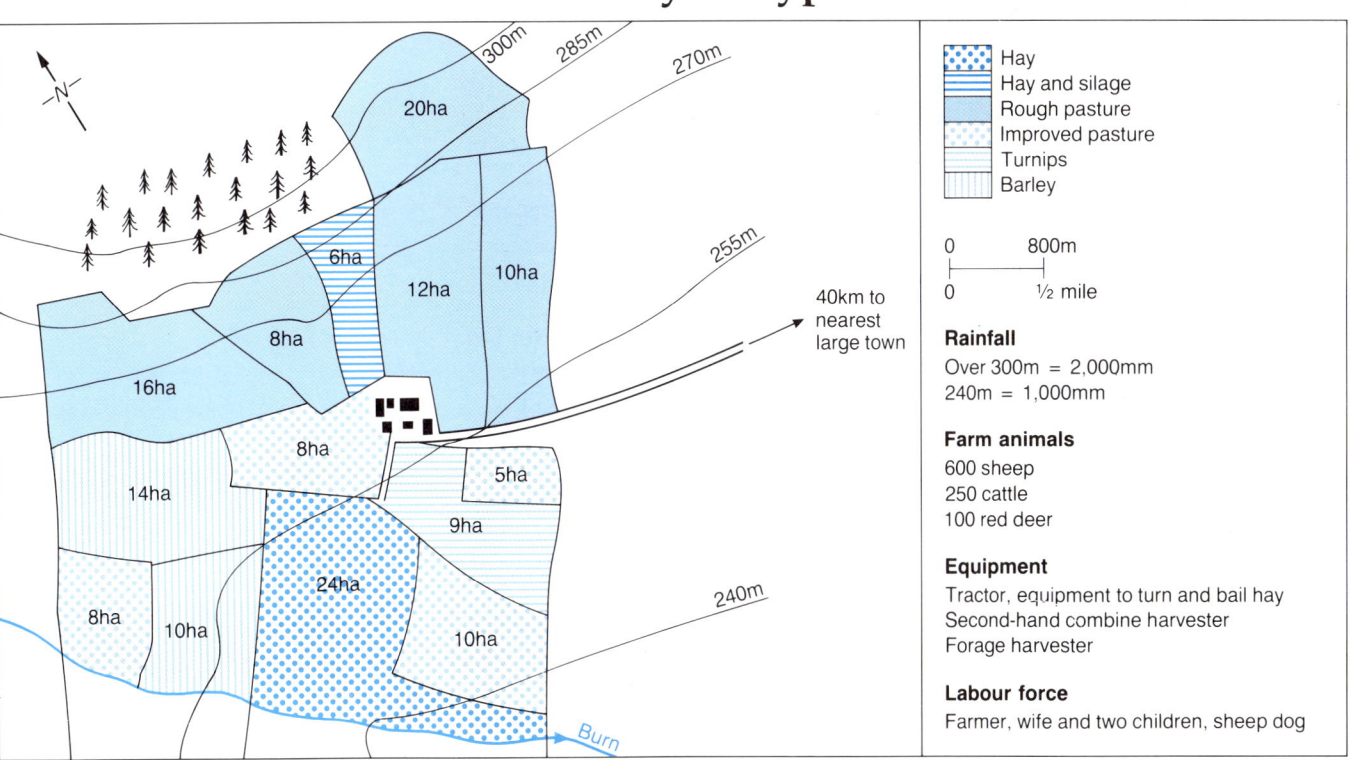

Key:
- Hay
- Hay and silage
- Rough pasture
- Improved pasture
- Turnips
- Barley

Rainfall
Over 300m = 2,000mm
240m = 1,000mm

Farm animals
600 sheep
250 cattle
100 red deer

Equipment
Tractor, equipment to turn and bail hay
Second-hand combine harvester
Forage harvester

Labour force
Farmer, wife and two children, sheep dog

Figure 4.4 A Scottish hill farm

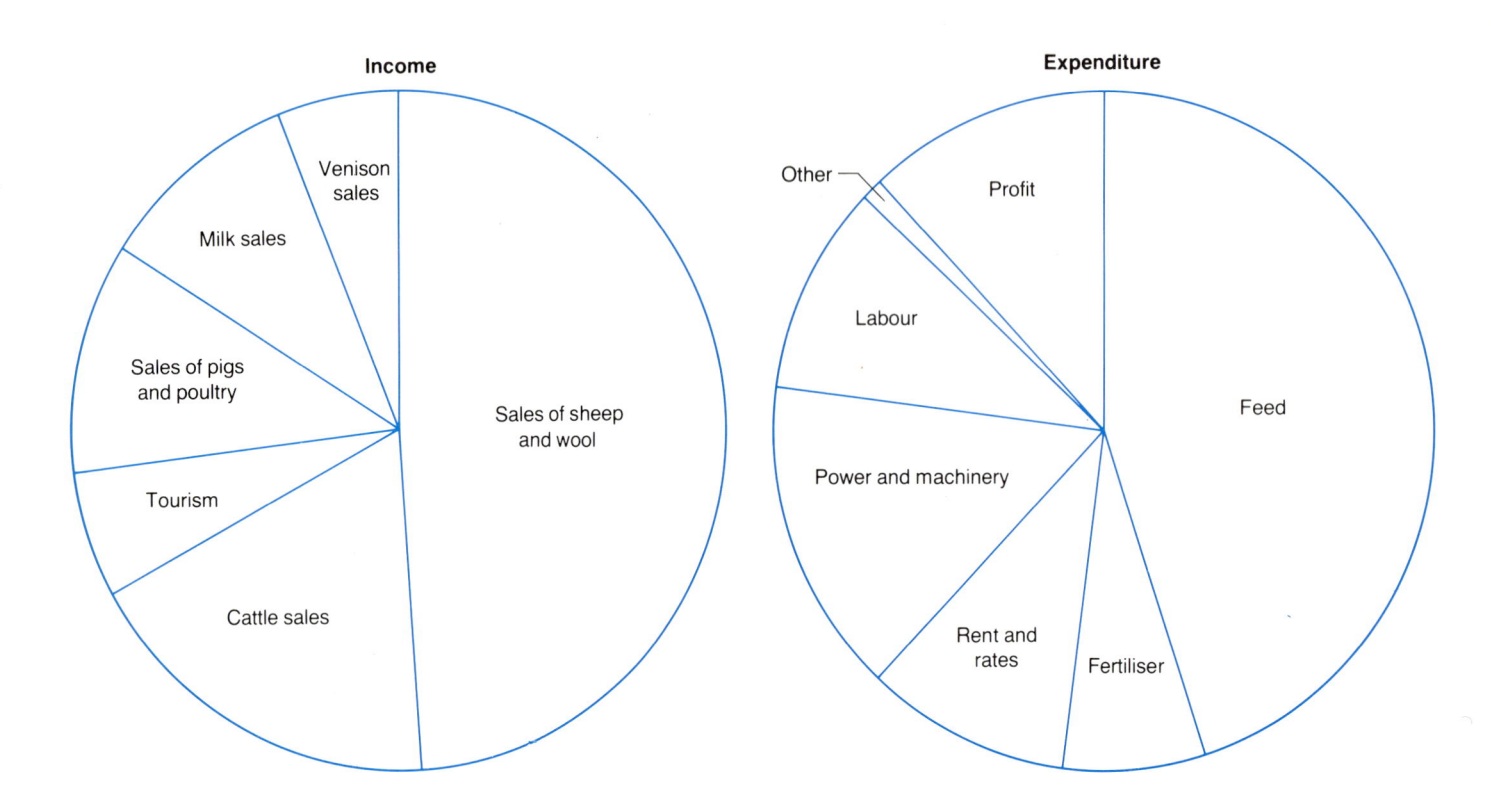

Figure 4.5 A Scottish hill farm: income and expenditure

Figure 4.4 shows the layout of Bellnoe Farm in the central Highlands of Scotland. This is an area of rocky mountain crags, steep slopes, little flat land and deep glens cut by rivers. The weather here is very changeable, with low temperatures for most of the year (January average 3°C, July 13°C) and lower temperature at high altitudes (1°C fall for every 75 metres). The first snow sometimes comes in October and may stay for fifty days. In winter, hours of daylight are short, but they are long in summer. These higher areas are also wet (2,000 mm of precipitation per year) and have only a short growing season of five to six months.

The aspect of the land, that is, its position in relation to rain, sun and wind, is important, with sunny south-facing slopes providing the best potential for farming and settlements. Even during the summer, frosts may develop in sheltered hollows, and high winds can damage plants and buildings, unless shelter belts of trees are planted.

The best land is found near the river, where the soil is sandy, well-drained and fertile. It is suitable for arable crops and improved pasture. On the lower hill slopes the soil is poorer-quality boulder clay, which can be improved by draining and by adding fertilisers and lime to reduce acidity. Here farmers grow some root crops or use the land for improved pasture.

Above 300 metres cultivation ceases as the soils are thin, acid and infertile. This is rough grazing for black-faced sheep. However, the farmers are not alone in the Highlands. Large areas of land are taken up by forestry, or HEP (Hydro Electric Power) sites, and camping and walking are popular with summer visitors.

The farmer of Bellnoe has taken advantage of government and EC grants to drain the lower hill slopes, and sow the land with better-quality pasture grass. Artificial fertilisers and animal manure are applied to all fields on the lower slopes and valley floor, in order to increase yields. Grass from the fields on the lower slopes and beside the rivers is cut for hay or silage, whilst some turnips and barley are grown as winter-feed for the animals.

The farmer also raises a few chickens for their eggs and meat, red deer for their venison, and takes in bed and breakfast visitors during the summer season.

Farming is not easy in this harsh, wet upland environment, particularly with problems of unreliable weather, and rising costs of fuel (for tractors etc.) and animal feed (the farmer has to buy in extra feed every year to supplement the home-grown hay, oats, barley and turnips).

Questions

1. Roughly how large in area is the farm?
2. Roughly calculate the percentage of the farm which is:
   a) rough grazing;
   b) arable;
   c) improved pasture.
3. What area of land is devoted to each of the main crops?
4. Why are the arable fields to be found on the *lower* slopes?
5. What are the four main sources of income to the farmer? what are his main costs?
6. How else does the farmer try to increase his income?
7. Look at the calendar diagram (Fig. 4.6). How long do the sheep spend on the hills?

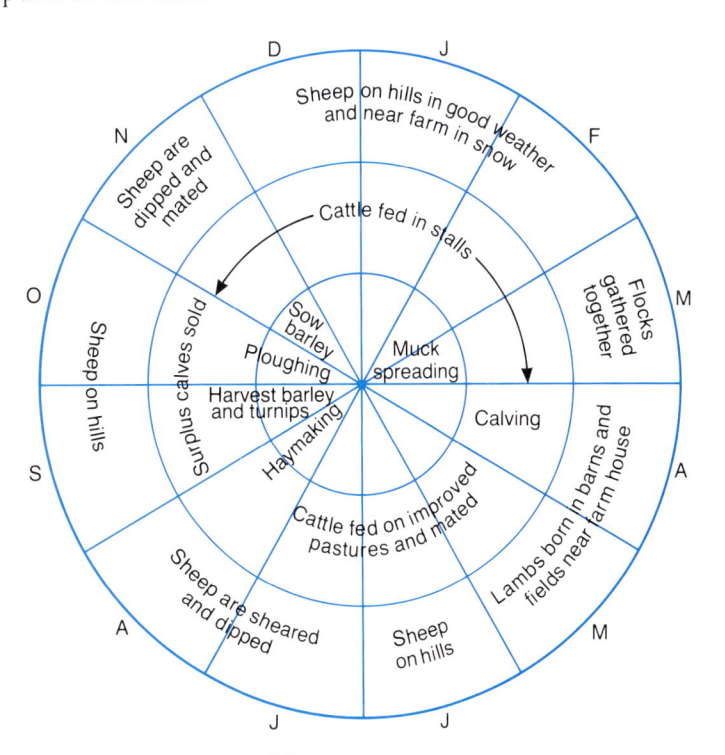

Figure 4.6 A year on a Scottish hill farm

8. How long can cattle be grazed out of doors?
9. Why are the sheep brought down from the hills?
10. Why are the hills not used for cattle rearing?
11. From the information in this case study, draw a diagram of the hill farm to show inputs, processes and outputs.

Case study: Brookfield Farm – a West Midland dairy farm

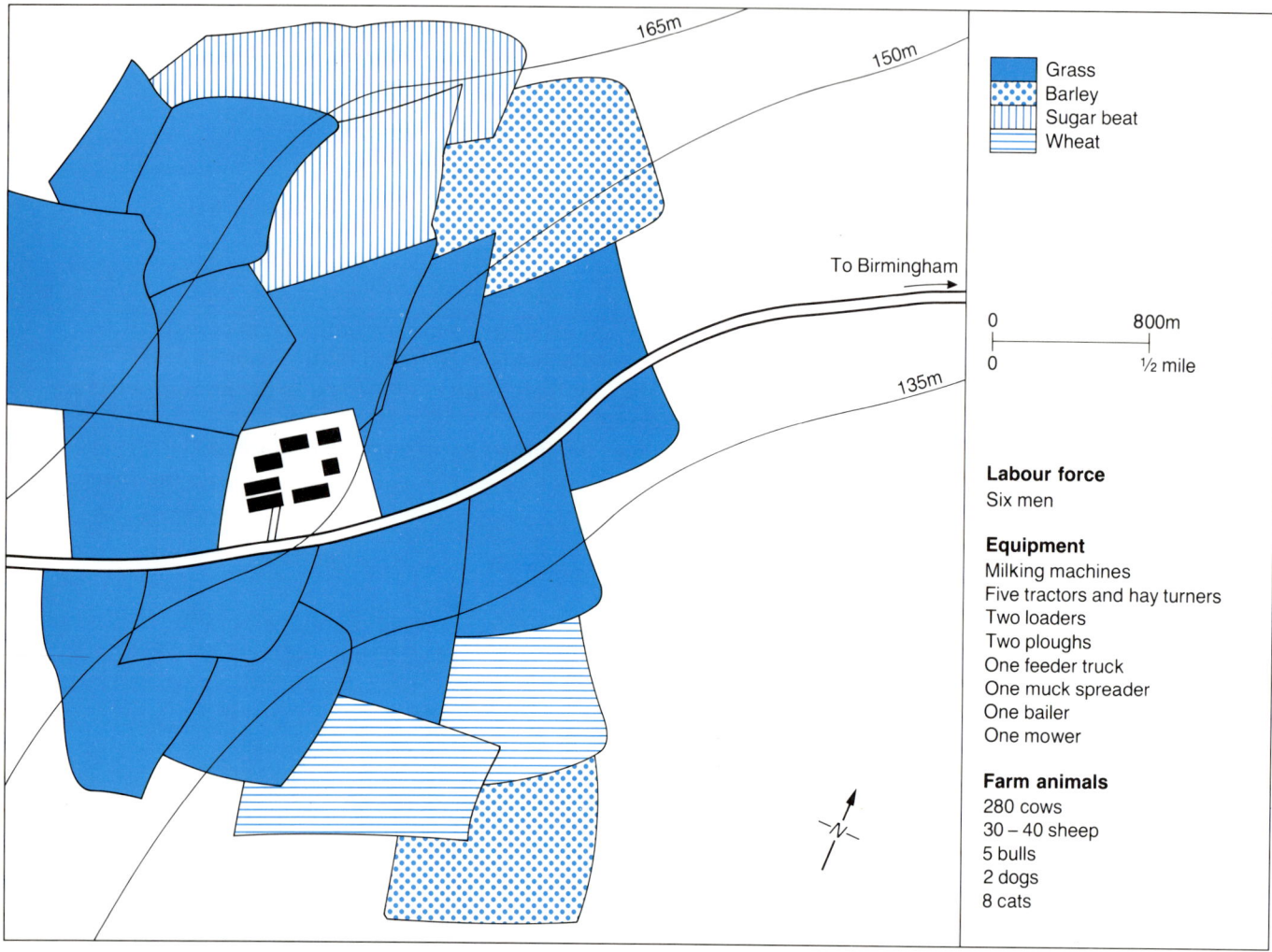

Figure 4.7 Brookfield farm: a dairy farm

Legend:
- Grass
- Barley
- Sugar beat
- Wheat

Labour force
Six men

Equipment
Milking machines
Five tractors and hay turners
Two loaders
Two ploughs
One feeder truck
One muck spreader
One bailer
One mower

Farm animals
280 cows
30 – 40 sheep
5 bulls
2 dogs
8 cats

Brookfield Farm is situated in Worcestershire, some 20 kilometres west of Birmingham. Dairy farming in Britain tends to be found in areas where grass grows well, so western regions with moderate rainfall, mild winters and cool summers are often important. Other dairying areas, such as parts of Kent, are based on heavy clay soils which are difficult to plough, but the most important locating factor is the need to consume milk fresh, so any area near a large town may become a dairy region. In fact, improved transport, such as larger lorry tankers and the building of motorways, means that London obtains fresh milk from areas over 600 kilometres away. In the more remote areas of the United Kingdom, such as parts of Scotland and Northern Ireland, milk is made into cheese and butter.

On Brookfield farm the cattle are milked three times a day, at 4.00 a.m., 2.00 p.m., and 10.00 p.m. In order to handle the 280 Friesian cattle a new milking parlour has been built, capable of taking sixteen cows at a time. Here they can be milked and fed on concentrates in only 15 minutes. The farm has two cowmen, who specialise in milking the animals. Each cow produces 30–35 kilos of milk per day. A tanker lorry collects the milk from the large refrigerated tank on the farm, to transport it to the Unigate Dairy, 18 kilometres away in Birmingham.

Agriculture 37

The cattle are kept near the farm all year, in order to save time, so most fields near the farmhouse are grass (see Fig. 4.7). Other fields, further away from the farm, grow wheat, which is sometimes sold, or at other times fed to the cattle. These fields may also be used for barley and sugar beet (for animal fodder), and grass, which is used for grazing or cut for silage. The cattle can usually graze outdoors until November, when they are brought in to the barns where silage and other fodder crops are available. Animal feed still has to be bought in, and it is expensive.

In addition to the cattle, the farm has between thirty and forty sheep, which help to keep the pasture grass short in winter and free from weeds. In February these sheep are sold for meat.

Figure 4.8 Brookfield farm: income and expenditure

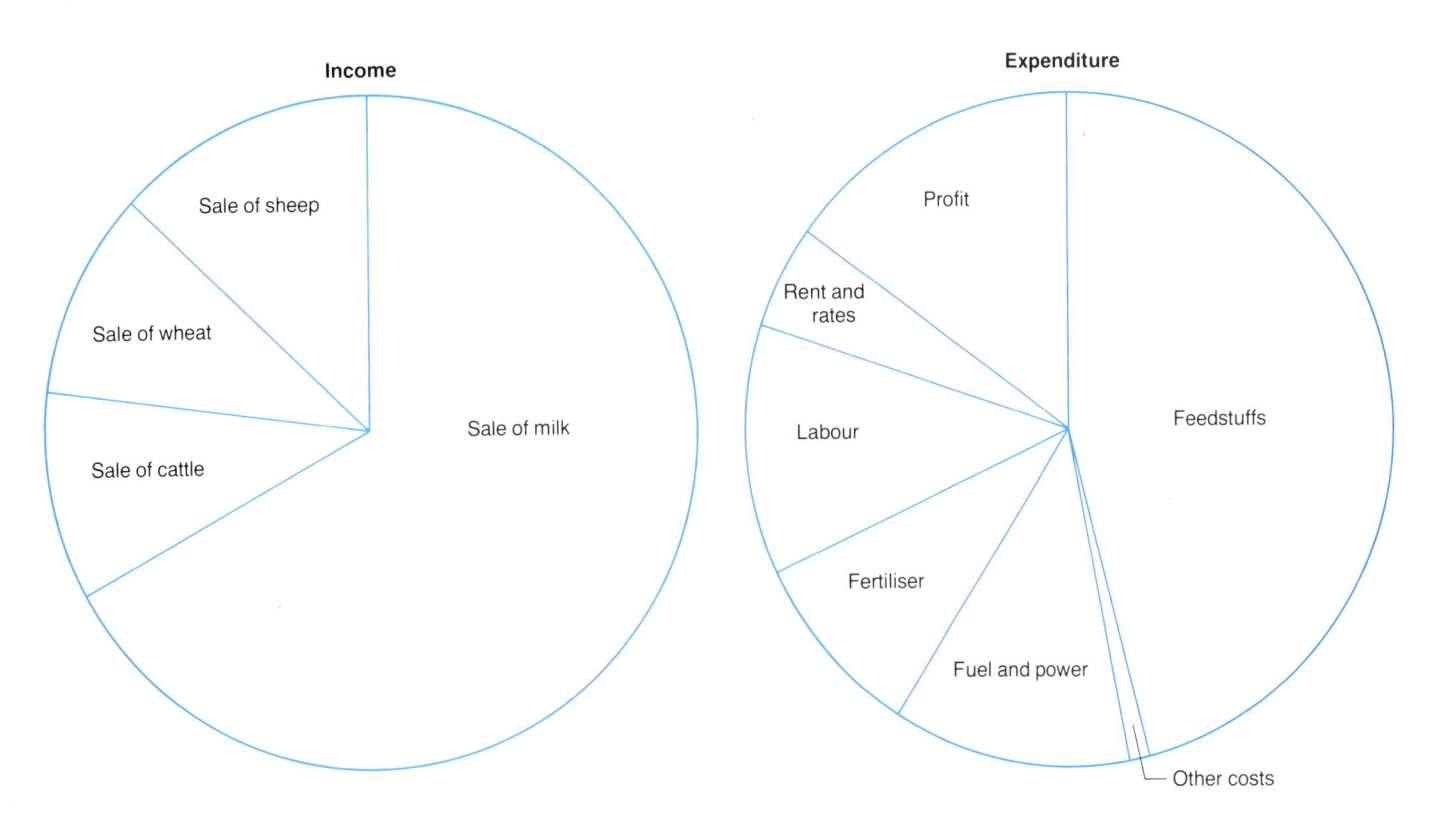

Income

- Sale of sheep
- Sale of wheat
- Sale of cattle
- Sale of milk

Expenditure

- Profit
- Rent and rates
- Labour
- Fertiliser
- Fuel and power
- Other costs
- Feedstuffs

Questions

1. Study Figs 4.4 and 4.7. Compare Brookfield Farm with the Hill Farm under the following headings:
   a) farm size;
   b) crops grown;
   c) percentage to total area given to each crop;
   d) farm animals reared (numbers and types);
   e) farm machinery;
   f) number of employees.
2. What are the main sources of income on Brookfield Farm?
3. What are the three largest items of cost? How might these be reduced?

Case study: Market gardening

One distinctive form of British farming uses much less land than either arable, hill, or dairy farming, but stands out by its particular locations, by its intensity and by its equipment.

This is market-gardening, the growing of vegetable and fruit crops on plots of 2 or 3 hectares of land, often using glasshouses, artificial heat and many fertilisers. There are pockets of market-gardening on fertile soils all over Britain. Many of them originally grew up because of their closeness to a large urban centre which formed a ready market for their fresh produce. The Lee Valley north of London is one such example. But these days, improvements in road links mean that the produce can be quickly transported all over the country.

Two traditional centres of market-gardening have been the Scilly Isles and the Channel Islands, both of which have milder winters and earlier spring weather than the mainland. This milder weather allows them to grow a wide range of vegetables, fruits and flowers, and to have them ready earlier than other places in Britain. (Guernsey tomatoes and flowers from the Scilly Isles are well-known 'early' crops in many markets and shops in urban areas.)

These crops are sent by air transport to their urban markets; the expense of this is offset by the relatively high prices which are paid for the 'first' crops of the new season. Even a few days' lead in getting crops ripe can make a considerable difference to the market gardener's income, since the prices fluctuate widely as more supplies come on to the market.

Figure 4.9 A market garden: income and expenditure

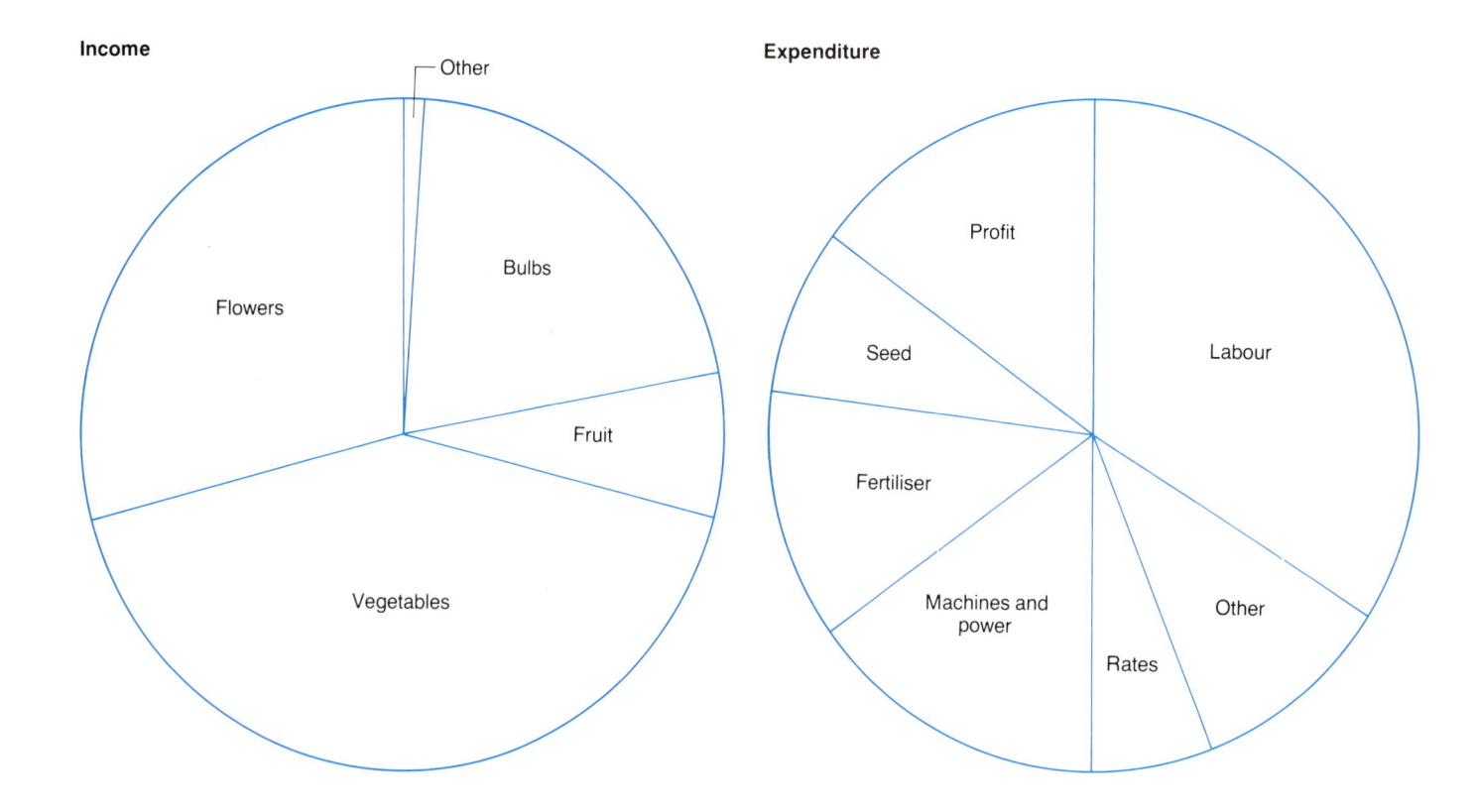

Agriculture 39

Figure 4.10 Glasshouses in Guernsey, Channel Islands

Questions

1. How many separate farms can you identify in Fig. 4.10?
2. Look at Fig. 4.9. How do the items of farm expenditure compare with other types of farming?
3. Here is a list of some of the crops grown on market gardens in the Sandy area of Bedfordshire. Which ones would you choose to grow if you farmed on a market garden there?
   Lettuce, potatoes, tomatoes, asparagus, chicory, peppers, carnations, daffodils.

40 A Geography of Contemporary Britain

Database: farming

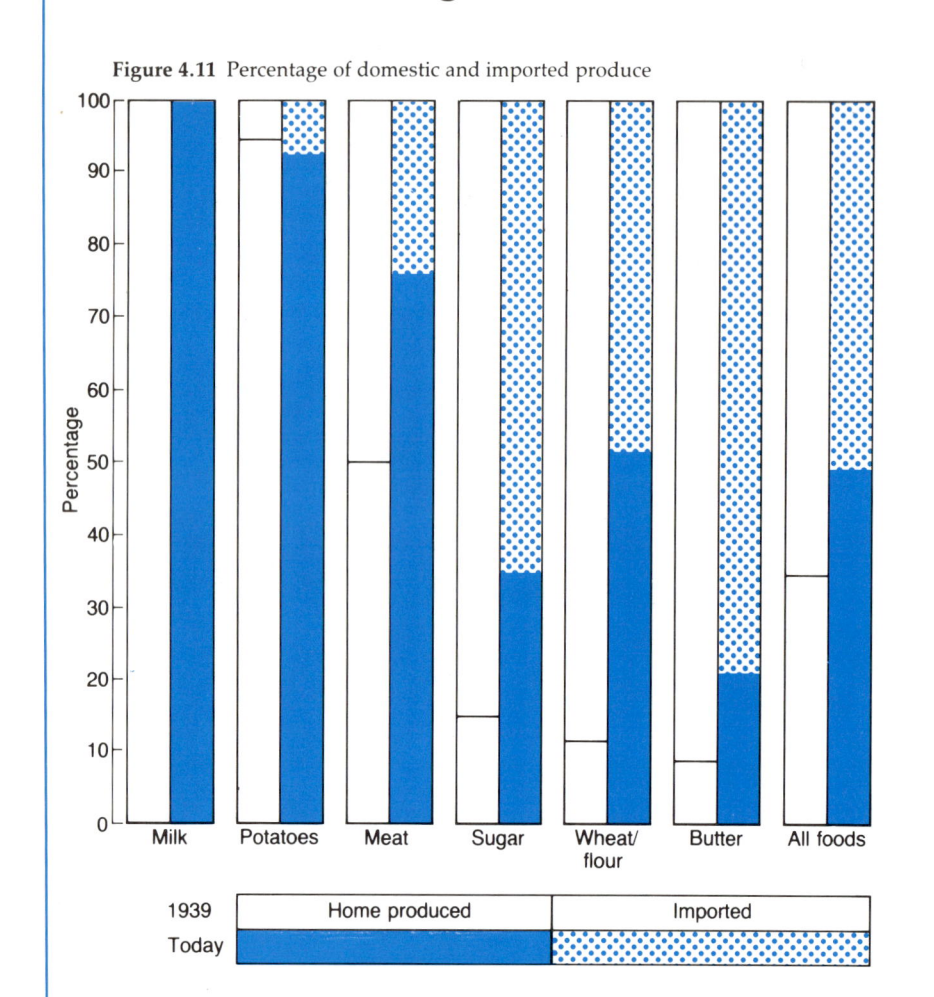

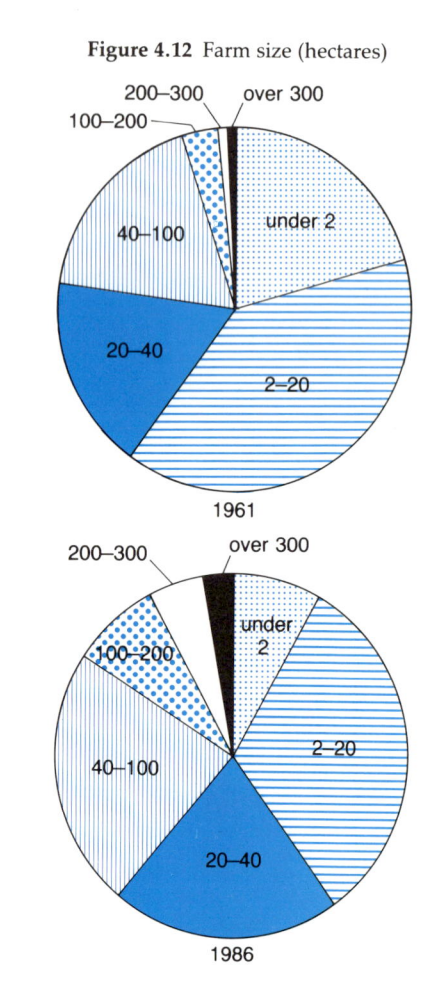

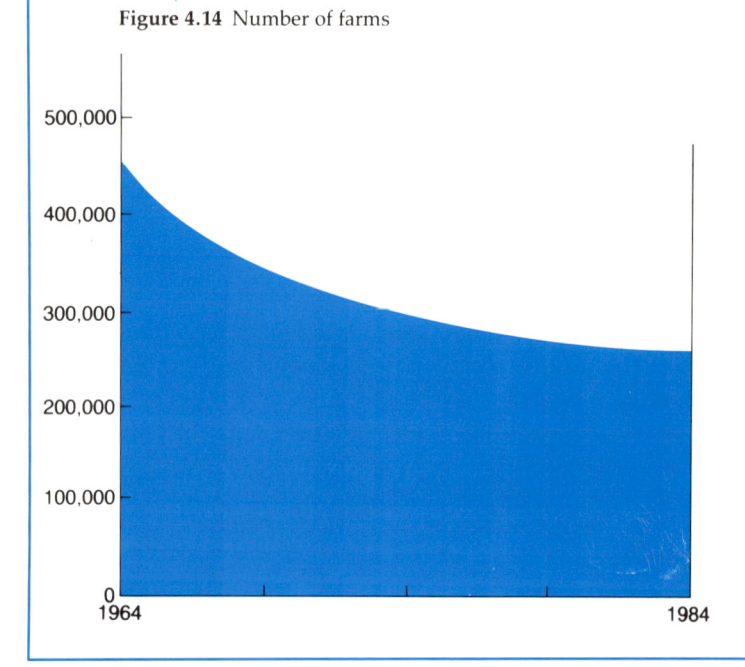

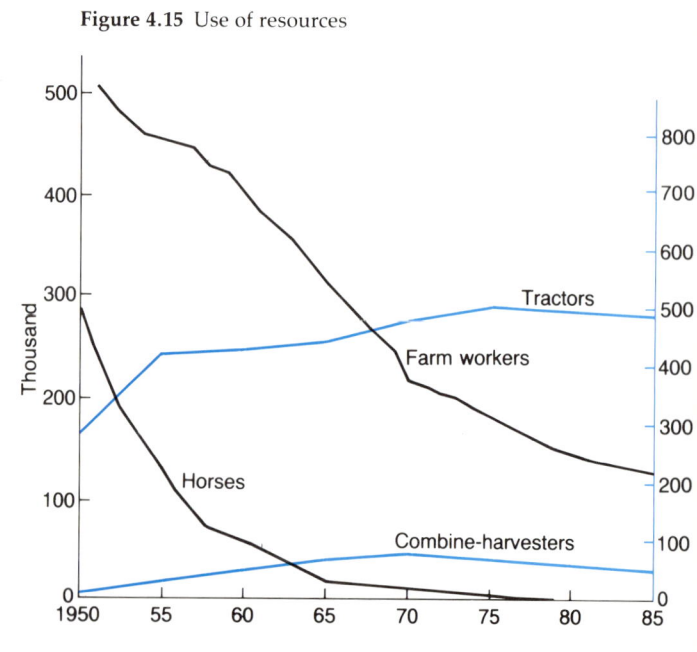

Figure 4.11 Percentage of domestic and imported produce

Milk, Potatoes, Meat, Sugar, Wheat/flour, Butter, All foods

1939 Home produced | Imported
Today

Figure 4.12 Farm size (hectares)

1961

1986

Farm size categories: under 2, 2–20, 20–40, 40–100, 100–200, 200–300, over 300

Figure 4.14 Number of farms (1964–1984)

Figure 4.15 Use of resources (1950–85)
Tractors, Farm workers, Horses, Combine-harvesters

Figure 4.13 Area of arable crops

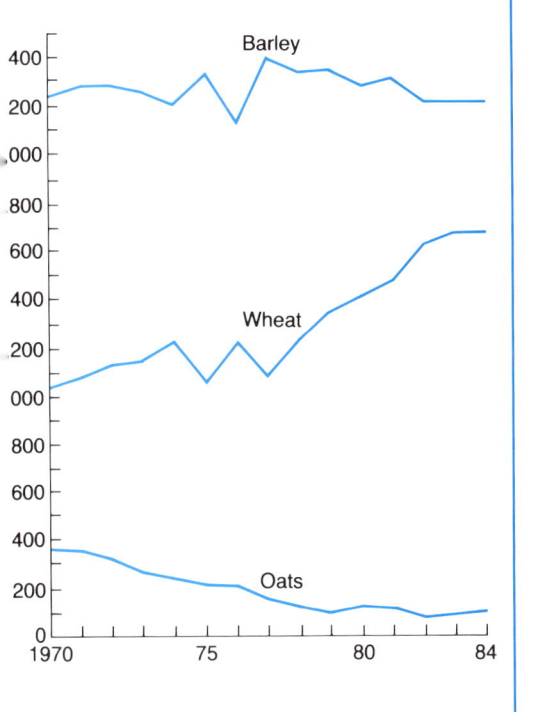

Figure 4.16 Yields of arable crops

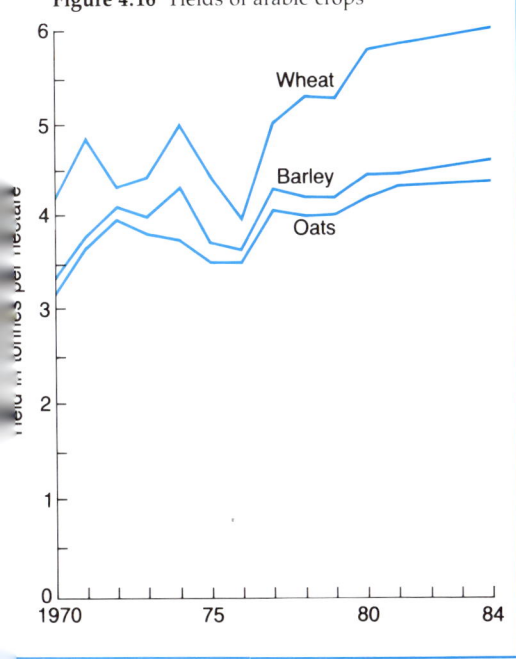

Workbase

1. Look at Fig. 4.11 and answer the following questions:
   a) Of which product has Britain always produced everything it needs?
   b) By what percentage has domestic meat production increased since 1939?
   c) What percentage of sugar was imported in 1939? How much is imported today?
   d) What is the percentage change of home-produced wheat since 1939?
   e) What is the percentage change of home-produced butter since 1939?
   f) Of what product do we import more today than in 1939?

2. Study Figs. 4.12–4.16 carefully and then write a paragraph summarising the changes in British farming since 1950 using the following headings:
   a) farm size;
   b) number of farms;
   c) number of people employed on farms;
   d) mechanisation;
   e) changing yields;
   f) changing patterns of crop production.

3. Classify the following list of farming factors into:
   a) inputs (land, labour or capital);
   b) processes;
   c) outputs.

Milking parlour	Rent	Animal feed	Milking
Silage	Milk	Grazing	Calves
Improved seed	Pesticides	Boiler fuel	Electricity
Drainage	Rainfall	Sheep	Hay

4. Look at the map (Plate 38) showing the distribution of the main types of farming in Britain.
   Take each type of farming listed on the map, and:
   a) describe the areas of Britain where it is found (use an atlas to help you);
   b) explain the pattern of distribution by referring to Plates 33–36.

5. In 1984, the Nature Conservancy Council estimated that since 1946 Britain had lost:

   95 per cent of its herb and flower-rich meadows;
   50–60 per cent of all heathland;
   50 per cent of fens and wetlands;
   30–50 per cent of ancient deciduous woodland; and
   30 per cent of upland grassland and heath to farming or housing.

   Should we be concerned by this loss, or is it the acceptable price to pay for economic prosperity and progress?

6. Many farmers are now turning to 'multiple-use' of their farmland and buildings in order to fully utilise their property. Stables and cowsheds are being turned into small industrial units, fields into golf driving ranges, and so on. What kinds of multiple-use might be opposed by planners and local residents?

Chapter 5
Forestry

(a) **Figure 5.1(a–f)** The uses of timber

(b)

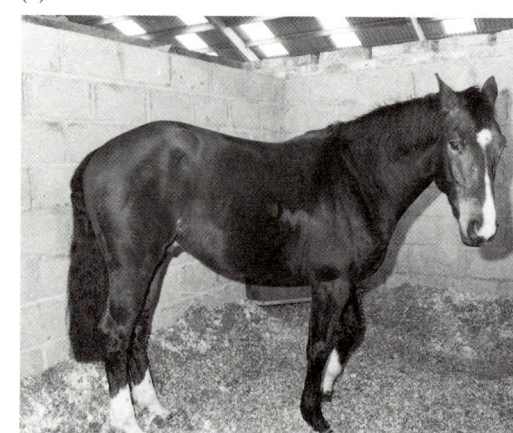

(c)

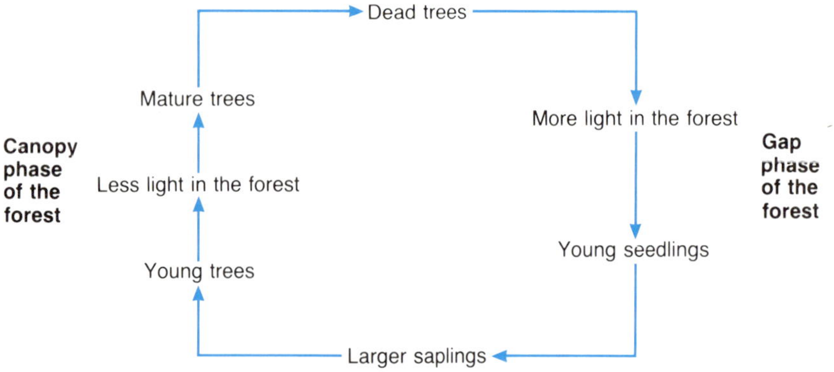

Figure 5.2 The cycle of forest regeneration

```
              Dead trees
         ┌──────────────────┐
         │                  ▼
    Mature trees      More light in the forest
         ▲                  │
Canopy   │                  │            Gap
phase  Less light           │          phase
of the in the forest        │          of the
forest   │                  │          forest
         │                  ▼
    Young trees         Young seedlings
         ▲                  │
         │                  │
         └── Larger saplings ◄┘
```

(d)

(e)

In the United Kingdom 8.5 per cent of the land is covered by forest, half of which has been planted within the last forty years. Britain's forests are a very valuable resource, as Fig. 5.1 illustrates.

There are two main types of timber – hardwood such as mahogany, teak and oak, which come from deciduous forests, and softwoods such as pine, spruce and larch, which are grown in coniferous forests. Before 5000 BC most of Britain, except the very highest, steepest and wettest areas, was covered by forest. It is difficult to be certain what the early forests were like, but there were probably open glades within the forest where the cycle of regeneration was in operation (see Fig. 5.2).

(f)

The changing forest cover

Fig. 5.6 shows how the forest cover has expanded and contracted according to changing political, social and economic circumstances. For instance, there was a great decrease in the forest cover during the eighteenth century when the agricultural revolution allowed new methods to be used and more land was needed.

The Forestry Commission

During the First World War nearly one-third of Britain's depleted stocks of timber was consumed. German submarines had made imports very difficult, so domestic forests had to be cut. By 1919 there was general alarm in Britain at the low level of timber stocks, so the Forestry Commission was set up with the main aim of increasing Britain's forest reserves. During the 1920s and 1930s a start was made by planting new areas of woodland. But this was interrupted by the Second World War when further inroads were made in the forested areas. Since 1950, however, both the forest area and amount of timber produced have both expanded, as Figs 5.4 and 5.5 illustrate.

Forestry expansion – good or bad?

The Forestry Commission has had to acquire land in order to sustain the expansion of the industry. Most land in Britain is expensive because it is in great demand. The only large areas of relatively cheap land suitable for tree planting are in the highland areas of the country, particularly parts of Wales and Scotland.

As a result many hill areas throughout the United Kingdom have been covered by forest. This has led to objections because some glorious views of open countryside have been replaced by closed ranks of coniferous trees. Some ramblers complain because the new forests cut across old paths and access becomes restricted.

In order to increase timber production as quickly as possible, the Forestry Commission planted the fast growing coniferous trees such as pine, fir and spruce. These trees retain their needles most of the year and so, unlike deciduous trees, do not lose their leaves in autumn. However, some people object to views of long rows of uniform conifers, thinking they are boring and dull, tending to make a dark, drab landscape.

There are other objections to planting more coniferous trees:

- Large areas of conifers are not natural to the British landscape and they are creating a very uniform, alien landscape.
- Planting conifers on open moorlands means that when the trees form a canopy the natural heath and moorland vegetation dies and is replaced by a covering of pine needles and a few mosses. The main danger is that rare plants, animals and environments, such as blanket bogs or valley mires, will be destroyed forever.
- Planting a few species of tree may make an attack on them all by pests and diseases more disastrous. Spraying with pesticides may kill wildlife.
- Coniferous forest plantations do provide a habitat for wildlife new to the area, for example birds such as chaffinch, wren and woodpigeon. But the loss of open moorland may mean that birds, such as merlin, golden plover and greenshank, disappear with the loss of their habitat.

But remember:

- Britain imports 90 per cent of its timber, so this is a high cost on the balance of payments. Growing more of our own timber would reduce this cost.
- By the year AD 2025 a 90 per cent increase in the world demand for timber is forecast, so Britain must produce more.
- Britain produces its timber on only 8.5 per cent of the land area, as opposed to an average 21 per cent of land covered by forest in EC countries.

Case study: Grizedale

Not only is forestry itself changing rapidly, but equally the role of the Forestry Commission has expanded beyond the mere provision of timber. One forest, Grizedale (extending over 3500 hectares of land between Coniston Water and Lake Windermere) in the Lake District illustrates the great variety of tasks that the Forestry Commission has to fulfill.

Stabilising soil on steep slopes
In a mountainous area like this, with steep slopes and heavy rainfall, tree roots help to bind the soil together and prevent erosion.

Conservation of wildlife
The forest provides an important habitat for squirrels, and both roe and red deer. Grizedale beck has brown and sea trout and salmon, and natural tarns are home for greylag geese plus mallard and teal ducks.

Recreation and education
- Car parks and picnic centres, together with a Visitor and Wildlife Centre.
- Forest trails and walks.
- Photo safari and observation hides.
- Angling club and pony trekking.
- Camping, self-catering chalets.
- Forest theatre, hotel and restaurant.

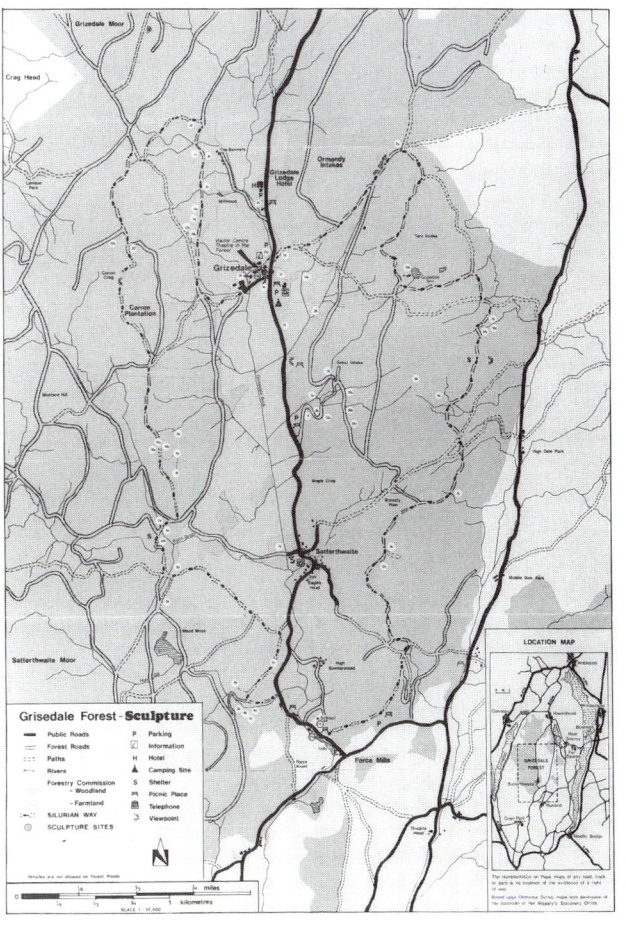

Timber production
There is a growing local market for fencing stakes and posts, whilst the pulp mill at Washington and several local mills continue to demand Grizedale timber. 10,000 tonnes of timber are produced each year, of which 15 per cent are sawmill logs, 40 per cent paper and pulp, 35 per cent posts and stakes, and 10 per cent assorted products.

Providing Employment
The forest is managed by a chief forester, one head forester three foresters, a head ranger and one full-time and two part-time office workers. There are also thirty forest workers and two part-time cleaners.

Helping farmers
Trees can provide shelter, helping farmers produce better crops and stock in such a high, exposed area.

Database: forestry

Figure 5.3 A forest area

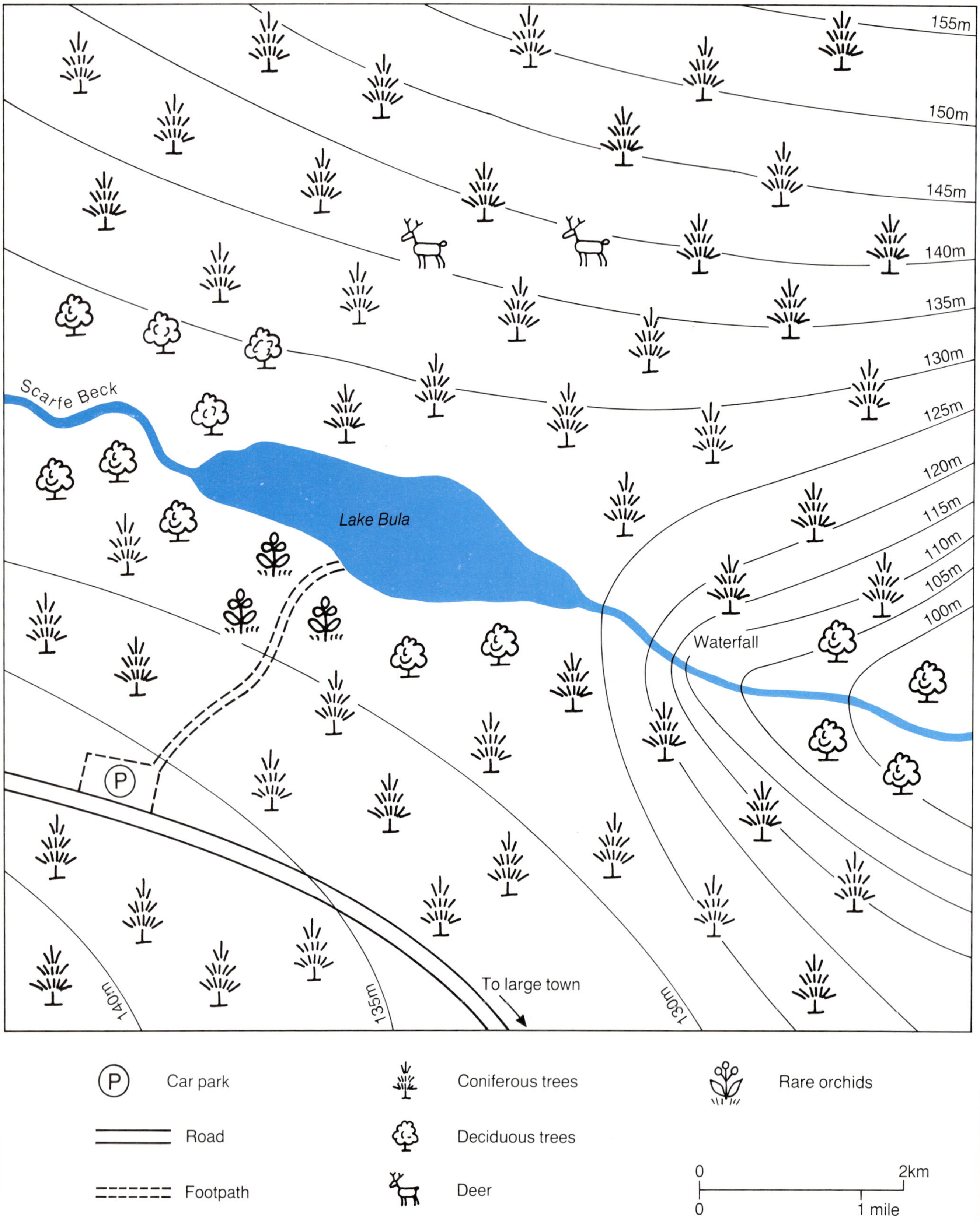
155m
150m
145m
140m
135m
130m
125m
120m
115m
110m
105m
100m
Scarfe Beck
Lake Bula
Waterfall
P
To large town
140m
135m
130m
Car park
Road
Footpath
Coniferous trees
Deciduous trees
Deer
Rare orchids
0
2km
0
1 mile

Workbase 1

Opening up the forest: a decision-making exercise

The Forestry Commission has decided to open the area shown on Fig. 5.3 to the public. This plantation lies about 40 kilometres from a large town of 500,000 people. The Commission sent out a questionnaire asking 'do you think there should be any of the following features in the forest?' The results are shown below.

	Percentage of people who said yes
More paths to the lake	96
Walks around the lake	94
Deciduous trees near paths and the main road	87
More forest walks	85
Better roads into the area	67
More toilets	65
Picnic areas	58
Caravan sites	56
'Hides' to observe wildlife	51
Refreshment facilities	50
Camp sites	37

You have to redesign the layout of the area to include some (or all) of the features listed above. You need to decide:

1. If all the facilities are to be provided.
2. How many of each facility will be built without spoiling the natural beauty of the area.
3. How much each project would cost (see list below).
4. What you can provide on a total budget of £250,000.

You can then redraw the map locating each facility using the correct symbol.

Project	Cost (£)
Car Park (60 cars)	6,000
Toilet block	22,000
Caravan site (50 vans)	110,000
Camping site (150 tents)	90,000
Restaurant	50,000
Picnic area	4,000
Access road (cost per km)	8,000
Footpath (cost per km)	400
Hide	300

Database: forestry

Figure 5.4 Forested area (Forestry Commission land)

Year	Thousands of hectares
1950	170
1955	400
1960	510
1965	640
1970	690
1975	800
1980	910

Figure 5.5 Timber production by Forestry Commission

Year	Thousands of cubic metres
1950	260
1955	320
1960	460
1965	500
1970	1 000
1975	1 200
1980	1 500

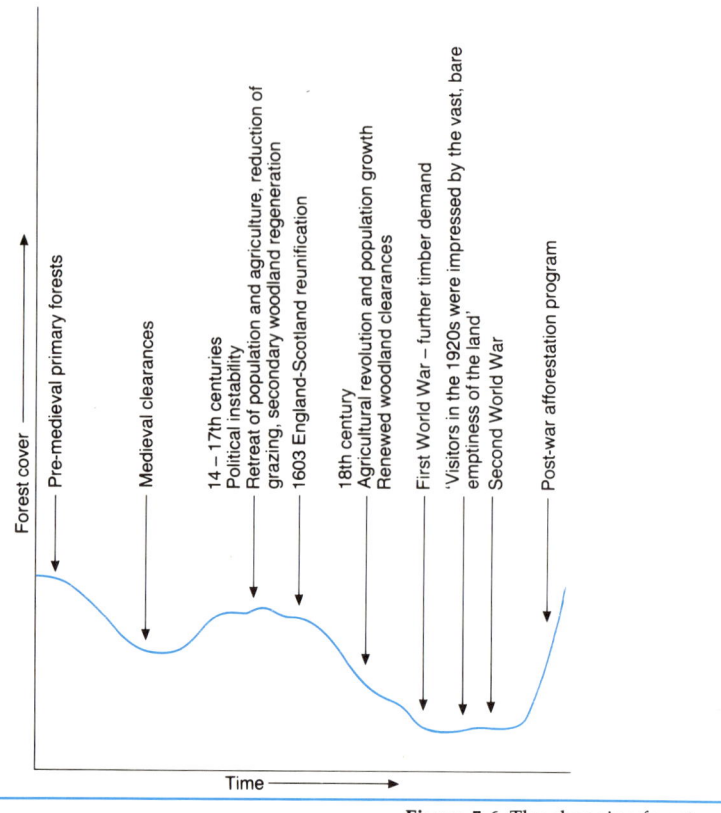

Figure 5.6 The changing forest cover

Labels on Figure 5.6: Pre-medieval primary forests; Medieval clearances; 14–17th centuries Political instability Retreat of population and agriculture, reduction of grazing, secondary woodland regeneration; 1603 England-Scotland reunification; 18th century Agricultural revolution and population growth Renewed woodland clearances; First World War – further timber demand; 'Visitors in the 1920s were impressed by the vast, bare emptiness of the land'; Second World War; Post-war afforestation program

Workbase 2

1. Look at Fig. 5.2 and explain in your own words (prose or poetry) the growth of a forest canopy.

2. Make a list of the uses of wood in the home. What newer alternative materials have replaced wood for some purposes, and what advantages do they have over wood?

3. Study Fig. 5.6 and make a copy of it. Add the following labels at the correct points:
   a) The expansion of Britain's navy (e.g. Nelson's fleet) requires the felling of large areas of forests.
   b) Population growth in the twelfth century leads to further forest removal, because of the need for farmland and fencing.
   c) Forestry develops to provide charcoal for smelting iron (used for 300 years until 1760).
   d) Early man cuts down trees to provide houses and fuel, and to clear the land for settlement.

4. Using Figs. 5.4 and 5.5
   a) Construct two graphs to show the changing area under forest and timber production.
   b) If present trends continue, how many hectares of land will be planted by the Forestry Commission by AD 2000?
   c) What is the percentage increase in the output of timber since 1955?

5. Give some examples of cases where the different roles of the Forestry Commission may conflict with each other.

Chapter 6
Mining and quarrying

Mining and quarrying in rural areas: saving jobs or the environment?

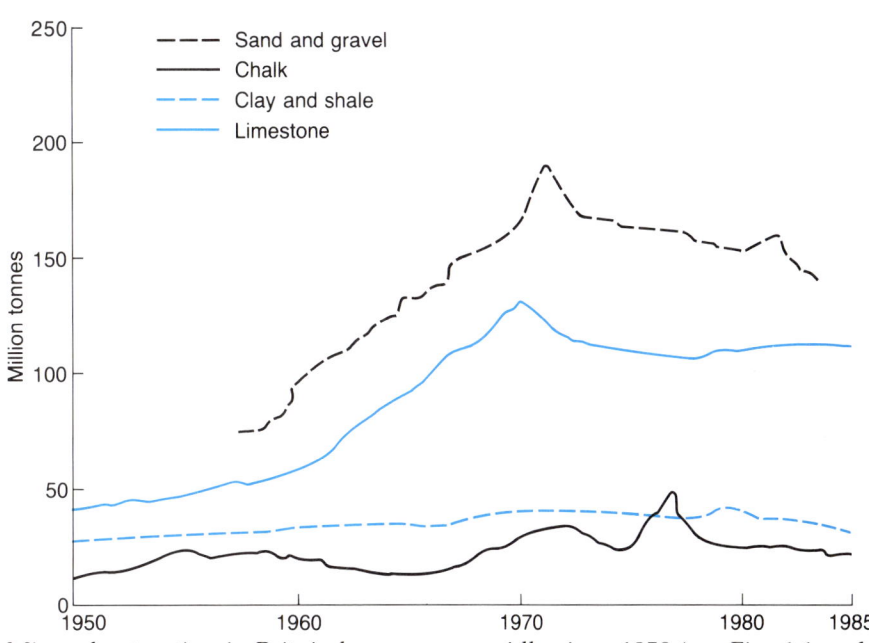

Figure 6.1 Mineral production in Britain

Mineral extraction in Britain has grown rapidly since 1950 (see Fig. 6.1 and Plate 39). This growth is the result of the needs of urban housing and redevelopment, of road improvement schemes and of motorway construction – all of which have created a demand for minerals, especially for concrete.

Concrete is made from ● cement (made from chalk or limestone)
and ● aggregates (which consist of
sand and gravel *or*
crushed limestone *or*
crushed sandstone *or*
artificially-made material

So there has been a massive expansion in the mining (underground) or quarrying (by 'open-cast' methods) of minerals such as limestone, chalk, sands, gravels and granite.

Quarrying and mining are not new to Britain. The Romans, for example, mined lead in the Pennines and tin in Cornwall. But there has been a vast increase in mineral extraction. There are now many unsightly quarries, spoil heaps, storage areas, and processing plants, and they cannot all be disguised by tree belts or embankments. Up to 2,000 hectares of land each year are now taken over in this way.

The activity is increasing rather than declining. The growing economic value of oil and potash has also encouraged recent searches in rural environments all over Britain.

Case study: the Yorkshire Dales

One example of mineral extraction is the limestone quarrying of the Yorkshire Dales. Figure 6.2 shows the location of the main quarries and the resulting traffic flows. At present only 10 per cent of all quarry products leave the area by rail. Quarry operators are reluctant to switch to rail transport because it is very expensive to install new railway lines and sidings. This expense would commit the company to the long-term use of the site, together with a high output (to repay the costs) and greater reliance on more distant markets. At present, therefore, the quarrying industry prefers the greater flexibility offered by road transport. However, lorries are becoming larger and they represent a source of environmental damage, as well as a potential danger to other road users.

Figure 6.2 Quarry traffic in the Yorkshire Dales

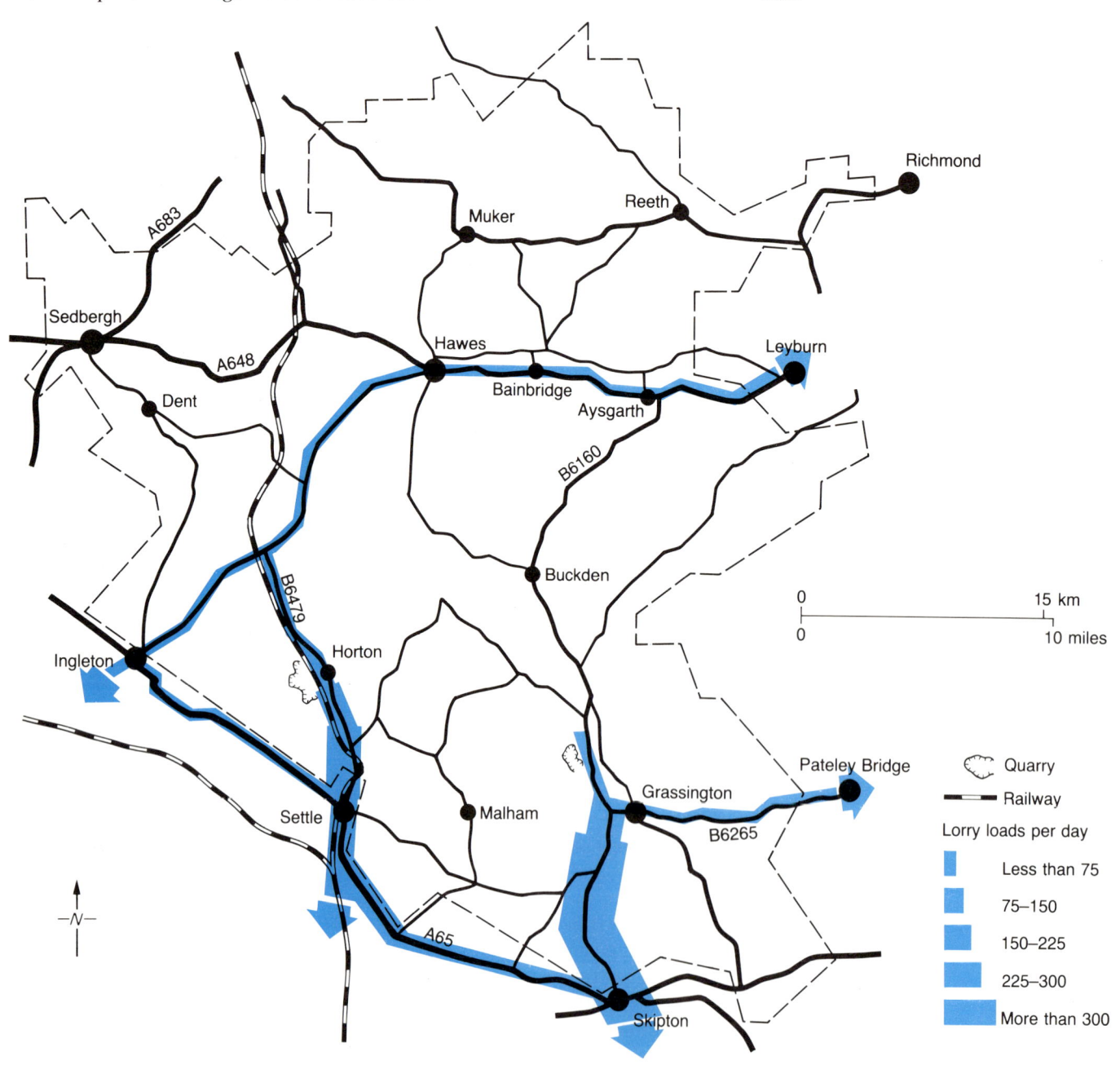

Mining and quarrying 51

Figure 6.3 Horton Quarry, Yorkshire (see map Fig. 6.2)

Questions

1. What type of limestone is being quarried in this area?
2. Which sections of which roads have the greatest problems from quarry traffic?
3. How might the roads be improved to cater for heavy lorries? What would be the effect of this on the character of the local countryside?
4. Look at Fig. 6.3. Make an outline tracing of the photograph. Mark on your tracing a) the crushing plant, b) lime burning, c) waste tips, d) area previously mined and now flooded, e) trees planted to screen the quarry. Describe how you think the area might have looked before the quarry came (look at the area around the quarry).

In order to quarry the very pure Yorkshire limestone the rock is first blasted loose, and then crushed into smaller fragments which pass through screens to sort them into sizes. The limestone is then burned to concentrate the lime content. When cool, it is stored in special containers called hoppers, before transport by lorry to the cities and farms.

At first, quarrying was welcomed in the area because it brought new jobs, but now people are not too sure. These are some of their views:

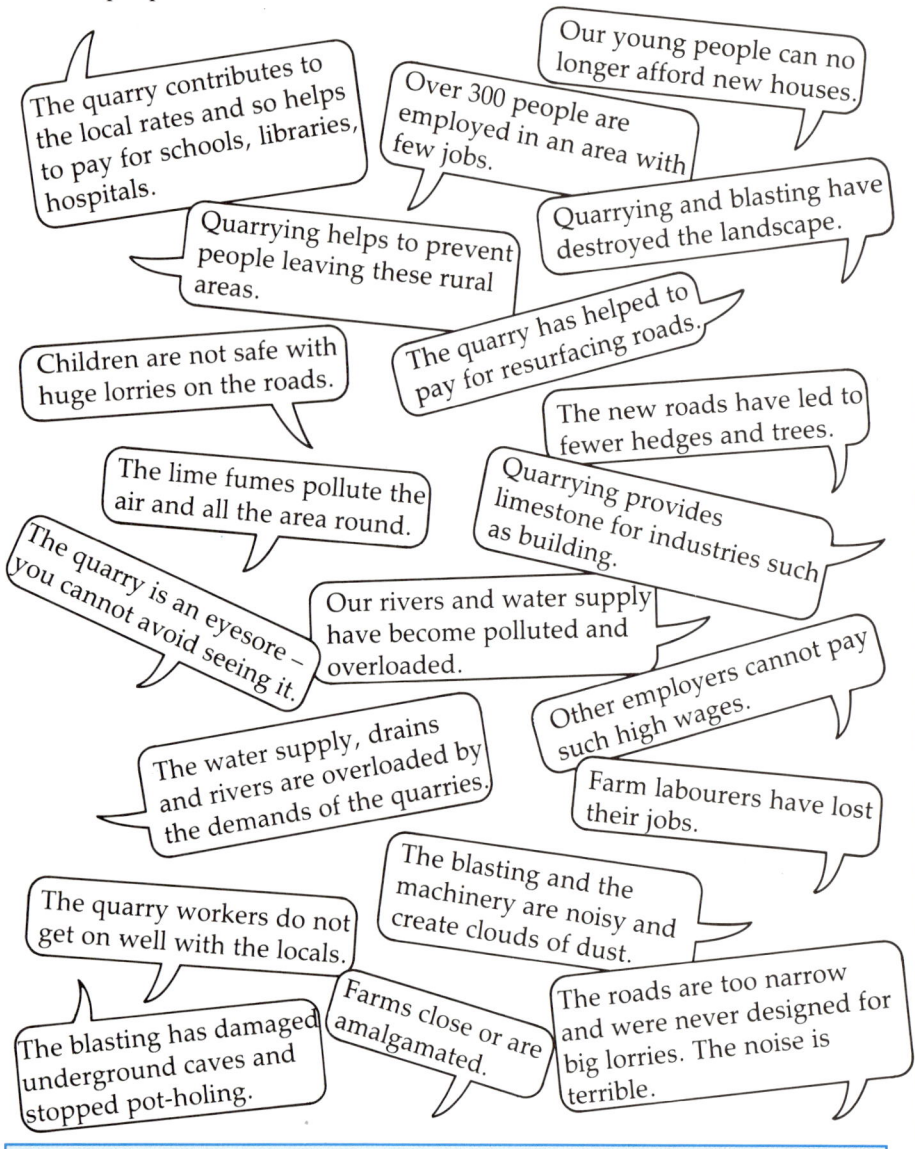

- The quarry contributes to the local rates and so helps to pay for schools, libraries, hospitals.
- Over 300 people are employed in an area with few jobs.
- Our young people can no longer afford new houses.
- Quarrying helps to prevent people leaving these rural areas.
- Quarrying and blasting have destroyed the landscape.
- Children are not safe with huge lorries on the roads.
- The quarry has helped to pay for resurfacing roads.
- The new roads have led to fewer hedges and trees.
- The lime fumes pollute the air and all the area round.
- Quarrying provides limestone for industries such as building.
- The quarry is an eyesore – you cannot avoid seeing it.
- Our rivers and water supply have become polluted and overloaded.
- Other employers cannot pay such high wages.
- The water supply, drains and rivers are overloaded by the demands of the quarries.
- Farm labourers have lost their jobs.
- The quarry workers do not get on well with the locals.
- The blasting and the machinery are noisy and create clouds of dust.
- The blasting has damaged underground caves and stopped pot-holing.
- Farms close or are amalgamated.
- The roads are too narrow and were never designed for big lorries. The noise is terrible.

Figure 6.4 Two faces of Caistron; a) the gravel wo[rks]

b) the nature reserve

Wasting scarce resources?

The Yorkshire limestone is particularly pure, being 95 per cent calcium carbonate. Unfortunately, only 20 per cent of the limestone is used for those purposes which specifically require such pure limestone, such as steel-making, cement, paper and glass manufacture, sugar refining and agriculture. The remaining 80 per cent is used as aggregate for road building, or cement production, yet many other materials could be used for these two processes. The danger is that such quarrying operations not only destroy the national heritage at an accelerating rate, but are wasteful of a non-renewable resource of considerable economic value to the nation.

Putting things right

One way to reduce the waste of limestone would be to mine more sand and gravel for aggregates. The largest deposits of sands and gravels are found in south-east England, with Hampshire, Oxfordshire and Berkshire the largest producing counties. Some sands are compacted into solid rock and others are soft deposits left by rivers and glaciers which covered Britain thousands of years ago. Some are even remains of ancient beaches (in the Fens and Plain of York) from when the sea covered more of the country.

Sand and gravel in wet areas is extracted by suction pumps and dredgers, or even floating cranes and grablines. In dry sites, tractor shovels, scrapers, bulldozers and bucket excavators are used. After extraction, the material is sorted into sizes, washed and prepared for sale. Some sites have a ready-mixed concrete plant, others prepare sand for builders or road building.

These sites have similar problems of noise, pollution and dust to the limestone quarry but the industry is aware of the need to replace the countryside after use, as Fig. 6.4 on Caistron (Northumberland) shows.

It was a bright, February day, mild after a sharp frost, with sunlight glittering on the lakes, and the soft russet, red and gold colours of trees and bushes merged into the rolling hills of the Northumbrian countryside. Lapwings flickered overhead and large flocks of starlings and jackdaws wheeled in tight formation. On the lakes to the right swam pochard, tufted duck, goldeneye and goosanders. On the left reared the gaunt skeleton of a gravel digger.

For this was Caistron, a working gravel pit in the valley of the River Coquet, the brainchild of Ian Hornsby, managing director of The Ryton Sand and Gravel Group. The story of Caistron goes back to 1968 when the company was thinking of applying for planning permission to work the area, and the restoration of the land after extraction had to be considered. Recreational facilities such as sailing and fishing were rejected as being unsuitable for the area. Then Ian Hornsby had the idea of transforming it into a nature reserve 'to create the best possible environment for birds'.... No less than 120 different species have been recorded on the reserve, which is probably one of the best breeding areas for tufted duck in the north of England, and an important winter roost for greylag geese, which can number 500–600. Many birds, particularly oystercatchers, also use Caistron as a staging post as they travel up the river valley.

It is all very well for managers to have ideas, but ideas must be implemented and interest sustained throughout the project. Caistron's staff take an enthusiastic interest in the welfare of the birds. Each year oystercatchers and ringed plovers lay their eggs on the shingle which is being worked, so the men go to great lengths to work around the nests, and to avoid disturbing the birds. The driver of the digger carefully shapes and sculpts the islands after extracting the sand and gravel, and Neil Telfer, apart from working for the production side of the business, also acts as reserve warden.

Existing trees, such as the alders and hawthorns which are scattered on the flood plain are usually left, and other trees are planted, and a stone wall was built on one of the islands to provide an excellent shelter and nesting site. In this way a varied habitat has been created, with a large amount of gently sloping shoreline, much more attractive to birds than the large expanse of water, with comparatively steep banks, of the usual disused gravel pit.

Birds magazine, RSPB

Workbase

1. The major effects of any environmental change are often calculated by a method called **impact assessment**. The gains and losses are listed under major headings, and also given 'weightings', depending on how important the authors of the table believe them to be.

    Below you will see an impact assessment sheet for the Yorkshire Dales partially completed. Copy it out in your own notebook and complete it by filling in the spaces and by giving your own weightings to the factors which you list as either gains or losses

   Gains

		Weighting
Economic	More employment	___
Social	Improved bus services	___
Environmental	Improved, wider roads	___

   Losses

		Weighting
Economic	Loss of farming jobs	___
Social	Overloading of water-supply, drains and sewers	___
Environmental	Loss of trees and hedges	___

2. Consider the views on page 52. If you were a government inspector, conducting an enquiry into the possibility of mining in the area, which views would you count the most important, and why?

Chapter 7
Water supply

Water is vital to all forms of life, both animal and vegetable. The human body is two-thirds water, ranging from bones which are 33 per cent water, to the brain which is 85 per cent water. If you lose 10 per cent of your body water you will not be able to walk. Lose 20 per cent, and you will die unless given very rapid treatment. Yet we tend to take water for granted, except in drought years such as 1976 and 1984.

Problems with water supply

Our water supply comes from rain, or its frozen forms, hail or snow, but it tends to fall a) at the wrong time and b) in the wrong place.

At the wrong time

Precipitation (i.e. mainly rain, hail, sleet, snow) falls in roughly equal amounts in winter and summer. Quite a lot of the summer precipitation evaporates *but* this is just the time of peak demand for water for irrigation, drinking, and bathing etc. Hence, farmers are not merely concerned with the rain which falls in a year, but how *much* of that water becomes available to the plants. Some water is lost by evaporation and so is not available to the plants. The '**water budget**' is in surplus when precipitation is greater than losses by evaporation, and is in deficit when evaporation exceeds precipitation. Figure 7.1 shows the annual soil moisture deficit in the United Kingdom, i.e. those areas, where on average, evaporation exceeds precipitation.

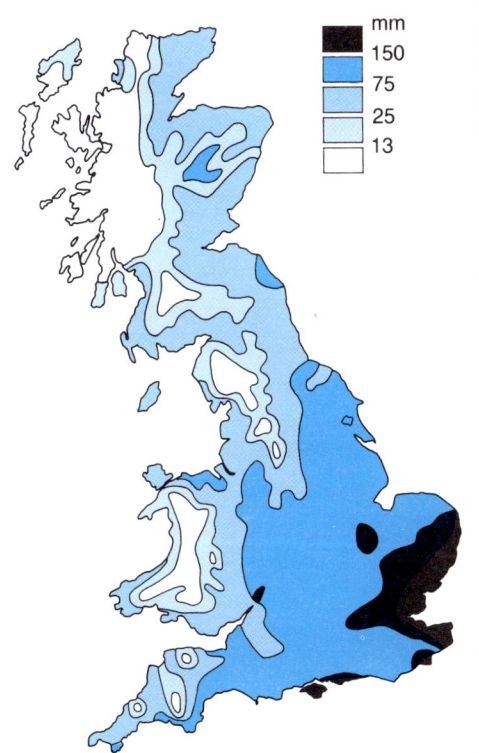

Figure 7.1 The average annual soil moisture deficit in Britain

In the wrong place

Most precipitation falls on the hills of North and West Britain (see Plate 35). These are thinly populated areas, with an average annual precipitation of about 2,700mm. In contrast, the densely populated Midlands, and South-East, where there is most demand, only receive some 500mm.

Because of these two problems of time and place, we have to store winter rainfall for use in summer. This water may be stored either:

a) Underground

Water can be stored in porous or permeable rocks, such as limestone, chalk and sandstone. These rocks may form an aquifer (see Fig. 7.6) where the impermeable rocks (e.g. clay) trap the water in the porous or permeable rocks. In this case, wells and bore-holes (narrower and deeper holes than wells) have to be used to reach the water. Springs may occur at the junction of the permeable and impermeable rocks and are another source of water supply.

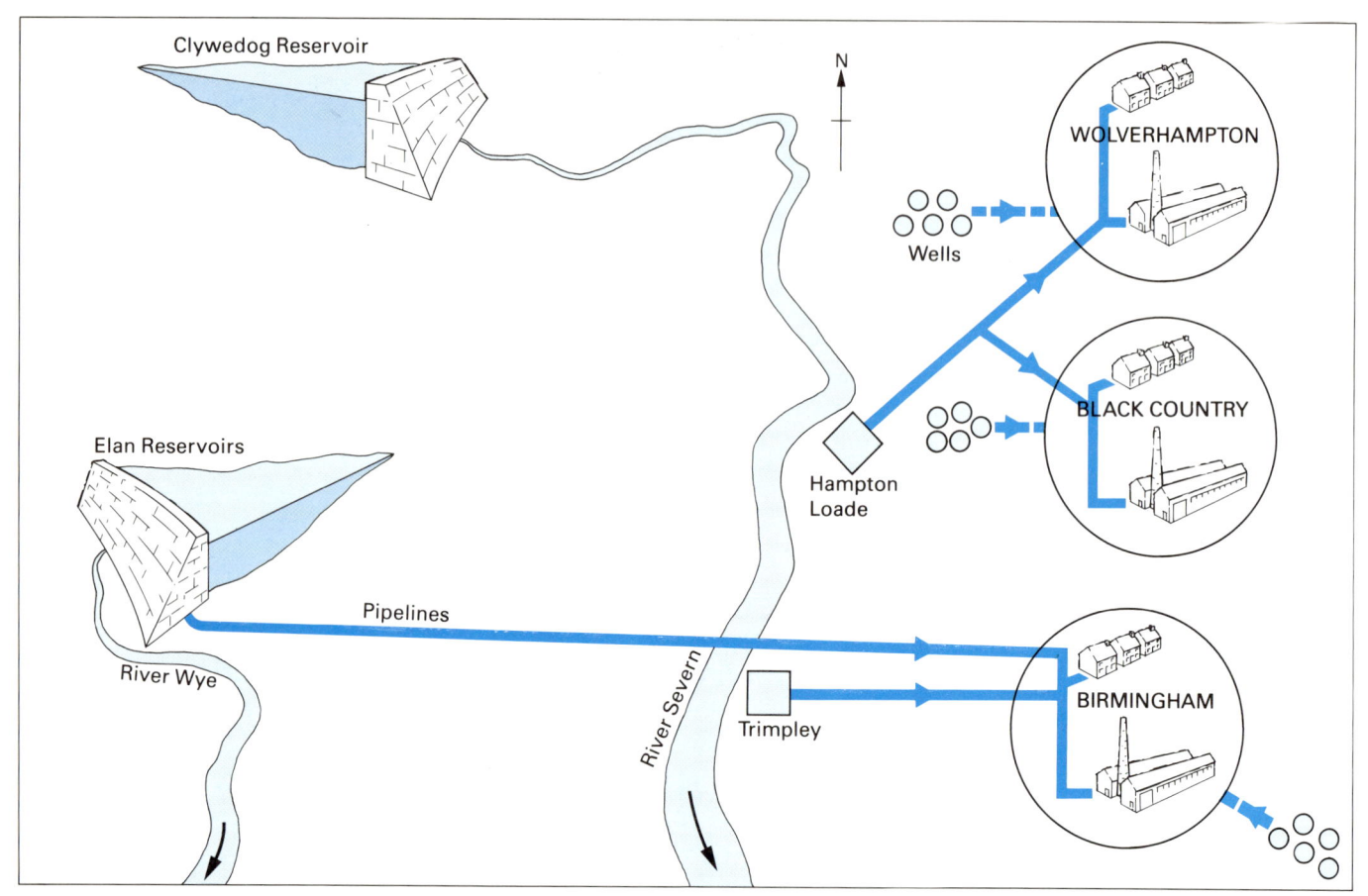

Figure 7.2 Birmingham's water supply and its origins

b) Above ground

Because there are not enough aquifers in Britain water may be stored in reservoirs. It is collected during the winter when the reservoirs fill, and then is released in summer to supplement the flow of water in rivers. Water is piped from reservoirs to areas of demand, which may be many kilometres distant, eg Birmingham obtains much of its water from reservoirs built over 150 kilometres away in the Elan and Clywedog areas of Wales (see Figure 7.2).

Wales is a particularly good area for developing water storage because it has a) high annual rainfall, partly due to its mountainous nature; b) low annual temperatures, so low rates of evaporation; c) large areas of impermeable rock, so little water drains away underground; d) narrow, steep-sided valleys which make suitable sites for dams; e) large areas which are only thinly populated, so not too many people lost their homes and their land when the areas were flooded.

Building reservoirs to increase water supplies inevitably involves conflicts. The following are some of the points of view expressed about plans to build a new reservoir at Carsington, near Derby in the East Midlands.

'As a local farmer I resent the loss of such valuable farmland, which will be under the waters of the new reservoir.'

'The East Midlands is an area of low rainfall and we need to ensure adequate water supplies for homes, farms and factories for the next thirty years. The reservoir will do this job.'

'My house will disappear under the water so I have had to find a new home, when I was quite happy in the old one.'

'Important wildlife sites will be lost when the area is flooded.'

Other sources of water supply

Other sources of water include schemes which extract supplies direct from rivers, for example at Trimpley on the River Severn in Worcestershire, which supplies Birmingham and the West Midlands.

Water from springs, wells, bore-holes or reservoirs has to be transported to the place of demand, and because water is so heavy, and distances often large, then transport is expensive and difficult. For example, the West Midlands needs 1 900 000 000 litres of water every day, but a large road tanker can only carry 20,000 litres and a railway tanker wagon only 50,000 litres. So most water has to be pumped along pipelines and transport is usually the most expensive part of water supply. Once the water has been transported it usually needs treatment to remove impurities and to kill germs, so that it is safe and fit to drink. Only then is the water released into the network of pipes bringing water to homes, offices, farms and factories.

Water consumption

a) Water in the home

In a typical day, one person may use:
55 litres flushing the toilet;
50 litres for personal washing and bathing;
18 litres for washing clothes;
15 litres for dish washing and general cleaning;
13 litres watering gardens, washing the car etc.;
 9 litres for drinking and cooking;
This adds up to 160 litres per day, in other words, half a tonne of water.

b) Water in industry

Water is also consumed by all industries and is frequently more important as a locating factor than energy. It takes about 7 litres to brew a pint of beer, a tonne of newsprint takes 45,500 litres, and a daily newspaper takes 9 litres. Water may be used either to cool plant and machinery in the factory, or may be part of the manufacturing process, as with paper, textiles and chemicals.

c) Water in agriculture

Water is used to irrigate crops, for washing and sterilising equipment, as drinking water for animals, and for carrying away waste products.

d) Water and play

Water is a vital part of our recreation. People flock to rivers, streams and lakes for fishing, swimming, boating, and water sports.

e) Water in public use

Water has to be available in both towns and the countryside for fire fighting, street cleaning and for parks, ponds and public gardens. Used water is directed through the sewers to the water reclamation works for purification. Ten regional water authorities were created in 1973 to manage water resources on a large scale. Each is responsible for water conservation and supply, sewage disposal, pollution control, land drainage, flood prevention, water recreation and fisheries. Water uses can be considered to be either complementary (i.e. both uses are possible) or conflicting (see Fig. 7.8).

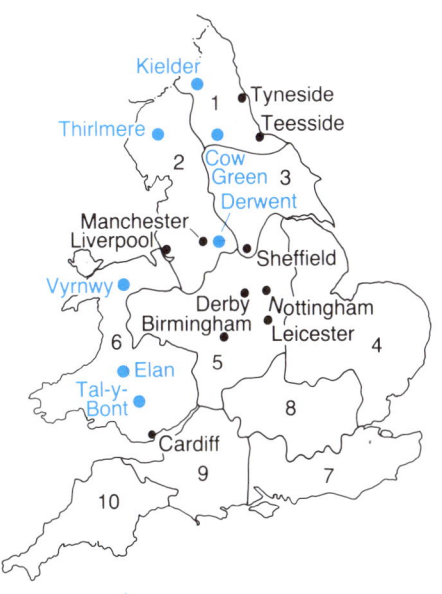

Water authorities
1 Northumberland
2 North-West
3 Yorkshire
4 Anglian
5 Severn-Trent
6 Welsh
7 Southern
8 Thames
9 Wessex
10 South-West

● Major reservoir

Figure 7.3 Water authorities in England and Wales

Case study: the Derwent Reservoir

The Derwent Reservoir is on a tributary of the River Tyne in north-east England. It is an example of a scheme where a planned use of resources tries to balance the conflicting demands for water.

The reservoir supplies water to over one million people on Tyneside and Wearside. Because it is close to large urban areas many day trippers visit the reservoir and so three car-parks (with picnic sites and toilets) have been built, as well as six lay-bys.

These sites are located away from the nature reserve, a stretch of sheltered water at the western end of the reservoir, where wildfowl are left undisturbed. Power-boats have been banned from the reservoir, but facilities for sailing (a clubhouse, slipway and car-park) and for fishing (shelters, toilets and car-parks) have been built at the eastern end of the reservoir. The result is a multi-purpose water scheme designed to maintain a balance between uses of the reservoir, the preservation of the natural environment, and the supply of water for thousands of homes.

Figure 7.4 The Derwent reservoir and its amenities

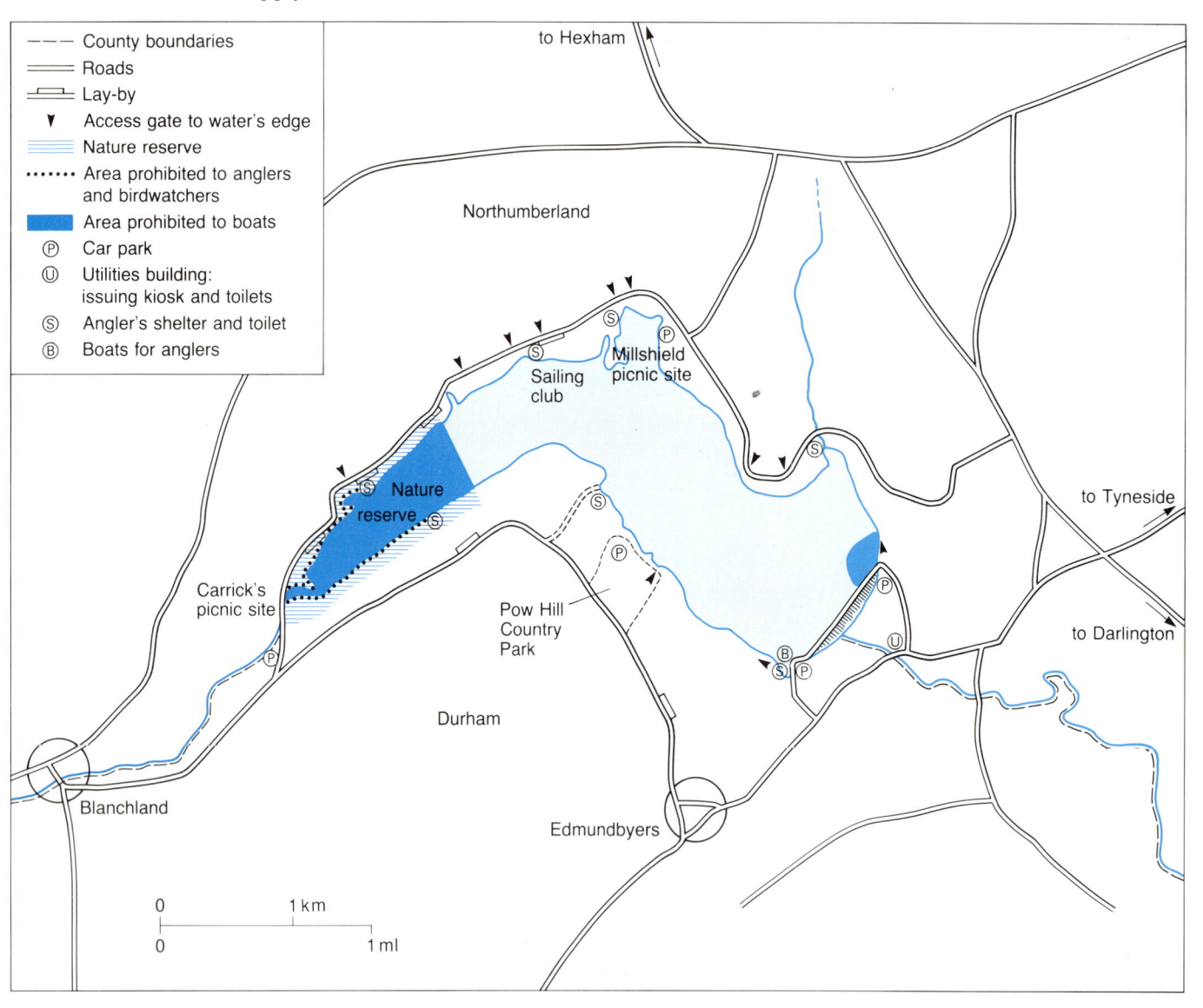

Pollution

Used water may contain many sorts of pollutant, e.g. grease, acids, poisons, inflammable liquids, sulphides, detergents, phenols, chlorinated solvents. The polluted water has to be taken to the sewage works where it is treated to remove all the impurities, before being returned to the river.

Figure 7.5

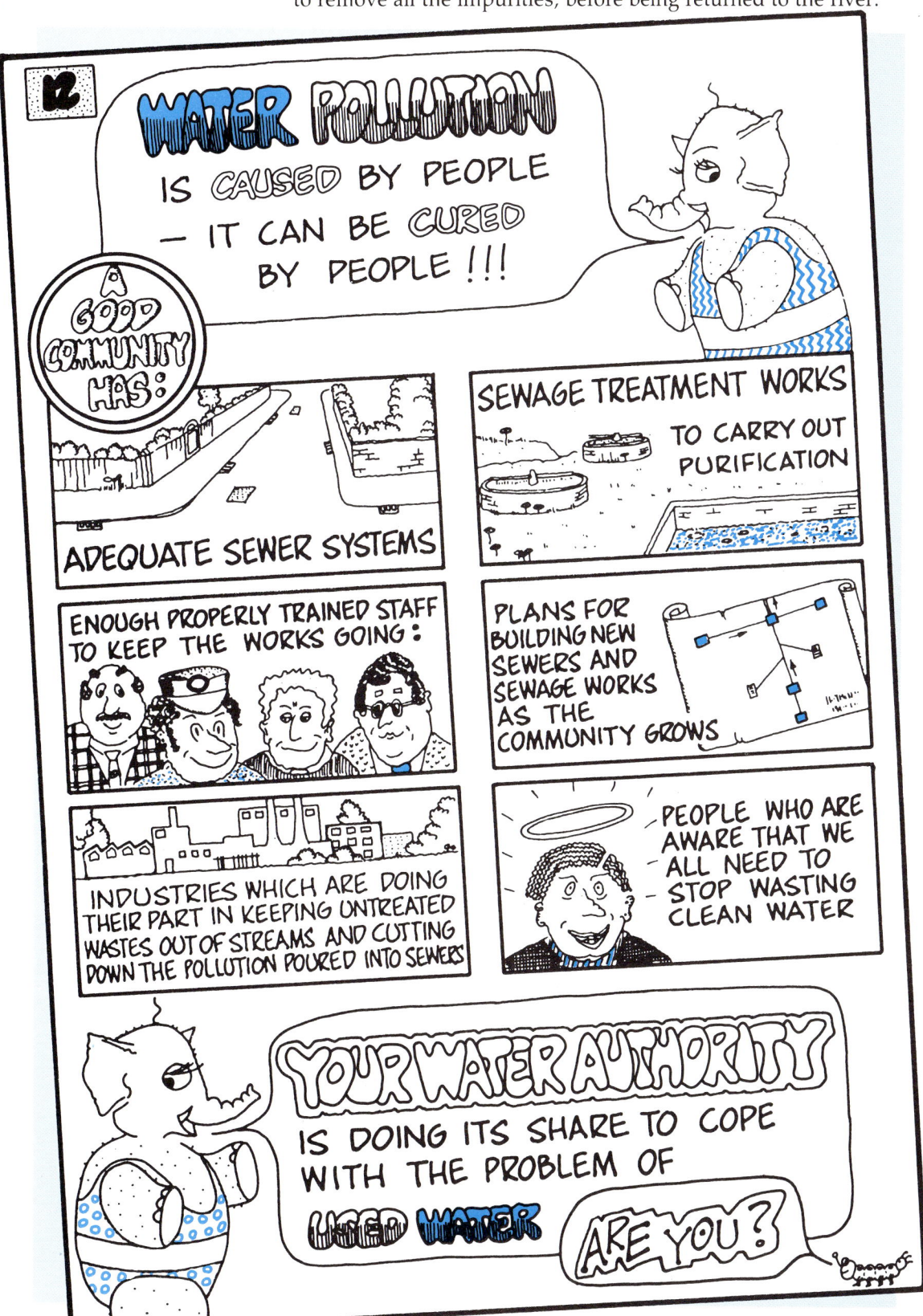

Drought

'Drought' is often difficult to define. To the farmer or gardener it means two to three weeks with no rain, so that the ground dries out and crops suffer. 'Drought' affecting water supply means a longer period over which rain has been in such short supply that there is not enough to replace water taken from reservoirs, rivers and wells. Normally water authorities expect a drought every forty to fifty years, but the weather can be very variable and 1976 and 1984 were particularly dry summers in Britain.

Between March and August 1984 England and Wales only received 270 mm of rain, making it the third driest period this century, after 1976 (204 mm) and 1921 (268 mm). One particular feature of the 1984 drought was the relative dryness of Wales in comparison to England. Rainfall in Wales from March to August 1984 was only 284 mm (compared with 279 mm in 1976), while by contrast England over the same period received 264 mm (compared with 191 mm in 1976). The 1984 drought was a particular problem for those water authorities such as the North-West and the Severn Trent which have water collection areas in Wales.

One result of the drought was that by August 1984 the Elan Valley area of Wales was short of 17,200,000 gallons of water, i.e. enough to supply Birmingham for thirty weeks at normal rates of consumption. Heavy rainfall in Wales from September to December 1984 helped to refill the Elan Valley Reservoir and end the restrictions on the use of water, such as bans on watering by hosepipes, filling swimming pools and mechanical car washes.

Plate 9 St Neots, Cambridgeshire. The picture shows a visible rural-urban frontier but this country town is a suburb of London is some respects. There are many daily road and rail commuters to London, 80 kilometres away.

Plate 10 Oxfordshire. Why have farmers been so anxious to remove hedgerows and make fields larger? What possible *dis*advantages may this cause?

Plate 11 A traditional farm.

Plate 12 A china-clay pit near St Austell, Cornwall. In what industries is this raw material principally used?

Plate 13 Haweswater in the Lake District; this 1984 picture shows evidence of the old hamlet of Mardale, drowned by the lake. Can you find it?

Plate 14 Hadrian's Wall in Northumberland, now a favourite route of walkers. For what purpose was the wall first built?

Plate 15 Thorpe Park, near Staines. A new leisure park created from derelict land and flooded gravel pits.

Plate 16 A diamond of trees planted by the Forestry Commission in Scotland. Why do you suppose that plantations like these are sometimes strongly opposed?

⑨

⑩

(1)

⑫

13

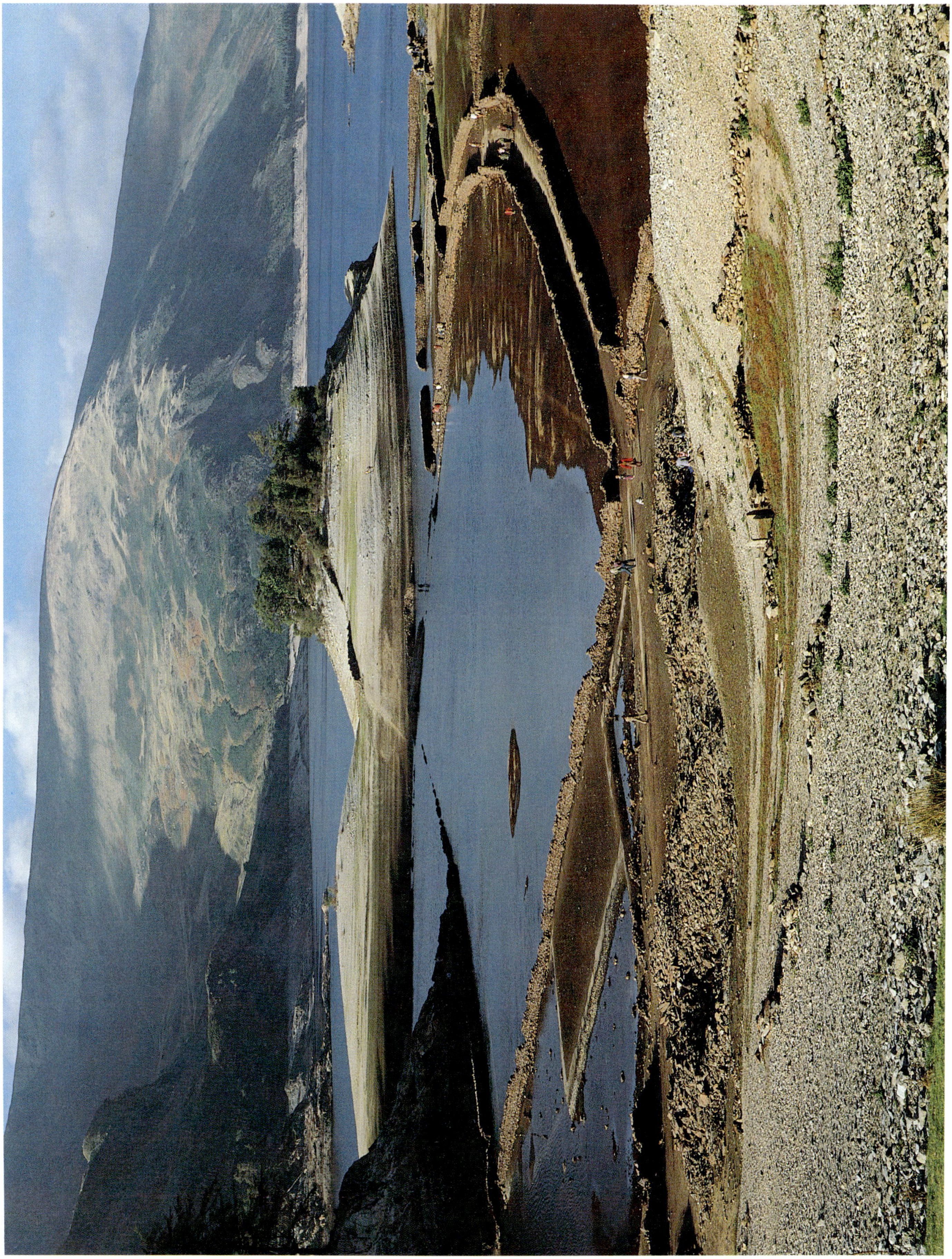

⑭

⑮

⑯

Future water supplies

The water authorities in Britain have to cater for a rising demand for water from industry, agriculture and the home. They need to be able to collect and store this water adequately and distribute it quickly and effectively to areas of greatest need.

These are some of the issues and problems which they face in seeking to provide increasing amounts of water:

a) New reservoirs

Building new reservoirs is controversial, may take up to ten years and can be very expensive. Water authorities do not automatically plan to build many new reservoirs after a single drought year. Too many reservoirs can be as bad as too few, because money spent building them could be spent on other projects such as new hospitals or new roads.

b) Water meters

Some people argue that all homes should have water meters, just as they have gas and electric meters. People would pay for the water they use. Some areas of Britain already have water meters, and in general water consumption does fall slightly when people realise how much they are using. However, meters have to be installed and read at regular intervals, and this might increase water costs by 50 per cent.

c) Stopping leaks in the system

As much as 25 per cent of all water treated may be lost before use. It escapes through leaks in the system which distributes water in England and Wales.

d) Water re-use and re-cycling

Water can often be used more than once, for example industry can use water after a city has finished with it, rather than use the city's drinking supply (especially in those industries like engineering, which do not require high quality water). And water heated by power stations can be used to heat hospitals and public buildings.

e) Desalinisation of sea water

Sea water can be distilled to produce suitable drinking water. However the process, at present, is very expensive and is hardly used in Britain where other alternatives are more readily available.

f) Estuary barrages

Another solution to long-term water supplies would be to construct barrages across estuaries such as Morecambe Bay, the Wash, the Solway Firth and the Dee estuary. The water behind such barrages would gradually turn fresh as river waters, flowing into the area, diluted the original sea water.

g) Water grids

A water grid would allow water to be moved from areas with a surplus to areas of high demand. On a regional level there are such grids, for example in the Severn Trent Authority a pipeline from Coventry to Leicester allows the movement of water from the West to East Midlands, or vice-versa. There are proposals for a National Water Grid but such a scheme would be so expensive that at present it remains just an idea.

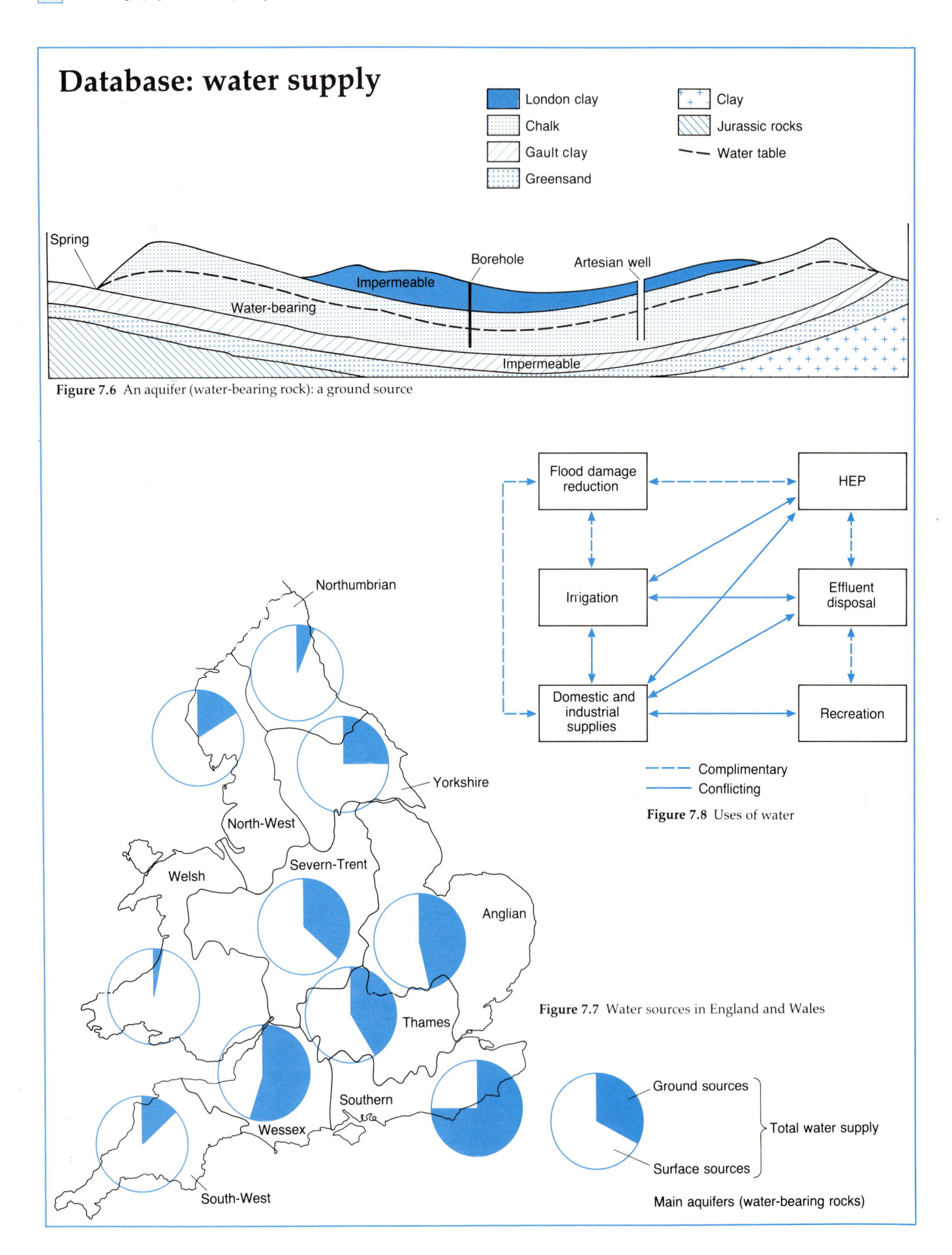

Database: water supply

Figure 7.6 An aquifer (water-bearing rock): a ground source

Figure 7.7 Water sources in England and Wales

Figure 7.8 Uses of water

Workbase

1. Fig. 7.7 illustrates the distribution of aquifers (water-bearing rocks) in Britain and the proportions of total water supply derived from these by each water authority.
   Rank the water authorities according to the proportion of their total supplies coming from aquifers.

2. On page 56 you can read the views of some people concerned about the plan to build a new reservoir at Carsington, near Derby. Write down the views that might be expressed by the following people:
   a) a brewing company, who wants to build a new factory near Derby;
   b) a family with a holiday cottage in the area which is to be flooded;
   c) a local water-sports club;
   d) a local firm of earth-movers and demolition experts;
   e) The local branch of the Royal Society for the Protection of Birds.

3. Look at the information about the use of water in the home (page 57). Write a short feature article for a newspaper *or* devise a poster to encourage people to use less water. Suggest how water may be saved without loss of standards of hygiene.

4. Study Fig. 7.8 and identify the main conflicting uses of water. Explain the nature of the conflict and which use may be likely to gain priority.

5. If a farmer takes water from a river during a drought, what do you think might be the consequences for:
   a) people in a city downstream which takes drinking water from the river;
   b) wildlife in the area;
   c) power stations, dependent on river water for cooling processes;
   d) local anglers and sailing clubs.

Chapter 8
Leisure and the countryside

Nowadays we spend less time 'at work' than we used to. The time spent on paid work has fallen from 70 hours per week in 1850 to 40–44 hours per week on average in the 1980s. There is more time for **leisure**. Those who are unemployed have leisure whether they want it or not.

The demand for increased leisure and recreation facilities dates from the 1950s. This is because:
- after the Second World War paid holidays and a five-day working-week became widespread for workers;
- a rising standard of living produced more surplus money to spend on leisure;
- the growth of car ownership has vastly increased 'personal mobility' (1939 – 2 million cars in Britain, 4 million driving licences 1980 – 15 million cars in Britain, 23 million driving licences);
- people have tended to have less children and so have decreased the time spent on domestic activities and tasks.

It is also notable that in the late 1980s there are over 10 million people who have 'retired': which is 2.5 times as many as in 1950.

Changing holiday patterns

The idea of holidays is not new; the Romans had spa resorts such as Bath. But from the eighteenth century onwards British royalty (and the wealthy) became interested in 'taking the sea waters' at places such as Brighton. This practice increased greatly with the development of the railways in the nineteenth century. Many more people from all walks of life could now travel long distances quickly and relatively cheaply. Lines linked great urban centres with seaside resorts such as Blackpool, Southend, Scarborough, Weston-super-Mare and Ayr. Visitors went for day trips or week-long holidays, staying in boarding houses or small hotels.

Since the 1950s, increased car ownership, longer holidays and more wealth have led to people visiting 'areas' (such as the West Country, or the Lake District) rather than a specific town. They tend to spend a single night at a resort and then move on. The increased numbers of people going overseas is balanced by large numbers of foreign tourists coming to tour Britain.

Though some holiday-makers still stay in hotels, an increasing number go to self-catering flats, or youth hostels, or use caravans or tents. There are many more people now visiting rural areas for day or weekend visits. The result is a growing demand for recreation provision in the countryside (such as information centres, accommodation, campsites, car-parks, etc.). This would prevent the situation revealed in a recent roadside survey of caravans on holiday, which found that at least one-third had already spent a night at a roadside lay-by or an unauthorised location.

Leisure and the countryside

National Parks and Country Parks

As the choice of holiday locations has become wider, the Government has become concerned about the possible long-term damage to areas which are exceptionally beautiful. In 1949 an Act of Parliament created the idea of National Parks. National Parks were set up to preserve and enhance the existing landscape. They provide facilities for public open-air recreation, whilst seeking to preserve wildlife, historic buildings and the local economy.

Much of the land in National Parks remains privately owned, but there are restrictions on development. The parks service provides information about the facilities in the areas and the park ranger can help, guide, advise and warn.

In 1967, the Government also established Country Parks. These areas vary greatly in size (from 7 hectares to 1,273 hectares) and in environment (former quarries, grassed-over tip-heaps, abandoned railway land, areas of farmland). They are not on the massive scale of National Parks, but they provide areas for country walks and recreation close to large towns and cities.

Figure 8.1 Clumber Country Park, Nottinghamshire

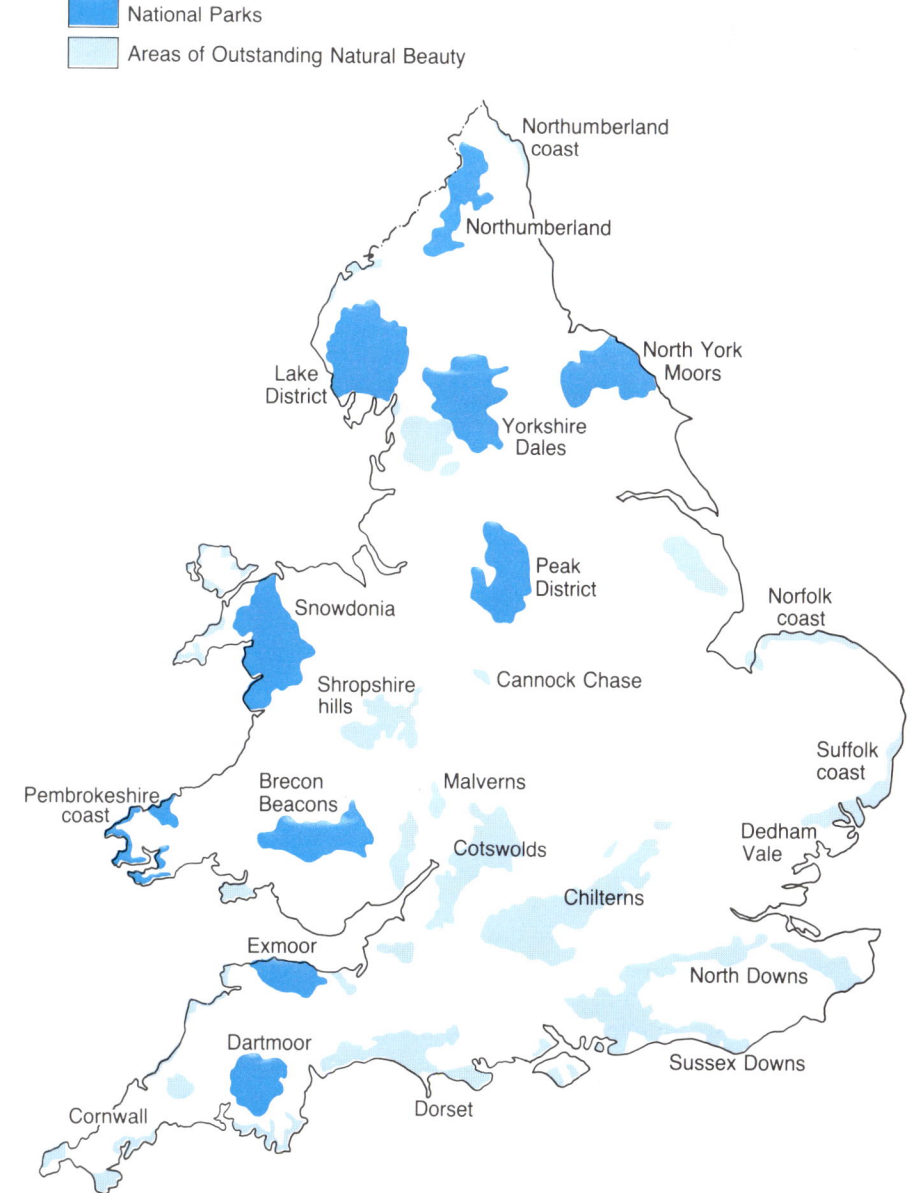

Figure 8.2 National Parks and Areas of Outstanding Natural Beauty (the Norfolk Broads have recently been added)

How many is too many?

Some visitors to Country Parks only use them in the winter, because they feel that they are too crowded on summer weekends; even National Parks are sometimes over-crowded at popular beauty spots at the height of the tourist season, despite their large areas. The question arises – when is a park 'full'?

Capacity is the amount of use we can get from a resource, but it can have different meanings:

a) **Ecological capacity** is the term used when the number of visitors to an area is so great that environmental damage is caused (crumbling footpaths, worn-out grass areas, etc.)

b) **Physical capacity** is the number of people who can actually use a park on any one occasion (people realise that a park is 'full' in this sense as they sit in a very long traffic jam on an entrance road or at a car-park).

c) **Perceived capacity** is the term used for the maximum number of people who can use the park at any one time before everyone's level of pleasure begins to fall, because of the over-crowding that they feel. (It may happen especially on a beach.)

Honeypot sites

The biggest capacity problems occur at **honeypot sites**, named because tourists flock there 'like bees round a honeypot'. Here the danger is that the attraction itself will be severely damaged or destroyed by the numbers of people who come to see it.

Snowdon is an example. The great number of walkers (the average is over 2,000 on a summer day) are wearing away paths, deepening gullies, and dropping litter as they climb the mountain. They find it hard to avoid each other most of the time. And their pets often frighten the mountain sheep.

Similarly, Stonehenge is now suffering from soil erosion as a result of receiving 700,000 visitors each year. The ancient stones now have graffiti. So there is now a plan to build a simulated Stonehenge at a place nearby, leaving the real one to a little peace and quiet.

Figure 8.3 Country parks in the UK

Planning for leisure

If too many people visit a particular site in the countryside they *all* lose satisfaction. Rural resources are easily spoiled, so it is important to try and *plan* the use of these resources, in order to achieve a balance between resource conservation and the needs of the people.

In the past, decisions about use were often left to the people who actually owned the places or resources in question, and this is still partly true. However, since 1946, when the first Town and Country Planning Acts were passed, the Government has become more involved in how resources are used in the countryside for the benefit of all. However, different ministries, such as the Ministry of Agriculture and the Department of the Environment, may not always speak with the same voice. But the aim is to see that the nation benefits as a whole, that the rights of individuals and groups are protected, and that the environment is left intact for future generations to enjoy.

… Leisure and the countryside

Case study: North York Moors

The North York Moors National Park covers 1,432 square kilometres of north-eastern Yorkshire and south-eastern Cleveland (see Fig. 8.2). Its landscape varies from heather-covered moorlands on the highest areas giving way to bracken-covered lower slopes and small woods, to small fields in the valley bottoms, where farms have stone walls and hedgerows. The pattern is broken here and there by large plantations of conifers. There is more intensive farming on the southern plateau and a coastal area of steep cliffs to the north-east. This is an area of scenic grandeur. It is also an area in which conflicts of land-use often occur.

Figure 8.4 North York Moors National Park

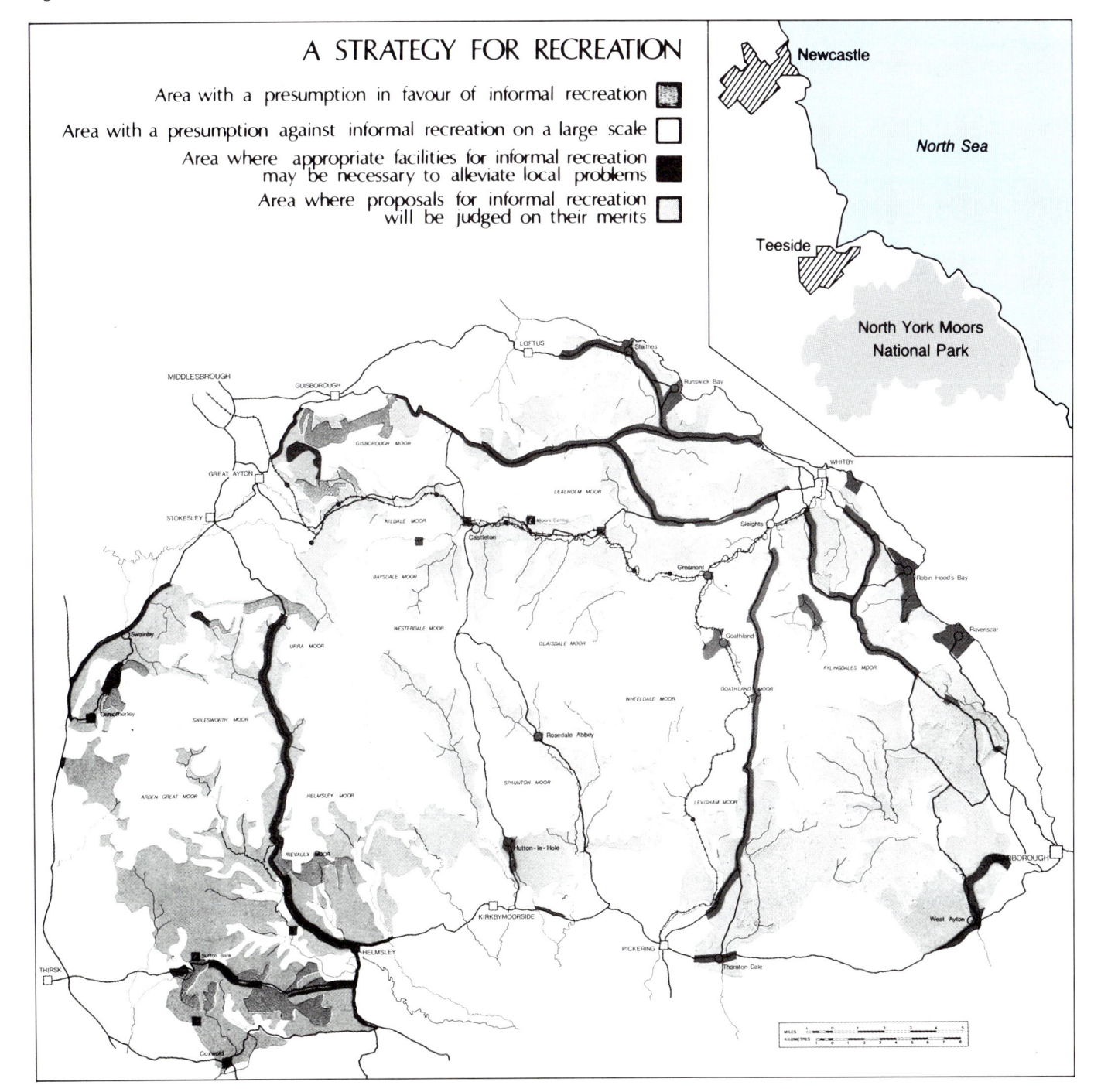

A STRATEGY FOR RECREATION

- Area with a presumption in favour of informal recreation
- Area with a presumption against informal recreation on a large scale
- Area where appropriate facilities for informal recreation may be necessary to alleviate local problems
- Area where proposals for informal recreation will be judged on their merits

Sources of conflict: farming

The North York Moors is an area where farmers live and work, often struggling to earn a living against the harsh winters in this part of England. Most of the land is privately owned and the increasing farm costs (of fuel, fertilisers, etc.) have forced farmers to look for ways to increase their income by keeping more sheep or cattle.

In order to do this farmers have been ploughing up the moorland, draining it, fencing it and sowing higher quality grassland for better grazing. But such reclamation work is expensive as it requires deep ploughing, and the use of large amounts of lime and fertiliser. At present, grants are available for this reclamation from the Ministry of Agriculture. It is estimated that a third of the present moorland is good enough in quality to be converted to pasture. But this would reduce the open landscape and result in the loss of some quite rare plants, animals and bird life. The scale of recent moorland change can be seen in Fig. 8.5.

Year	Rough pasture Hectares	%	Improved farmland and woodland Hectares	%	%change for Rough pasture
1853	70,246	49	72,613	51	−3.6
1895	67,711	47	76,259	53	−0.2
1904	67,563	47	76,406	53	+0.7
1950	68,044	48	75,926	52	−15.4
1963	57,330	40	86,640	60	−9.7
1974	51,793	37	88,994	62	−1.7
1979	50,935	36	90,510	63	−1.5
1983	50,056	35	90,720	64	

Figure 8.5 Changes in North York Moors land use

Farmers point to increased production and higher income as the conversion from moorland to pasture has taken place; others point to the loss of habitat for wildlife, and the destruction of the beauty of the landscape.

In other parts of the moors, bracken is invading abandoned fields; it grows very quickly and prevents the original moorland vegetation of heather and mosses from re-establishing itself. Bracken is of no use as animal feed, and fields infested by it quickly become useless.

There is thus a changing **moorland edge**: over the years cultivation has sometimes expanded into the moorland; at other times either bracken or moorland vegetation reclaims abandoned fields.

Resolving the conflict

The North York Moors National Park Authority is caught in the middle of the conflict between the farmers and the 'environmentalists'. It has to protect the natural beauty of the park but must also consider the needs of agriculture.

It has offered a) to buy land from farmers to prevent further ploughing; b) to pay farmers *not* to plough up land.

But most farmers do not want to sell their land, and ask for greater sums of money than the Park Authority can provide. Though many farmers are aware of the benefits of conserving their moorland, they feel that they should be free to make their own decisions about whether or not particular fields should be conserved or not.

The NPA does not have the legal power to stop farmers ploughing up moorland, nor does it have unlimited sums of money. It is thus criticised by some people who claim that it is failing to 'protect' the National Park.

> ## Questions
>
> 1. Do you think farmers in National Parks should be quite free to do as they like with their own land?
> 2. Is it important to conserve the habitat of wildlife? If so, should we do so whatever the cost?
> 3. If you were appointed an independent assessor to judge the merits of both sides in this conflict, how would you put matters in your report?

Sources of conflict: forestry

Eighteen per cent of the open moorland has been converted to plantations of conifers in the last thirty years, – with the intention of increasing commerical timber production. It is estimated that over 85 per cent of the remaining moorland could also be planted in this way. But these areas have a dramatic visual impact, and change the pattern of vegetation and wildlife, as well as restricting access for walkers.

Resolving the conflict

The Forestry Commission consults with the National Park Authority in order to try and meet these problems. As a result it now seeks to:

- plant more deciduous trees, especially along roadsides;
- establish woodland management schemes for areas of remaining deciduous forest;
- split the areas of conifers into blocks, which are felled in rotation, so as to avoid massive damage to the visual aspect of the landscape;
- develop forest walks, picnic sites and information points.

Sources of conflict: tourism

As many as 140,000 visitors may come to enjoy the North York Moors on a fine summer Sunday; eleven million visitors can be expected in a year. This creates a problem managing patterns of receation so as to allow people to enjoy themselves and yet avoid damage and degradation to the landscape Different people have very different ideas of what they want from a visit to a National Park, as a recent survey shows.

Group 1 (29.5 per cent of the total)

These visitors stop at main tourist sites, such as Robin Hood's Bay, Sutton Bank, Goathland, Helmsley and Hutton-le-Hole (each of which may receive over 600 people on a summer Sunday). People in this group are attracted by a 'holiday atmosphere' and seek companionship rather than peace and quiet. They expect car-parks, toilets, shops, cafes and entertainments to be available.

Group 2 (21 per cent of the total)

This group arrive by car, and park on their own or in small groups. They are interested in walking or picnicking in quiet, beautiful places. They require safe car-parking but few other facilities.

Group 3 (28 per cent of the total)

These visitors travel *through* the park, though stopping for a while at viewpoints to enjoy the scenery. They are heading for another destination, such as Whitby or Scarborough. They require only 'transit' facilities.

Group 4 (20.4 per cent of the total)

This group do a circular tour of the park but may not stop to get out of their vehicles. They require only a good road system (the responsibility of the highway authority, not the National Park authority).

Group 5 (1.1 per cent of the total)

A small percentage of visitors, who may not own cars, use two railway lines and a public bus service. They require walks, trails and other facilities near the stations and bus stops.

Group 6 (percentage of total not known)

Some groups enjoy the moors for specialised recreation, such as hang-gliding or motor-cycle scrambling. This may need control in both location and duration to avoid annoying other park users.

Group	Description	Percentage of total
Group I	Stopping visitors (main areas)	29.5
Group II	Stopping visitors (dispersed)	21.0
Group III	Through traffic	28.0
Group IV	Circular tours	20.4
Group V	Public transport	1.1
Group VI	Specialist recreation	Not known
	Total	100

Figure 8.6 Visitors to the North York Moors National Park

Questions

1. Which of these groups is most easy to please? Which is most difficult?
2. If you were putting resources into tourist facilities in the National Park, what would you spend most of your money on?
3. Is it more important to satisfy tourists than farmers?
4. Below are listed three more potential sources of conflict. Write a short piece for each of them, setting out 'Some ideas for resolving conflicts'. Some possible headings might be 'Monitoring change', 'Persuasion', 'Allocation of areas', 'Prohibition'.

Source of conflict: mining and quarrying

Within the park there is quarrying for potash, limestone, sand and gravel. The industry provides employment for about 150 people in small villages. The quarrying may, however, cause disturbance by traffic, blasting, dust and resultant pollution. Important wildlife habitat may be damaged and some people think that quarries are an 'eyesore' on the landscape.

Source of conflict: the coast

The coast of the National Park is an area of great beauty with some of the highest cliffs in England. There are small fishing villages at the foot of small wooded valleys, with open rolling moorland above them. But pressure on the coast as a resource and conflicts of interest arise from the following:

- the erosion of cliff walks by large numbers of hikers and ramblers;
- the threat of oil pollution from tankers passing offshore;
- the conversion of cottages to holiday homes, leaving fewer cheap houses for local people;
- the differing needs and activities of water-skiers, and bird-watchers, yachtsmen and power-boat racers.

Source of conflict: water catchment

There is currently only one reservoir in the park. But as the demand for water rises in surrounding urban areas, pressure builds up for more valleys to be dammed for reservoirs. This would drown some of the best valley-bottom farmland, and also flood some farms, cottages and small villages. Supporters of the proposals argue that the reservoirs would not only provide better water supply for the whole area, but also be an extra resource for fishing, boating and water-sports. Better roads would be built to help construction of the dam and reservoir, and these would remain as a resource for visitors afterwards.

Figure 8.7 Part of coastal scenery of the North York Moors National Park, Robin Hood's Bay

Measuring landscapes

In order to resolve conflicting demands for the countryside, planners need to assess the importance of preserving certain areas. They have therefore developed various techniques for **measuring** the quality of different landscapes, so that some can be designated 'very beautiful and not to be changed' and others (for example) 'not especially worth preservation'.

An example of this is shown in the photograph and annotated sketch, Figs. 8.8 and 8.9. Try the same sort of assessment for the photograph Plate 11. An example of the kind of scale from which a 'landscape score' is calculated is shown opposite.
If you disagree with the values in this scale, see if you can make up one which seems more satisfactory. Try it on some other pictures in this book.

Figure 8.8

Leisure and the countryside 73

Land-use
Wild landscape, e.g. marshland, heather	+ 10
Varied landscape, e.g. woods, hedges, fields	+ 7
Farmland with trees	+ 2
Farmland with no trees	+ 1
Blocks of coniferous forest	− 2
Urban or industrial area	− 8

Landforms
Mountains	+ 10
Hills	+ 8
Undulating land, with low hills	+ 6
Plateau	+ 4
Lowlands	0

Other scores
Add 2 if there is water in the distance
Add 4 if there is water in the foreground
Add 5 if it is coastal area

Figure 8.9

Database: leisure in the countryside

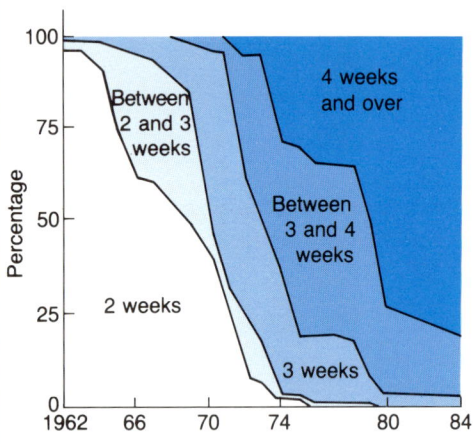

Figure 8.10 The length of paid annual holidays in Britain

Park	National Trust	Forestry Commission	Water authorities	Min. of Defence	National Park	Other	Private
Brecon Beacons	3.4	6.7	4.0	–	1.5	–	84.4
Dartmoor	1.7	1.9	–	5.0	3.0	1.0	87.4
Exmoor	9.0	1.7	–	–	1.9	4.5	82.9
Lake District	17.0	5.0	7.0	–	1.8	–	69.2
Northumberland	0.5	18.0	1.0	23.0	–	–	57.5
North York Moors	–	11.6	–	1.0	1.0	–	86.4
Peak District	5.0	0.8	14.0	–	1.5	–	78.7
Pembrokeshire Coast	3.3	1.0	–	5.0	–	–	90.7
Snowdonia	9.0	10.5	1.0	–	–	6.5	73.0
Yorkshire Dales	1.0	–	–	–	–	–	99.0

Source: Countryside Commission

Figure 8.11 Land ownership in National Parks (percentages)

Figure 8.12 Top 20 visitor attractions in Britain

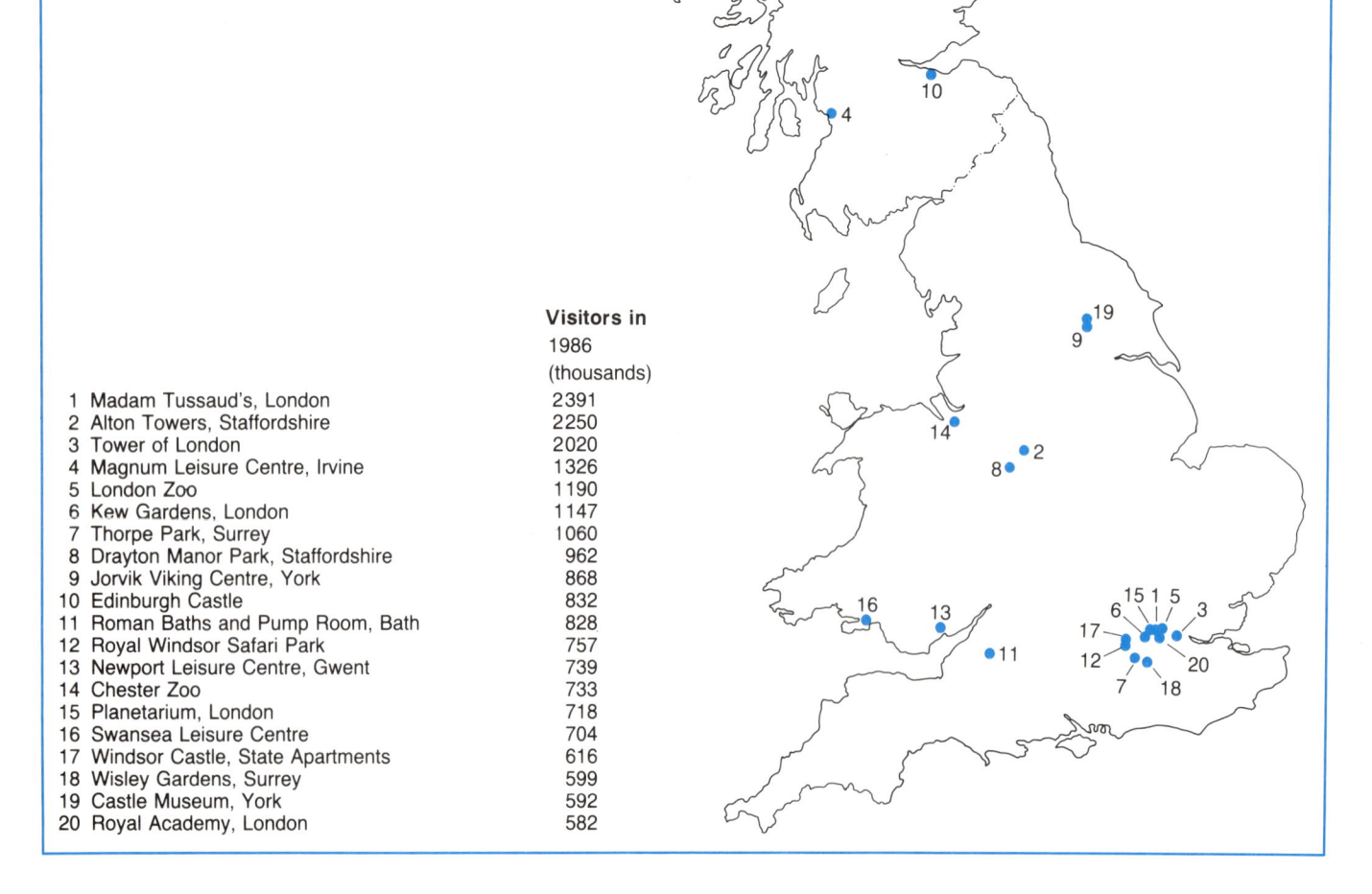

Visitors in 1986 (thousands)

1	Madam Tussaud's, London	2391
2	Alton Towers, Staffordshire	2250
3	Tower of London	2020
4	Magnum Leisure Centre, Irvine	1326
5	London Zoo	1190
6	Kew Gardens, London	1147
7	Thorpe Park, Surrey	1060
8	Drayton Manor Park, Staffordshire	962
9	Jorvik Viking Centre, York	868
10	Edinburgh Castle	832
11	Roman Baths and Pump Room, Bath	828
12	Royal Windsor Safari Park	757
13	Newport Leisure Centre, Gwent	739
14	Chester Zoo	733
15	Planetarium, London	718
16	Swansea Leisure Centre	704
17	Windsor Castle, State Apartments	616
18	Wisley Gardens, Surrey	599
19	Castle Museum, York	592
20	Royal Academy, London	582

Workbase

1. Look at Fig. 8.10 – the length of paid annual holidays.
   a) Describe in a paragraph the change in the length of paid annual holidays in Britain since 1961.
   b) Write another paragraph about the likely effect of these changes on rural areas.

2. A survey in 1951 asked people what means of transport they used to go on holiday; the survey was repeated in 1984, with the results as shown below

	1951	1984
Car	27%	73%
Bus/coach	27%	12%
Train	46%	12%
Other	Less than 1%	3%

   a) What have been the main changes and why?
   b) What modes of transport will be significant in the 'Other' category?
   c) How will such changes affect a National Park?

3. Look at Fig. 8.2 – National Parks and Areas of Outstanding Natural Beauty
   a) List the National Parks and AONBs, and identify the ones which are nearest to where you live
   b) Why are Londoners more likely to visit AONBs than National Parks?
   c) Do you know of any other areas which you think could be suggested for inclusion in these categories?

4. Look at Fig. 8.11 – land ownership in National Parks.
   a) Which is the largest single landowner in all the National Parks put together?
   b) Compare the ownership pattern in the Peak District National Park with that in the Yorkshire Dales National Park by means of a pie diagram. Explain the differences.
   c) Why might the Ministry of Defence require land in National Parks?

5. Look at some maps of your own area. Using your own local knowledge and the evidence of the maps, identify an area which might be set aside as a Country Park, if there was agreement with the landowners.

6. Look at Fig. 8.12 which shows Britains Top 20 visitor attractions in 1986. Which other attractions known to you might now be challenging for a place? Why might this list not be completely reliable?

Part III Britain's urban areas

Three out of every four people in the United Kingdom live in towns or cities, but the buildings and the environments in which they live may differ greatly. The tall tenements of Glasgow are unlike the semi-detached villas of Ilford; the Georgian parades of Bath are unlike the inner-city terraces of Salford.

Yet all these urban environments have grown within the last two hundred years, mainly as a result of changes in living styles brought about by the industrial revolution. Even those towns which did exist before the 1750s were much smaller in size and population than they are now.

The development of steam-power and the use of engines in factories impelled industry to organise on a larger scale. Factories needed more workers as production expanded to meet the growing demands of national markets; so workers were drawn from the countryside by the lure of higher wages. They came to live in houses within walking distance of the factories in which they were employed.

Then as the railway network developed, the possibility of a daily journey to work beyond walking distance arose. Railways were the first form of **mass transport** and they allowed towns to expand in size, as large new estates were built with room for at least a small garden to each house. The development of the petrol-driven combustion engine at the end of the nineteenth century gave a further impetus to the expansion of urban areas; horse-buses were replaced by petrol-driven ones. The development of the tram and, later, the trolleybus (using electricity as a source of power) also encouraged town growth.

By the end of the Second World War (1945) some towns had grown so big that the nation became concerned about their continued sprawl. Successive Governments introduced planning acts which created **green belts** around the urban areas. There were also efforts to rebuild inner-city areas which had begun to decay. But the increased ownership of private cars means that many people live a considerable distance from their places of work in the 1980s, even in *another* urban area, many kilometres away.

The hierarchy of settlements

Settlements differ in size from the isolated house or pair of houses on a country roadside to areas populated by millions. A broad classification of settlements by name is given below.

Population size	Name	Other features
1–10	Isolated houses	
11–100	Hamlet	Usually does *not* have a church
101–1,000	Village	Usually has a number of shops
1,001–100,000	Town	
100,000–1,000,000	City	The historic definition of a city would require a cathedral
1,000,000 and above	Conurbation	Several towns and cities joined together

Britain's urban areas

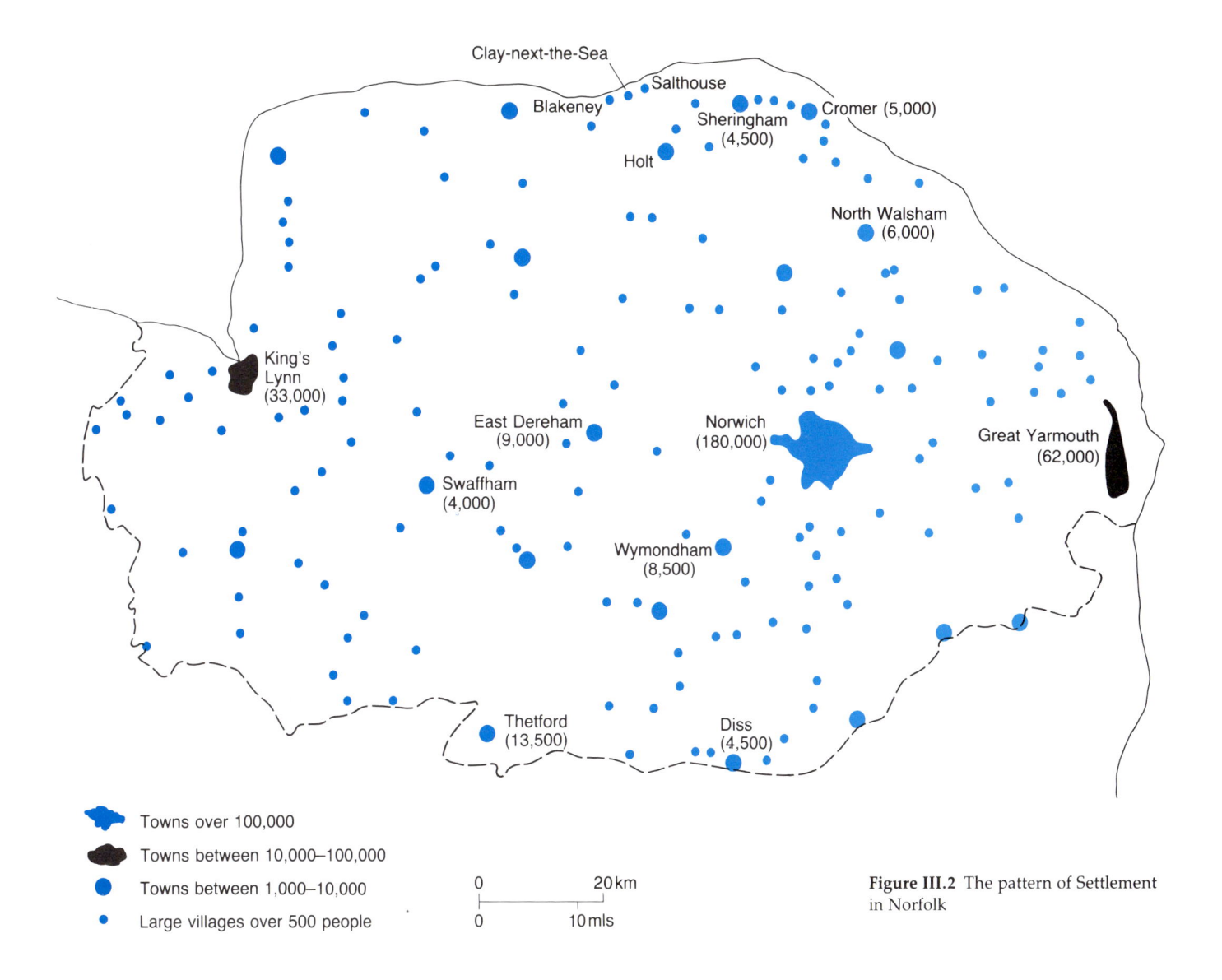

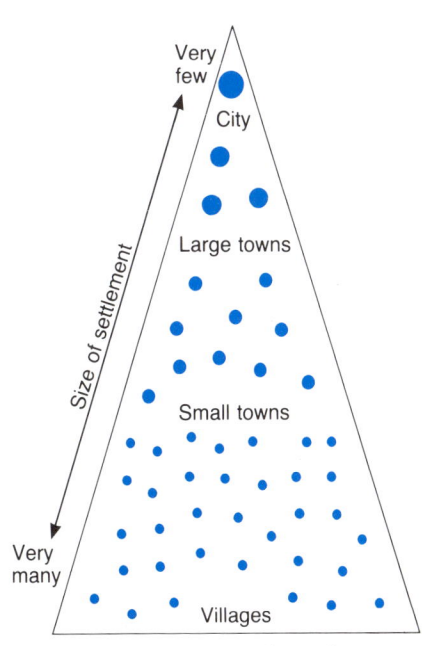

Figure III.2 The pattern of Settlement in Norfolk

Legend:
- Towns over 100,000
- Towns between 10,000–100,000
- Towns between 1,000–10,000
- Large villages over 500 people

Towns shown on map:
- Clay-next-the-Sea
- Salthouse
- Blakeney
- Sheringham (4,500)
- Cromer (5,000)
- Holt
- North Walsham (6,000)
- King's Lynn (33,000)
- East Dereham (9,000)
- Norwich (180,000)
- Great Yarmouth (62,000)
- Swaffham (4,000)
- Wymondham (8,500)
- Thetford (13,500)
- Diss (4,500)

Figure III.1 The settlement hierarchy

(Pyramid showing, from top to bottom: City (Very few) → Large towns → Small towns → Villages (Very many); Size of settlement decreases downward)

On a perfectly even landscape you might expect to find a pattern of cities, towns, villages and hamlets as shown in Fig. III. 1, but hardly anywhere is so flat and free from other influences that this pattern works out in practice. Fig. III. 2 shows the pattern in Norfolk. In some parts of Britain there is little settlement of any kind.

The original locations for these settlements usually lies many hundreds of years back in history. An initial settlement set up by Saxons, Vikings, Romans or Normans has become the base for later growth; sometimes the name of the village betrays its origins (see Fig. III. 3).

Place-name element	Meaning	Origin and date
Caster or chester	castle	Roman 55BC–AD 450
ing	settlement	Saxon
ham	village	Saxon
ton	homestead	Saxon
hurst	wood, hill	Saxon
thwaite	meadow	Norse
by	farmstead	Norse
bury, borough	fortified place	Saxon

Figure III. 3 Origins of British place names

The shape of urban areas

Villages are often in distinctive shapes: **nucleated** around a village green, **linear** along a single street, or **nodal** at the four arms of a cross-roads.

In the same way towns and cities can be roughly classified. The individual characteristics of the physical site on which the settlement was founded, and other historical factors (who originally owned the land, whether or not the railway came early and was allowed into the centre of town) make each one individual in character. However, some general patterns emerge. Attempts to show some of these general patterns produce 'models' as in Fig. III. 4. These models are often known by the name of their authors. Each of these models identifies a **central business district** (CBD), an inner-city area, and outer suburbs.

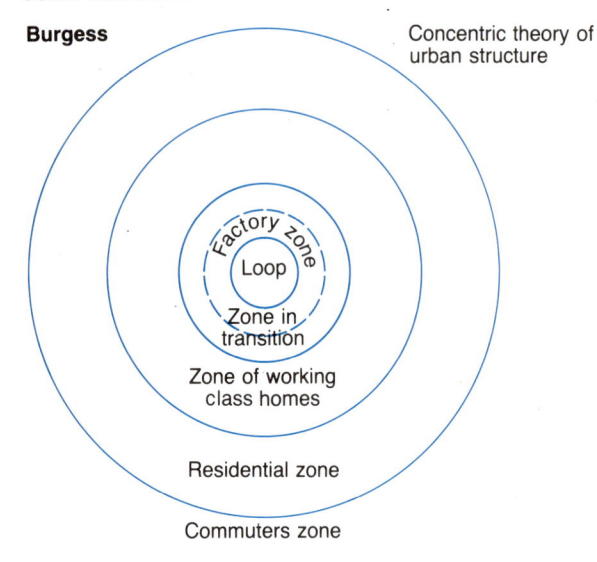

Figure III.4 Urban structure models

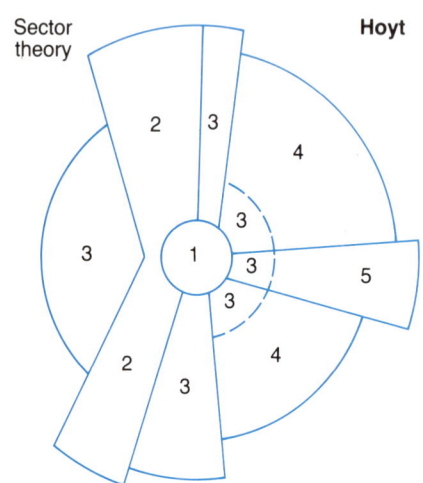

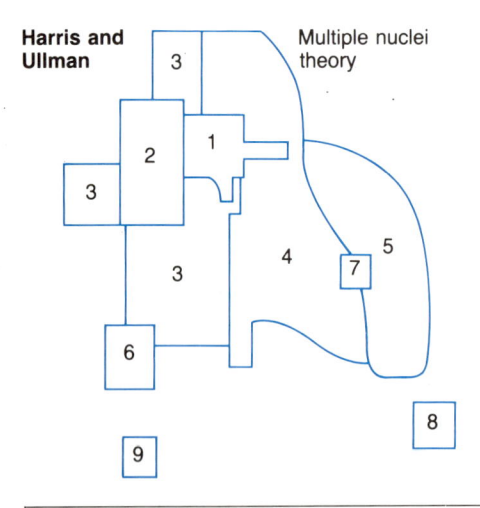

Burgess — Concentric theory of urban structure
- Loop
- Factory zone
- Zone in transition
- Zone of working class homes
- Residential zone
- Commuters zone

Hoyt — Sector theory

Harris and Ullman — Multiple nuclei theory

Mann

Key (Hoyt and Harris and Ullman):
1. Central Business District
2. Wholesale light manufacturing
3. Low class residential
4. Medium class residential
5. High class residential
6. Heavy manufacturing
7. Outlying business district
8. Residential suburb
9. Industrial suburb

Key (Mann):
1. City centre
2. Transitional zone
3. Zone of small terrace houses in sectors C and D; larger by-law houses in sector B; large old houses in sector A
4. Post-1918 residential areas with post-1945 development on the periphery
5. Commuter villages
A. Middle class sector
B. Lower-middle class sector
C. The working class sector (main council housing areas)
D. Industry and lowest working-class sector

Questions

1. Can you identify these major divisions in the city nearest to where you live? Does the city also have sectors (as in the Hoyt model) and more than one CBD (as in the Harris and Ullmann model)?
2. Draw a transect diagram across a city you know, showing the main kinds of buildings which you find in each zone.

Chapter 9
How a conurbation grows

If you look at a map of Britain you will see that there are seven large urban areas which are usually considered to be the major conurbations. Over one-third of all Britain's population is contained within these seven areas.

The oldest and largest of these areas is London and we shall look more closely at its development as an example of the way in which urban areas grow and change through time.

There was probably a small **hamlet** of encampments on the River Thames even before the Romans came. But the Roman armies, coming from the south, found a place where the River Thames was shallow enough to wade across. They established a defensive camp on the north side of the river, near two low gravel-capped hills. The hills made a good defensive site, and so – having chased or frightened away the original inhabitants – the conquering army built a wall around their own settlement and barracks. They called it Londinium. This area was nothing more than a large **village** and today is only a tiny part of the great London conurbation. But it is the part known as the old 'City of London' and in places parts of the old Roman wall can still be seen. Some street names also give clues to the placing of the walls and the gates which surrounded the city until medieval times.

The population grew, and eventually (in much more peaceful times, after the Romans had withdrawn) settlement developed outside the city walls. Workers' dwellings grew up to the north, a port to the east developed, and some large country houses – amidst hunting land – were built to the west. Another settlement (Westminster) grew up further upstream; the settlement of Southwark also grew on the south bank of the river.

A riverside track led between the City and Westminster. It was called the Strand (a word meaning beach), since it was once at the water's edge. Today it is one of nation's most famous streets, joining the western edge of the old City of London to Westminster. But it is no longer at the water's edge. Can you suggest the reason why?

In the sixteenth century London's population increased four-fold. The lands of the monasteries became available for housing outside the city walls, and the trade and wealth of Britain grew fast. Though the Great Fire of London (1666) destroyed many of the older wooden buildings, it allowed a massive rebuilding programme, using stone. The genius of Sir Christopher Wren created many fine buildings, including St Paul's Cathedral. London – by now the capital of Great Britain – grew in its trade and financial activities (concentrated in the old City) and in its administrative ones (concentrated in and around Westminster). The two settlements merged and grew together. London's south bank growth remained small for another hundred years – until beyond 1750.

Question

What single piece of building was needed to make the south bank grow as quickly as the settlements on the north side of the river?

A Geography of Contemporary Britain

Figure 9.1 The growth of London

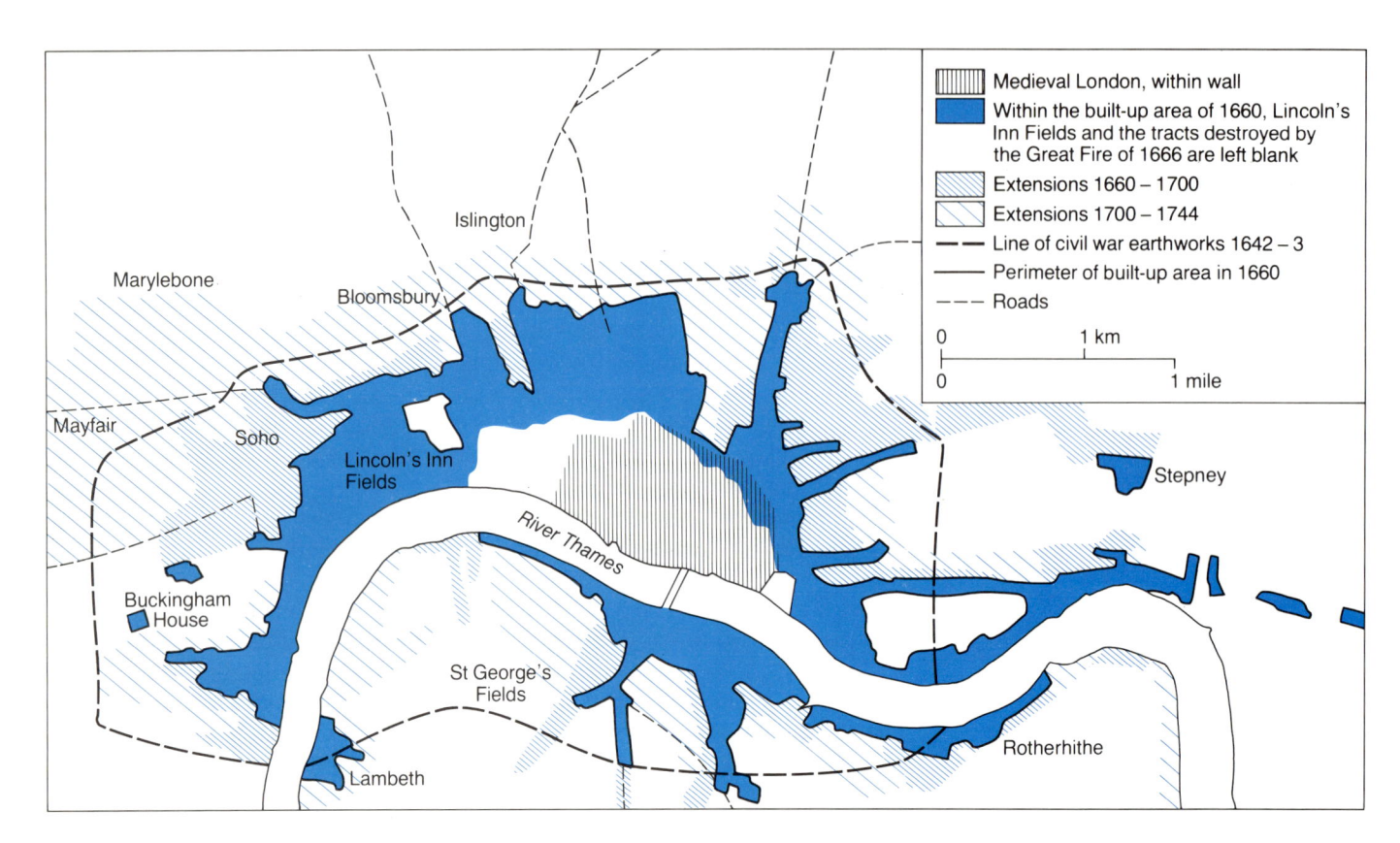

By the eighteenth century fine crescents and squares of houses had been built amongst trees and parks by architects such as John Nash and William Cubitt. In these houses lived the merchants who profited from the increasing trade of the port of London, the Government Civil Servants, Members of Parliament and the court officials.

The nineteenth century was to bring great changes, however. The harnessing of steam power to the railways encouraged a rapid growth of lines and stations from 1830 onwards. The railways would make it possible for London to expand further because now the trains could be used to bring people daily in to work from areas beyond walking distance.

From Westminster Bridge

In 1802 William Wordsworth, standing on Westminster Bridge composed these famous lines:

> Earth has not anything to show more fair:
> Dull would he be of soul who could pass by
> A sight so touching in its majesty:
> This City now doth, like a garment, wear
> the beauty of the morning; silent, bare,
> Ships, towers, domes, theatres, and temples lie
> Open unto the fields, and to the sky;
> All bright and glittering in the smokeless air.
> Never did sun more beautifully steep
> In his first splendour, valley, rock, or hill;
> Ne'er saw I, never felt, a calm so deep!
> The river glideth at his own sweet will:
> Dear God! the very houses seem asleep;
> And all that mighty heart is lying still!

Figure 9.2 The view from Westminster Bridge, 1988

Wordsworth's sister Dorothy made this comment on the same scene:

> We mounted the Dover coach at Charing Cross. It was a beautiful morning. The City, St Paul's, the river and a multitude of little boats made a most beautiful sight as we crossed Westminster Bridge. The houses were not overhung by their usual cloud of smoke, and they were spread out endlessly; yet the sun shone so brightly, with such a fierce light, that there was even something like the purity of one of nature's own grand spectacles.

Question

Do you think that the Wordsworths would still find the view from Westminster Bridge 'a sight so touching in its majesty' now? Compare the view above with a similar one taken at night, Plate 17.

> I walk my beat before London Town
> Five hours up and seven hours down
> Up I go till I end my run
> At Tide-end-town, which is Teddington.
> Down I come with the mud in my hands
> And plaster it over the Maplin sands.
> But I'd have you know that these waters of mine
> Were once a branch of the River Rhine
> When hundreds of miles to the East I went
> And England was joined to the Continent...
>
> From *The River's Tale* by Rudyard Kipling

The inner-city: terrace ribbing

The growth of London beyond Westminster and the old City accelerated rapidly after the railways had come. The changing base of Britain's industry (see also Part IV) was stimulating the growth of factories and their growth was accompanied by housing for their workers.

Figure 9.3 Terrace-ribbing; Kilburn, North London

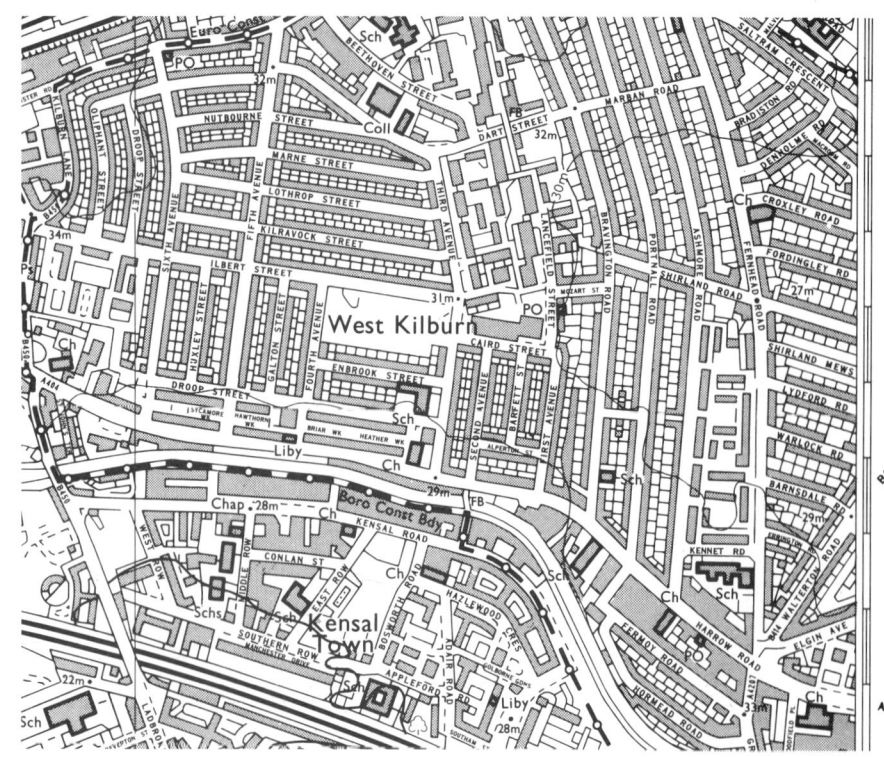

Figure 9.4 Ordnance Survey Greater London, Kilburn Scale 1:10 000 © Crown copyright

The Romans had built a straight road out from the centre of London to the north-west and called it Watling Street. It changed its name in the nineteenth century and became called Edgware Road – taking its name from a small village on the road, 25 kilometres out of London.

By 1900 the tight terraces of houses had progressed 15 kilometres up this road, already swallowing the small country villages of Kilburn and Cricklewood. Factories were built close to the railway in order to take advantage of the goods yards. By the turn of the century the motor-bus and the tram were passing up and down the Edgware Road, and lorries were also taking their share of factory products on the roads.

Life in the inner-city

The poet John Betjeman described the inner-city in the early twentieth century in his poem 'Parliament Hill Fields':

> Rumbling under blackened girders, Midland, bound for Cricklewood,
> Puffed its sulphur to the sunset where that Land of Laundries stood.
> Rumble under, thunder over, train and tram alternate go,
> Shake the floor and smudge the ledger, Charrington, Sells, Dale and Co.,
> Nuts and nuggets in the window, trucks along the lines below
>
> When the Bon Marché was shuttered, when the feet were hot and tired,
> Outside Charrington's we waited, by the 'STOP HERE IF REQUIRED',
> Launched aboard the shopping basket, sat precipitately down,
> Rocked past Zwanziger the baker's, and the terrace blackish brown,
> And the curious Anglo-Norman parish church of Kentish Town.

The inner-city terraces of the nineteenth century still stand in many roads today, but their original owners have moved on to other places – mostly outwards to newer housing in the outer suburbs.

The terrace houses were the cheapest available to many newcomers who came to Britain in the 1960s from the new Commonwealth. Attracted here by the prospect of jobs in London's hospitals and transport system, they needed to find somewhere to live. So Kilburn and Cricklewood today are multi-cultural communities and the range of shops and facilities reflect this.

Figure 9.5 Londoners all

Some of the factories in this area have now closed and been relocated elsewhere. The local councils and the central Government have been keen to see this happen, since it helps to re-zone areas in a more satisfactory way.

But these authorities also need to provide grants to help upgrade the housing to modern standards. The houses lack garage facilities and there are relatively few play and recreation spaces. These difficulties affect many similar inner-city areas in cities and conurbations throughout Britain.

Life in Kilburn

This is how a Kilburn resident (who lived there from 1915 to 1936) remembered conditions:

> We lived in a road of little terraced houses which opened straight on to the street. Our house had been divided into two flats; we only had one proper bedroom and Mum and Dad slept in that. Two girls slept in the back room and my younger brother had a put-u-up in the scullery. We never had people to stay overnight – but then most of our friends lived very close by.
>
> We had no car, nor even a bicycle. Father was a painter and decorator and he would walk to Belsize Park each day to pick up his handtruck and then go off to his job. Most mornings Mother would go shopping in the Kilburn High Road. We'd get groceries in the Home and Colonial Stores but there were also little roadside stalls where you could buy delicacies like a juicy bowl of dripping!
>
> At the weekends, we would walk up to the railway station on Kilburn High Road and go for a ride out into Hertfordshire. 'Metroland' they called it. They would give you maps to show you where you could go for a good day's ramble. And sometimes there was the excitement of a fair on Hampstead Heath or at the Welsh Harp at Hendon.
>
> When I married, we moved further out. We saw a house at Colindale with a front and a back garden and liked it very much. It backed on to Hendon Aerodrome. I was sorry to leave Kilburn in many ways; it was such a happy community.

Councillor Linda Bellos, former Leader of Lambeth Council

Britain faces a major housing crisis which is based on rapidly rising rents and house prices, and too few new homes to meet soaring demand.

The Government hopes to tackle this crisis by encouraging more private landloads to rent their empty properties, but this will not happen. Between 1979 and 1987, private lettings shrunk by 550,000 properties despite attempts (through the 'Assured' and 'Shorthold' tenancy schemes) to give greater power and profit to landlords and thus make renting more attractive to them.

So much for the private sector, but what about council housing? The To-

CONTRASTING VIEWPOINTS
'How can we best ensure all are housed properly?'

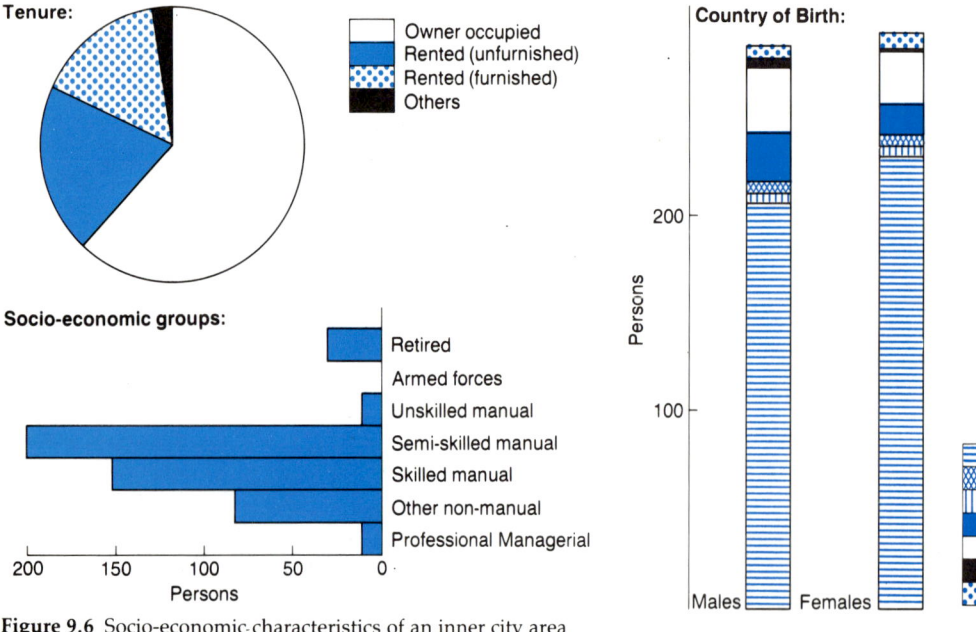

Figure 9.6 Socio-economic characteristics of an inner city area

ries insist that councils cannot continue as giant landlords because as a society we cannot afford it. I would insist that councils can and must continue to play such a role but that role has to change substantially.

The role of local authorities as landlords was not developed to give power and comfort to the poor and underprivileged, but to fend off the worst aspects of poverty and slum housing after the First World War. But simply removing slum conditions or providing affordable homes has not proved enough to meet people's expectations.

We should be offering homes which do not all look the same, homes whose gates need not be painted a regulated colour, and homes which can be improved and renovated by the tenant (with appropriate financial assistance) without the fear of the tenancy being removed at a later date. And, of course, we should offer a decent repairs and maintenance service, but for this we need adequate resources.

And since these are rights which those who own their own homes can enjoy, why should they be denied to working class tenants on council estates? These are the rights of self-expression, self-determination and self-pride which encourage people to feel a part of their estates, and assume greater responsibility for their lives.

The role of local authorities as landlords should be to facilitate those rights, for all people regardless of income, or any of the prejudices which bedevil the private sector.

Rt Hon William Waldegrave MP as Minister for Housing and Planning

I believe that freedom of choice is the key to good housing. Many people, quite naturally, prefer to own their own home. This gives them both a stake in maintaining the quality of their home and the community as a whole. The 1980s have seen an upsurge in the numbers of people who own their own homes. Thanks in part to the Conservative Government's Right to Buy policy which gave council tenants the right to buy their own homes — 2 million more than in 1979.

However, there will always be those who, for different reasons, either do not want or cannot afford to buy their own home. For these people, I believe that the great nineteenth-century housing reformers were right when they argued that the best way to ensure the best possible standard of rented housing was to support people not buildings. For many people who rent their houses or flats, the levels of rent have in the past been kept unrealistically low. Everyone should be enabled, if necessary by subsidy from the Government, to pay a realistic price for their housing. In that way, the owners of the properties have enough money to keep them up and maintain the quality of the housing stock as a whole. Low rents — whether in the private or public sectors — simply mean that properties fall into disrepair.

By supporting individual people in this way, we can also ensure a greater freedom of choice for them about where and in what kind of housing they want to live. People will be willing to offer houses and flats for rent if they know they can get realistic levels of rent in return and more money will be available to plough back in to building new properties for rent. The housing association movement will have an increasing role to play, I believe. This means that people who would rather rent their home, or cannot afford to buy, will find it easier to find a home. And when people can choose where they live, they can also demand higher standards; freedom of choice means better housing for everybody.

The outer suburbs: villa studding

Eight kilometres further on from Cricklewood on the Edgware Road stands Edgware itself; once a small village where G.F. Handel played the organ in the village church and wrote a famous piece of music after watching the blacksmith at work. Edgware was not much affected by development until the coming of the electric train – the Northern Line reached Edgware in 1924. Electric trains first came into use in the 1890s, but it was another twenty years before tunnelling techniques developed enough to allow them to run in deep tubes beneath the London clay. These deep tunnels enabled them to run *beneath* the existing pattern of houses and roads in central London and to remain underground until they reached open countryside. But the lines were then extended outwards – to Epping, Cockfosters, Ruislip and Hounslow, as the present-day London Underground map will show.

When the line came to Edgware it was built mainly through open fields, but the strong advertising of developers was already advancing the delights of a 'town house in the country' (see Fig. 9.7). The London County Council built a vast new estate of houses for tenants at Burnt Oak (the station was sub-titled with the name of the estate 'Watling') and at Edgware itself there were shrewd plans for expansion.

Figure 9.7 A London Transport poster advertising the 'delightful prospects' of the suburbs in north-west London

Planning shops in Edgware

George Cross describes the planning of the shopping parade at Edgware in the early 1920s.

> Multiple traders are very much like sheep in the way they follow one another, but unlike sheep, they do not go astray. It was then I was fortunate enough to get an interview with that great and charming business man, J.B. Sainsbury. . . . He was interested in Edgware but he rather fancied the main road he said. My shop plans were no good to him; they always built their own premises on land they purchased, and would never rent. If I cared to offer him a 24-foot site at a nominal price, he might consider it.
>
> I knew that if only I could say Sainsbury's had bought a plot other traders would follow suit, and I asked him what he considered a nominal price. 'Oh, a couple of hundred pounds, or say ten pounds a foot' he replied. 'But' I objected, 'that would be giving it away.' 'Well, wise people have done that before now' was his rejoinder. It did not take me long to make up my mind. 'You can have it at your own figure if you will let me put up a board stating it has been sold to you' I said. . . .
>
> It is impossible to overestimate the value of traders like Sainsbury to a new parade of shops, and with this card to play I laid siege to other desirable firms. . . . My next coup was MacFisheries [who] were obviously anxious to become a neighbour of Sainsbury's and W.H. Smith's . . . next came the Manor Farm Dairies. . . . It soon became apparent to me that with this shop scheme I should make another substantial fortune. . . . I should drag the trade from the main road and what was more, keep it. . . . On the 18th August 1924 the first passenger train was run on the Tube from Charing Cross to Edgware. . . . The effect of the opening of the Tube and the building of the shops on the Edgware Manor Estate was like the sun ripening the harvest. . . .

In a few brief years the areas between the electric train stations were filled with rows of neat semi-detached houses; villas studded the landscape

How a conurbation grows 87

Figure 9.8 Edgware 1926

Figure 9.9 Edgware 1930

Figure 9.10 Ordnance Survey Greater London, Edgware Scale 1:10 000 © Crown copyright

with more space between them than the earlier closer-ribbed terraces. The developers tried to provide interest and variation by planning the streets in different patterns. Small cul-de-sacs and areas of green land were interspersed in these estates – at Edgware this was the case on the council-owned and planned Watling estate as well as the private developments which surrounded it.

These outer suburban houses were built cheaply enough for them to be bought by families moving out from the inner-city and now able to use the electric train to commute to work to the City or the West End. Today, some of these houses begin to show their age, but they usually have enough space and good enough construction to allow the building of extensions and garages, if they were not provided in the first place.

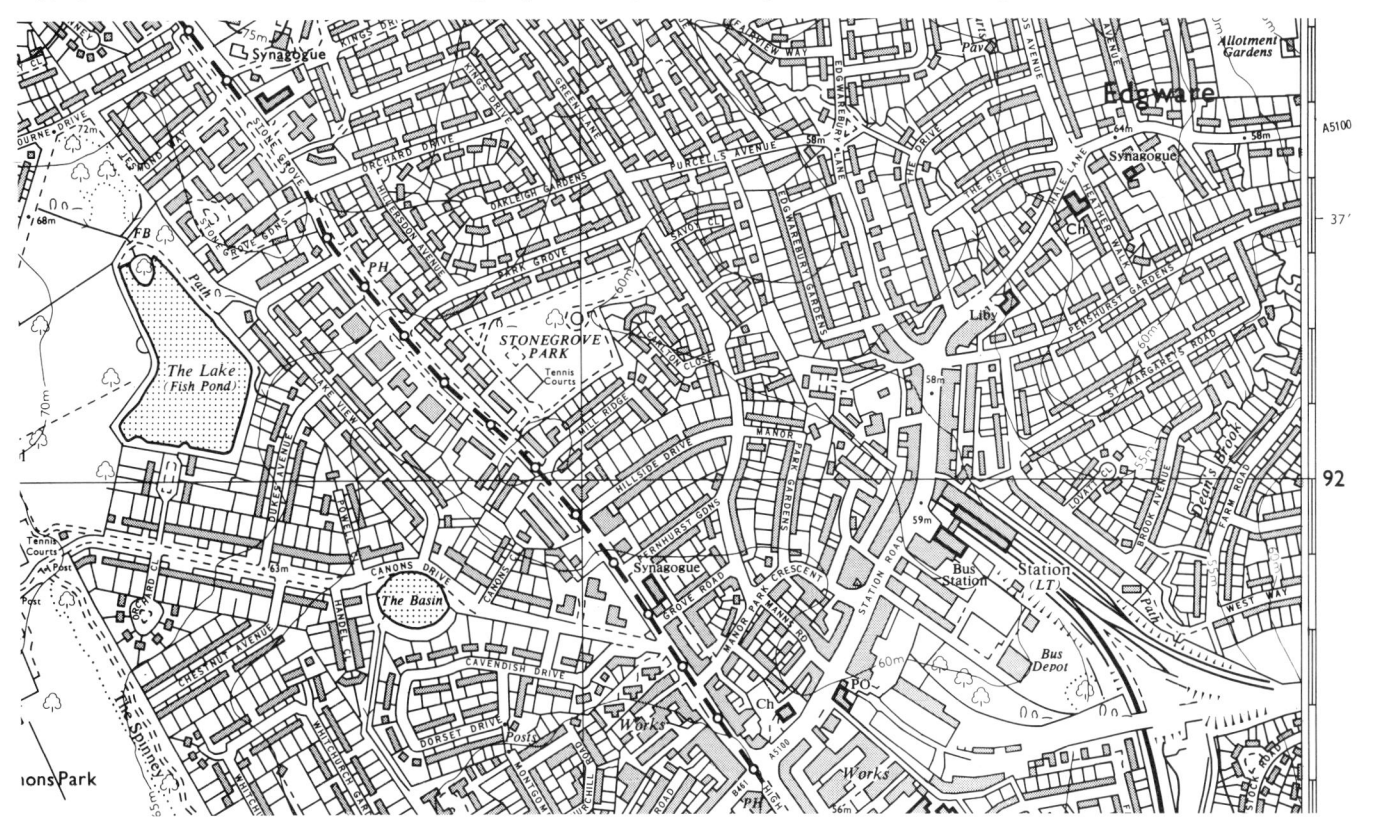

Life in the suburbs

John Betjeman comments on life in the Suburbs in his poem 'Middlesex'.

> Gaily into Ruislip Gardens
> Runs the red electric train
> With a thousand Ta's and Pardon's
> Daintily alights Elaine;
> Hurries down the concrete station
> With a frown of concentration,
> Out into the outskirt's edges
> Where a few surviving hedges
> Keep alive our lost Elysium – rural Middlesex again....
>
> Gentle Brent, I used to know you
> Wandering Wembley-wards at will,
> Now what change your waters show you
> In the meadow lands you fill ....

Figure 9.11 Selected elements of the geography of North-West London

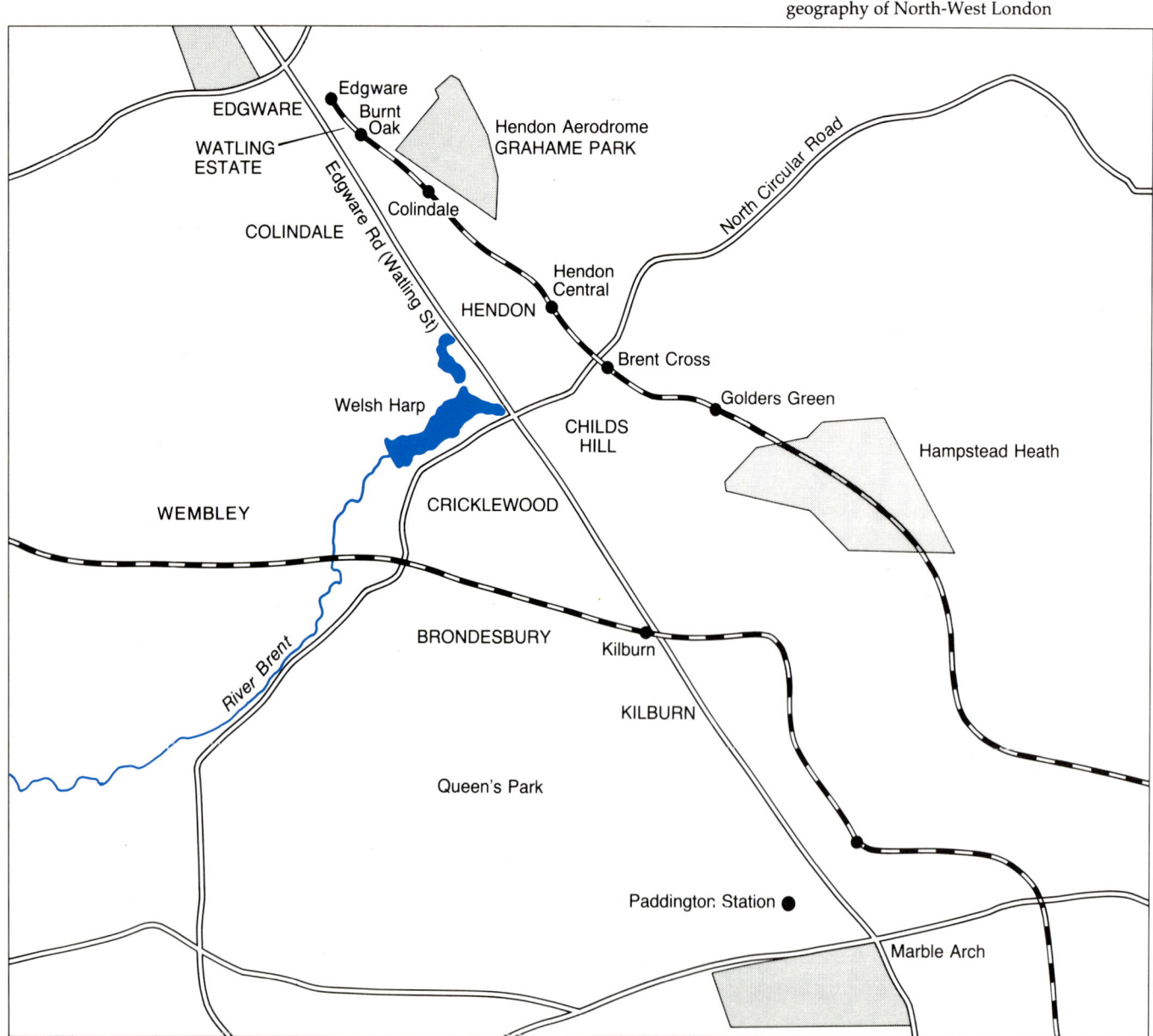

Castles in the air: block clumping

One of the stations on the Northern Line between Golders Green and Edgware is Colindale. For a week each year in the 1930s its usual throng of suburban commuters was swollen to enormous proportions by the crowds who flocked by train to the Hendon Air Pageant. Hendon Aerodrome had been founded in green fields in the earliest days of flying (around 1910) and had become the home of some small aircraft factories (notably one owned by Claude Grahame-White), and then a Royal Air Force station.

As the suburbs grew up all around it Hendon Aerodrome remained an oasis of green. But after the Second World War it was clear that the aerodrome was now too small to be useful for the faster and bigger planes which were being developed. So eventually Hendon Aerodrome was developed into a housing estate.

The development happened in the 1960s and by then builders had developed new techniques of construction which allowed them to build bigger and higher than they had ever done before. The cost of land was very high. So it was not surprising that when the new Grahame Park estate was developed there should be 'tower-blocks' interspersed with other houses.

It was claimed that these tower-blocks provided services for residents at a much cheaper cost (because things such as electricity and gas were all being provided in one building) and that they provided more spectacular views and comfort, compared with the cramped terraces and small villas of the earlier suburbs. For a time these 'castles in the air' were seen as very fashionable places, since they were set in spacious green surrounds and looked impressive.

The idea of building tower-blocks was also developed in some inner-city areas. In the places where housing was decaying quickly (areas often called 'twilight zones') some Councils thought it best to bulldoze down whole roads of houses and start again.

Figure 9.12 Hendon aerodrome — air pageant 1936

Figure 9.13 Hendon aerodrome 1988 — now the Grahame Park estate

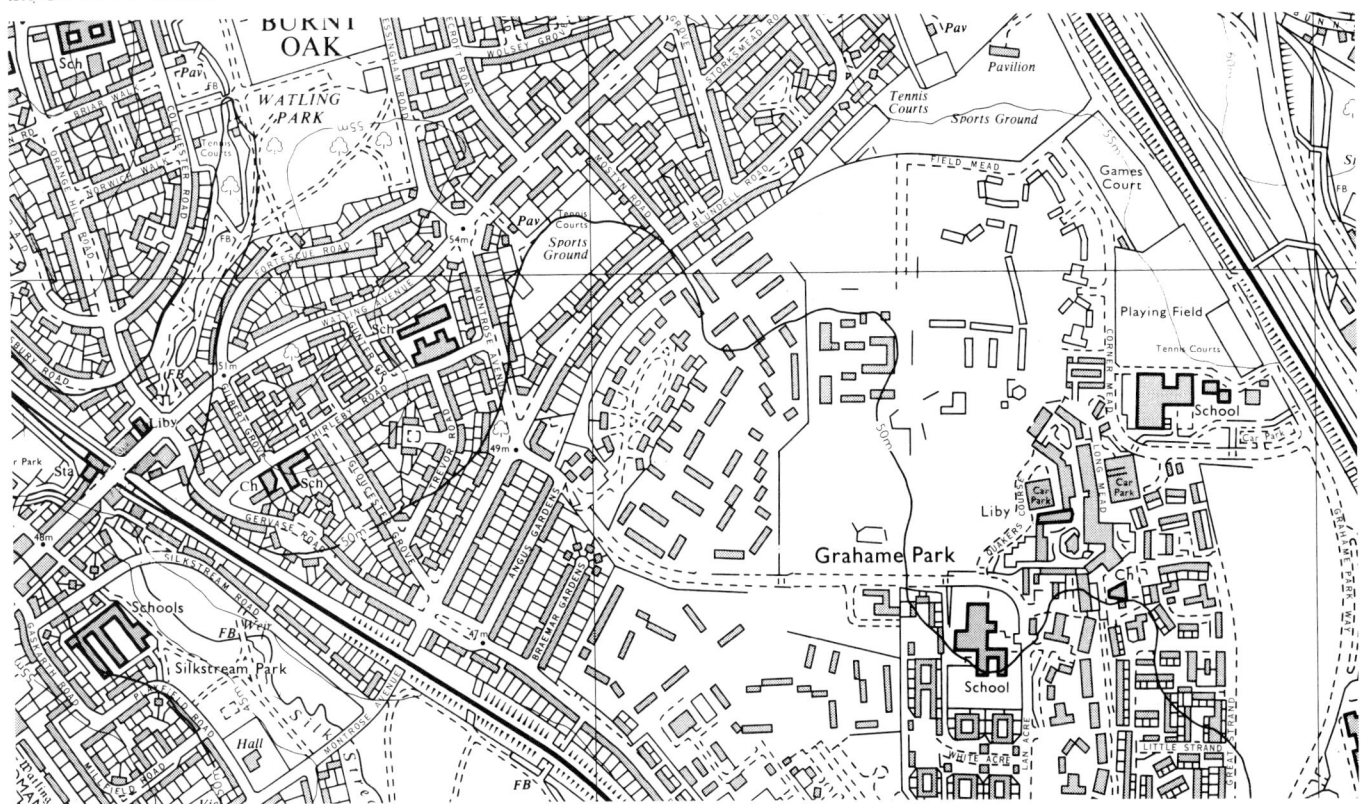

Figure 9.14 Ordnance Survey Greater London, Grahame Park Scale 1:10 000 © Crown copyright

In order to keep the density of population as high as before, and re-house all those who already lived in the neighbourhood, they built tower-blocks in the inner-city. In Birmingham this was done extensively – so that nothing of some of the nineteenth-century Birmingham suburbs is now visible.

In London many tower blocks were built in the eastern boroughs near the Docks and in the inner south London boroughs. Sheffield also built a massive high-rise development called Park Hill which dominated the centre of the city. In Newcastle a development called the Byker Wall was created.

A severe gas explosion in a tower-block called Ronan Point in East Ham, London, created severe doubts about the safety of these high-rise buildings. Those who lived there also began to complain of the difficulties of getting out if the lifts were not working. Some areas became vandalised and were the territory of gangs and muggers. A long lonely walk down a corridor was feared by elderly residents, especially late at night.

The block-clumping made quite an impact on the city landscape, but already, after only twenty years, some of the tower-blocks are being pulled down. They did not prove as cheap as it was hoped and their constant need of repair is a source of irritation to those who lived in them.

Life in the tower-blocks

From 'The Planster's Vision' by John Betjeman.

> I have a Vision of The Future, chum,
> The workers' flats in fields of soya beans
> Tower up like silver pencils, score on score:
> And Surging Millions hear the Challenge come
> From microphones in communal canteens
> 'No Right! No Wrong! All's perfect, evermore.

Harsh reality of city flats — the view of a tower-block dweller

I have lived in a damp council flat for two years. Here we sit like birds in the wilderness, 20 flats to a floor, 15 storeys high, separated by dim concrete corridors and icy stairs. All the flats are square like slabs of dirty cake with windows. My low-ceilinged walls are wet and mould thrives on them. Puddles collect on the window sills. Clothes in the wardrobe rot. Life is harsh here. At first I had the milk delivered but had more bottles stolen than I drank. Our private lives are very private except that you can hear every word of even slightly raised conversation in bordering flats. I am constantly woken by either shouted oaths, slammed doors or Rod Stewart full volume, all carried out at 2 o'clock in the morning but hopefully not all together. I now have two locks, a chain and a bolt on my door. My son has nowhere to play. His sole companion is a six-year-old from three blocks away. Life for the local kids is bleak. Boredom equals vandalism. The only telephone box has few panes and cannot be relied upon. The bus shelter is an eyesore. My dear old cat has had her whiskers cut with scissors. The folk in floors above me litter the space beneath my windows. They empty their ash trays, even their cat trays. The spirit of the next door neighbour as practised in old terraces is gone. The garden and washing line used to be reasons to talk and meet. Recently I met the man in the flat opposite for the first time – I have lived here two years! I know only two women on this estate. The others are shadows – they do not speak or smile.

Figure 9.15 From *The Guardian*

Changes in the city

The inner-city

The houses nearest the city centre, many terraced, are usually the oldest. Residents may have lived there for many years and have deep roots in their local community. But faced with major repairs to a decaying property, they may eventually choose to go to a newer house further away from the city centre, if they can sell at a good price.

Those who pay such a price may have the money available to **refurbish** the old property. In London, young professionals who earn high salaries in banking, advertising, and finance, have **gentrified** whole streets of terraced houses in this way, in districts such as Islington, Kennington and Canonbury. It is a great advantage for them to avoid **commuting** long distances to their work each day.

In other areas, the reverse happens. Councils may decide to purchase compulsorily decaying central areas of poor housing in order to make room for new road-schemes or car-parking. The area assumes an air of desolation and the remaining residents lose hope in their community and their environment. Simon Barnes, a journalist, describes one particular inner-city:

> Wolverhampton, like so many medium-sized provincial cities, is a depressing place. It seems to have given up being a town, at least in the middle, and set itself up as a shrine to the internal combustion engine. The place seems swathed in ring roads designed to co-ordinate tastefully with the giant cantilevered stand in the football ground – itself an emblem of folly, a monument to football's great age of self-delusion in the 1970s.
>
> So many provincial towns seem to have been subjected to violent centrifugal force; everything has whizzed from the middle to the rim, pushing the outer edges ever further back. There are times when I believe that all England will become a suburb of itself, as the towns grow hollow at the heart and the suburbs grow proud and fat and push ever further into the Green Belt.

The suburbs

The suburban villas do not yet need replacement, though the huge growth in motor-vehicle ownership shows up the problems of those houses without room for a garage. Side-street parking and a general increase in commuting to work by private car have created many suburban traffic problems. In the inter-war period, and in the first twenty years after the Second World War, many large council estates were built to provide housing for those who could not afford to buy a house. The houses on many of these estates have since been offered for sale to those who already live in them, and many have chosen to become property-owners. This **privatisation** has led to a more varied look to many of the estates, as owners carry out individual improvements and extensions to houses formerly built to a regular pattern.

The development of planning controls has meant that there have been relatively few large suburban developments in recent years. Extra population has been diverted away to 'new towns' and 'overspill towns', well beyond the limits of the city.

Plate 17 London — the Central Business District taken from the south bank of the River Thames. Notice the dome of St Paul's Cathedral (left) and several tall modern office blocks (right). From the map on page 98 can you identify the bridge in the foreground?

Plate 18 The inner city — terrace ribbing, old housing and new. The terraced houses are nineteenth century in age; behind them towers a new office-block built in the 1970s on a piece of redeveloped land.

Plate 19 The suburbs – a street in Harrow, North London. Compare this photograph with Plate 18; note the differences in a) distance of houses from the road b) provision for vehicles c) style of houses. Suggest a date for the building of these houses.

Plate 20 The outer city – an aerial view of the Grahame Park Estate, Mill Hill, North London. The estate was built on the site of a former aerodrome in the 1960's; the location is closer to Central London than Heathrow or Gatwick. Can you suggest why it was not developed as London Airport? Note the buildings of the Battle of Britain Museum (left) and the RAF Museum (right) which are a reminder of the areas's former use.

Plate 21 Beyond the city – an out-of-town superstore. If you were searching for a site for a superstore what would be the locational factors which would be most important to your company?

Plate 22 A New Town. A striking aerial view of the patterned housing developments of an area in Telford, Shropshire. What are a) the advantages b) the disadvantages of living in a new town?

Plate 23 Market-day in the centre of an old-established regional centre, Ripon in Yorkshire. Would you prefer to shop here or in a centre such as that shown in Plate 21? Why?

Plate 24 A pedestrian precinct. Here a street once busy with vehicles has been 'pedestrianised'. Are there any *problems* that this might cause?

(47)

(18)

⑲

20

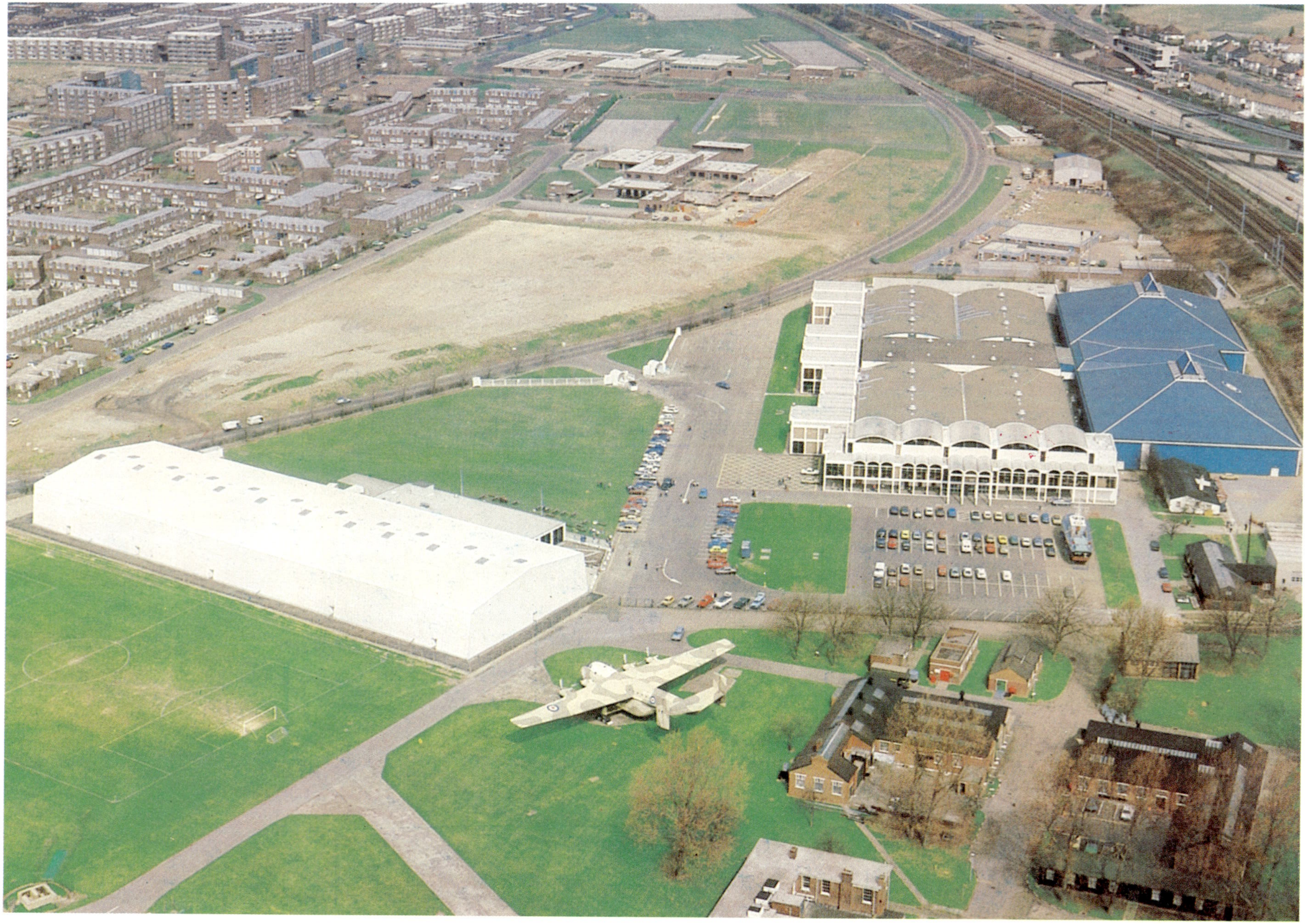

21

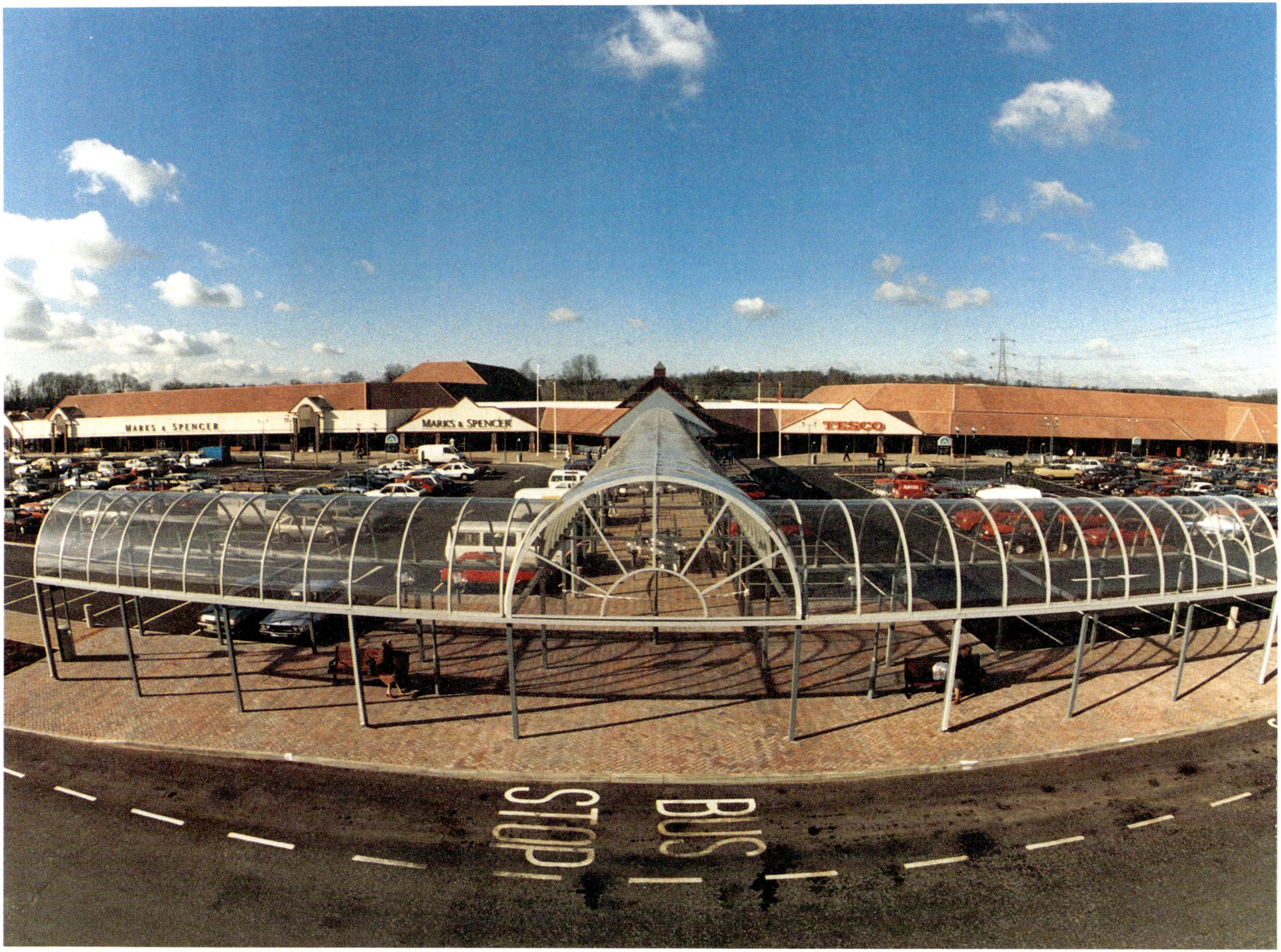

22

23

24

The tower-blocks

Though the most recent addition to the townscape, the tower-blocks have not been successful in many areas. The Mozart estate in Queen's Park, near the Edgware Road in North-west London, is a good example of the problems. It won a Department of Environment housing design award in 1973. Blocks of flats, inter-connected by walkways, surrounded a small shopping centre, public housing and housing office.

In 1986 the local Council spent thousands of pounds on repairing damage caused by vandals, who could escape easily through the warren of walkways if challenged. The pub was closed, many of the shops were boarded up and the shopping centre became a desolate place.

The Council listened to the proposals of a geographer, Alice Coleman of King's College, London, who had researched the problems of high-rise living. They took her advice and decided to knock down the walkways and re-shape the estate in a different way. In 1988, similar plans were proposed for the high-rise blocks of Grahame Park, Hendon.

Dreams borne by desolation

THIS morning a crane will remove 15 metres of high-level walkway connecting Naylor House and Grover House on the Mozart Estate in Queen's Park, north west London – and change the lives of 2,000 people for whom a planners' Utopia has become a paradise for vandals. There will be no fanfare of trumpets. But there should be. As the top brass of Westminster Council stand among the squalor and watch the crane bring the walkway crashing down, the ideas of one woman, urban geographer Alice Coleman, of London University, will become a reality....

In a study of 4,000 blocks of flats in London – housing 250,000 people – Miss Coleman discovered 15 danger factors which, if incorporatd into the design, were directly responsible for crime, vandalism and anti-social behaviour.

The high-rise comes top of the table. Open walkways, corridors, and entrances from the street are serious danger factors. Those grassy open spaces, that look so good on the plan, turn into places where no one wants to go.

Miss Coleman's ideal is homes for people that are not open-plan, but have both privacy and access to the community.

She maintains: 'We are turning out little savages when we need not. The ideal family home is one with a garden that leads out of the kitchen. The child plays outside, where he feels safe and develops his self-confidence.'

Heaven, to Miss Coleman, is the street of urban semis, and she gets very angry when this is disparaged. The bay window gives you a view out, strangers do not lurk about on your doorstep, low garden fences mean you can chat to your neighbour.

Her recommendations should transform life on the Mozart Estate. Small houses are to be built on the open spaces that have become wastelands. Streets are to be built again through the estate. Each block is to be surrounded by a wall, with one entrance.

Little gardens are to be created, wherever possible. Windows that once looked in to the estate will now look out.

Says Peter Walters, deputy district housing officer: 'We hope to turn Mozart into a popular estate.'

Mrs Winnie Plunkett, vicechairman of the tenants' association, moved into Tilleard House 11 years ago. She has watched the show-piece estate disintegrate and will not now go out alone at night on her own.

What she looks forward to is the return of the community spirit she misses so much. 'This open plan means that too many outsiders come through the estate,' she says. 'Soon we will have our privacy.'

Figure 9.16 *Today*, 20 March 1986

Plans for inner-city change

In many of Britain's conurbations (Fig. 9.24) decay in the inner urban areas has become so widespread that it has become a matter for national concern. Reports from churches and charities have drawn attention to many social and environmental problems and called for major investment in their renewal.

Figure 9.19 Hay's Wharf as it is now promoted

Hay's Galleria is London's new shopping and eating experience - the focal point of London Bridge City. The site on which Hay's Galleria stands has an extremely vivid history. It became the Thames River's most famous Wharf, serving the whole of the British Empire. A triumph in modern engineering, Hay's Galleria has been carefully constructed to conserve a sense of the past. The original dock, where tea clippers once moored, has been sealed over and a spectacular glass and steel roof covers the Galleria.

Spectacular views of the Thames and beyond, makes it one of the most thrilling environments that London has ever seen. Much more than a place to shop, it's somewhere to meet friends, to sit, chat and look around. It's an exciting mix of offices, apartments, shops and eating places. Just a few yards from Hay's Galleria, you'll find the Cottons Centre beneath which is a superbly equipped leisure centre. Facilities include squash courts, a swimming pool, gymnasium and sauna. And for the first time in 300 years it will soon be possible to take a riverside walk from London Bridge to Tower Bridge.

So come and discover London's latest and most exciting landmark.

Figure 9.17 Hay's Wharf 1925

Figure 9.18 Hay's Wharf 1988

How a conurbation grows 95

To meet these problems, the Government has set up a number of Urban Development Corporations with direct responsibility for revitalising particular areas. The first, and best-known of these is the London Docklands Development Corporation (LDDC), set up in 1981. It has £200,000,000 to revive the area which was once the hub of Britain's international trade.

Figure 9.20 (below) St Katherine's Dock in 1968

Figure 9.21 (bottom) St Katherine's Dock today

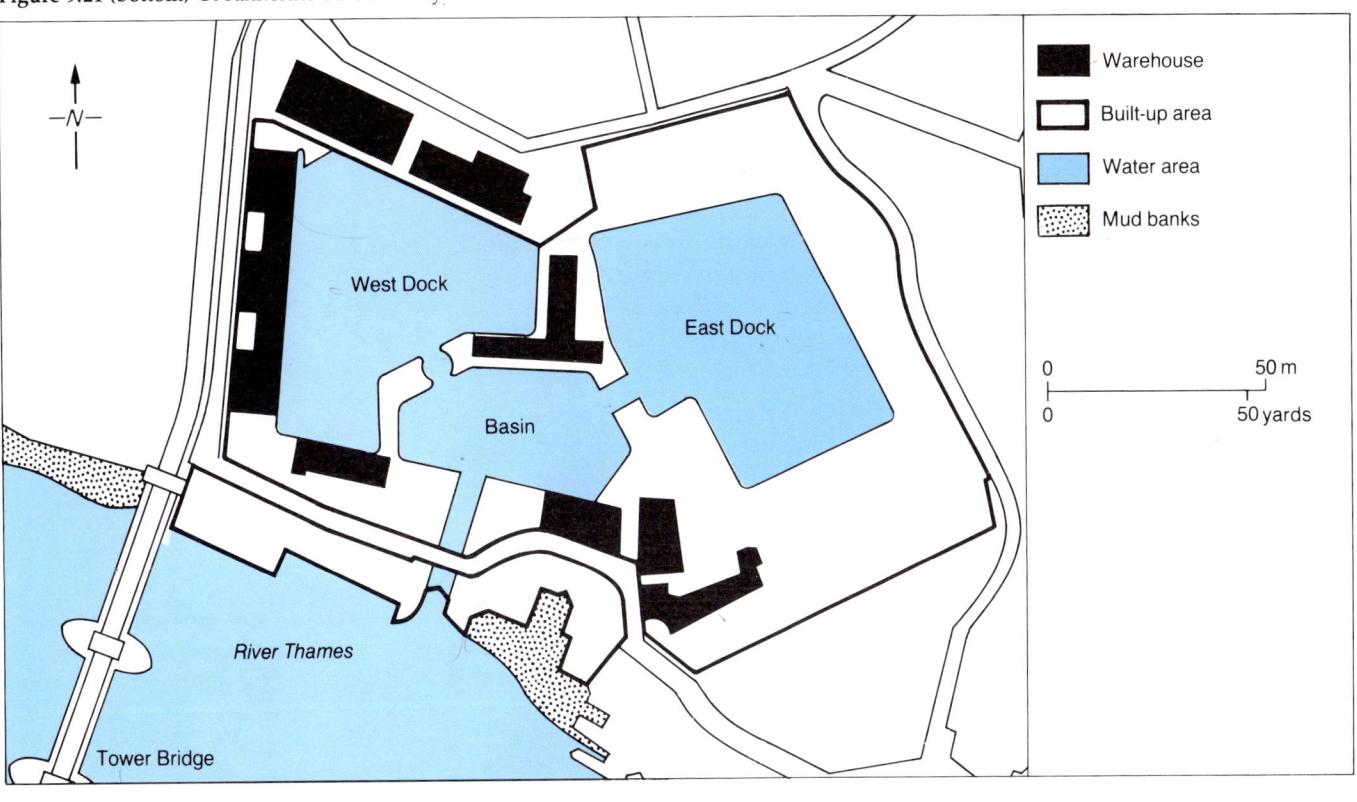

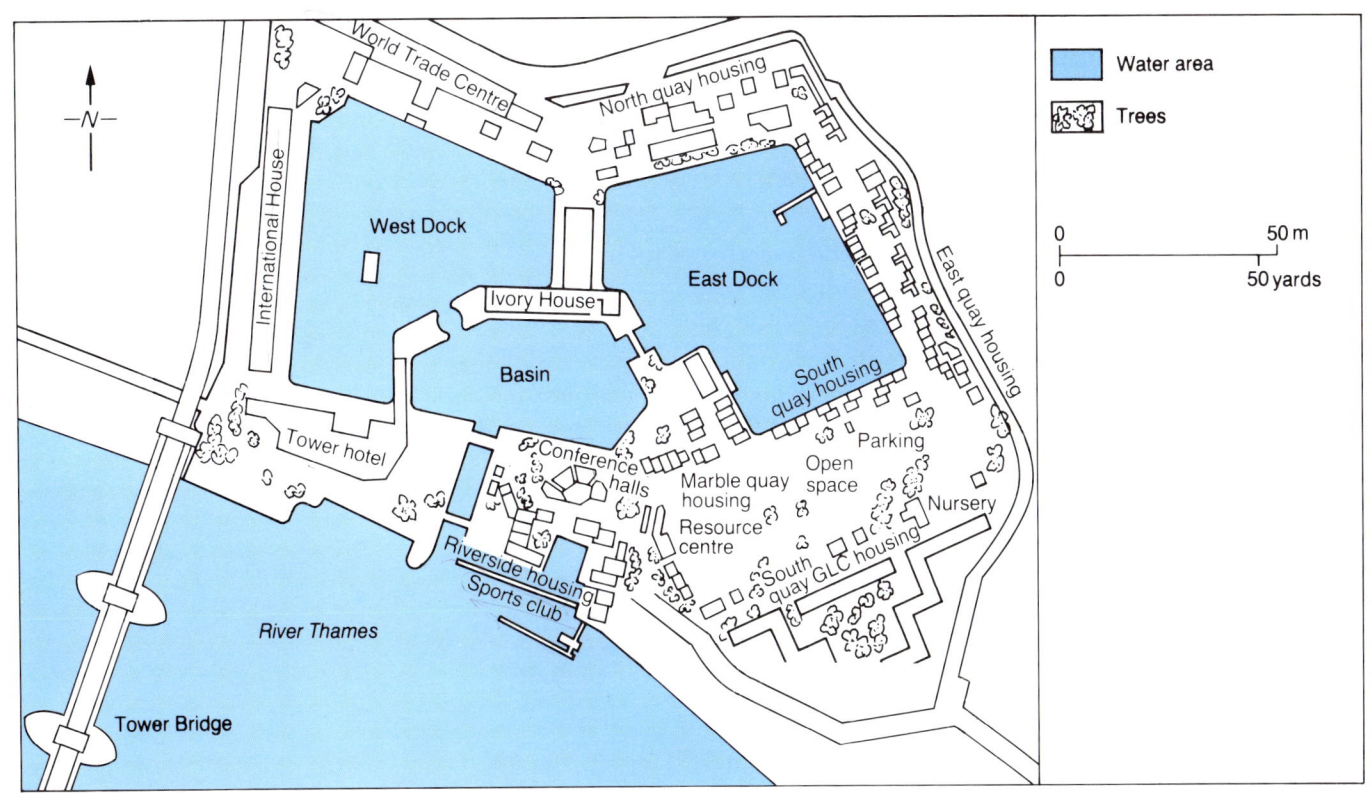

The extensive dockland areas have lain unused for twenty years, following the movement of dock activity further downstream to the deeper water ports on the Thames estuary. Now the LDDC aims to redevelop the area downstream of Tower Bridge into a thriving community again.

These are some of its plans:

- It is hoped to increase the population of the area by 25,000. Already there are a number of new riverside apartment blocks in the Limehouse and Wapping areas. Critics argue that these are much too expensive for existing residents to move to, and that there should be more emphasis on cheaper housing.

- By rate and rent incentives the LDDC is attracting new business to the area. Several national newspapers are moving their editorial offices and their printing works from Fleet Street to the Docklands, and taking on new technology in the process. One huge new works in Wapping, owned by Rupert Murdoch, has already been at the centre of controversy, picketed by workers who are now no longer needed because of new automated processes. A television complex, Limehouse Studios, has been opened in old dock buildings.

- There are many new office developments in the area. Some, like the Canary Wharf complex in the Isle of Dogs, are being built from scratch; others are taking over old dock warehouses and administrative buildings.

- New transport links are making the area more easily accessible. A new Docklands Light Railway links the area to the existing London Underground system at Bank Station. There is a new STOL airport sited in the area of the Royal Docks.

The plans for inner-city change do not always command universal agreement between those who are involved. There have been several examples of conflict between those who want to see inner-city sites redeveloped for housing and those who believe that commercial use would be more profitable and beneficial in the long-term.

The Hay's Wharf site – just south of London Bridge and within the LDDC area – is a good example of the tug-of-war which sometimes take place.

Hay's Wharf: timetable of events

1978   Hay's Wharf Ltd, a shipping firm, decides to vacate its site. They sell the land to the St Martin's Property Company who design a scheme for 200,000 square metres of offices.

1980   A public enquiry is held. A Government inspector hears the arguments for the scheme from the developers and from local community groups (who oppose it and want to see the site developed for housing). The local Council at this stage supports the developers.

1981   The inspector rejects the developers plan. The Government minister responsible overrules the decision and gives permission for the scheme to go ahead.

1982   The local Council now changes its mind and supports the opponents of the scheme.

1983   A new proposal for offices is put forward. This time it is put forward through the London Docklands Development Corporation. (The LDDC has power to decide planning applications without going through the longer mechanisms of public enquiries and community hearings.)

1984   The minister responsible agrees to the revised scheme. Local community groups still remain opposed.

CONTRASTING VIEWPOINTS

'Is the Docklands Project the best way to revive the inner city?'

London Docklands Development Corporation

London's docklands stretch for eight miles along the river from London Bridge to past the Thames Barrier. One hundred years ago, the docks were prosperous and growing with plenty of other local industries.

Yet by 1981, Docklands showed all the signs typical of inner city decay. The docks had all closed, the old industries gone, losing 18,000 jobs in the previous eight years. Unemployment reached 30 per cent. Nearly all housing was rented and in increasingly bad condition. Public transport was limited and the roads poor. There was little of anything left to benefit the local community.

Since then the London Docklands Development Corporation has been set up and has begun to turn the tide. More than 10,000 new jobs have been introduced. The largest private housing programme in Britain is well under way. New roads have been built, a new railway will soon be opened and a new airport is about to be completed. So far, £2,242 millions are being spent by private industry alone; 'levered' by just £297 million of public money. The resultant 'leverage' ratio of 9 to 1 is high and increasing.

What is the key to Docklands' success?

Although set up by the government, the LDDC is small, strong and single-minded. It has avoided the problems of red-tape, clumsiness and slow reaction of many central and local government departments.

Yet it also has a longer-term vision and broader perspective than private companies. By using public money on crucial projects such as roads and railways and special training schemes for school-leavers, the LDDC has encouraged companies from all over Britain to come to Docklands, bringing with them jobs, the stimulus for better housing and the means to improve the environment.

After decades of decline, Docklands now has a future in which all can share. This has only been made possible by the creation of a single-minded development agency providing a partnership between the public and private sectors.

Ian Mikardo, retired Labour MP

The London Docklands Development Corporation is a copy of the New Town Corporations which were set up, some years ago, to build new towns in empty areas with very few people in them.

It was therefore fair enough to give each of those Corporations wide-ranging powers to do virtually what it liked without consulting local people, because by definition there were, in its area, no local people to consult.

But the London Docklands Corporation was given the same dictatorial power over an area in which 50,000 people were already living. Those people could, through periodic elections of councillors, control the borough councils who had previously administered their area.

They have no such powers over the Docklands Corporation, which has therefore ridden roughshod all over them.

It has taken the land which was available to build houses for them and sold it to developers to build expensive housing for yuppies that no local people can afford. It has blocked the access of those people to the riverside which is their greatest environmental treasure. It has created jobs for commuters to come in from outside, and a light railway to carry them to and from work, but it hasn't made any reduction in the high level of unemployment amongst the local people.

Reviving the inner city demands more than piling bricks and mortar and steel and concrete on to it: it demands reviving the *community*, the local people. And that is precisely what the Docklands Corporation has *not* done.

Database: city development

Name of bridge	Date of building	Name of bridge	Date of building
London	1176	Chelsea	1858
Westminster	1750	Victoria (railway)	1860
Battersea	1771	Lambeth	1862
Blackfriars	1796	Battersea (railway)	1863
Vauxhall	1816	Blackfriars (railway)	1864
Waterloo	1817	Hungerford (railway)	1864
Southwark	1819	Cannon St (railway)	1866
Wandsworth	1823	Albert	1873
(New) London Bridge	1831	Tower	1894

Notes Bridges west of Wandsworth are not included.
Later came tunnels east of Tower Bridge.

Figure 9.22 London's bridges
The key to the development beyond the site of the City of London lay in the provision of bridges over the river to the southern bank and (in the nineteenth century) the development of railways.

Figure 9.23 London's railway termini

Name of railway terminus	Major railway company using it	Date of opening	Main destinations beyond London
Euston	LNWR	1838	Manchester, North-West, Scotland
Paddington	GWR	1838	Wales, West, South-West
Waterloo	LSWR	1848	South coast and South-West
Fenchurch Street	LT & S	1854	South-East Essex
Kings Cross	GNR	1852	Yorks, North-East, Edinburgh
Victoria	LB & SCR	1860	Sussex coast
	LC & DR		Kent
Cannon Street	SER	1864	Kent
Charing Cross	SER	1865	Kent
St Pancras	MR	1868	Midlands, Yorkshire
Liverpool Street	GER	1874	East Anglia
Marylebone	GCR	1899	Midlands, North

Figure 9.24 British conurbations

Name of conurbation	Population size (approx)	Major historic centres
Greater London	6,696,000	City of London, Westminster
West Midlands	1,000,000	Birmingham, Wolverhampton, Solihull
Greater Manchester	700,000	Manchester, Salford
Merseyside	600,000	Liverpool
West Yorkshire	500,000	Leeds, Bradford
Tyne and Wear	500,000	Newcastle
Clydeside	1,000,000	Glasgow

Figure 9.25 Passengers carried by London transport 1950–65

	Per year			
Year	Red (city centre) buses (passengers in millions)	Green (country) buses and coaches (passengers in millions)	Underground railways (passengers in millions)	Private cars licensed in London area (in 000s)
1950	3,535	305	695	480
1953	3,330	329	672	600 (approx.)
1956	2,918	318	678	803
1959	2,470	286	669	1,050
1962	2,215	270	668	1,546
1965	1,896	236	657	1,920

Figure 9.27 London's bridges

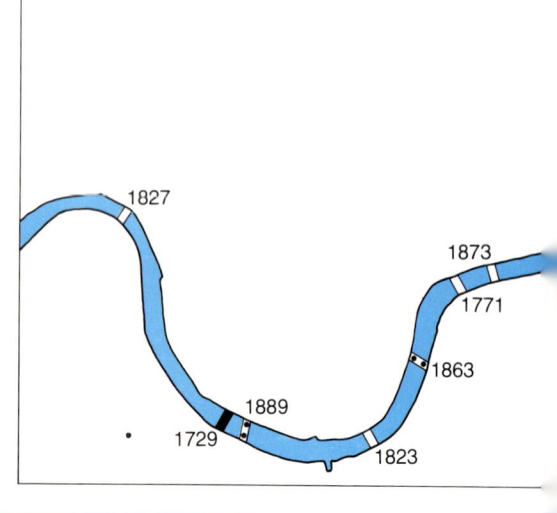

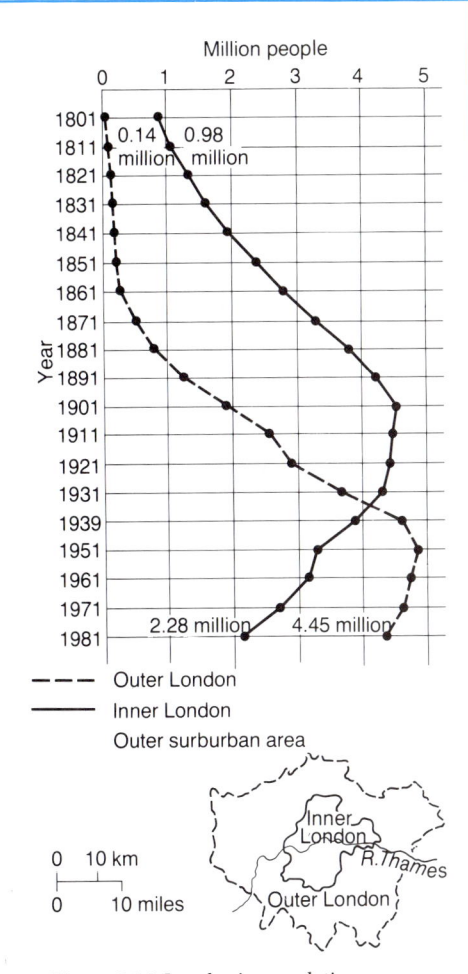

Figure 9.26 London's population 1801–1981

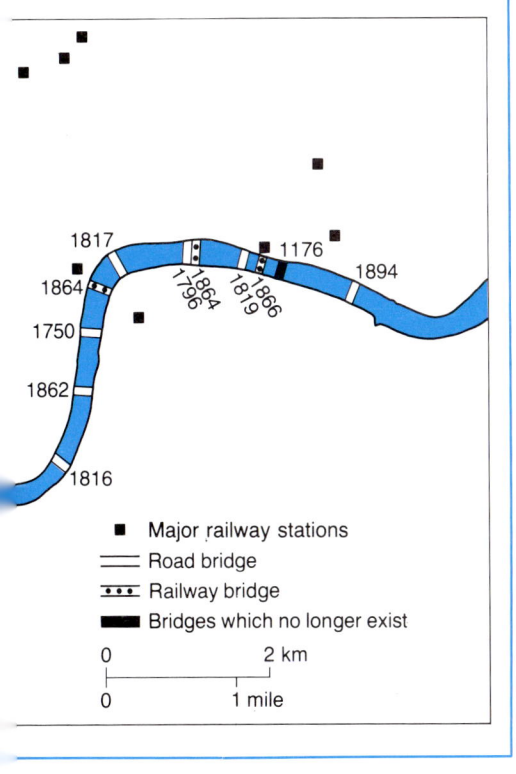

Workbase

1. On the Fig. 9.27 bridges over the Thames and the locations of London railway termini are marked but not named. Figs 9.22 and 9.23 provide more information about them. Using a London A–Z, public transport map, or atlas, if necessary, match the tables to the locations on the map. Identify correctly each bridge and terminus.

2. Make a copy of Fig. 9.27. Mark each bridge and terminus by its name. Put a number by each one, to show the order of their origin. (eg London Bridge would be '1'; Westminster Bridge '2' etc).

3. On your map (see Q2) mark in as many of the following locations as you can, using available maps *or* (if you prefer) personal knowledge;
   Houses of Parliament   Buckingham Palace   Oxford Circus
   The British Museum   St Paul's Cathedral   London Docklands
   The Festival Hall   The Mansion House   The Tower of London
   The Post Office Tower

4. Draw a graph to represent the information in Fig. 9.24 (British conurbations). Consult an atlas map of Britain to make sure that you know where these conurbations are and could locate them by memory on a blank map.

5. Consider Table 9.25 (Passengers of LT 1950–65)
   a) Is there any difficulty in presenting these figures on a single graph? If so, how could it be solved?
   b) Prepare a diagram which shows the inter-relationship of the four tables as clearly as possible.
   c) Write a paragraph to explain how you think the changes in the figures are caused and related.

6. Consider Fig. 9.26 (graph of London's population, 1801–1981).
   a) How do the other tables in this database help to explain the reasons for the curves of this graph?
   b) How would you expect the lines of the graph to continue in 1991, 2001, 2011, 2021? Give reasons for your answer.

7. Which other areas of Britain seem closest to becoming 'conurbations'?

Chapter 10
Shopping

Centres and their influence

Just as the size of urban areas varies, so does the size of shopping centres. In a small village there may be only a single general store, which sells all kinds of goods, but has no links with any of the major retailing organisations. In a market town or suburb there may be several parades or streets of shops, including some supermarkets, department stores, and branches of well-known major retailers.

In a major city or conurbation there will be many streets of major shops, and some purpose-built shopping centres, which cover almost every item that could be needed. Here, specialist shops lie alongside major branches of the big chain stores, as well as a range of medium-sized stores.

Consider these items: a loaf of bread; an expensive outdoor coat; a pot of paint. Which would you most likely buy in your local store? Probably the loaf of bread. This is a **convenience** or **low-order** item, since you expect to buy it fairly frequently and want a convenient place to buy it from, close to your home. A local store is almost certain to supply such basic needs as bread, milk, tea sugar and fresh vegetables.

Figure 10.1 Home locations of shoppers visiting Exeter Shopping Centre

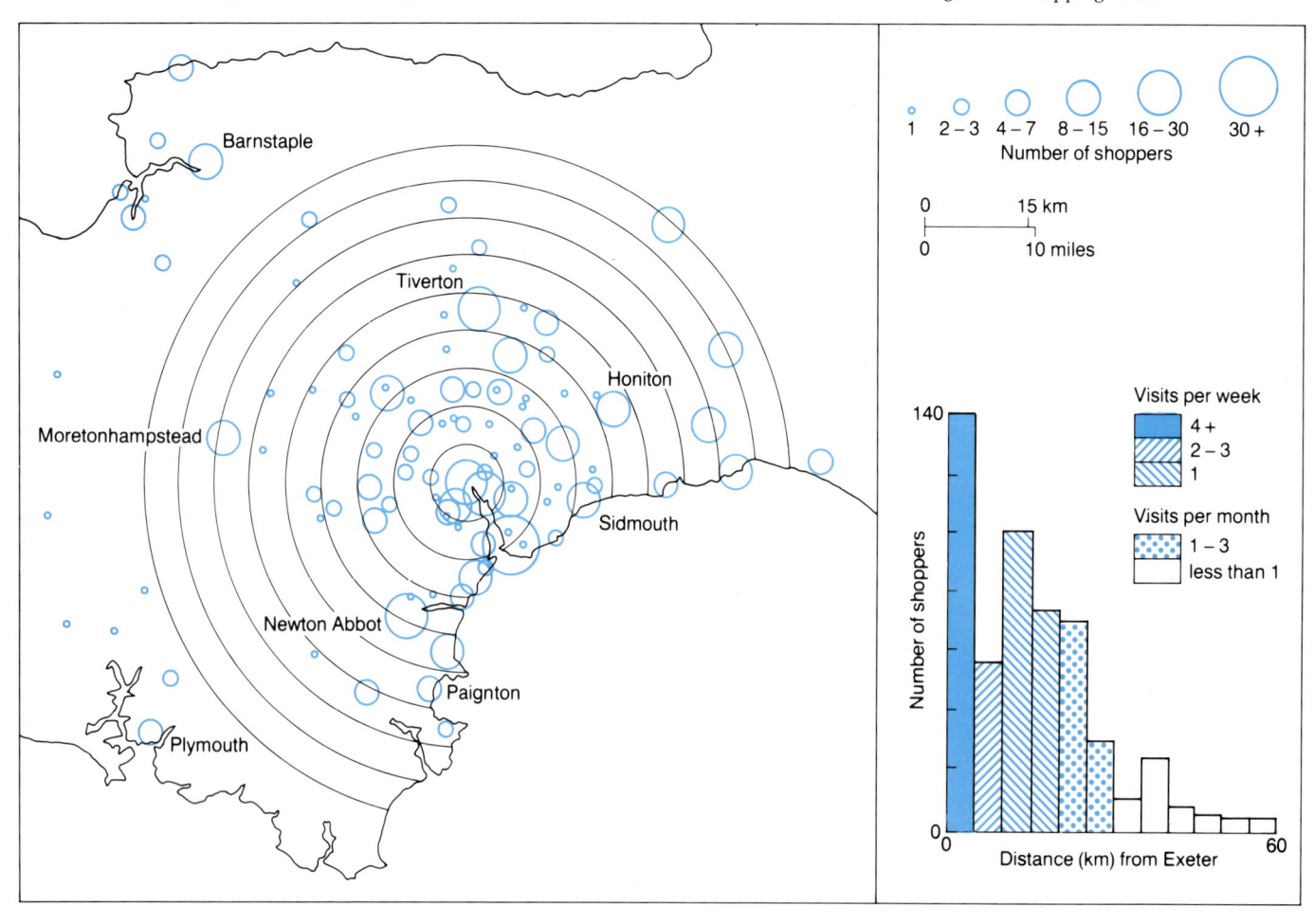

You would buy a pot of paint less frequently. Your local store *might* have the brand and the colour you want, but in many places you could not be certain. Yet would you go all the way to the centre of the city for it? Perhaps the nearest suburb or town will have a hardware shop from which you can get the type of paint you want. This is a **middle-order** good, since we buy it less frequently than the daily or weekly purchase.

The expensive outdoor coat is probably a once-a-year purchase at the very most. You may think that a trip to the nearest major urban centre is worthwhile for this, in order to give yourself the choice that you want. Shops selling **high-order** goods of this kind are not scattered widely; they tend to cluster in city locations, knowing that customers are likely to make a special trip to compare prices and qualities and to obtain what they want.

Thus each of these types of shops has a different area from which it draws its custom: the village stores will have a relatively small **hinterland**; the hardware shop will have a wider one; the expensive clothes shop a quite extensive area of influence.

Downtown in the CBD

If you go to a large city, you will find all kinds of shops within the **central business district**. It will include those which sell bread and paint, as well as those which sell coats.

But in the very heart of the downtown areas, the shops selling food and everyday convenience goods are unlikely to be found. Their weekly income is not likely to be enough to pay for the high rents which are found at the 'centre' of the town. Shops which sell expensive goods will have a high income and profit margin, and will therefore tend to cluster at the **peak land value intersections** – the main crossroads or central market squares of these large areas.

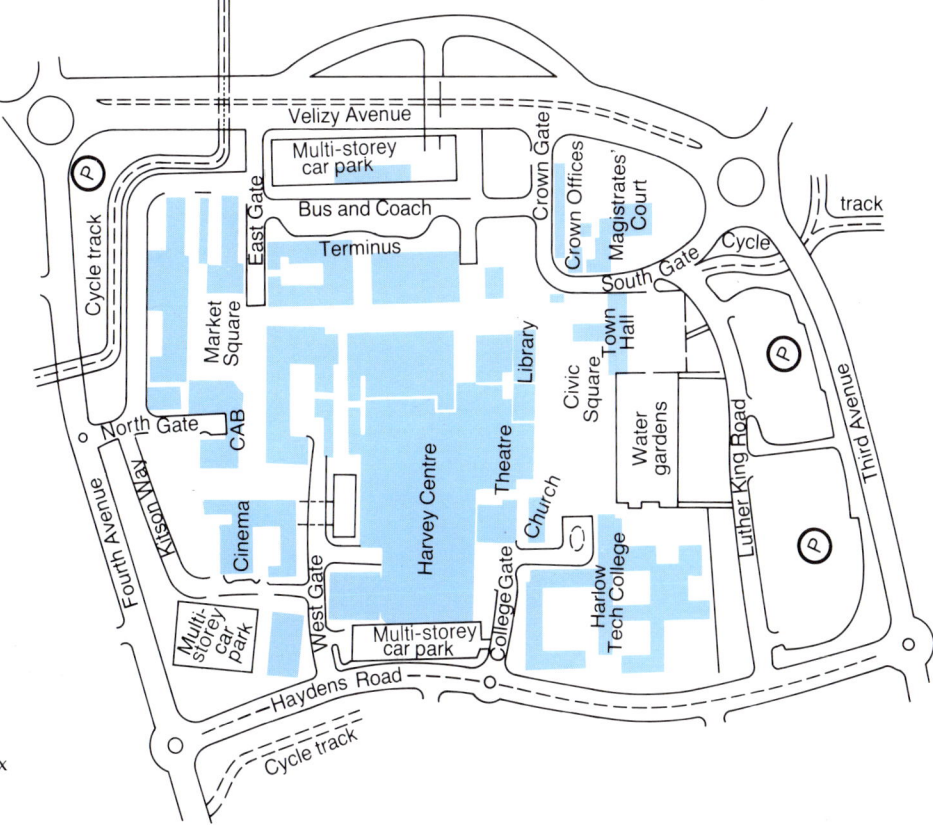

Figure 10.2 Plan of the CBD, Harlow, Essex

There is a difference between those shops in the CBD which generate custom of their own accord – those to which shoppers make a special trip – and those which rely on passing trade. Shoppers are likely to make a deliberate journey to a shop like Marks and Spencer or Boots; shops where they buy their bread or notepaper are much less likely to be a result of a special journey. So there is a great advantage in having a convenience goods shop on the stretch of road between two large stores, since the **pedestrian density** is likely to be high, and the number of casual shoppers who call in to buy will therefore be greater.

Pedestrian densities often, but not always, decrease away from some central landmark in the shopping centre; sometimes factors like the width of the pavement or the bleakness of the whole street can unconsciously deter shoppers from going to shop in a particular street.

Banning the traffic

Another big problem for 'downtown' CBDs in recent years has been the problem of traffic. The difficulty of finding a parking space has become a regular problem for many families who do their weekly shopping at the weekend, and in some cases there may not *be* a parking space to find, for at least a kilometre radius from the city centre.

Some towns and cities have invested heavily in multi-storey car parks, but there is not always the room to build them, or the suitable access roads for cars to get in and out of the car parks easily. It is possible for some families to spend as much time queueing to get into a multi-storey car park near the town centre, as it is to do the shopping.

Another solution which has been tried is to provide park-and-ride services from car parks on the fringes of the town. The hope is that shoppers will use a public minibus or coach service from the car park to the CBD.

Figure 10.3 Melton Mowbray, Leicestershire; the market square is also the central business district and has the peak land value intersection

Figure 10.4 Plan of the area of Melton Mowbray shown in Fig. 10.3

The pressure of traffic in some town centres – notably historic ones with narrow streets – has led to **pedestrian precincts**. The most extreme forms of these ban all traffic from the town centre; others allow traffic to circulate around the centre on a ring road. A milder form of **semi-pedestrianisation** allows buses, taxis, unloading lorries, bicycles and vehicles for disabled people to use the central area, but not private cars.

Some shopkeepers worry that pedestrian precincts may reduce their trade, but there is no doubt that they make the centre of towns more pleasant to shop in. 'The interesting thing about Guildford', said one Surrey shopkeeper, 'is that it is very noisy for most of the week when traffic passes through the centre, but you can hear the clip-clop of your own feet on Saturdays when traffic is banned!'

Some newly-developed areas have tried to plan the segregation of traffic and shoppers from the very beginning. At Milton Keynes, in Buckinghamshire, there are extensive car parks close to the shops, but the modern city centre is totally pedestrianised and covered against the elements.

The retail revolution

Figure 10.5 Tesco hypermarket, Blackburn, Lancashire

The congestion of downtown CBDs has led to the promotion of shopping in out-of-town locations, far away from other aspects of urban living. The first of these out-of-town locations were built by individual stores (such as the Carrefour superstore near Bristol) but later a number of stores began to combine forces to provide for a variety of shopping needs. These supermarkets or hypermarkets are often located near a major road or motorway intersection; they usually ensure that there is plenty of room for hundreds of cars to park nearby.

The idea originated in the USA (where they are called shopping plazas), but has quickly become popular in Britain as private-car ownership has spread through the population.

More recently even bigger schemes have been developed. The Metrocentre built between Gateshead and Sunderland on Tyneside is a site of 46 hectares, developed on the otherwise barren wasteland of an old power-station ash-tip. It is twice the size of the Brent Cross shopping centre in north-west London and has 7,600 free parking places.

There are 140 shops within the centre (170,000 square metres of buildings) including the biggest Marks and Spencer store in Europe. The centre has created 6,000 new jobs in an area of high unemployment.

John Hall, director of Metrocentre, describes how the centre has reacted to changes in society:

> 'Today we are seeing fundamental changes in society. People are buying different goods from those they used to, and they are buying them in a different way. They do it now by motor-car and the city centre doesn't cater for the motor-car. There isn't the space.
>
> The MetroCentre is not just about shopping. It is about how people spend their leisure time. What I have tried to do is bring the outdoors indoors, to create the sort of atmosphere you get in a square in a town in Portugal. If you go into the Eldon Square shopping centre [in central Newcastle] there is hardly anywhere to sit down. Here you can sit in the garden court, you can stroll, you can have something to eat – and soon there will be a fantasy funfair, entertainers and bands and a palm court where caterers will offer dishes of a dozen different countries.'

Figure 10.6 Inside the Metrocentre, Tyne and Wear

David against Goliath?

Against such a giant as Metrocentre, can the single small shop survive? Perhaps not, if it is in a dull and drab city centre. Dr Russell Schiller, a research land agent, believes that, overall, city centres will eventually lose trade to out-of-town centres, but that those cities with historic distinction and attractive architecture will survive.

Another factor turning the tide against the small shopkeeper is the way in which big multiple stores now control more and more of the packaged goods market – selling their own brands and often using particular offers of cut-price goods to entice shoppers into their store. (This is known as the **loss-leader** approach – when a particular item is deliberately sold at a loss in the belief that profit will be made on other goods which the shopper is likely to buy in the same shop.)

But village shops are fighting back, after a period in which their numbers were declining at the rate of 100 a year. (There are about 12,000 shops which are the only providers of food and general produce in a particular settlement.)

Shops close for many reasons. Some merge with another shop; others are turned into a home when the owner retires; some just never have enough customers to provide any kind of profit for the owner, in order to pay the overheads.

However, more and more small village shops are banding together in self-help associations, in order to buy in bulk and achieve the same kind of economies as big supermarket chains. They also pride themselves on offering a personal, friendly service which may more than offset a few pence more on the prices of their products, when allied to the saving in transport costs for local people.

And they have also been cheeky to their bigger competitors. One day a few years ago a group of village shopkeepers in Hampshire launched a daring dawn raid of a new supermarket in Southampton which was offering bread at half-price as its loss-leader. The shopkeepers bought up every loaf on the shelves and were re-selling them in their own shops an hour later! They kept the raiding **parties** in action until the supermarket decided to go back to normal pricing!

Figure 10.7 The small shop

Database

Figure 10.8 Hypermarkets and superstores in the UK: 1.1.87. Top 30 stores: gross floorspace ranking

Retailer	Address Location	Gross Fl'space (sq. ft.)	Trading Fl'space (sq. ft.)	Year of opening
Savacentre	Merton, London	200,000	100,000	Planned
Savacentre	Calcot Reading	182,000	81,000	1981
Asda	Watford	180,000	65,000	Planned
Carrefour	Patchway, Bristol	178,000	90,000	1978
Savacentre	Basildon Town Centre	166,000	74,000	1980
Savacentre	Washington Town Centre Tyne and Wear	162,000	78,000	1977
Savacentre	Warley	158,000	64,000	1980
Tesco	Weston Favell Centre	150,000	105,000	1974
Carrefour	Minworth, Birmingham	148,000	70,000	1977
Savacentre	Gillingham	148,000	70,000	1978
Carrefour	Chandlers Ford	140,000	70,000	1974
Carrefour	Metrocentre Gateshead	132,000	77,000	1986
Tesco	Basildon	130,000	82,000	1978
Savacentre	Cameron Toll Centre, Edinburgh	130,000	68,000	1984
Carrefour	Merry Hill Centre, Dudley	120,000	71,000	1986
Carrefour	Caerphilly	118,000	55,000	1972
Gateway	Cwmbran	117,000	68,000	1986
Carrefour	Telford	117,000	52,000	1973
Co-op (Portsea Island Mutual)	Littlepark, Portsmouth	115,000	65,000	1980
Asda	Ellesmere Port	113,000	49,000	1984
Gateway	Washington, Tyne and Wear	112,000	68,000	Note 1
Gateway	Livingston, Scotland	112,000	67,000	Note 1
Gateway	Bournemouth	111,000	74,000	Note 1
Gateway	Warrington	109,000	73,000	1986
Gateway	Cumbernauld	108,000	65,000	Note 1
Co-op (CWS South East)	Broadstairs	107,000	67,000	1977
Co-op (Norwest Pioneers)	Wythenshawe, Manchester	106,000	49,000	1979
Co-op (United Co-operatives)	Blackpool	106,000	54,000	1979
Asda	Brunstane, Edinburgh	105,000	57,000	1984
Gateway	Killingworth, North Tyneside	105,000	68,000	Note 1

Notes:
1. Store temporarily closed at 1st January 1987 due to refurbishment.
2. Year of opening is the year the store first opened with the current floorspace and/or retailer.

Source: The 1987 List of UK Hypermarkets and Superstores, URPI P1, 1987

There is no completely agreed set of definitions in relation to what different sizes of shop are called. The following should be a useful rough guide, however.

Shop
A small single-unit space for retailing goods, usually under 1,000 sq ft in size, and often with personal 'counter-service'. 'Corner-shops' are often sited amidst residential housing; collections of small shops are found in suburban shopping 'parades' or in the historic 'High Street' areas of a town (the original CBD).

Supermarket
A medium-sized retailing space (over 1,000 sq feet in trading area, but under 25,000 sq ft). Usually self-service with a check-out desk. Many supermarkets are predominantly food stores.

Superstore
A large-size retailing space (over 25,000 sq ft in trading area, but under 50,000 sq ft). Self-service, but with specialist counters. May sell other merchandise (clothes, records, DIY, etc).

Hypermarket
A very large retailing space (over 50,000 sq ft in trading area). Self-service. A wide variety of merchandise sold.

'Shopping complex' or 'shopping mall'
A collection of separate retailing spaces within a modern purpose-built area. Some small specialised shops, some large supermarkets. Usually traffic-free, under-cover and providing rest and refreshment area.

Workbase

1. Consider the definitions of different types of retailing spaces.
   a) Which is the nearest i) superstore ii) hypermarket iii) modern shopping complex to your school?
   b) It is proposed to locate a new hypermarket somewhere in your local district. Suggest a 'best location' for such a store, assuming that ownership and planning matters can be resolved. Write about the factors which you consider in taking this location as your choice.
   c) Imagine you are an owner of a small shop in a suburban 'High Street', selling records, videos and tapes. How would you set out to attract customers to your shop, given that there are superstores and hypermarkets on the edge of town selling the same products as yourself?

2. Look at Fig. 10.8.
   a) Create a combined map/graph to show the information which the table contains.
   b) Suggest explanations for i) the difference between gross floor space and trading floor space.
   ii) the spatial pattern which emerges.

3. 'The coming of the superstore and the hypermarket can bring nothing but benefit for the average shopper'. Do you agree with this statement? Write a reasoned essay in support of *or* against it.

4. Assume that you have been given the brief to design a new large, covered 'shopping mall' for your local central business district.
   Draw up the rough plan of the mall, which you would like to see, showing the geography of the mall, the kinds of retail outlets which you propose (and their best positions), and the associated arrangements for parking (which will be required by planning law).
   Present your proposals to a group of others in your class; decide which is the best proposal in your group and exhibit this on the display-boards on the classroom wall, or make a presentation to the whole class. Make a decision about which should be the winning shopping mall design in the 'Class Design Competition'.

5. Compare the photograph and the shopping plan of Melton Mowbray on pages 102–3. Are there any large supermarkets in this central area of the town? Where would be a favourable site for a supermarket on the map (Fig. 10.4)?

Chapter 11
Other urban areas

Green belts

The spread of the suburbs was so fast in the inter-war years that many hectares of countryside were covered with neat tree-lined suburban avenues. This began to worry governments and after the Second World War more strict controls on development were introduced. Planning Acts were passed through Parliament so that farm and parkland could not be developed without due consideration by a local Planning Authority.

Sir Patrick Abercrombie, drawing up a plan for London in 1947, proposed the idea of **green belts** around the city, which would never be built on. They could be used for farmland and recreation (i.e. playing-fields) but they were not to have offices, factories or housing in fresh amounts. Other cities adopted this idea with variations – some opted for **green wedges**.

The green belt idea undoubtedly prevented the ceaseless sprawl of new housing – even in London there is some green belt land (at Totteridge) only 15 kilometres from the centre of the West End. But more recently the idea has come under threat:

- firms seeking more attractive environments for their employees want to move to 'green-field sites' in the countryside;
- green belt land is a clear target for large shopping-chains which want large sites on which to build superstores with plenty of car-parking;
- some housing developers want to build new housing estates in pleasant countryside (just as they did in the 1930s when there were no planning controls);
- there are proposals to build 'theme parks' and 'leisure centres' on green belt land, in order to provide more organised recreational opportunities for urban dwellers.

Figure 11.1 An early photograph of Letchworth, Hertfordshire — the first 'garden city'

New towns for old

At the turn of the century, a far-sighted pioneer planner, Ebenezer Howard, developed the idea of a '**garden city**' which was to combine countryside features (trees, large gardens, leafy avenues with grass verges) with the facilities of a town. The people of the town were to own their own land as a community, and plough back any profits from it into community developments – such as the building of a sports centre or meeting hall.

Howard's ideas were put into practice in Letchworth and Welwyn in Hertfordshire and eventually proved successful, though they have never been repeated in exactly the same way.

After the Second World War, and the introduction of green belts to stop urban sprawl, thoughts turned again to Howard's idea of building **new towns**. In 1947 the Government designated sixteen sites for new towns and set up special development corporations to organise each one. They were often based around existing village or town sites (as at Stevenage and Bracknell), but usually had separate facilities built and a variety of housing-

Figure 11.2 Ebenezer Howard created this famous diagram in 1902

Other urban areas 109

estate designs in different parts of the town. Industry was encouraged to take up sites in new factories specially built in planned industrial areas on the edge of the town.

Most 'Mark 1' new towns sought to weave green 'wedges' or areas of parkland into the town plan. Housing-estates were formed into neighbourhoods, each with their own small parade of shops which sold convenience goods. The more high-order goods were sold in the larger shopping centre, built at the heart of the new town.

Looking back, the planners made some mistakes:

- the large growth in car-ownership was not forseen, and so there were not enough garages;
- industrial areas suffered traffic congestion at certain rush-hour times;
- the towns looked monotonous and unattractive for several years.

One plan for a new town in Scotland – Cumbernauld, between Edinburgh and Glasgow – had a different plan. It crowded housing together in attractive but high-density layouts, within walking distance of the town centre. A complete system of pedestrian paths connected the areas to the centre, passing over or under all the roads on which vehicles moved. This 'Mark 2' design of new towns was more easily accepted in Scotland where high-density town living in high tenements had been more widespread than in England.

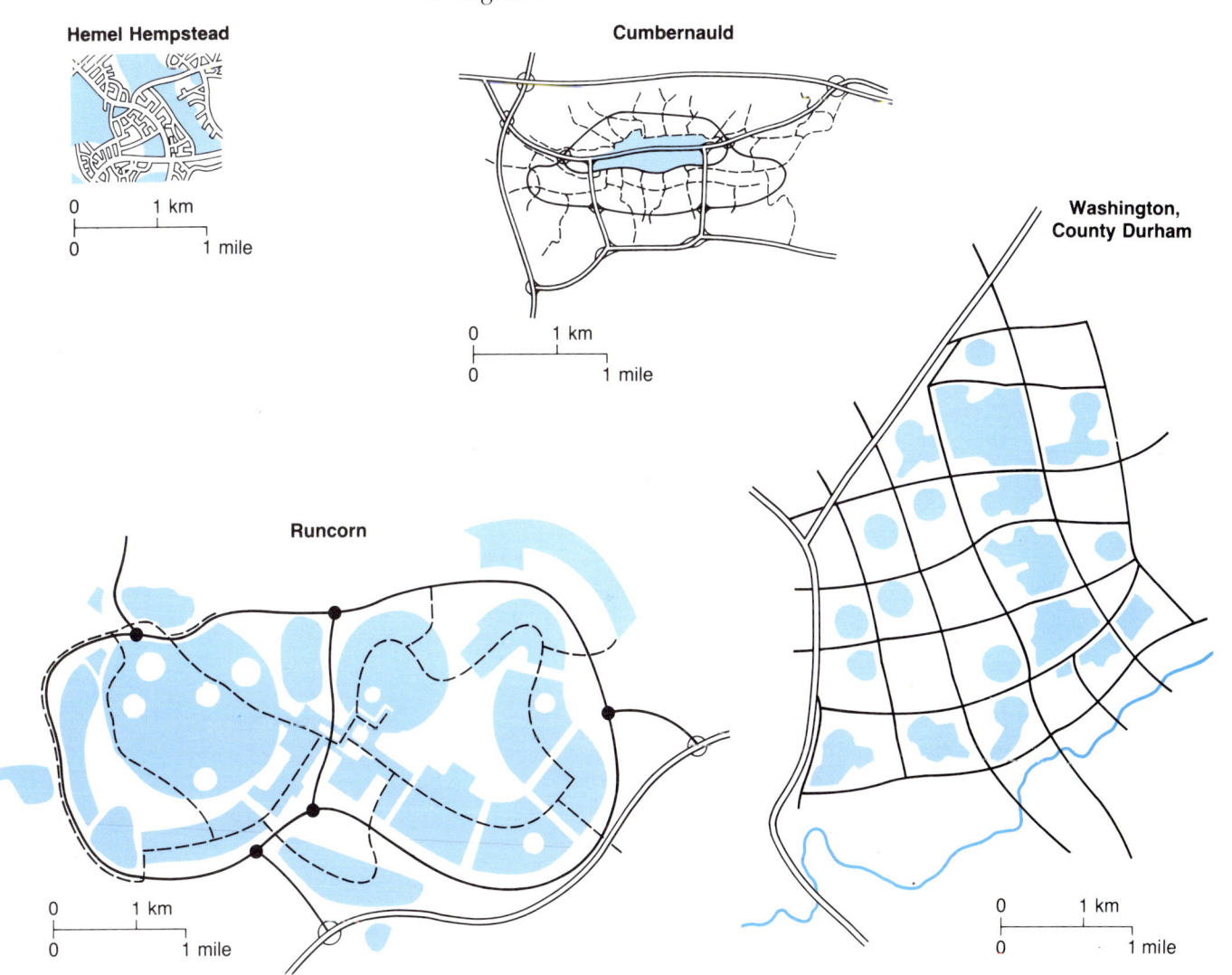

Figure 11.3 The changing shape of neighbourhood units in New Towns (blue = parkland)

The 'Mark 3' new towns built in England in the 1960s (e.g. Redditch and Runcorn) remained with the neighbourhood principle and tried to use restricted 'bus-ways' to provide linkage between homes and the centre.

But the 'Mark 4' new towns, built in the 1970s and 1980s have accepted the fact that many people will use their cars. They have provided an overall road grid which criss-crosses the town and allows maximum use of vehicles, Cars, however, are excluded from the city centre, although they can park very close to it. The housing estates are deliberately built with room for grass and trees around them. (For examples see Washington and Milton Keynes.)

Some of the more recent proposals were aimed at expanding *existing* towns, such as Northampton and Peterborough, rather than creating a town from scratch. Since 1975, with the decrease in population growth, there has been less pressure to move people from existing urban areas to new towns; indeed some cities are trying to tempt people *back* to their inner-areas with new housing developments.

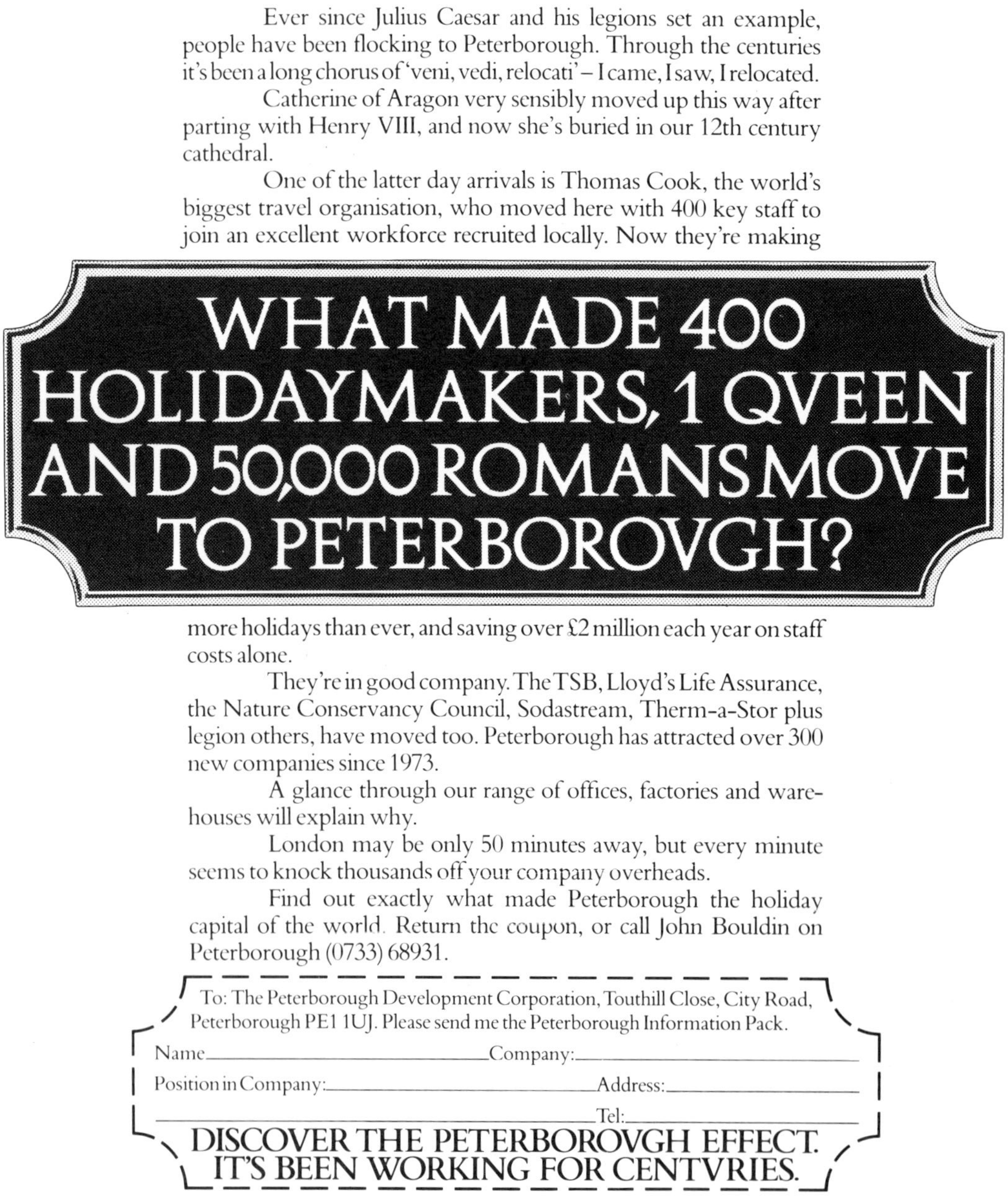

Ever since Julius Caesar and his legions set an example, people have been flocking to Peterborough. Through the centuries it's been a long chorus of 'veni, vedi, relocati' – I came, I saw, I relocated.

Catherine of Aragon very sensibly moved up this way after parting with Henry VIII, and now she's buried in our 12th century cathedral.

One of the latter day arrivals is Thomas Cook, the world's biggest travel organisation, who moved here with 400 key staff to join an excellent workforce recruited locally. Now they're making

WHAT MADE 400 HOLIDAYMAKERS, 1 QVEEN AND 50,000 ROMANS MOVE TO PETERBOROVGH?

more holidays than ever, and saving over £2 million each year on staff costs alone.

They're in good company. The TSB, Lloyd's Life Assurance, the Nature Conservancy Council, Sodastream, Therm-a-Stor plus legion others, have moved too. Peterborough has attracted over 300 new companies since 1973.

A glance through our range of offices, factories and warehouses will explain why.

London may be only 50 minutes away, but every minute seems to knock thousands off your company overheads.

Find out exactly what made Peterborough the holiday capital of the world. Return the coupon, or call John Bouldin on Peterborough (0733) 68931.

To: The Peterborough Development Corporation, Touthill Close, City Road, Peterborough PE1 1UJ. Please send me the Peterborough Information Pack.

Name_____ Company:_____
Position in Company:_____ Address:_____
Tel:_____

DISCOVER THE PETERBOROVGH EFFECT. IT'S BEEN WORKING FOR CENTVRIES.

Figure 11.4 An advertisement for Peterborough

Other urban areas

Figure 11.5 Aspects of Cambridge

Case study: Cambridge

There has been a settlement at Cambridge for nearly 2,000 years. The Romans built a camp on a small hill by the River Cam and used it to fortify a crossing-point of the river. In Saxon times the town flourished as a market, and it grew to be a centre for the region around it.

Students, disgruntled with conditions at Oxford, trekked across the country to Cambridge in the thirteenth century, seeking a quiet place for their studies. They and their teachers set up the first 'colleges' in ordinary houses, the forerunners of the thirty colleges which today make up the modern Cambridge University. Today there are over 10,000 students in the city in term-time, a considerable addition to the 100,000 other residents of Cambridge. Their usual mode of transport gives Cambridge the nickname 'Cycle City'.

The Colleges soon sought to have their own buildings for residence, for worship, and for social purposes, and so today places such as King's College Chapel and Trinity College Old Court are visited by many tourists interested in the history and architecture of the place. The tourist-centre function adds many more thousands of people to Cambridge in the summer, in addition to those who live there through the year.

The attractive landscapes near the river have been preserved because the colleges own the land; on the eastern side of the city, however, there have traditionally been some agricultural industries linked to the farming country which predominates in the East Anglian region.

The recent electrification of the railway line from Liverpool Street to Cambridge has reduced the journey time to one hour between London and Cambridge. This has increased the possibility of commuting daily to the metropolis and pushed up house prices in and around the city. The M11 Motorway and the planned expansion of Stansted Airport (35 kilometres from Cambridge) have also increased the accessibility of Cambridge.

But perhaps one of Cambridge's most significant changes began only in 1970. Some of the earliest computer firms in Britain (Acorn, Sinclair) began here, and there has been a mushroom-growth of other '**high-tech**' industries since (see Fig. 11.7). Cambridge has become a growth point of the so-called **sunrise industries** in Britain – and many people believe that the nation's future prosperity depends on their success.

The so-called 'Cambridge Phenomenon' of growth in these areas has come about because:

- Cambridge University and other research institutes around the city provided a ready pool of both resources and advice;
- there were locational advantages in being near London;
- purpose-built business and science parks were provided so that new firms could start up with a minimum of difficulty;
- there were environmental attractions in the city and surrounding areas of 'green-field' sites.

Figure 11.6 Umemployment in Cambridge and Britain as a whole

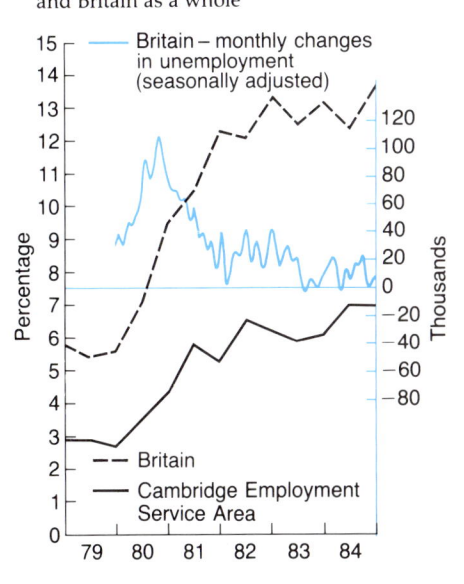

Figure 11.7 High-tech firms starting up in the Cambridge area since 1970

Year	Number of firms
1970	15
1971	9
1972	4
1973	10
1974	13
1975	8
1976	14
1977	16
1978	39
1979	24
1980	30
1981	44
1982	46
1983	54
1984	46

Figure 11.8 Industrial and technology sites in Cambridge

Legend:
- Industrial
- Research and development
- Warehousing
- Research Park

And, of course, once growth began, the effect was cumulative. Other firms followed the innovators or were generated from them, 'babies' of the original parents. There are now over 350 high-tech firms in Cambridge.

The Cambridge Science Park is just one of a number of sites around the city which was built to provide purpose-built accommodation for small but high-skill enterprises. Trinity College, Cambridge, owned land on the outskirts of Cambridge close to the northern by-pass. It provided a landscaped 'park' with different sizes of industrial unit, and central facilities which all could share.

But though these firms are at the frontiers of research and new technology, they do not employ great numbers of people. Computers and industrial robots are in use, and those who do work in high-tech are usually highly qualified and skilled in specialist ways.

Questions

1. In what ways are the Cambridge unemployment figures affected by the growth of high-tech firms – both directly and indirectly?
2. Can you suggest both advantages and disadvantages of having many high-tech companies on the same science park?
3. What disadvantages can you see for other residents of the Cambridge region?

Case study: Consett

Before iron-ore was discovered in the area in 1839, the area around Consett, in the hills of County Durham, was covered only by a few scattered farming cottages. In a few short years, however, the iron-ore deposits and the plentiful coal nearby transformed the area into a town of 30,000 people, largely dependent on the giant iron and steelworks built by the Consett Iron Company.

The works dominated the town both physically and economically. It was on a 250-hectare site and belched out great clouds of red iron oxide dust from its chimneys – even the local goats went pink from its effects. At the time of the Great Exhibition of industrial achievement (1851) Consett was called 'the greatest iron works in the kingdom', and it produced one-tenth of the nation's steel by the 1880s. It has given raw material for Sydney Harbour Bridge, Blackpool Tower, the Queen Mary liner and Polaris submarines.

The Consett Iron Company built rows of neat terraced houses for its workers, owned the local shops and public houses and even the nearby collieries. Consett was the classic 'company town'.

But the iron-ore proved uneconomic to work by the 1940s and Consett looked to imported ores. The old open-hearth furnaces of the works were less efficient than the newer oxygen converters, despite the highly skilled workforce.

Figure 11.9 Consett — the gasholder falls

Figure 11.10 Consett, County Durham; blast furnaces working through the night

When Britain's steel companies were nationalised after the Second World War, Consett was seen in perspective against other locations. Coastal steelworks now seemed to have the advantages. And, faced by cheaper steel from overseas and other metals (notably aluminium), Britain's steel industry was faced with over-production. In 1980 British Steel decided to close down the Consett Works.

3,700 jobs at the works were lost overnight; soon afterwards some other Consett industries (dependent on the locally produced steel) also closed, adding another 2,000 to the jobless. The works were speedily demolished. Consett had been 'de-industrialised' within a few months.

The Government has set up a development scheme to attract other kinds of industry to the town, but those which have come have employed people in tens and twenties rather than thousands. The biggest new factory – Derwent Valley Foods, which makes a popular brand of crisp – employs only ninety people. The local hospital and council offices are now the biggest employers. Many of those who were employed at the steelworks have to face the prospect of long-term unemployment, if they stay in Consett.

The long hours without a job have produced a spate of do-it-yourself house improvements in some parts of Consett; and the houses (some scrubbed and sand-blasted) have cleaner exteriors now that the continuous red pall of smoke has gone. But against the environmental gains must be balanced the economic problems.

Some workers migrated away to other towns in search of work; others have accepted a long and costly 30–50 kilometre journey to other places to find work. The new Nissan car plant at Washington has offered some hope for those willing to commute. And the community of Consett tries to rebuild:

'We've got clean air all right – but we've had to pay one hell of a price for it' (an ex-steelworker).

'Industry isn't going to come back. We mustn't support that myth' (a councillor).

'The he-man who used his muscles all day at work, came home to change before going out to drink ten pints to replace the sweat he'd lost – he's gone. The women are more of a force. I've seen a number of families now in better shape because the husband and wife have time to appreciate each other' (a social worker).

'Life in Consett is just like a lull – you're waiting for something to start again' (a steelworker's wife).

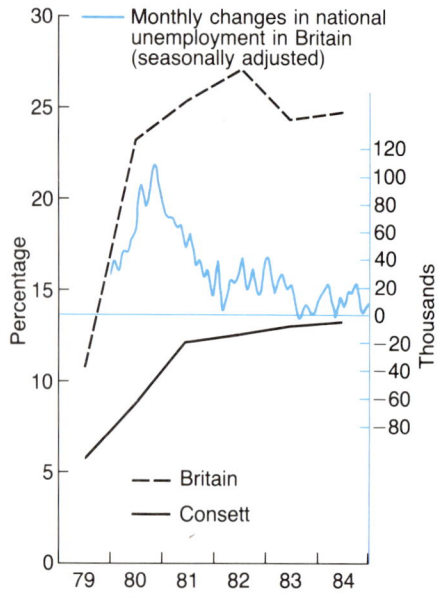

Figure 11.11 Unemployment in Consett

Figure 11.12 Consett — a new industry

Questions

1. Could Consett have a high-tech future like Cambridge? Prepare an advertisement to list the town's advantages for a prospective high-tech employer.
2. Is the loss of the steelworks an advantage or a disadvantage for Consett long-term?
3. Plot the employment figures for Cambridge and Consett on one graph.

Chapter 12
Urban living? Country living?

It would be mistaken to imagine that nowadays the town 'ends' where the bricks and mortar stop. Many people who work and shop and take their leisure in towns live many kilometres away.

Bus services run out to neighbouring villages and many who live 15–30 kilometres away can drive in daily to their nearest urban centre, if they have their own transport. The electrification of many railway lines allows high-speed commuting across the countryside. It is possible to live on the coast at Clacton, Ramsgate, Brighton or Bournemouth and still work in London each day. Even more important, the telephone (and, in the future, the computer terminal) weave an invisible web of communication between those who work in the town and those who *appear* to live and/or work in the country.

Looked at in this way, the boundaries of large urban areas like London and Birmingham, Liverpool and Manchester, Glasgow and Edinburgh, Cardiff and Bristol, Nottingham and Sheffield extend to meet each other. Commuters living in the same village may even go to two different cities for their daily work.

Is this urban living or country living?

City of the future

The writer H.G. Wells could see the possibility of this pattern of living even at the beginning of this century:

> Many of [the] railway-begotten 'giant cities' will reach their maximum in the coming century [and] in all probability they ... are destined to such a process of dissection and diffusion as to amount almost to obliteration, so far, at least, as the blot on the map goes, within a measurable further space of years. These coming cities will not be, in the old sense, cities at all; they will present a new and entirely different phase of human distribution.
>
> We are ... in the early phase of a great development of centrifugal possibilities.... A city of pedestrians is inexorably limited by a radius of about four miles ... a horse-using city may grow out to seven or eight.... Is it too much ... to expect that the available area for even the common daily toilers of the great city of year 2000 ... will have a radius of over one hundred miles?
>
> The city will diffuse itself until it has taken up considerable areas and many of the characteristics of what is now country.... The country will take itself many of the qualities of the city. The old antithesis will ...cease, the boundary lines will altogether disappear.... To receive the daily paper a few hours late ...will be the extreme measure of rusticity, save in a few remote islands and inaccessible places. 'Town' and 'city' will be, in truth, terms as obsolete as 'mail coach'.... We may call ... these coming town provinces 'urban regions'.

Commuter villages

Commuter villages have grown up, on, or near good transport links to local towns and cities. The commuters travel to and from the city every day for their work, and only return to the village in the evenings and at weekends. One such commuter village is Hagley, near Birmingham in the West Midlands (see Figs 12.1 and 12.2)

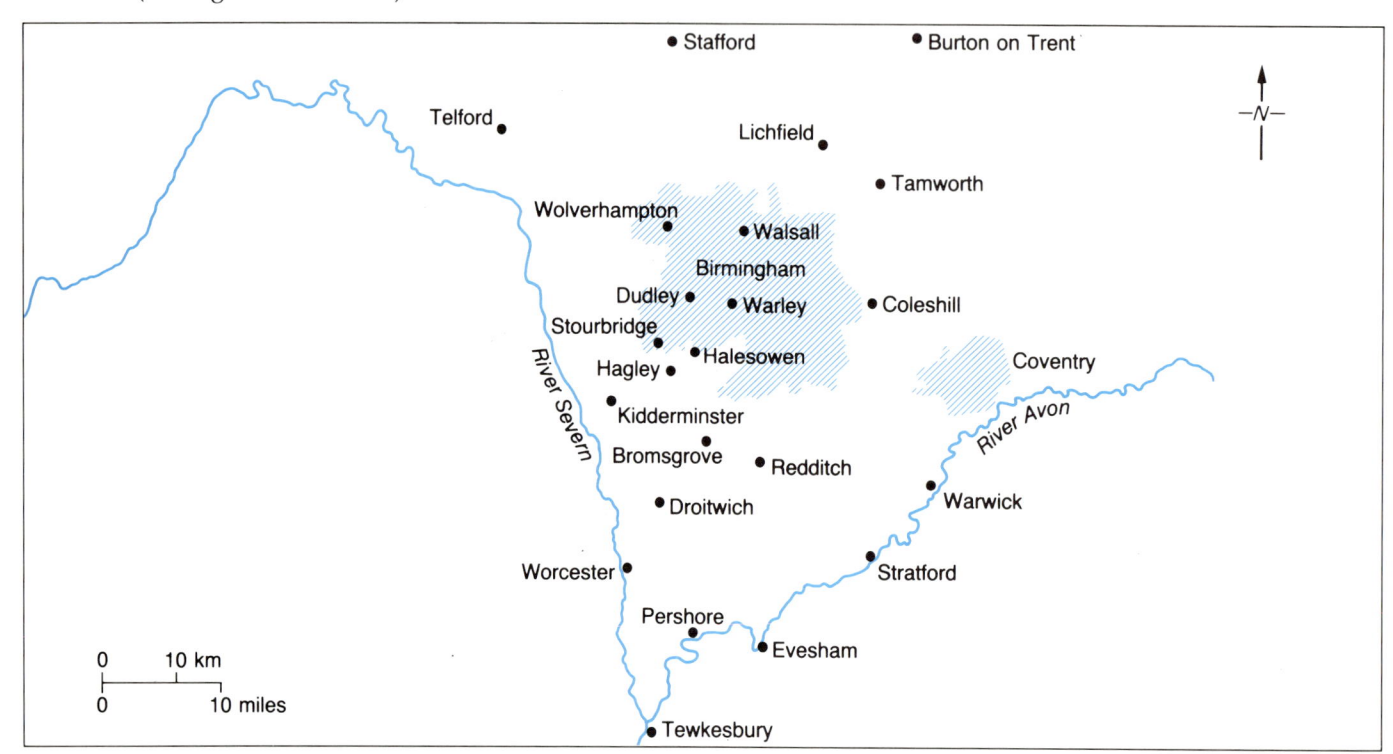

Figure 12.1 The West Midlands and Hagley

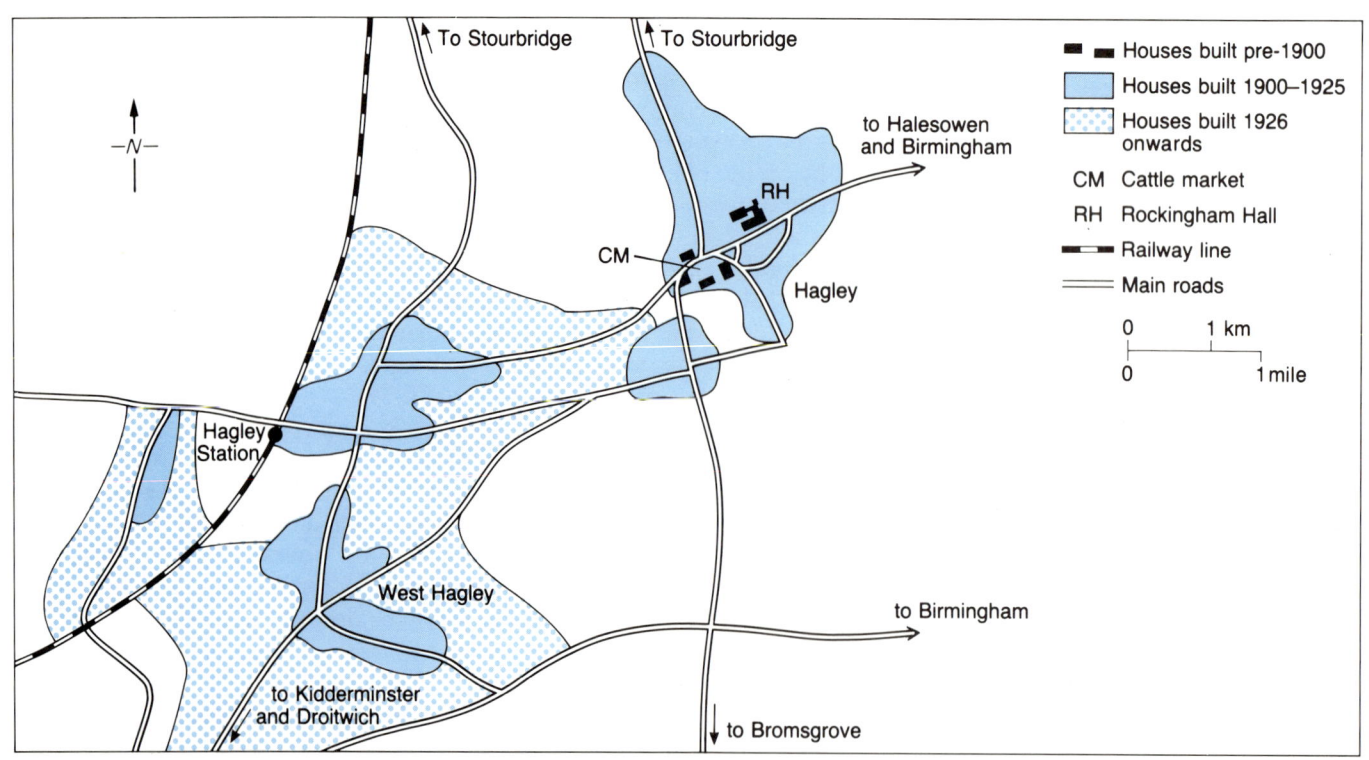

Figure 12.2 The growth of Hagley

This is what one old-age pensioner remembers of the changes she has seen in Hagley:

> I remember, in the 1920s, Hagley was such a small, pretty village. The centre of the village was the cattle market [see Fig. 12.2] where animals from the surrounding farms were regularly auctioned. Birmingham and the towns of the Black Country seemed a long way away. We did nearly all our shopping in the village and only took the train in to Birmingham two or three times each year. Lord Lyttelton lived in Hagley Hall and several villagers worked as servants there, or as farm labourers. All our children went to the local school and the clergyman and schoolmaster were important people in our community.
>
> Things began to change in the 1930s as people from Birmingham and the Black Country began to move out. They wanted a bit of peace and quiet, with good clean air and lots of trees. The newcomers sometimes built new homes on small estates, or bought older houses and cottages and renovated them. Most of the new development was along the roads leading to Stourbridge, Kidderminster and Birmingham. Fortunately there were not too many newcomers at this time, so they settled in to the community quite well.
>
> After the 1950s, though, it all changed drastically. Lots more people could afford to run a car and wanted to live in the countryside. The regular train service to Birmingham attracted even more people and big new roads were built to Birmingham and the Black Country. As more and more people moved into the village, so more shops opened and houses were converted in to shops, or knocked down to make car-parks. Lots of new housing-estates have been built as the farmers found they could sell their land at a good price, so the village has grown squarer in shape as the gaps have been filled in. The newcomers have swamped us locals. They tend to have more money than us, and to have contacts with each other, not the original residents, so we do not mix much. A lot of old houses have been bought and renovated but the old cattle market has gone to make way for a dual carriageway and new houses. Hagley has changed so much you can scarcely recognise it is the same place it was forty years ago.

Figure 12.3 A Welsh holiday home near Llanberis, Gwynedd destroyed by arson in 1986

Second homes

This pattern is taken furthest by those who have two homes – perhaps a flat in London which they use during the week and a house in the country which they use at weekends. Or, those who live and work in a large conurbation, may save up money to buy a small cottage in the countryside, which they use for holidays.

Though this may seem a pleasant form of life (**for those who can afford it**) it is much disliked by many village dwellers, since **second-home owners** may force up the price of local housing and make it more difficult for those working in country areas on low wages to stay in their own communities. There have been recent cases of damage to second-homes by irate villagers, whilst their owners have been absent.

Second homes may be seen as a danger by some villagers but others see them as an advantage. In Fig 12.4, one local council, in the Yorkshire Dales, is considering the arguments for allowing more abandoned cottages to be sold to outsiders as second homes.

Questions

1. Since second homes became important in villages in places like the Yorkshire Dales and Wales:
   a) which groups of people have become richer?
   b) which groups of people have become poorer?
   c) which groups of people have remained the same?
   d) which groups of people have become more influential?
   e) which groups of people have become less influential?
2. Suggest some ways in which the problems resulting from second homes might be solved if villagers, second home owners and developers could agree to co-operate. For example:
   a) developers might agree to build cheaper homes for local people;
   b) developers might try to attract industry to the area to provide jobs for locals;
   c) developers and the Council might agree to provide a regular, cheap bus service for local people.

What other possibilities are there? What are the difficulties involved?

'Incomers' threat to Dales

IN the past few years the 150 villagers of Preston-under-Scar, which lies in the Wensleydale country of north Yorkshire, have been deprived of their shop, post office and village hall, the nearest pub is now two miles away.

The changes in the population have been no less unsettling. Of the 48 houses in Preston, 19 belong to 'incomers' and six are holiday homes.

Another family of incomers is expected shortly. Builders are at work on a house that, when completed, will sell for more than £40,000, well beyond the reach of any local couple.

The uncertain future of many of the villages in the Dales and on the moors is a pressing concern of planners at North Yorkshire county council's headquarters in Northallerton, who have compiled a special report on their plight for the Development Commission, the Government Agency for Rural Affairs.

Mr Peter Davies, assistant planning officer, said; 'We are just asking them to recognise the facts of life. One of the unfortunate characteristics of the Dales and the moors is that young people are leaving, and we want to reverse the trend before it's too late.

It starts with jobs, of course – agriculture has declined in that respect, and it's difficult to get manufacturers in – but there are great problems with housing and transport. There are some places where you literally cannot get a journey to work even if you have a job, and when you can, the cost's heavy.'

The report shows that the daily return fare from some Wensleydale villages to the nearest town is as high as £4.50. It shows also that Preston is only one of 188 villages without a shop and suggests that half the shops and many of the post office in other villages are at risk because takings are so low.

The planners are reticent about the activities of landowners and developers, who have contributed to the problems in some districts, but more out-spoken villagers and Labour politicians attack them.

Mrs Dorothy Turner, of Scruton, on the edge of the Dales, has pinned to the village notice board a copy of a letter which she wrote last week to the local Press, complaining: 'The houses built in our villages are not built for village people; the people who really belong to the villages cannot afford these houses. Would the developers build if they were obliged to build homes for young villagers at affordable prices? I think not.

'Wolves prowled around the villages of ancient Britain, but wolves could be controlled and eventually exterminated. Today we have developers. I'd prefer wolves.'

Figure 12.4 *The Observer*, 28 August 1983

Regional differences

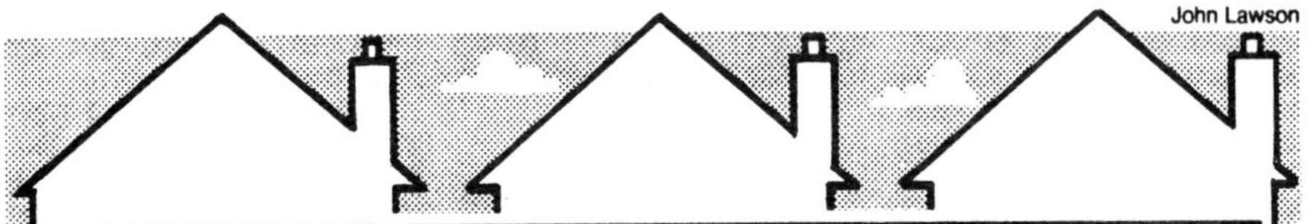

CAN THE HOUSE PRICE BOOM CONTINUE?

Average regional house prices at mortgage completion, £

		North	East Anglia	Greater London	South east	West Midlands	Scotland
1985	Q1	22,736	29,159	39,753	37,880	24,140	25,531
	Q2	22,969	30,641	43,689	39,771	26,257	27,562
	Q3	22,848	32,124	44,995	41,126	26,694	26,959
	Q4	22,607	33,669	47,593	42,602	25,919	27,438
1986	Q1	22,591	33,760	49,289	44,508	26,675	27,424
	Q2	24,331	34,370	53,254	46,561	27,461	27,535
	Q3	26,653	36,967	57,816	50,696	29,511	29,065
	Q4	23,724	38,502	57,723	51,049	29,563	28,778
1987	Q1	25,523	36,344	59,613	51,936	28,703	27,080
	Q2	27,016	40,516	63,626	55,204	32,503	30,997

Source: The Building Societies Association and Department of the Environment

Figure 12.5 House prices in Britain, 1987

As Fig. 12.5 shows there are quite considerable differences in the amount which you would have to pay for the same kind of house in different parts of the country.

This reflects not the actual value of the house, or the intrinisic beauty of the environment, but the relative value which house-buyers put on a particular place at a particular time.

At present this difference tends to make house prices *higher* in the South-East of the country, because more people want to buy these houses. This is because industry and commerce is doing relatively better there and offering better wages.

Someone once said that if the EC had been located just off the Outer Hebrides, it would have adjusted the economic balance of the country nicely. As it is, the influence of the capital city, London, down in the South-East, always tends to tip the scales towards that area.

But there are sometimes other factors which cause a turn in the regional differences. When the North Sea oil and gas boom was at its height, there were many industries and businesses setting up branches in north-east Scotland. The economy of Aberdeen and its region blossomed – and house prices in the area shot upwards because of the competition for the existing stock of houses. It takes time for the supply of new houses to meet such sudden surges in demand, and there are often difficulties in getting planning permission.

At the other end of the scale, houses in towns and villages where coal mines have recently closed are difficult to sell. One ex-South Wales miner, moving to Cambridgeshire in 1986 for a job as a school-caretaker, was fortunate in being given a house to rent in the school grounds by the local education authority. But after a year he had not sold his terraced house in the Rhondda – even for a price as low as £10,000. In London, such a house would have been worth £40,000. In time, however, the pendulum may swing back. The high price of housing in the South-East is beginning to deter some people from taking jobs there; if firms suffer shortages of labour, there is an incentive to re-locate in another area — and so firms which are not strongly tied to a raw material or market influence may move out. Some Government departments have already been re-located in this way, in places such as Swansea and Newcastle.

Database: urban areas

Some researchers (Tony Champion and Anne Green) computed a 1986 index of towns on the following basis:
1. Percentage of current unemployment in an area (weighted × 2)
2. Percentage increase in employment 1971–78
3. Percentage increase in employment 1978–81 (recession years)
4. Percentage increase in population 1971–81
5. Percentage increase of households with two cars or more

No more recent data on employment or change in population was available at the time. 280 'Local Labour Market Areas' of Britain were used as the basis for the survey.

A similar index was computed for 1987, but this time more statistics were available to use:
1. Percentage unemployment rate (current)
2. Median length of unemployment spells
3. Percentage employment in hi-tech industries
4. The 'economic activity' rate (% employed or *seeking* work)
5. The price of an average house
6. Percentage change in unemployment rate 1984–87
7. Percentage change in total employment 1981–84
8. Percentage change in hi-tech employment 1981–84
9. Percentage change in population 1981–85
10. Percentage change in price of a house 1982–86

Using the same 280 LLMA's, this time the 'top towns' and 'bottom towns' were as follows:

In 1987, the researchers also produced a table which concentrated on the indices of change (the factors listed 6–10). Below are listed some of the interesting variations between the 'general index' and the 'change index'

Figure 12.10

		General index position	Change index position
East Anglia and the Midlands	Corby	46	6
	Wisbech	130	29
	Cambridge	6	8
	Tamworth	227	114
	Telford	137	48
	Birmingham	168	163
The North	Burnley	180	280
	Bury	154	236
	Preston	133	235
	Consett	268	119
	Middlesbrough	217	136
	Leeds	145	204
The South	London	38	56
	Milton Keynes	1	1
	Winchester	31	92
	Bristol	81	117
	Plymouth	122	75
	Redruth & Camborne	261	165
Wales	Holyhead	280	274
	Ebbw Vale	202	99
	Wrexham	216	118
Scotland	Aberdeen	108	172
	Edinburgh	134	214
	Glasgow	210	239

Figure 12.6 Top twenty 1986

1. Winchester
2. Horsham
3. Bracknell
4. Milton Keynes
5. Maidenhead
6. Basingstoke
7. High Wycombe
8. Aldershot & Farnborough
9. Bishop's Stortford
10. Aylesbury
11. Hertford & Ware
12. Crawley
13. Haywards Heath
14. Woking & Weybridge
15. Guildford
16. Newbury
17. St Albans
18. Reading
19. Aberdeen
20. Bury St Edmunds

Figure 12.7 Top twenty 1987

1. Milton Keynes
2. Newbury
3. Didcot
4. Welwyn
5. Aldershot & Farnborough
6. Cambridge
7. Huntingdon
8. Hertford & Ware
9. Basingstoke
10. Woking & Weybridge
11. Crawley
12. Andover
13. Bracknell
14. Reading
15. Guildford
16. Aylesbury
17. Stevenage
18. High Wycombe
19. Reigate & Redhill
20. St Albans

Figure 12.8 Bottom twenty 1986 (*lowest* first)

1. Consett
2. Mexborough
3. South Shields
4. Coatbridge & Airdrie
5. Hartlepool
6. Sunderland
7. Bathgate
8. Liverpool
9. Irvine
10. Birkenhead & Wallasey
11. Greenock
12. Port Talbot
13. Peterlee
14. Middlesbrough
15. Corby
16. Gelligaer
17. Wigan
18. Dumbarton
19. Glasgow
20. Ebbw Vale

Figure 12.9 Bottom twenty 1987 (*lowest* first)

1. Holyhead
2. Mexborough
3. Barnsley
4. Pembroke
5. Cardigan
6. Stranraer
7. Doncaster
8. St Helens
9. Mansfield
10. Neath
11. Liverpool
12. Smethwick
13. Consett
14. Arbroath
15. Ffestiniog
16. Hartlepool
17. Banff & Buckie
18. South Shields
19. Sheffield
20. Redruth & Camborne

Figure 12.11 New towns in Britain and their population change

New towns	Population 1981	% Population change 1961–71	1971–81
Scotland			
Glenrothes	32,700	114.4	19.6
Cumbernauld	47,702	545.5	35.3
Livingston	38,594	902.0	184.5
East Kilbride	70,259	98.6	10.6
Irvine	32,852	36.1	42.7
Wales			
Cwmbran	44,876	32.2	7.6
The North			102.6
Washington	50,899	25.3	9.5
Newton Aycliffe	36,826	28.4	4.2
Peterlee	22,756	63.9	22.0
Chorley	54,775	12.9	42.1
Skelmersdale	43,464	121.0	78.1
Runcorn	64,117	26.6	
The Midlands			
Telford	103,786	30.0	30.4
Redditch	66,854	19.0	63.1
Corby	47,773	32.9	−0.5
The South			
Milton Keynes	106,974	42.5	102.0
Stevenage	74,381	56.0	10.9
Welwyn	40,496	15.0	0.1
Harlow	79,276	45.4	1.5
Basildon	152,301	45.9	17.7
Hatfield	25,160	23.6	−0.8
Hemel Hempstead	76,695	27.2	10.0
Bracknell	48,752	65.9	27.7
Crawley	73,081	25.1	6.9

Workbase: urban areas

1. Read the descriptions of how Figs 12.6 and 12.7 and 12.8 and 12.9 were compiled. Do you think the basis of the 1987 tables was better than the 1986 one? If so, why?

2. Using an atlas, identify the location of the 'top twenty' towns for 1987. Classify them by the five regions used in Figs 12.10 and 12.11.
    Identify the location of the 'bottom twenty' towns for 1987. Classify them by the five regions used in figs 12.10 and 12.11.
    Do Figs 12.8 and 12.9 provide evidence for a 'north-south divide' in Britain?

3. Consider the two tables of 'top twenty' towns. Which towns appear in both tables?
    For what reasons may a town appear in one table and not the other?

4. Figure 12.10 shows selected towns from different regions. Their index position (out of 280) is shown on a general index and on a change index. The change index is comprised of factors 6–10 listed above Figs 12.7 and 12.9.
    Group the towns into three categories:
    a) those with a change index figure much higher than a general index figure;
    b) those with a change index figure much lower than a general index figure;
    c) those with a change index and general index figure about the same.
   Which of the three groups should be most concerned about their future?
   In what circumstances does a low general index figure not matter very much?

5. Do you think that this way of describing towns has much meaning? Who would be most interested in the index figures?
    Are there other factors which should be taken into account in deciding 'top towns' and 'bottom towns'? If so which ones?
    What data could be obtained easily to reflect these other factors?

6. Figure 12.11 shows population change in Britain's new towns.
    Indentify the location of these new towns, using an atlas.
   Do any of these towns appear in the 'top twenty' or 'bottom twenty' lists? From which region do they come?
    Which of the new towns had the greatest percentage increase in population growth in the periods 1961–71 and 1971–81?
    Many new towns have closed primary and secondary schools in the last decade. If there is evidence of population growth in the new towns, why should this be happening?

Part IV Britain's industry

Britain was one of the first nations to become **industrialised**. The early adoption of new inventions in manufacturing and transport in the nineteenth century, coupled with new sources of power (steam, electricity, the internal combustion engine) led to the development of large factories, and the mass production of goods. In turn, this raised the standard of living for the nation, through improvements in living conditions and the wealth generated by trading with other countries.

Many of these other countries also seek the route of industrialisation in the twentieth century, in the belief that it will make them less dependent on selling agricultural crops (tea, coffee, wheat) which are often subject to unsettling changes in the world price. They believe that industry will make them a richer more stable society in which there will be 'mass consumption' of goods produced.

One notable theory about industrialisation suggests that an economy has to be pushed along until it reaches take-off – the moment when there is enough industry in the country for it to grow naturally by itself (see Fig. IV. 1). Take-off leads to growth and to 'maturity'. Maturity implies a high standard of living, a stable economy and the mass consumption of goods. What happens *beyond* that is something which Britain may be the first to discover, since she was one of the first to industrialise.

Industry is usually thought of as **manufacturing** things; i.e. raw materials (or component parts) are brought together and **processed** (or assembled) to make a **finished product**. The finished product will always have a greater value than the separate raw materials or components (think of a car, as an example).

Industrial activity is knowns as **secondary** activity to distinguish it from **primary** activity (farming, fishing, mining, etc.) which is concerned with producing the raw materials themselves. Those in **tertiary** activity do not produce a visible end-product but are involved in a service of some kind (train drivers, policemen, doctors, journalists, etc.)

Fig. IV. 2 uses these categories and shows how the employment structure of the United Kingdom has changed between 1801 and 1981.

Questions

1. Why do you think we sometimes take a more general meaning of the word 'industry' these days?
2. Can you think of a *fourth* sector of economic activity (beyond primary, secondary and tertiary) in which increasing numbers of people work?
3. To which sector of economic activity does a) the agriculture industry, b) the leisure industry, and c) the civil service belong?

As Fig. IV. 3 shows, manufacturing industry (secondary activity) was at its most important in the nineteenth century in Britain. In recent years it has declined rapidly. Between 1965 and 1985 it lost three million jobs. This

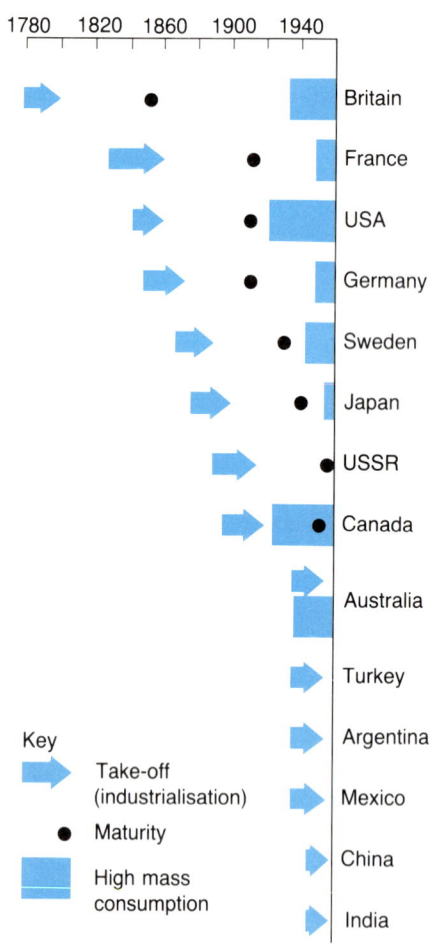

Figure IV.1 Rostow's ideas about when different nations entered the various stages of his theory of development

Date	Primary	Secondary	Tertiary
1801	49	30	21
1851	22	53	25
1901	10	45	45
1951	4	48	48
1981	2	39	59

Figure IV.2 The changing employment structure in the United Kingdom (1801–1981)

decline has been described as the **de-industrialisation** of Britain (see Chapter 15). The great industrial conurbations (such as Manchester, Tyneside and Glasgow) that grew in the nineteenth century now have factories unoccupied and large numbers of people who are unemployed. Where factory buildings have been knocked down there are now large, empty-looking areas of derelict land.

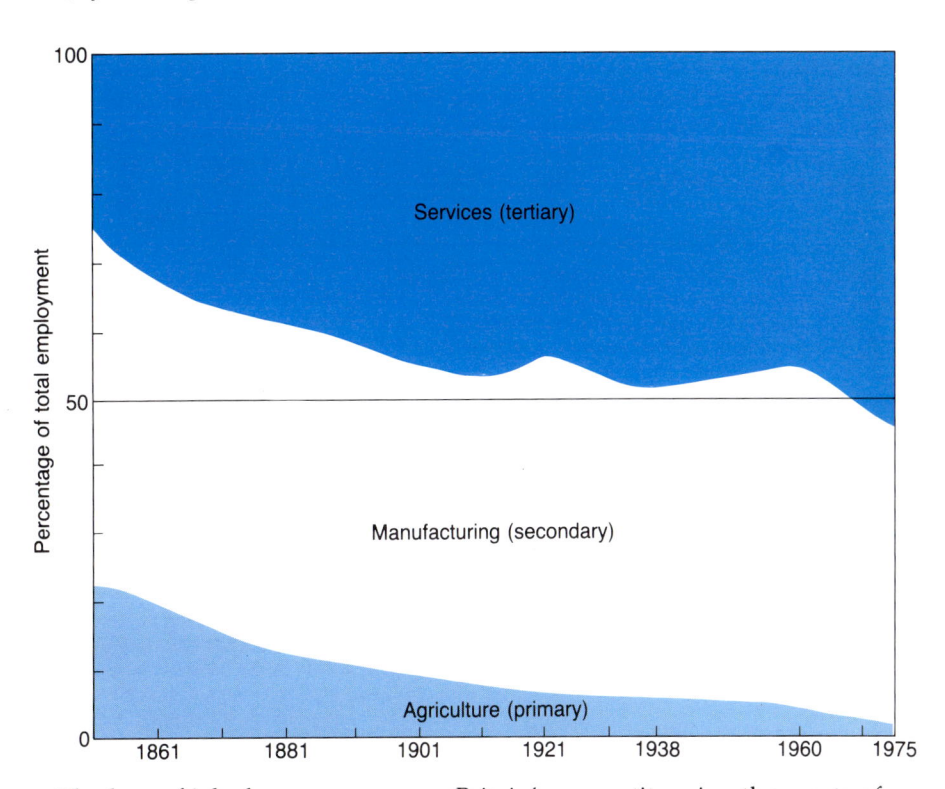

Figure IV.3 The changing employment structure in Britain 1871–1976. (The statistics for 1851–71 are for England and Wales only.)

The loss of jobs has many causes. Britain's competitors in other parts of the world (notably Japan and Korea) have been able to produce goods more cheaply because of lower wages; they have also suffered less from stoppages in production. The early industrialisation of Britain has meant that some industries have been handicapped by old buildings and outdated machinery. The structure of the management and marketing of firms has not always been flexible enough to react quickly to changes in demand for a particular kind of product.

But the loss of jobs has not always meant a loss in production. In some industries computers and robots now do the jobs which human beings once did; mechanisation of processes has meant more efficient production. In this way industry is experiencing the changes felt by farmers at an earlier time – farms now produce more than they ever did with *fewer* workers than they have ever had (mainly because of new and bigger machinery).

In Britain, most economic growth is now in the tertiary sector, where people employed in banks, shops, offices, and the tourist industry continue to grow in number.

The importance of location

The changes in Britain's industrial base have had different effects on different places. We need to ask some key questions:

- Are some manufacturing industries closing or reducing jobs faster than others?

- Are some manufacturing industries expanding and increasing jobs?
- Are some locations in Britain apparently 'better' than others for modern industry?
- Are some locations in Britain very unsuitable for modern industry?

You can probably think of other questions too – for instance the comparison of opportunities for men and women in different places, the difference in quality of jobs (and pay) from place to place, and so on.

The following table (Fig. IV. 4) contains four 'headings' which you can match with the questions above. Use the information in the table to help you to understand more about the present state of Britain's industry.

Heading	Details	Example
Declining industry	Sometimes known as 'traditional industries'; often very old and large-scale; many redundancies; often suffering from competition from newly industrialised countries.	Steel industry: between 1977 and 1983 British Steel cut its workforce by 120,000, a 56 per cent loss of jobs. Also shipbuilding, textiles, heavy engineering.
Growth industry	'New industries'; many small firms sometimes using highly skilled labour.	Electronics, high-tech industry, computers and telecommunications.
Declining areas	The old industrial conurbations based upon the coalfields in northern England, Scotland and Wales; also the inner-cities.	Merseyside, Tyneside, Clydeside, Birmingham, South Wales. In the USA old declining areas are now known as the 'Rust Belt'.
Growth areas	Suburban industrial estates; accessible areas with 'good' environments.	Milton Keynes (and the other new towns); the M4 corridor; 'Silicon Glen'; East Anglia, especially around Cambridge. In the USA the growth areas are in the South and West, the 'Sun Belt'.

Figure IV. 4 Britain's industrial pattern

Plate 25 A painting by William Bell depicting traditional industries on Tyneside.

Plate 26 A typical townscape formed in the days of the Industrial Revolution. A cotton mill in Oldham, Lancashire and surrounding workers' housing.

Plate 27 A large industrial building of the 1930s; the Firestone tyre factory on London's Great West Road.

Plate 28 Robots on a 1980s assembly line.

Plate 29 'Invisible production'. Brokers at work in the London money market; trading by computer has now replaced the face-to-face dealing which used to take place on the Stock Exchange.

Plate 30 Swindon – a nineteenth century picture.

Plate 31 Swindon – a modern view.

Plate 32 London's Isle of Dogs, once dockland, now has many offices and service industries.

✠ Whatsoever · thy · hand · findeth · to · do · do · it · with · thy · Mig[ht]

In the NINETEENTH CENTURY, the Northumbrians show the World what can be done with Iron and Coal.

29

27

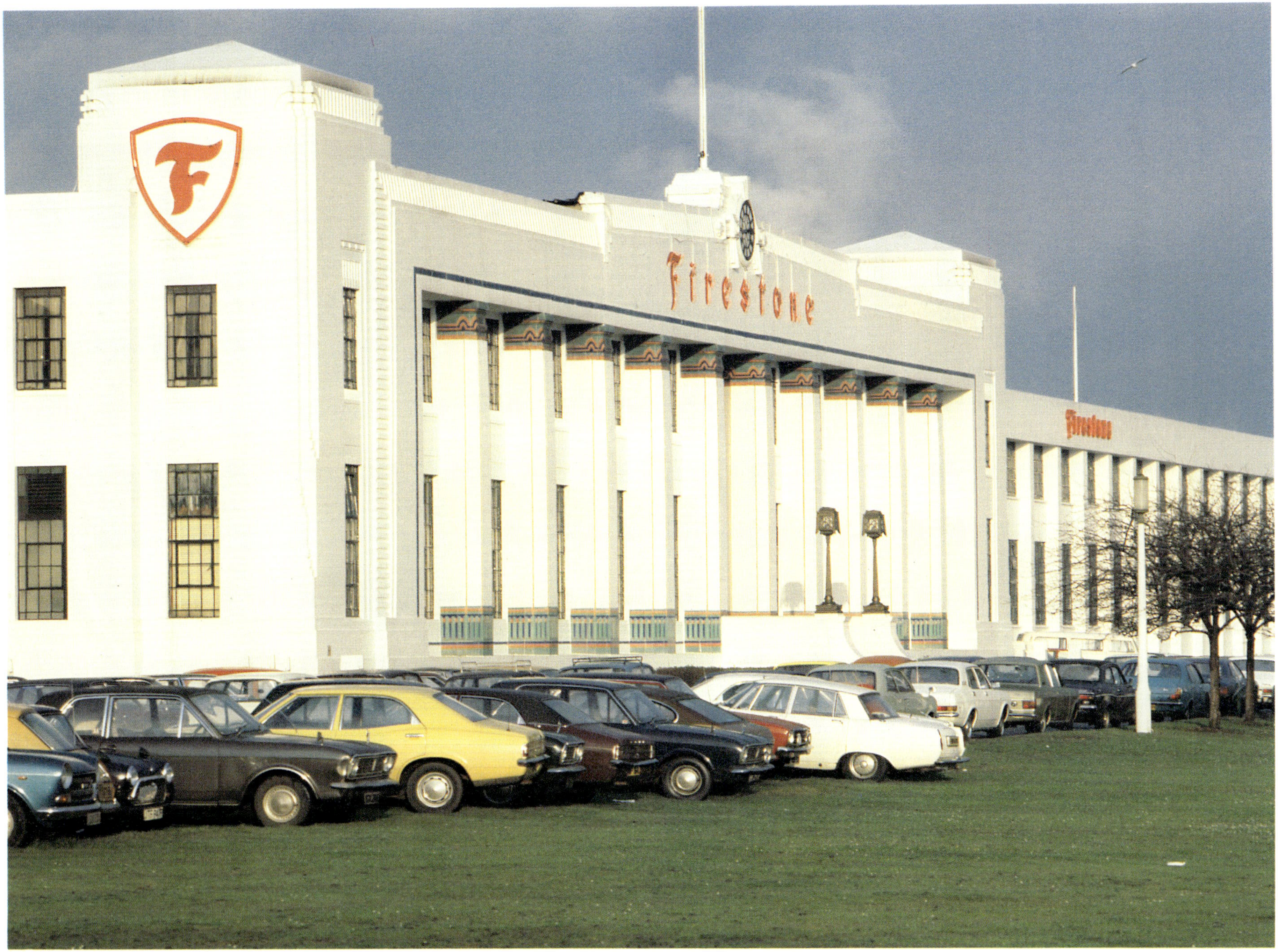

28

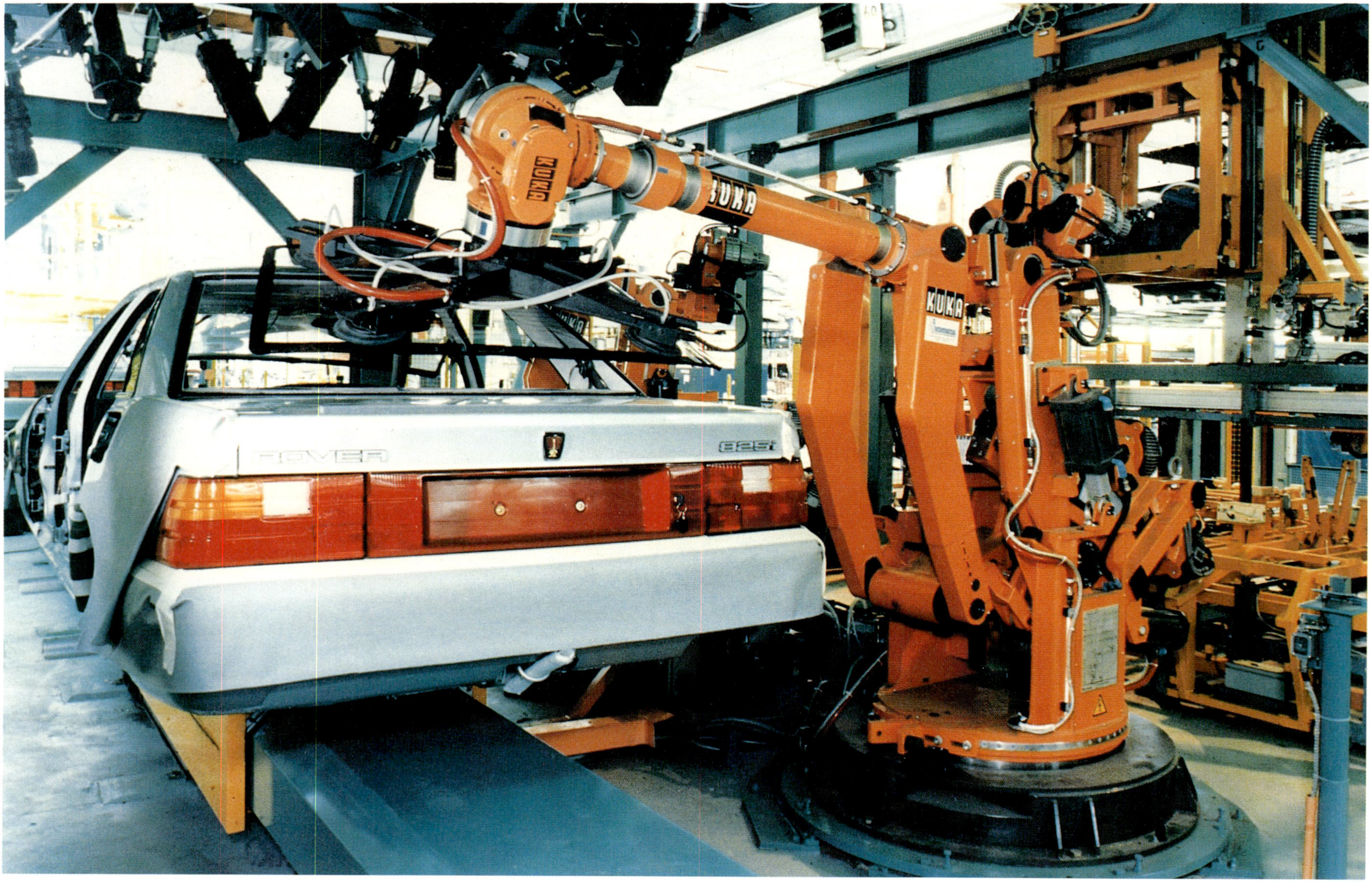

29

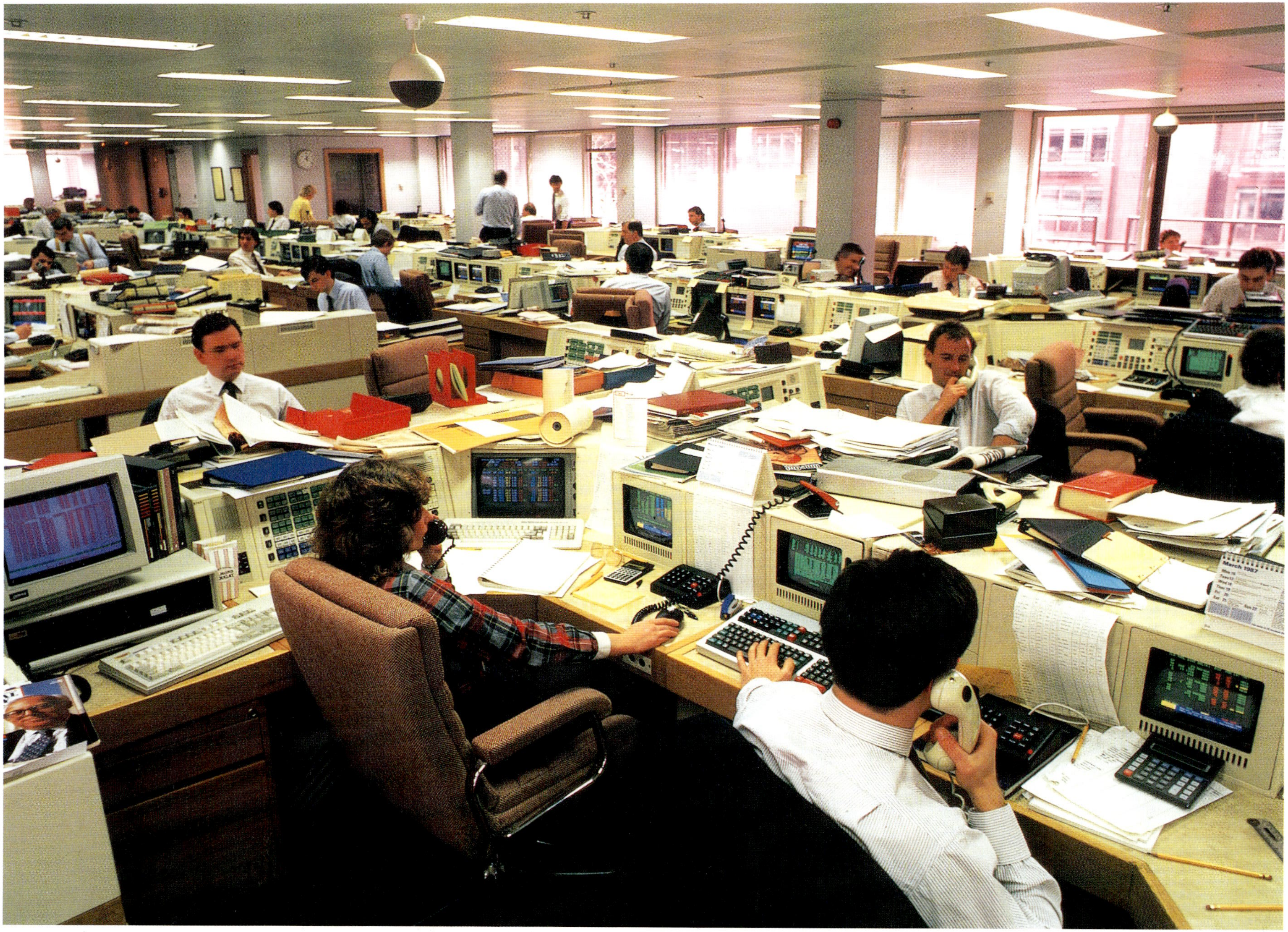

(38)

31

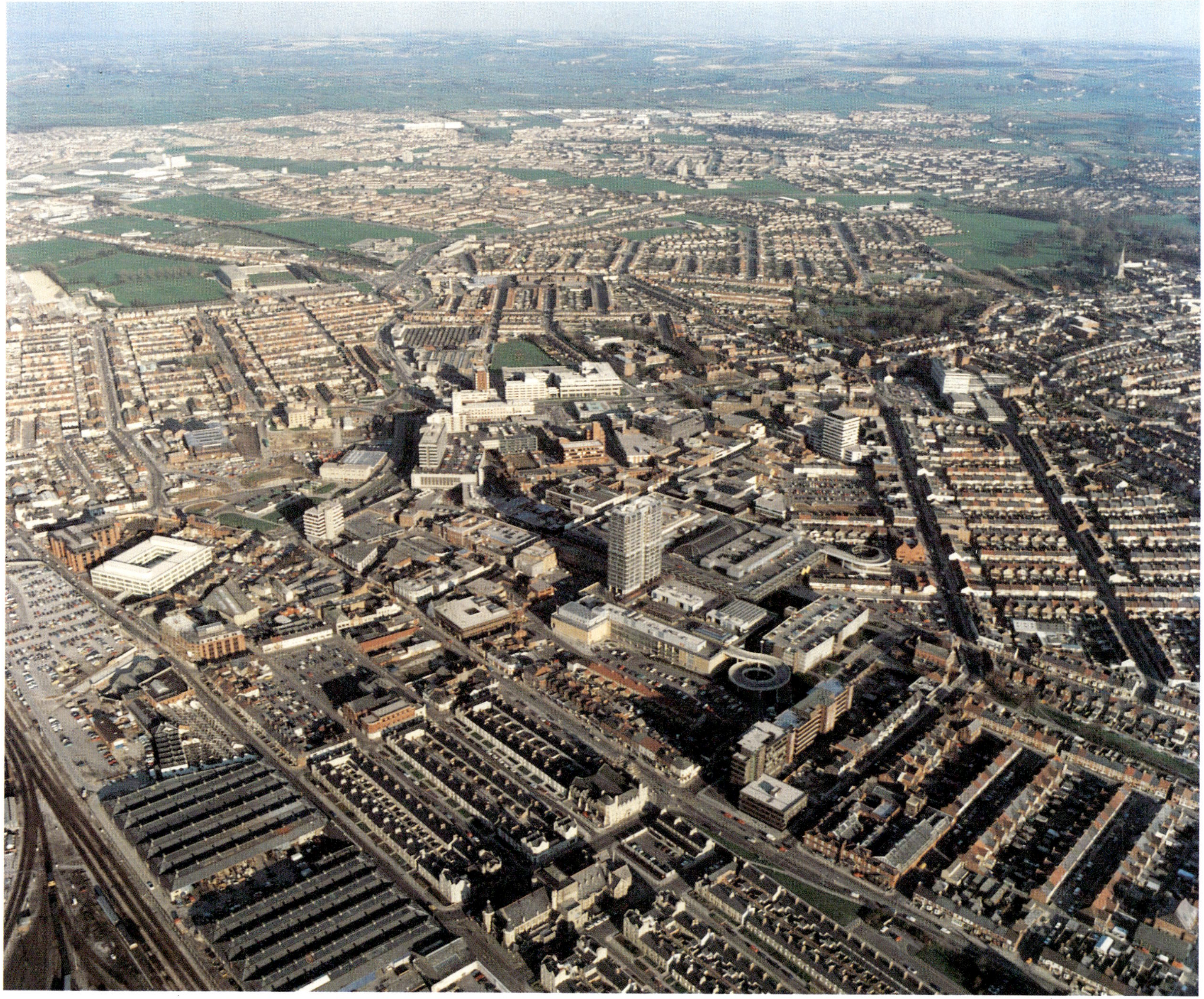

32

Chapter 13
Traditional manufacturing industries

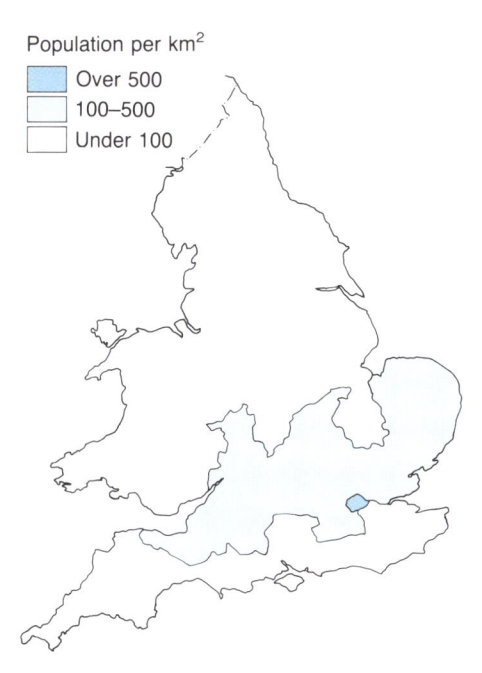

Population per km²
- Over 500
- 100–500
- Under 100

Figure 13.1 Population in 1740

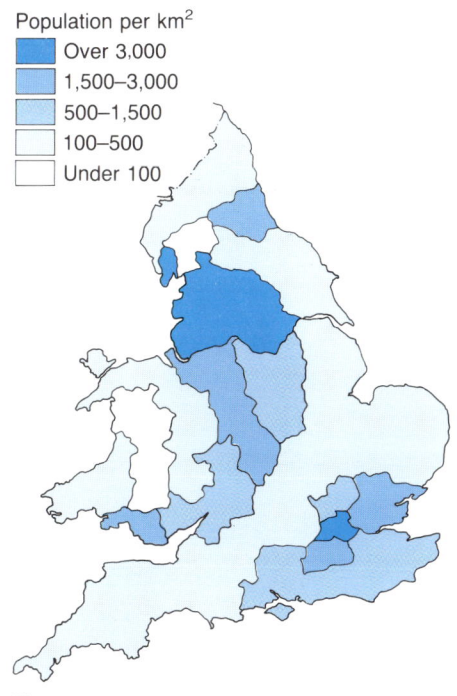

Population per km²
- Over 3,000
- 1,500–3,000
- 500–1,500
- 100–500
- Under 100

Figure 13.2 Population in 1900

Industrialisation in Britain

The traditional base of Britain's industries has been declining since about 1950. The effects on a society whose standards of living are mainly supported by industrial wealth have been severe. These effects have also been felt by other long-established industrial nations in Europe.

The phrase 'traditional industrial base' describes those industries which were first set up at the time of the first industrial revolution (which is usually reckoned to date between 1760 and 1840). Before this period there were small 'cottage' industries which used wind or water power or small-scale charcoal furnaces. The development of the use of coal for smelting (first developed at Coalbrookdale in Shropshire by Abraham Darby in 1709) and to power steam engines changed both the scale and the location of industries. From then on goods could be made in greater numbers more cheaply in large factories. The first large major industrial locations of this period occurred on or near their source of power – the coalfields.

The process of change

It soon became clear that there were higher wages to be had in the factories than in the villages – even if the conditions were not so pleasant. People moved to the newly-built areas of housing around the factories, seeking employment in the factory system.

- Before 1750   20 per cent of Britain's population (which was then about ten million) lived in cities.
- By 1900   77 per cent Britain's population (which had then risen to about forty one million) lived in cities.

The two maps (Figs 13.1 and 13.2) show the change in population location and density over this period. Industrialisation and urbanisation went hand-in-hand.

The main industries which developed at this time are known as **heavy industries** and they include the manufacture of iron and steel, of metal-working, chemicals, the processing of textiles (cotton and wool), and engineering. In all of them coal was of vital importance in driving the machines. Coal traffic, almost all of which was by rail until the internal combustion engine was developed around 1900, was a vital part of the economy. To minimise costs, the industries usually went to where the coal was.

The overall effect of Britain turning into a 'mature industrial society' by 1850 was an increase in its capacity to produce and sell many kinds of manufactured goods. In the years 1793 to 1847, when the population was doubling, output was doubling in half the time. The ouput of iron production increased four-fold in the same fifty-year period.

Analysing nineteenth-century industrial locations

The original industrial system was created by **entrepreneurs** (or financial risk takers), who attempted to look for locations for their new industries which would produce (if possible) maximum returns of profit for minimum costs. At the very start of the industrial revolution this decision was a process of finding a location where the total **costs of transport** (of the various raw materials used in manufacturing, and then moving the finished product to market) were *least*.

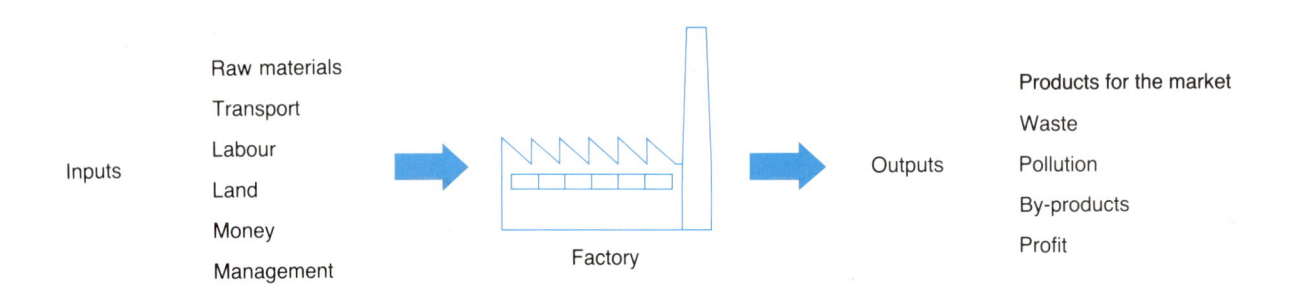

Figure 13.3 The factory system

The industrial system can be described by the means of a simple diagram (see Fig. 13.3) which outlines the **inputs** and **outputs**. The best location would be where the costs of assembling the inputs and distributing the products to market were at a minimum.

In the nineteenth century the processes of manufacturing (what actually happens within a factory) were inefficient and large amounts of coal were used to drive the machinery used in factories. Locations were therefore often **fuel based**. Despite gradual improvements in transportation (by road, rail and canal), the methods of transportation were still relatively costly and tied industries to the sources of coal. Those industries not directly related to the use of coal (such as shipbuilding and engineering) were also forced to assume a location next to the coalfields because they used the bulky products created by coal-based industries. Many industries saw that there was a common advantage to be gained from locating near to each other and using the same supplies of raw materials, services and transport. The realisation of these advantages (known as advantages of **agglomeration**) caused the massive concentration of both people and industries onto coalfield locations in Britain. The growing towns and cities (which began to merge into **conurbations**) became huge markets for products of the developing industries, and therefore became even more attractive. This development of an **optimum location** was always, of course, in the hands of the factory owners. Since workers had to live near the factory in order to walk to work each day, their own housing clustered around the mill or other industrial building which provided their work and wages. Their own conditions were not optimum in either social or environmental terms.

Case study: nineteenth-century iron and steel industries

The raw materials of iron and steel manufacture are all bulky (iron ore, coal and limestone) and therefore there are considerable cost advantages if the industry can locate near to at least one of them. Over the past 200 years the nature of supply of these raw materials, and the amount of them used, has changed dramatically, affecting location of the industry.

Before 1800 iron-making was a cottage industry using local 'black band' iron ores and charcoal for smelting; therefore the Forest of Dean and Weald of Sussex were favourable locations, because they had supplies of both. In the early nineteenth century the invention of the blast furnace for smelting iron ore, and the exhaustion of local black band ores, meant that locations changed. Coalfield locations became important.

One advantage was that iron ore was often found in coal measures, making locational decisions easy – at this stage by far the majority of iron made was in just three regions, South Wales, the Black Country the Midlands and around south Yorkshire.

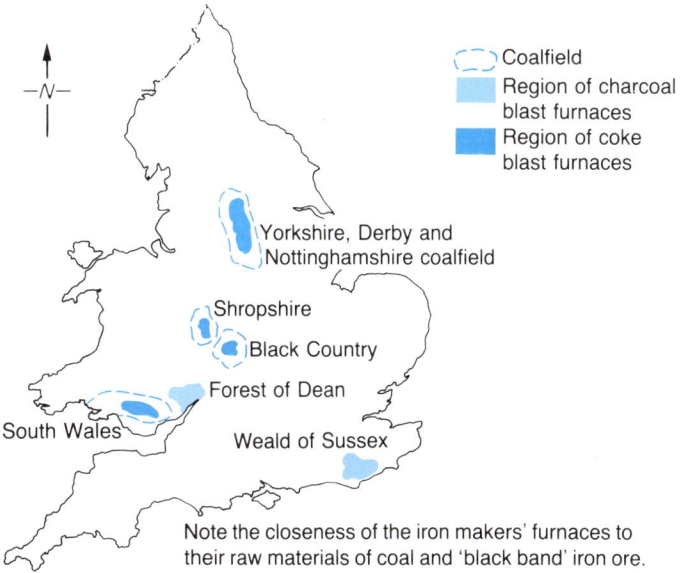

Figure 13.4 The location of iron making industry in early nineteenth-century Britain

Note the closeness of the iron makers' furnaces to their raw materials of coal and 'black band' iron ore.

After the middle of the nineteenth century the pattern of iron and steelworks being supplied with local iron ore and coal changed. Local supplies were becoming exhausted and although new discoveries of ore were still occuring in Britain, these were largely low-grade, with large amounts of impurities in them. Iron and steel makers were therefore persuaded to look for new locations for their blast furnaces, where the cost of transporting new sources of iron ore (and coal) were relatively cheap.

Fortunately the cost of transporting the raw materials used in making iron and steel had now decreased – due to transport being more efficient (and in effect cheaper) and because the recently-developed blast furnaces used less iron ore (and therefore coal) in making their finished product. In addition, high-grade iron ores were being transported from Spain and Sweden to Britain at very cheap rates, which meant that industrialists began to site their steelworks on the coasts. This avoided the extra transport costs that would now occur if inland locations were still used.

	1850	1875	1900	1925
Iron (000s tonnes)	9,000	16,000	14,000	10,000

	1870	1880	1900	1920
Steel (000s tonnes)	300	1,250	5,000	9,000

Figure 13.5 Production of iron and steel in the late nineteenth and early twentieth centuries

Case study: nineteenth-century textile industry

The textile industry of Britain was the first to adopt the machine process in manufacturing. Before the industrial revolution there were four major areas of textile production – East Anglia, the South-West, Lancashire and West Yorkshire. At this stage all the industries were croft (or cottage) industries; however, after about 1750, it became important for these industries to locate near to fast-flowing rivers both for water power and for washing yarn. This accounts for the early locations of the woollen industry in Lancashire and the West Riding of Yorkshire (see Fig. 13.6).

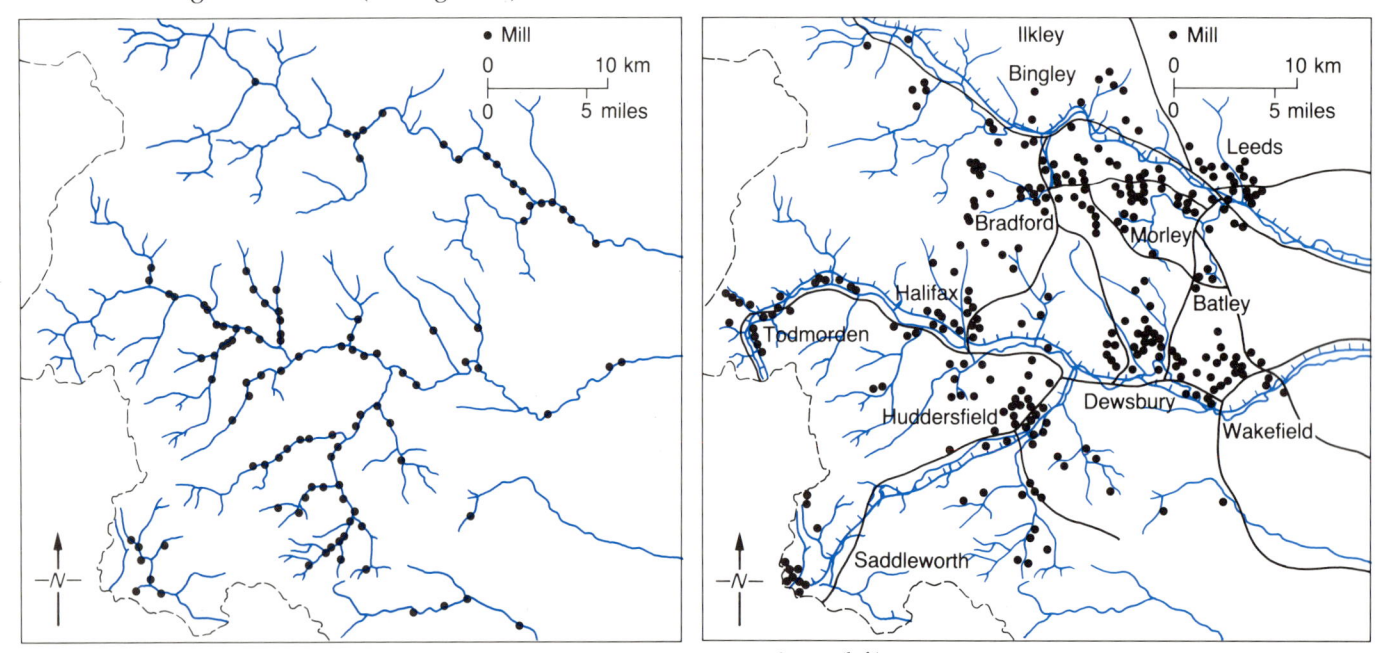

Figure 13.6 and 13.7 West Riding wool and textiles belt before the Industrial Revolution (left) and after (right).

With the invention of steam-powered machinery the locations of textile industries began to change, though wool manufacturers adapted much more slowly than cotton makers to the advances of the industrial revolution, largely because the workers were strongly opposed to changes that they saw damaging to their continued employment.

The woollen industry of West Yorskhire moved onto the Yorkshire coalfield and led to the creation of industrial towns such as Bradford, Leeds, Huddersfield and Halifax. Coalfield location began to spell the death of the previous water-powered processes and their river locations. At the same time, cotton manufacturing took on a greater importance than wool. Lancashire became the centre of cotton manufacture, using the ports of Liverpool and Manchester to supply cotton imports and then export the finished products. The dramatic increase in importance of the cotton industry can be seen in Fig. 13.8.

The South-West and East Anglia, which were the previous centres of wool making, declined, because they were too far away from the coalfields necessary to provide power for the new machinery. The continuing changes in the locations of textile factories during the industrial revolution is shown in Figure 13.7.

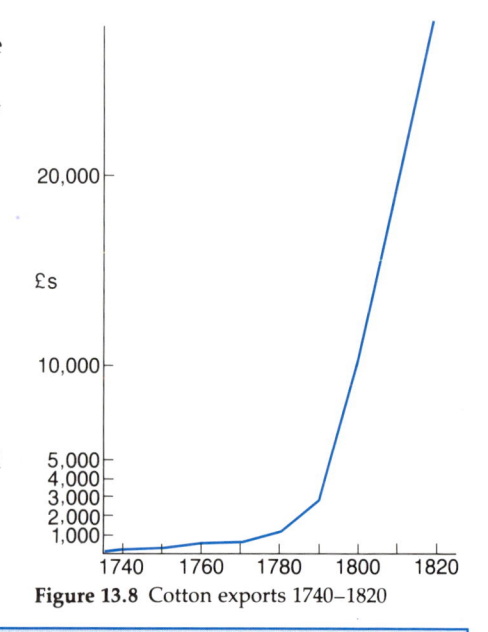

Figure 13.8 Cotton exports 1740–1820

The legacy of industrial working

Major changes in the location of many industries have occured since the industrial revolution – the nineteenth-century centres of manufacturing have now aged into old industrial regions; their advantages have often now gone and they are left as a legacy of the past. Analysed from the present day, many of the nineteenth-century choices of favourable industrial locations are now unattractive – they occupy cramped and congested sites, they no longer have supplies of essential raw materials, they are made up of small, unplanned factories using outdated machinery and methods, and often they have poor connections to services and markets. In addition, this legacy of the past has given these old industrial regions a bad image, especially amongst people with little or no first hand knowledge of these areas such as those living in the south of England.

How has this industrial legacy occurred? During the industrial revolution the economy grew quickly, but in uneven bursts. At times, Britain had high production from its industries and it enjoyed international trade and full employment. But when the economy was poor, there were low wages for workers, poor conditions and a decrease in demand for workers. Social conditions for industrial workers were mostly poor and remained so until the start of this century; the following poem outlines one of the injustices of children being used as industrial workers in Britain:

> The golf links lie so near the mill,
> That almost every day,
> The labouring children can look out,
> And see the men at play.
> Sarah Cleghorn, 'Portraits and Protests', 1917.

A full day's work was often over sixteen hours. Sometimes workers were not given any break-times and had to eat meals whilst working. There were no controls on the length of a working day and workers could work from one day into the next. Accidents were common in mining and manufacturing, and laws to increase safety and control child employment were almost non-existent.

Textile mills were the first to develop along modern lines, though conditions at this stage were very poor:

> ... it is dirty, unroofed, ill-ventilated, with machinery not boxed in, and passages so narrow that they could hardly be defined; it seemed more to be a receptacle of demons than a workhouse of industrious human beings.
> *Parliamentary Papers*, 1833, Vol. XX A1 38.

Mechanisation helped to produce greater quantities of products and to make them cheaper and so it was welcomed by the owners and managers of factories. But the factory conditions often remained poor.

Some factory workers also feared that the growth of machinery would eventually put them out of work, and so industrial unrest occurred when workers attacked machines and sought to destroy them. These workers were called Luddites, after one of their leaders, Ned Ludd, and the term is still applied to those who oppose industrial change.

The populations in industrial towns grew rapidly in the nineteenth century. Workers usually lived close to their factories so that they could travel quickly each day, on foot, to their places of work. But the pollution of air and water and the noise of factories was a hazard in these 'back-to-back' terraces which had often been built as quickly and cheaply as possible to house the workers. Sanitation was poor, water supplies were impure and overcrowding was a major social problem.

The exceptions to this were in the 'model' estates created by employers with a Christian conscience, such as George Cadbury (who built the suburb of Bourneville in Birmingham) and Titus Salt (who built Saltaire in Bradford).

Figure 13.9 Saltaire

T' master's mill town lives on

The mill buzzer no longer punctuates the working day and sends a tide of workers out into the street. The baths and washhouses have been demolished and the Sunday School is no more. These days some children even doubt that the stone lions rise at midnight and go down to the Aire to drink. Yet, overall, Saltaire remains remarkably unchanged, the most complete industrial model village in Britain.

Saltaire, now one of the star attractions for Bradford's surprisingly flourishing tourist industry, is accustomed to being in the limelight. Right from the start, it excited a great deal of international interest and admiration. And it was all, as Charles Dickens wrote, 'created by the genius and industry of one quiet man of business'.

Titus Salt had intended to retire and take up the life of a country gentleman. He had made his fortune in the worsted trade and by 1850 he was probably Bradford's wealthiest citizen and certainly its biggest employer. He'd served as mayor, worked to improve the conditions of 'the masses' and, more than most men, had earned a rest. Instead, he created Saltaire – partly, he said, that 'I might provide occupation for my sons' and partly because 'outside my business I am nothing – in it, I have considerable influence.'

He owned six mills in Bradford, a hellish city then, in spite of the efforts of men like Salt – overcrowded, polluted and cholera-ravaged. It also suffered from a severe water shortage and woollen mills needed quantities of water. Salt decided to bring all his operations together and to build for his workers a new Jerusalem. He decided to get out of town – a decision he was later accused of taking in order to avoid paying Bradford taxes. He chose a picturesque site at Shipley, conveniently placed on the railway, turnpike, river and canal.

Salt cared deeply about the welfare of his workpeople but he was also a hard-headed industrialist. The mill was the first building to go up (a second mill followed in 1868). A vast Italianate structure incorporating the most modern design features and latest machinery was completed within two years. A dining room was provided where workers could have their own food cooked free of charge or buy a plate of meat for 2d or soup for 1d.

On September 20, 1853, Titus's 50th birthday and the day he had previously set for his retirement, he presided over the opening of his new mill, christened the Palace of Industry. The work-people were brought by train from Bradford and 3500 guests sat down to a banquet.

After Mammon, God was served – and finely, too, with a distinguished Congregational church, facing the mill entrance across Victoria Street, Saltaire's main thoroughfare. The baths and washhouses were completed next: 12 baths each for men and women, naturally with separate entrances, plus a Turkish bath, and a laundry with a centrifugal wringer to eliminate the, to Salt, offensive sight of washing hanging outdoors and the domestic nuisance of steam and damp. (As it turned out, people preferred to wash themselves and their clothes at home and the buildings were demolished in 1894.) The elementary schools followed, described by the government inspector as having 'no rivals in the district'. For the sick and injured, Salt provided an infirmary and dispensary and for the elderly 'of good moral character and incapacity for labour', 45 almshouses were built, in the style of Italian villas. These were furnished and residents received a weekly allowance.

All this time, the houses were being built, 850 in all, streets named after the Queen and Prince Albert, members of the Salt family and Messrs Lockwood and Mawson, architects of Saltaire. Salt said the he 'hoped to draw around me a well-fed, contented and happy band of operatives. I have given instructions to my architects ... that nothing be spared to render the dwellings a pattern to the country'. He even consulted his workpeople about the size and facilities they wanted Everything was to be designed with sanitary principles in mind. The result was a sometimes dour, often attractive mixture of two, three and four-bedroomed stone houses, each with a living room, kitchen, pantry and cellar and a backyard with a privy, coalstore and ashpit – there were no back-to-backs in Saltaire.

Halfway up Victoria Street, Salt built the Saltaire Club and Institute, set back behind gardens adorned with two stone lions – a matching pair front the elementary school opposite. The Institute was 'intended to supply the advantages of a public house without its evils', Salt being convinced that 'drink and lust' were at the root of most of the evils of mankind.

For a few shillings a year, members could enjoy the well-stocked library and reading room, play billiards or bagatelle, relax in the smoking room, study art and science, attend concerts and lectures.

Across the river, Salt provided a splendid park with promenades, flower beds and shrubberies and a bandstand. For the more energetic and athletic, there were allotments, boating, croquet, archery and a cricket ground.

Sir Titus Salt died on December 29, 1876 and was laid to rest in his mausoleum attached to the Congregational church, becoming a Saltaire resident as he never had been in life.

If Salt were to rise up today and walk the streets of Saltaire he would find them pleasingly familiar and could congratulate himself that his noble experiment had stood the test of time. The village remains, externally, at least, almost as he left it: only the washhouses, the Sunday School and the old Wesleyan chapel have gone. The New Mill stands empty but the original building still produces fine quality cloth. Saltaire is not a dead monument to a great philanthropist. It is a living community.

Database: traditional manufacturing industries

Figure 13.10 The value of imports and exports of selected goods – Britain 1885 and 1984 (£m). The figures in brackets show the percentage of the *total* imports or exports for each year stated.

	1885		1984	
	Imports	**Exports**	**Imports**	**Exports**
Metals and ores	16 (4%)	26 (10%)	6213 (8%)	5241 (7%)
Textiles	67 (18%)	90 (33%)	5316 (7%)	2909 (4%)

Workbase

1. Read through the extract on Saltaire page 131.
   a) Why do you think that men like Salt and Cadbury thought it their duty to create such working conditions and communities in and around their factories?
   Were there benefits for owners, as well as for workers? If so, what were they?
   b) Do you know of any evidence to suggest that industrial towns such as Saltaire, Bourneville and Port Sunlight were more successful communities than other nineteenth-century towns?
   c) Are their similar ventures today? Give examples of any employers who provide *other* benefits besides employment to their workers.
   d) Draw up the design of an industrial town which *you* might have built, if you had been a wealthy and caring mill-owner in 1850. Label the community facilities which you would have wished to provide.
2. Look at Fig. 13.10, 'The value of imports and exports of selected goods in Britain; 1885 and 1984.
   a) Compare the value of imports and exports for both 'metals and ores' and 'textiles' for the two dates. Do you think either was a stronger industry in 1984? If so, why?
   b) What do the percentage figures suggest to you, concerning the importance of these two industries to the British economy *as a whole* at the two dates given?

Chapter 14
Twentieth-century manufacturing industries

Development and change

Many changes have occurred since the start of industrialisation in the nineteenth century. They have taken place as a result of several important processes which are explained below. These processes have been operating throughout the twentieth century.

Transport improvements

In the previous chapter on nineteenth-century manufacturing industry in Britain, the importance of transport to the location of bulk-reducing industries was shown. Transport costs of both raw materials (to factories) and finished products (to markets) were high. Many industries used bulky raw materials in large quantities (8 tonnes of coal were needed to process 1 tonne of iron ore in 1850). Transport was relatively slow and expensive in the early days of the industrial revolution.

However, since the early nineteenth century, there have been major improvements. Changes have occurred not only because of the needs of Britain's industry, but through the growth of trade within and outside Britain and through the rise in demand by the public for all kinds of manufactured products as the standards of living improved.

Great competition developed between different modes of transport. This was helpful to industry because it meant an improvement of service and lower costs. Transport cost began to lose its significance as the key factor in location for many industries, as industries became more '**footloose**'.

Figure 14.1 A 1908 picture of a new factory, Spirella, making women's corsets at Letchworth, Hertfordshire

However, some (such as the cement industry) still show clear signs of taking transport costs into account in their location.

Changes in technology, and improvements in the efficiency of many industrial processes, have also helped this footloose effect because new industries have only had to use (and therefore move) a fraction of the raw materials which they used to (1 tonne of coal was needed to process 1 tonne of iron ore in 1987).

Rationalisation

In **'capitalist'** or 'free market' economies, such as Britain, many industries are owned by individuals (shareholders). The shareholders take the risk that the industry may fail; but if it succeeds they are rewarded by profit income.

The **profit** made by manufacturing a product is reached by calculating all the costs (including 'overheads') per unit of the product and measuring this against the price for which it is sold.

From the very start of the industrial revolution risk-takers (sometimes known as entrepreneurs) were aware that keeping costs down was the surest way of making a business profitable. One way to do this is to **substitute** costs; for example, if a machine (costing the wages of two workers for a year) can do the job of three workers, it would clearly be profitable to buy the machine, rather than employ the three workers to do the job by hand.

Sometimes whole factories have been closed down in this way, when an industrialist has worked out that it will save money (i.e. boost profits) to concentrate production on fewer or newer factories. This process, known as **rationalisation**, has been quite a common feature of recent years, as industries have sought to stay in business during a national and world recession of trade.

But rationalisation which makes sense in economic terms may create considerable hardships in human terms. Those who have their industry rationalised are probably delighted if they stay in work and receive higher wages; but for others it means **redundancy**, and a search for a new job. Even when a firm provides a 'golden handshake' it may be a small compensation for the loss of a job which a worker liked and depended on.

Economies of scale

Closely connected to rationalisation is the idea of **economy of scale**. This is the saving made by an industrialist by increasing the scale (or size) of some, or all, of the processes used in manufacturing. For example, the decision might be made to manufacture a product not in many small factories but two or three larger, more efficient factories. Similarly economies of scale might be achieved by transporting raw materials, or products, not in small and costly units but in one large one. Transportation of crude oil shows how economies of scale have been reached over the last forty years.

The main aim in reaching economies of scale is to cut the costs of production and they have therefore often been seen as a part of the process of rationalisation.

External economies of scale

It is possible to achieve scale economies not only within one set of factories (i.e. all manufacturing the same product such as, say, paper) but also between different factories (paper manufacture, printing, ink making, etc.).

Figure 14.2 A 1928 picture of a new factory — Pyrene, making fire extinguishers at Brentford, Middlesex

Here many small industries can cluster together (or **agglomerate**) to make joint use of transport facilities, common services, component manufacturers and waste disposal, and therefore achieve economies of scale by behaving like one large unit.

Inertia

Some industries, even if they are not making as much profit from their location as they would from another, do not actually move to a better location. The 'best' (or optimum) location for any particular industry is virtually impossible to find because the conditions that make it so will be constantly changing. A location will alter over time due to changes such as:

- the construction of a new transport route that means the old location of the industry is no longer on the 'cheapest transport-cost location';
- a new market being established in a city nearer than the previous market;
- the discovery of a new source of cheaper raw materials;
- competition from another business putting a factory in the area.

Optimum locations therefore always change. Certain industries can definitely state that their location is now in a less profitable place than it once was, and that better locations exist elsewhere.

Inertia occurs because it is often too costly to move to this better location. Consider the cost of moving buildings, machinery, labour, services and re-routing transport to an entirely new location. The move would also take time, a valuable commodity to modern industry. The cost of moving therefore often outweighs the loss of profits that happens from the factory continuing to operate in its old location. Inertia may also be made stronger by the fact that movement of a factory causes considerable social problems and costs. The redundancies that factory closures cause are extremely damaging to communities, and people do not move freely and easily to new locations because of their existing family and friendship ties.

But industries cannot continue to operate in uneconomic locations forever. Inertia may eventually lead to factory closure.

Case study: the British steel industry

The steel-making regions of Britain have suffered over the past forty years from the legacy of their nineteenth-century locations, methods of production and markets. Often the problems have been blatantly apparent – for example, the exhaustion of local ore and coal, and the decline of markets such as shipbuilding. Steelworks have therefore had to adapt to changing circumstances, or close.

Inertia, rationalisation and scale economies in steelmaking

Many steelworks in Britain provided, in the 1970s, good examples of industrial inertia. The original advantages of their locations had gone, but it was too costly to move. The British Steel Corporation (established in 1967) realised that, due to widespread changes in the original factors of production (e.g. labour supply, raw material supply, methods of steelmaking, markets), the whole of the map of steelmaking had to be revised.

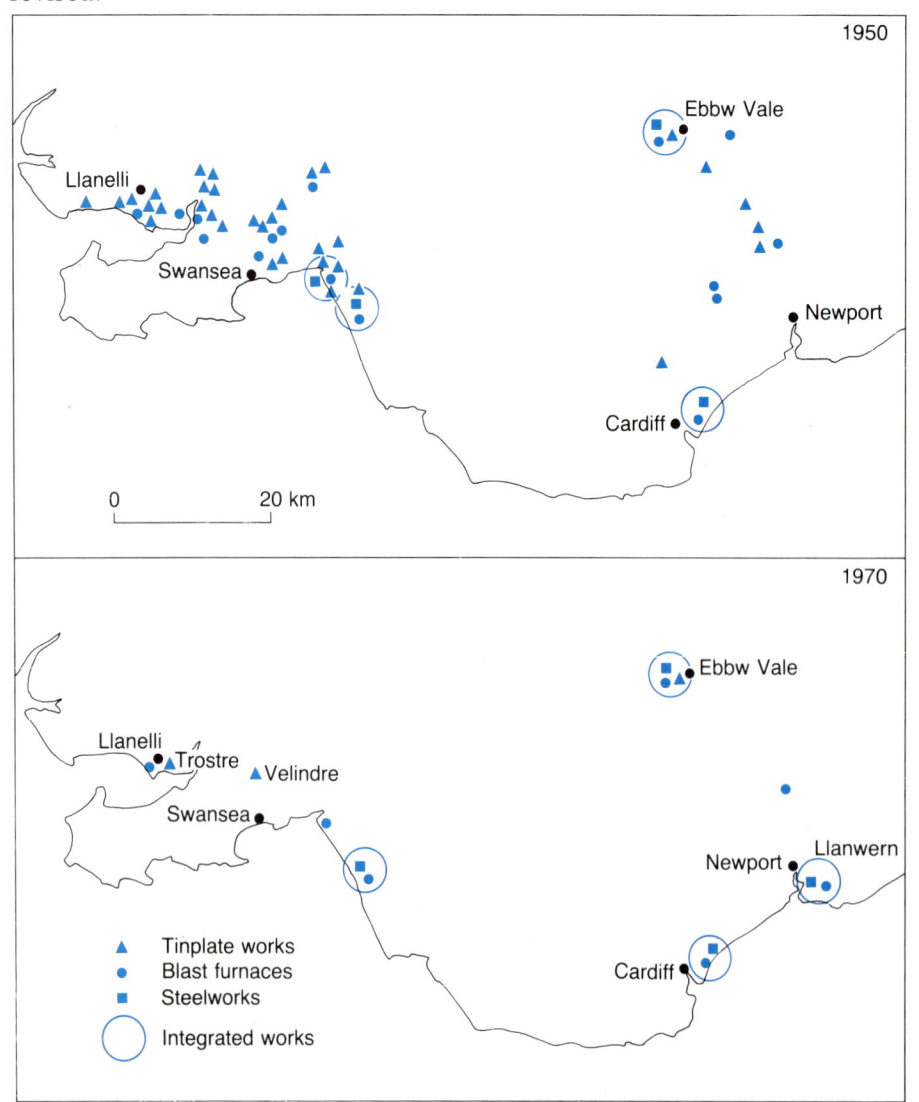

Figure 14.3 The rationalisation of the iron, steel and tinplate industries in South Wales, 1950–70

Twentieth-century manufacturing industries 137

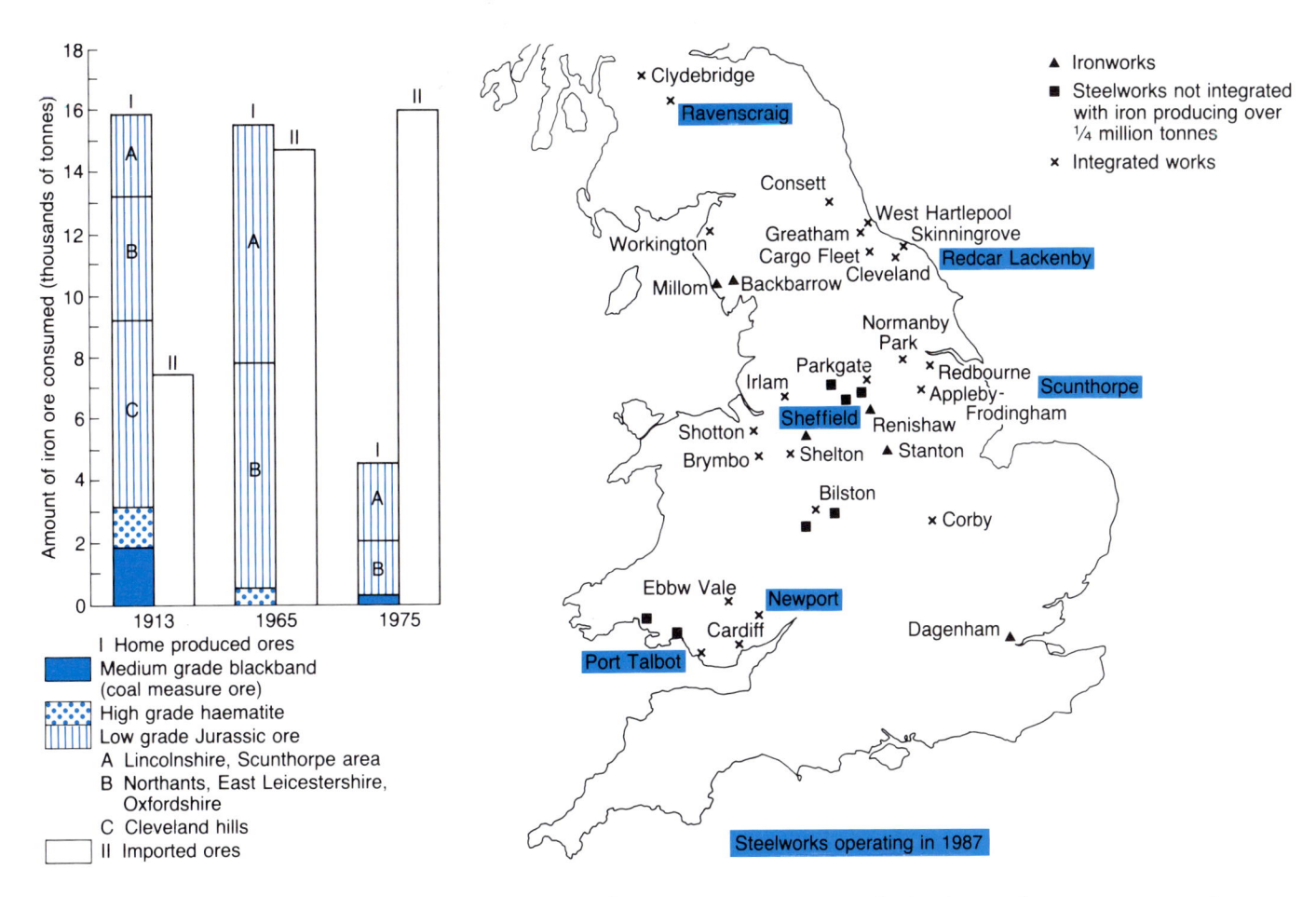

Figure 14.4 (above) Consumption of iron ore in the iron and steel industry, 1913–75

Figure 14.5 (above right) Iron and steelworks in the UK in 1967 and 1987

Supplies of iron ore were now mostly foreign and were transported on large ships at a fraction of the cost of moving iron ore across the land by railways. This suggested that the best location for steelworks in Britain would be coastal.

The large quantities of iron ore that could now be transported from foreign suppliers forced other economies of scale – the new steelworks would benefit from being much larger than previously, from being fewer in number and from becoming **integrated**. An integrated iron and steelworks is one which makes iron from iron ore and then directly transports it across the site to be made into steel straight away.

Rationalisation of the industry, both from the point of view of closing small, costly units and of introducing new methods of steelmaking and new techniques, has happened as quickly as possible. However, the consideration of effects of closures has slowed the process – for example, closing Consett, once the third biggest steelworks in Britain, caused major unemployment in an area that relied heavily upon this for its livelihood.

The speed and scale of rationalisation can be seen from Fig. 14.5, showing iron and steelworks in Britain in 1967 and their reduction to the six steelwords operating in 1981. 1967 was the year of **nationalisation**, with the creation of the government-owned British Steel Corporation. Rationalisation was already well underway before nationalisation, however.

British ores and coking coal cannot compete with the cheapness of those which are imported, forcing steelmaking locations to the coasts. At the same time, the decline in Britain's manufacturing industries has meant that the markets for steel are now increasingly *outside* Britain. The key British industries of shipbuilding and of the Midlands car industry have both declined. Industries of the South-East are now closer to foreign suppliers in Europe than to those in Britain itself!

The British steel industry in the 1980s

Britain's steel industry has been considerably rationalised, but it is now far more competitive. Production is now centred upon five major integrated steelworks – Llanwern, Scunthorpe, Ravenscraig, Redcar, and Port Talbot – which have advantages of scale and position. There are still problems: certain steelworks have difficulties with ore supplies (for example, Ravenscraig), some have outdated machinery and techniques, or were set up for reasons not wholly connected to creating steel at the cheapest price in the best location.

The 1970s saw the steel industry of Britain being dismantled. Throughout South Yorkshire, East Midlands, West Midlands and Wales steelworks were closed (including Bilston, Shotton, Corby, Consett, Ebbw Vale and Clydebridge) whilst some steelworks on coastal locations that did not have ports deep enough to take large iron ore ships also had to close (Cardiff, Irlam, Hartlepool). The workforce has fallen from 336,000 in 1967 to less than 100,000 after rationalisation in 1984, though labour productivity (the amount of steel made by each steelworker) has increased. This transformed the British steel industry from a loss-maker to a profit-maker.

Figure 14.6 The Port Talbot steelworks, West Glamorgan, Wales

Questions

1. Describe what conditions are required to make a favourable location for a steelworks in Britain (remember that the raw materials used are iron ore, coking coal, water, limestone and air).
2. What problems would inland integrated steelworks, such as Ravenscraig and Scunthorpe, suffer that coastal steelworks do not?
3. Local opposition to the closure of small steelworks is often very strong. Why do you think this is so?
4. Briefly describe how the favourable locations for iron and steelworks have changed over the last hundred years.

Case study: the British textile industry

The textile industry, often one of the first to establish in the industrial growth of a nation, is usually one of the first to be rationalised and possibly fall into decline in a mature industrial society. It is therefore something of a surprise that in Britain the textile industry stayed as one of the largest employers of industrial labour into the 1960s, although in the 1970s and 1980s the loss of workers was immense. By 1980 the workforce had been reduced, due to factory closure, to 300,000 – approximately one-third of the number employed in the early 1960s. The wool textile employment in West Yorkshire from 1972 to 1976 (Fig. 14.8) gives an accurate indication of this in just one region of Britain.

If we now consider the effect nationally, the dramatic nature of the loss of jobs over the decade of the 1970s due to rationalisation becomes clear. In Fig. 14.7 the reduction of workforce is indicated by different sectors of the textile industry.

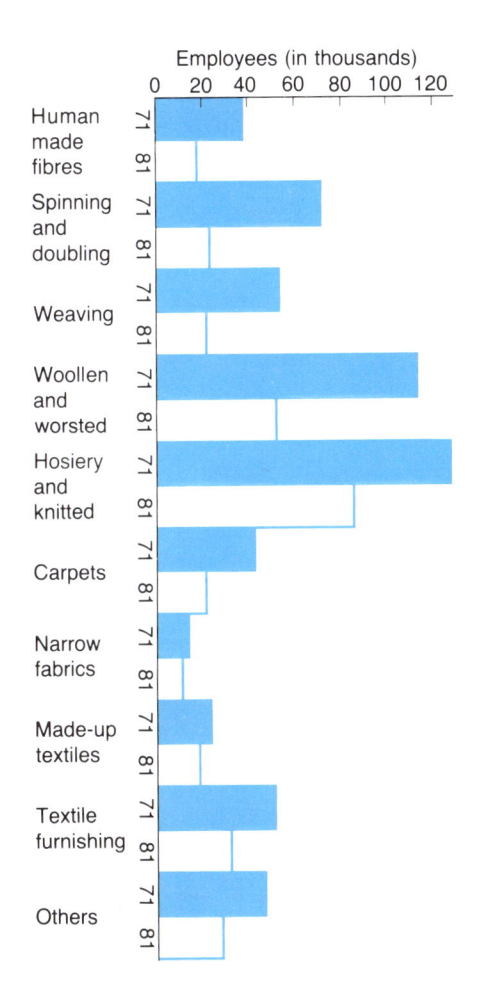

Figure 14.7 Employment in the textile industry in Britain, 1971 and 1981

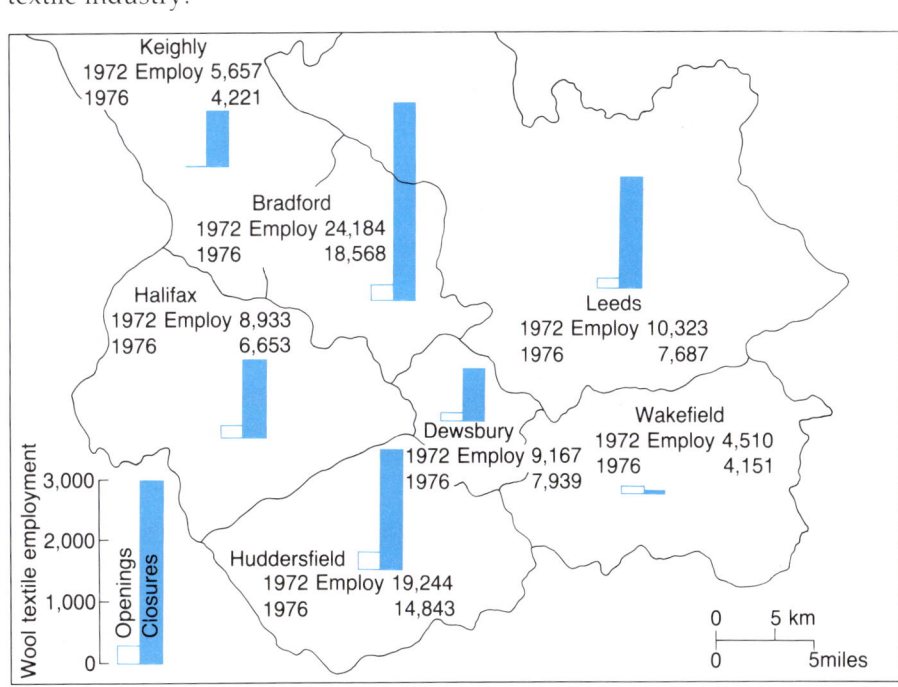

Figure 14.8 Wool textile employment in West Yorkshire, 1972–76 by functional region

Reasons for changes in the textile industry

The reasons behind the decline in the number of workers in the textile industry are complex. Different sectors of the industry have declined at different rates for different reasons. However, the conditions that have affected most of the industry can be summarised and act as a guide to understanding the general nature of change in textiles.

- Exports of textiles have not competed well with those of other foreign producers who have managed to produce cheaper goods.
- There has been a rise in cheaper imports of textiles to Britain from foreign producers.
- Poor and outdated management decisions have caused problems. In particular new markets have not been found and new techniques not been used.

Figure 14.9 Tartan cloth being woven on a modern loom, Huddersfield, Yorkshire

- Substitutions of human-made fibres (now over three-quarters of all textile production) have been made for natural fibres such as wool, cotton, jute and linen.
- An improvement of output per worker has been achieved, due to mechanisation.

The result of these changes has been that the cotton, jute and linen production of Britain has fallen markedly, although the production of high-quality woollen goods has not been so severely affected.

Current trends in the textile industry

The three main textile producing regions of Britain are now the East Midlands, Yorkshire and Humberside, and Northern Ireland, although each of these has experienced dramatic loss of labour. Since the 1970s the traditional characteristics of production have changed, so that no longer is the East Midlands recognised as a region specialising in knitwear and hosiery production, Yorkshire and Humberside wool producers or Northern Ireland a region for the manufacture of linen, as a previous generation of geography books descibed them.

Not only has the textile industry seen the most dramatic rationalisation of jobs of any British industry, there have also been major changes in the management structure. Although textile production was not nationalised (like the steel or the coal industry) it has seen a major merging of national firms, so that it now has a management structure similar to a nationalised industry.

Case study: the British motor vehicle industry

The motor vehicle industry in Britain in the early twentieth century took over the position of strength occupied by the iron and steel industries in the previous century. It began by entrepreneurs, like Morris and Austin, establishing industries using their own skills in light engineering as a basis for creating a manufacturing process. These skills were sometimes first gained by making bicycles or lawn-mowers.

Growth in the twentieth century

It soon became apparent that the most successful locations were those in the West Midlands and South-East, where:

- engineering skills already existed in the labour force;
- component manufacturers which could supply the motor industry were close by;
- large markets were available in the cities of the Midlands, in London, and in the South-East.

We must remember that the motor industry is an **assembly** industry – it uses numerous **components** for every vehicle manufactured. Therefore the industries must be located close to transport links to component makers.

In the 1930s and 40s the Midlands continued to strengthen its position and achieved scale economies by locating its small manufacturers close to each other, reducing transport, service and processing costs. Almost two-thirds of all vehicles produced in Britain came from this region in the late 1940s.

The post-war changes

After the Second World War demand for cars dramatically increased, because people could afford cars and wanted to be more mobile. Figure 14.10 reflects this growth.

In response to the increased demand for cars from the general public, the output of cars from British manufacturers rose. The Government directed some of this increase in production to areas away from the South-East and Midlands, especially to regions suffering from a lack of this type of industrial employment and a high unemployment rate. Thus Ford set up a factory in Halewood, Vauxhall in Ellesmere Port and Triumph in Speke (all in the Liverpool and Merseyside region), Talbot in Linwood (Glasgow) and various truck manufacturers located in South Wales and central Scotland.

Year	Vehicles (in millions)
1952	4.9
1957	7.5
1962	10.6
1967	13.6
1970	15.0
1975	17.2
1980	19.2
1985	21.1

Figure 14.10 Numbers of vehicles on Britain's roads

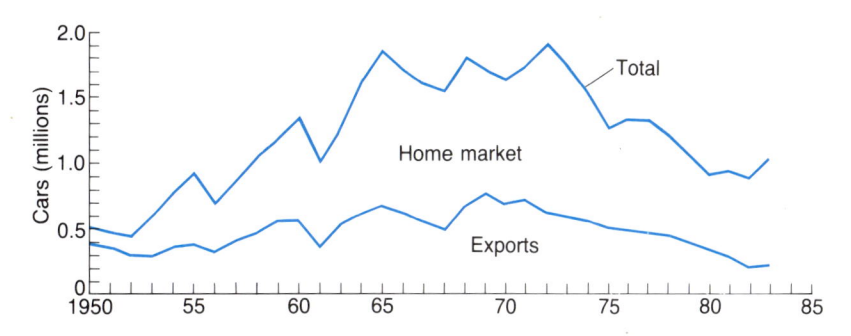

Figure 14.11 Car production in the UK

The 1970s – a decade of change

The British motor industry is now dominated by four firms (Ford, The Rover Group, GM-Vauxhall, and Peugeot) but each of these has suffered problems recently. There has been a reduction in the number of assembly plants (from thirteen in 1972 to eight in 1982) and this has been paralleled by a drop in production by about one-half.

Fig. 14.12 illustrates the way in which the motor vehicle industry has become concentrated and rationalised through the 1970s. These changes have obviously had an effect on the production of motor vehicles in Britain. The figures in Fig. 14.13 show certain trends, especially when we look at the figures for exports of vehicles.

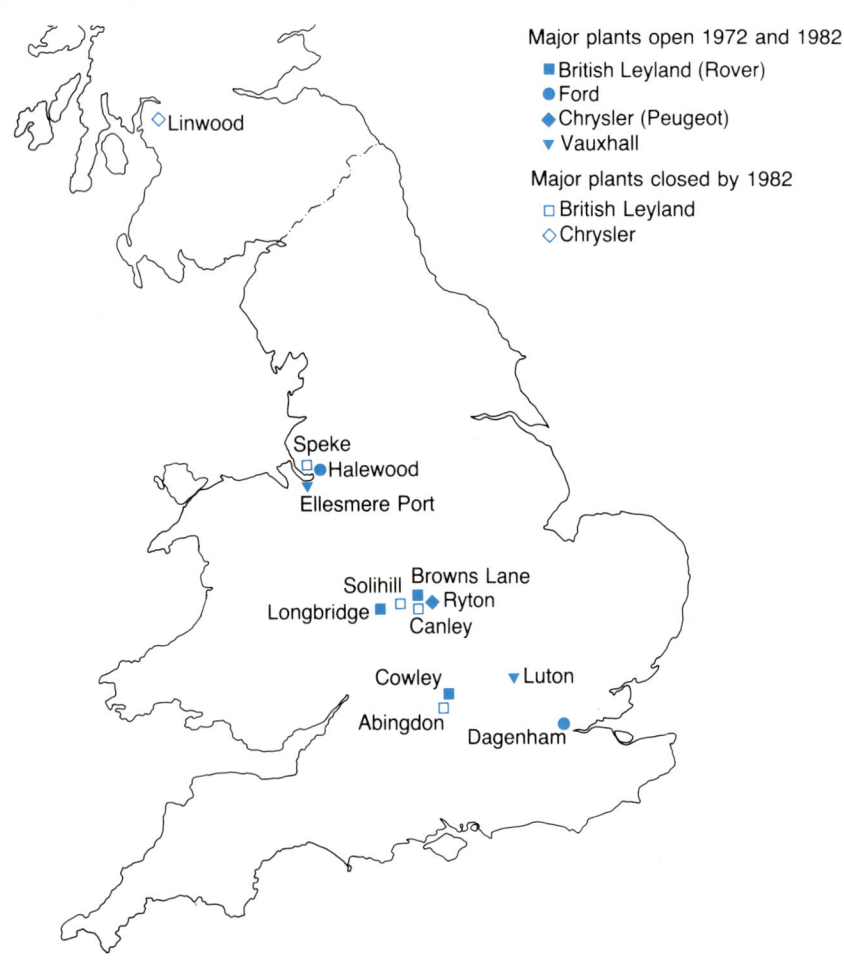

Figure 14.12 Major car assembly plants, 1972 and 1982

	Total	Markets	
		Home	Exports
1972	1,921,311	1,307,881	613,430
1982	887,679	661,814	225,865
% change	−53.8	−49.4	−63.2

Figure 14.13 Production of cars in the United Kingdom

As we can see from Fig. 14.13, the effect has been extremely rapid, over the space of ten years total production and sales to both home and export markets have declined by approximately 50 per cent (or over).

The British car industry therefore faces problems – foreign car producers (such as the Japanese) have taken over many markets both home and abroad, problems have occurred with labour and the amount each worker produces in larger plants, and low profits mean little investment of money. The factories that have been set up in development areas away from the Midlands and South-East, the traditional home of the car industry, have faced closure; two out of four have closed in the last ten years, Linwood in Scotland and Speke in Merseyside.

Both the older centres in the Midlands and South-East and the newer locations have suffered a loss of over 40 per cent of their workers in the last ten years. The current distribution of car workers throught Britain is shown in Fig. 14.14.

Region	People employed (in 000s)
West Midlands	161
South-East	150
North-West	71
Scotland	22
Wales	21
East Midlands	18
Yorkshire and Humberside	17
Northern Ireland	16
South-West	14
East Anglia	11
North	8

Figure 14.14 Number of people employed in vehicle manufacture 1981

Figure 14.15 The Austin-Rover factory, Longbridge, West Midlands

Questions

1. What factors caused the motor vehicle industry to locate originally in the Midlands and South-East?
2. a) The car industry is increasingly organised on a world scale by international companies. Discuss the effects of this on Britain.
   b) The Nissan Company, has built its new plant in Washington, near Sunderland. Try to find out its reasons for this decision.
3. Why do you think there were labour problems in the British car industry in the 1970s? What is it about production lines and car assembly techniques that perhaps leads to labour problems?
4. On a map of the United Kingdom place the figures from Fig. 14.14 as a bar on each region to show the distribution of employment nationally in the car industry.

Database: traditional manufacturing and twentieth-century industry

Figure 14.16 Employment by industry (1000's) in United Kingdom 1984

	Males	Females	Total
Agriculture, forestry and fishing	256	84	340
Energy and water supply industries	547	83	630
Extraction of minerals and ores other than fuels, manufacture of metals, mineral products and chemicals	642	153	794
Metal goods, engineering and vehicle industries	2,054	541	2,595
Other manufacturing industries	1,239	889	2,128
Construction	864	120	984
Distribution, hotels, catering and repairs	1,976	2,348	4,323
Transport and communications	1,038	266	1,304
Banking, finance, insurance, business services, leasing	968	912	1,881
Other services	2,258	3,925	6,183
All industries and services	11,841	9,321	21,162

Source: Department of Employment

Figure 14.17 Women's hourly earnings, by employment, compared to men's – 1984

Female police officer	91.3% of male hourly earnings
Female nurse	89.6% of male hourly earnings
Female laboratory technician	78.9% of male hourly earnings
Female sales supervisor	67.0% of male hourly earnings

Source: New Society 3rd October 1986

Figure 14.20 The location of Ford manufacturing and assembly plants worldwide

Argentina	New Zealand
Australia	Philippines
Belgium	Portugal
Brazil	South Africa
Canada	Spain
France	Taiwan
W Germany	United Kingdom
Japan	USA
Malaysia	Uruguay
Mexico	Venezuela

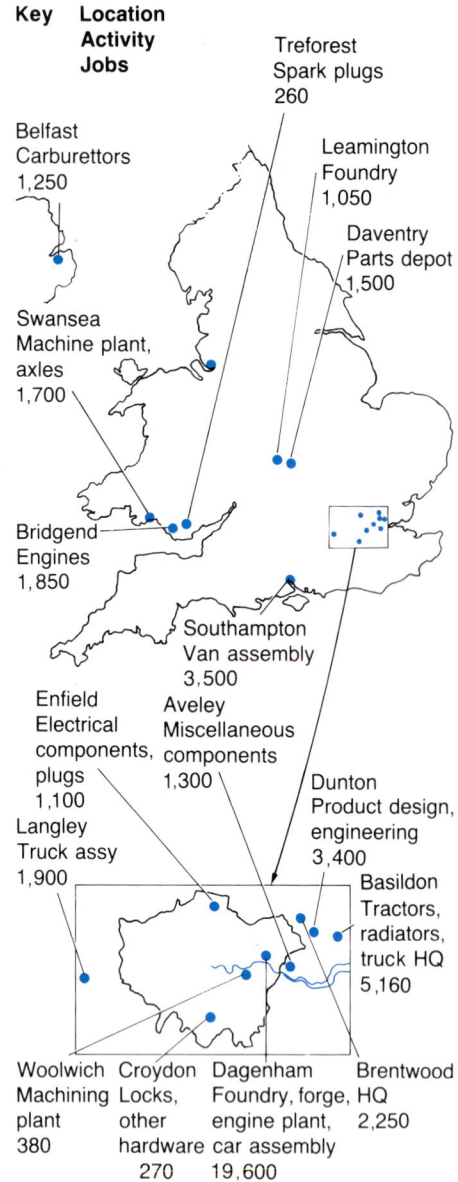

Key Location
     Activity
     Jobs

Belfast Carburettors 1,250
Treforest Spark plugs 260
Leamington Foundry 1,050
Daventry Parts depot 1,500
Swansea Machine plant, axles 1,700
Bridgend Engines 1,850
Southampton Van assembly 3,500
Enfield Electrical components, plugs 1,100
Aveley Miscellaneous components 1,300
Dunton Product design, engineering 3,400
Langley Truck assy 1,900
Basildon Tractors, radiators, truck HQ 5,160
Woolwich Machining plant 380
Croydon Locks, other hardware 270
Dagenham Foundry, forge, engine plant, car assembly 19,600
Brentwood HQ 2,250

Figure 14.18 Ford factories in Britain

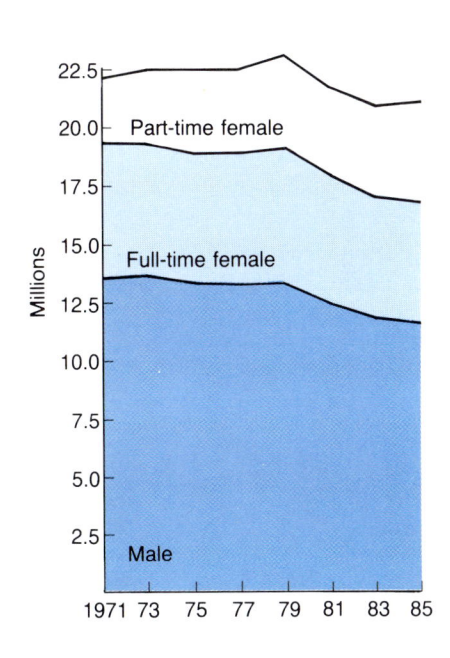

Figure 14.19 The growth of part-time work

Workbase

1. Figure 14.20 lists the location of major Ford Motor Company plants in Europe and the World. Identify the location of each of these plants, using an atlas, and create a rough world sketch-map to illustrate the caption' Ford – a multi-national company'.

2. Figure 14.18 shows the location of Ford Motor Company factories in the UK. Which factories do you think might be most vulnerable to complete closure, and why?

3. Ford (in partnership with Mazda cars) has decided to set up a £350 million factory in the developing (but deeply in debt) country of Mexico. What advantages are there for Ford in doing this?

4. Fig. 14.19 shows a growing amount of part-time labour in Britain between 1971–1985. Using this, and the information in Fig 14.16 write a paragraph on 'Britain's growing part-time economy'.

5. Consider Fig 14.16.
   a) In which industries are there the highest number of female workers?
   b) In which industries are there the highest proportions of female workers?
   c) What are the reasons for the past differences in male and female employment in some of the industries listed? Choose three industries and give your reasons.
   d) Do you expect such differences to continue in the future? Give reasons for your answer.

6. In some regions of Britain, there has been a sharp decline in traditional 'male-dominated' industries, but a rise in service industry employment. What effects may this have on the home life of some families?

7. Consider 14.17. Is there any justification for women being paid less than men? Why do you think that this is still the case in some industries?

Chapter 15
The second industrial revolution

De-industrialisation

Britain's highest unemployment totals this century have been recorded in the 1980s. Many people accept that unemployment is likely to stay at a very high rate for many years to come, because it is 'structural' to our economic situation. Britain's old industrial base has shrunk and the country may need to adjust to new conditions over a period of many years. The experience of a second 'industrial revolution' may be as important – and for some people, as painful – as the first.

Figure 15.1 shows clearly the rapid growth in unemployment during the 1980s for the whole of Britain. Figure 15.2 helps to show what the unemployment situation is like for areas within Britain. But even these figures do not show up particular towns and localities. Consett in County Durham has 27 per cent of its workforce unemployed; parts of London also have unemployment rates of over 20 per cent. The table, Fig. 15.3, suggests the problem has eased, though only slighty, in the period 1983–6.

	1978	1980	1982	1984	1986
United Kingdom	5.2	6.2	10.9	11.7	11.9
North	8.1	9.9	15.5	17.0	17.1
Yorkshire and Humberside	5.3	6.8	12.2	12.9	13.8
East Midlands	4.4	5.6	9.9	10.9	11.3
East Anglia	4.3	4.7	8.5	8.7	9.1
South East	3.6	3.8	7.7	8.4	8.7
South West	5.5	5.6	9.1	9.7	10.2
West Midlands	4.9	6.8	13.6	14.1	14.0
North West	6.5	7.8	13.6	14.5	14.5
England	4.8	5.7	10.4	11.1	11.3
Wales	6.9	8.4	13.8	14.2	14.5
Scotland	7.1	8.5	13.0	13.8	14.3
Northern Ireland	9.3	10.9	16.1	18.0	18.8

Source: Department of Employment.

Figure 15.1 Unemployment rates (percentages)

In the 1970s, when average unemployment rates were low (see Fig. 15.1.) the only places in Britain with serious job shortages (and an unemployment rate of approaching 10 per cent) were parts of the North, Wales, Scotland and Northern Ireland. The South-East had a surplus of jobs. By the mid 1980s there was no region which could be said to be free from the 'spectre of unemployment', although the southern half of the country is still cushioned to some extent.

The major reason for this unemployment is the rapid shrinkage of jobs in the traditional manufacturing industries. It is reflected by the fact that in 1983, for the first time ever, Britain imported more goods than she exported abroad. Britain is going through a period of **de-industrialisation**.

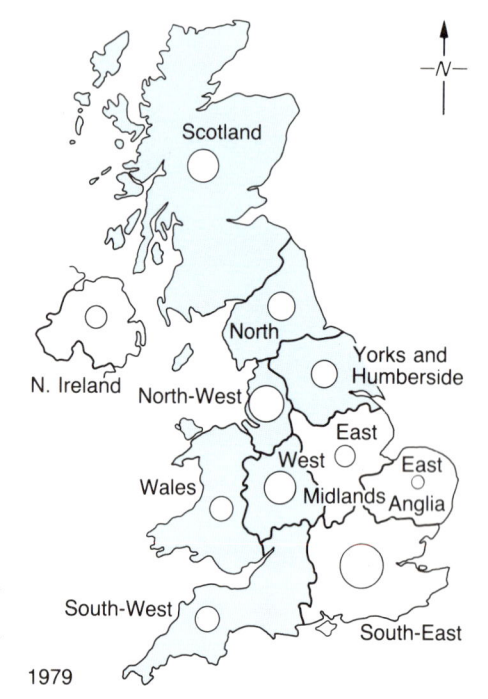

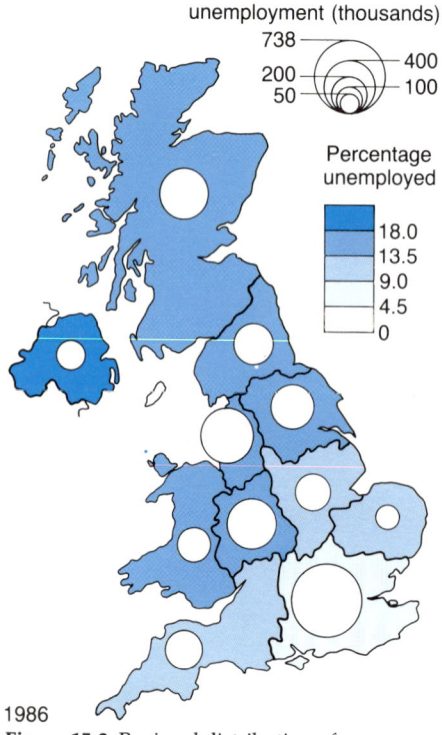

Figure 15.2 Regional distribution of unemployment, 1979 and 1986

Region	June 1979–May 1983	June 1983–May 1986
South-West	−84,000	+ 54,000
Wales	−145,000	− 30,000
West Midlands	−298,000	+ 78,000
South-East	−391,000	+269,000
East Anglia	− 15,000	+ 74,000
East Midlands	−132,000	+ 91,000
Yorkshire and Humberside	−240,000	+ 5,000
North-West	−374,000	− 41,000
North	−191,000	+ 20,000
Scotland	−204,000	− 12,000
Northern Ireland	?	?
United Kingdom	−2.071,000	+500,000

Source: Department of Employment

Figure 15.3 Britain's employment

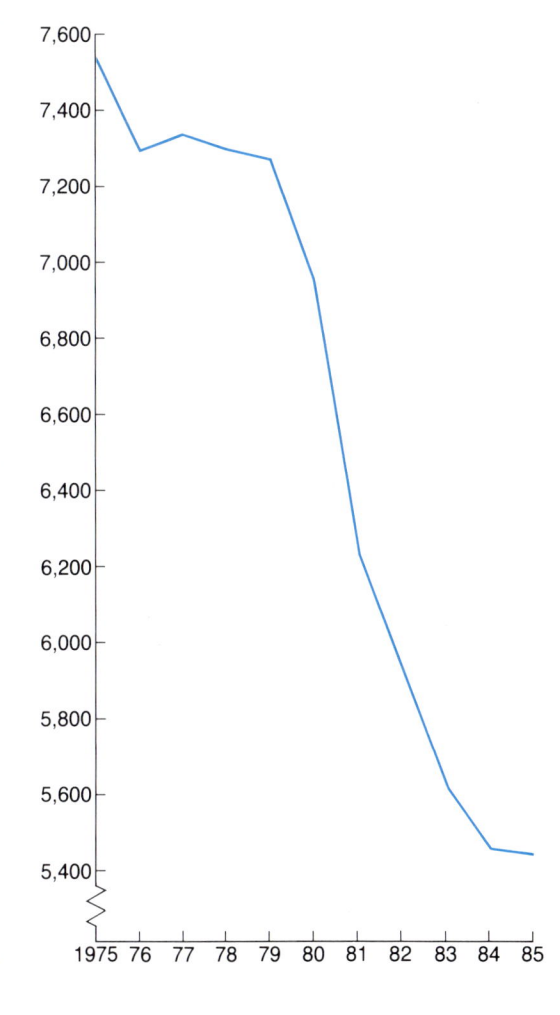

Figure 15.4 Employment in manufacturing in the UK, 1975–85

The reasons for de-industrialisation

No country would choose to de-industrialise and deliberately throw people out of work. But industries close and go bankrupt if they are no longer making the goods which people want, and if they are being pushed out of their markets by goods from other countries. If we allow a free market to goods from the rest of Europe, or from the rest of the world, we have to make sure that our own factories compete with them by making goods at a cheaper price and with similar quality. In recent years, the British consumer has tended to prefer German cameras, Japanese motorcycles, European fashion clothes and American machinery. The ease of transporting goods around the world makes international competition much fiercer than it was a hundred years ago. It is the choice of the consumer that decides which factories stay in business.

In Britain our own traditional industries have not found enough satisfied customers. Therefore some of our industries have had to rationalise. This means that a firm – or even a whole industry – cuts back on the number of factories in use or the amount of machinery in operation (and therefore on the number of people employed). The steel industry has undergone major rationalisation in recent years (see chapter 14) because the only way to stop losing large sums of money was to close down some of the older, less efficient works, despite the many problems which this caused for the communities which have long depended on them. By concentrating the manufacture of steel on to a few locations, the most modern methods can be used in the most economically-favourable places. The same story is true for chemicals, textiles, and motor vehicles. And as industries rationalise, so too do the coalfields which have traditionally supplied them – hence the closure of pits.

Restrictive practices by workers may also hasten closures. Headlines and articles such as those above are evidence of this. Some large international companies (such as Ford and ICI) rationalise their production not just within a single country such as Britain, but throughout a continent or throughout the globe. NEI (Northern Engineering Industries) is a creation of the 1970s. It came about when a number of engineering firms recognised that they might all go out of business if they did not combine and then reduce the total number of factories which they ran. They had to reduce their work force, but managed to maintain jobs for over half of their workers.

The other major reason for de-industrialisation and unemployment is **technical change**. Some firms which have *increased* their output and sales have done so whilst *reducing* the number of workers employed. In other words, productivity per worker (output) has increased. This is usually achieved through investment in new technology, which mechanises processes formerly done by hand; robots and computerised systems are now common sights in many manufacturing industries. Firms may be able to make a profit with the introduction of modern equipment – but jobs may nevertheless be reduced.

Figure 15.5 How the newspapers report job losses

Re-industrialisation

There is a theory that industry in a country like Britain experiences a sequence of 'booms' and 'slumps'. During the booms, investment increases so much that employment also increases; industry grows and everybody enjoys increasing wealth. During the slumps, industry and jobs decline; much rationalisation takes place and firms go out of business.

If this is true, then in the future we might expect a period of rapid expansion in industry ('re-industrialisation') to follow the present long slump. It is hoped by those who believe in the 'second industrial revolution' that Britain will expand rapidly in the '**new industries**'. The old, declining 'traditional' industries will be allowed to disappear and be replaced by the growing new industries which include micro processors and computers, bio-technology and other **high-tech** industries.

This hope is based upon what has happened in the USA. In California there is an area within Santa Clara County, near San Francisco, which has become known as Silicon Valley. This area has been the centre of a large number of developments in the micro-processor industry and has, between 1968 and 1978, generated 27,483 new jobs. Similar, but less dramatic, stories can be heard elsewhere in the USA's 'Sun Belt' which includes Texas, Arizona and Colorado, in addition to California. Cities such as Denver, Dallas and Houston are expanding very rapidly and are the industrial centres of the future, whereas elsewhere, the so-called 'Rust-Belt', cities like Detroit, Cleveland or Pittsburgh have serious unemployment problems, owing to the decline of the traditional industries of steel and motor vehicles.

Figure 15.6 Unemployment by state in the USA, 1981

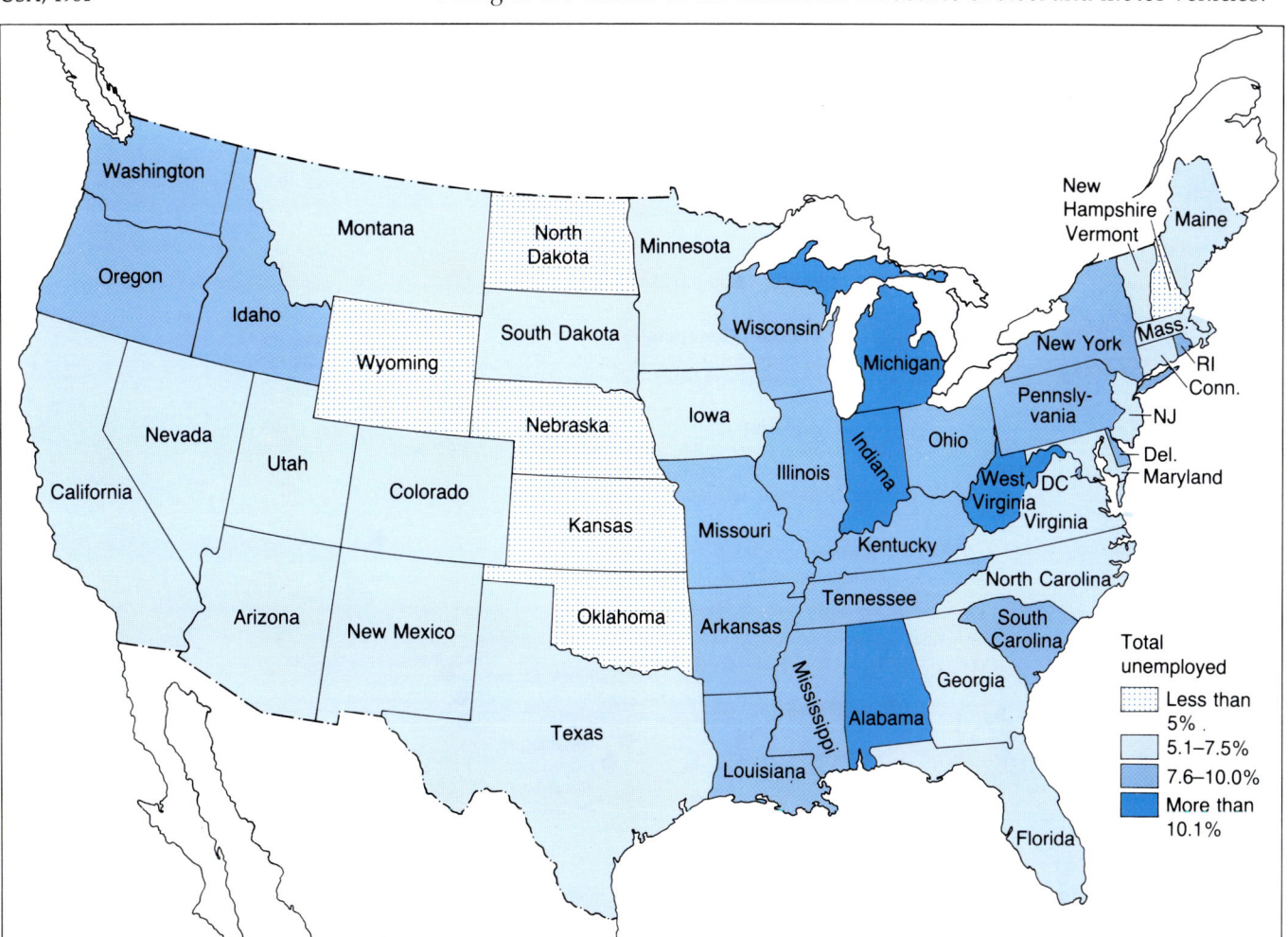

150 A Geography of Contemporary Britain

Questions

1. What do you think attracts high-tech industries to locations in the 'Sun-Belt'?
2. Do you think that the growth of these high-tech industries really provides job opportunities for unemployed workers in the 'Rust-Belt'? Try to give reasons for your answer.

One problem with re-industrialisation happening in a different region from the industrial decline is that unemployed workers have to move to get one of the new jobs. A greater problem, however, is that unemployed car workers or steel workers probably do not have the right **skills** to be employed in the new industry. People with the right 'high-tech' skills, though, are more **mobile** and are able to move to the new jobs which are found in attractive areas (with sun, mountains and the outdoor life). The firms themselves are very **footloose**, which means they have a great choice of location and, unlike older, traditional industries, are not bound by raw materials or even transport costs. So long as there are good roads, an airport and land available, any number of locations would do – so why not choose the most attractive?

Figure 15.7 Silicon Glen investment, 1980–84

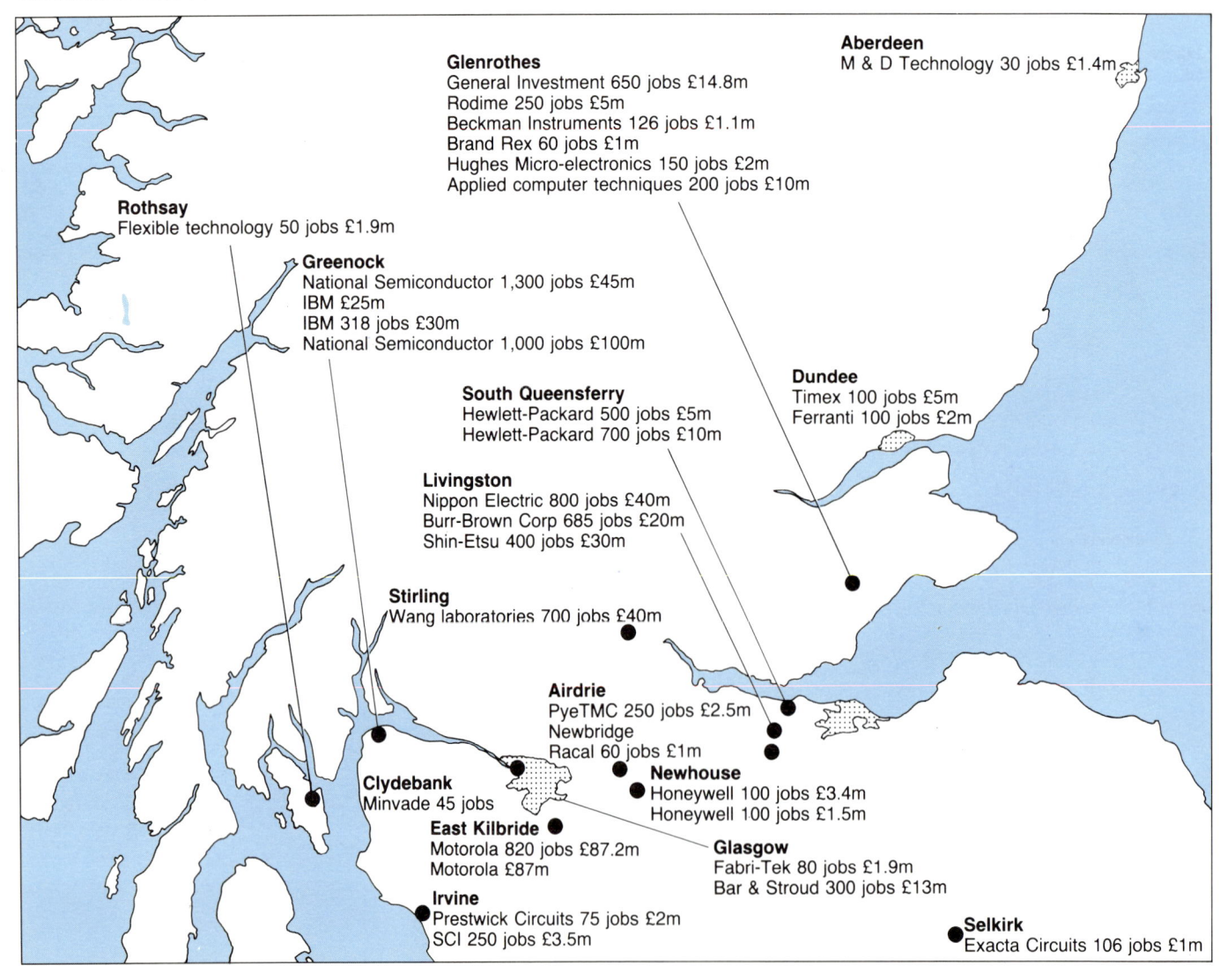

Aberdeen
M & D Technology 30 jobs £1.4m

Glenrothes
General Investment 650 jobs £14.8m
Rodime 250 jobs £5m
Beckman Instruments 126 jobs £1.1m
Brand Rex 60 jobs £1m
Hughes Micro-electronics 150 jobs £2m
Applied computer techniques 200 jobs £10m

Rothsay
Flexible technology 50 jobs £1.9m

Greenock
National Semiconductor 1,300 jobs £45m
IBM £25m
IBM 318 jobs £30m
National Semiconductor 1,000 jobs £100m

Dundee
Timex 100 jobs £5m
Ferranti 100 jobs £2m

South Queensferry
Hewlett-Packard 500 jobs £5m
Hewlett-Packard 700 jobs £10m

Livingston
Nippon Electric 800 jobs £40m
Burr-Brown Corp 685 jobs £20m
Shin-Etsu 400 jobs £30m

Stirling
Wang laboratories 700 jobs £40m

Airdrie
PyeTMC 250 jobs £2.5m
Newbridge
Racal 60 jobs £1m

Clydebank
Minvade 45 jobs

Newhouse
Honeywell 100 jobs £3.4m
Honeywell 100 jobs £1.5m

East Kilbride
Motorola 820 jobs £87.2m
Motorola £87m

Glasgow
Fabri-Tek 80 jobs £1.9m
Bar & Stroud 300 jobs £13m

Irvine
Prestwick Circuits 75 jobs £2m
SCI 250 jobs £3.5m

Selkirk
Exacta Circuits 106 jobs £1m

The second industrial revolution

A final point to remember is that now the high-tech businesses have been established in these 'Sun Belt' locations, they will almost certainly remain there and keep growing in number. The single most important reason for this is '**linkage**'. This means that there are huge advantages to new firms to be located near to – and have links with – other, similar firms. These linkages are usually known as economies of **agglomeration** (see page 126).

So, is there any hope of a Silicon Valley happening in Britain? There is in fact *no* sign of any area of high-tech industrial growth in Britain approaching the importance or size of the original Silicon Valley. However, there are three areas in Britain which have seen some high-tech industrial growth:

- The 'M4 corridor' between London and South Wales. In particular, towns like Reading, Swindon and Bristol have benefited.
- The Cambridge area of East Anglia.
- Between Glasgow and Edinburgh in Scotland. This area is perhaps the most spectacular of the three and is now often referred to as the 'Silicon Glen' (see Fig. 15.8). The article from *The Guardian* describes the exciting prospects for industrial growth in this area, and some of the problems such new industrial growth fails to solve.

Question

1. Using a good atlas to help you, identify some reasons why each of the three areas listed above has attracted new industrial growth.
2. Discuss with a partner, or with your teacher, the idea of 'linkage' mentioned previously. What kinds of useful links might a high-tech firm miss out on if it were located well away from other similar firms?

Figure 15.8 *The Guardian*, 6 March 1984

Chips boost creates 1,000 jobs

A thousand jobs are being created on Clydeside through a £100 million expansion of the American-owned National Semiconductor's microchip factory at Greenock, where unemployment is around 20 per cent – a figure which could rise above 30 per cent if the Scott Lithgow shipyard were to close.

But there will be few opportunities for redundant shipbuilders. At least 60 per cent of the jobs will go to women and around half the jobs will be for professionals: 30 per cent graduate engineers and 20 per cent qualified technicians.

Mr Manuel Yuan, the UK managing director of National Semiconductor, said that 200 people had been recruited already for the four-year expansion programme and another 800 would be needed by 1987.

He agreed with estimates that Britain has only about 1,500 engineers qualified for microchip production and said that the company would try 'desperately' not to start importing these specialists.

Mr George Younger, the Scottish Secretary, said the importance of the investment lay not just in the size – Scotland's biggest foreign investment in electronics so far – or in the job potential. Rather, it lay in National Semiconductor's commitment to maintaining its Greenock plant at the forefront of chip technology.

The plan involves a high level of automation and will include by next year the production of six-inch wafers. Wafers are the razor-thin circular slices of ultra-pure silicon on which chips are built. The bigger the wafer, of course; the bigger the number of chips that can be manufactured cheaply, although with increasing difficulty because of the fragility of the material. The standard size of wafer up to 1980 was three inches across, and that meant around 250 chips per wafer. Now the industry's standard size is four-inch.

The six-inch wafers of Greenock, carrying nearly 1,000 chips each, will probably be the first in Europe.

Scotland has Europe's largest collection of foreign-owned chip factories. The value of its electronics products has grown by 80 per cent since 1975, compared with 18 per cent for the UK overall. Yet Britain, because of its home computer boom, is suffering more than any other country in the current world-wide famine of microchips. UK firms urgently need at least 30 per cent more chips than they can buy.

The company has had a chip plant at Greenock since 1972 and has already invested about £75 million there – partly because the factory had to be completely rebuilt after a fire in 1977. It currently employs 1,050 people at Greenock, a 60 per cent rise since 1982.

Sir David Nickson KBE DL, former President, Confederation of British Industry (CBI)

Jobs and our standard of living depend on industry and commerce. Yet few people want industry next door to them.

Some basic industries almost choose their own sites. Homes we live in are composed of bricks or cement made from materials dug from holes in the ground, conveyed in vehicles made, in part at least, from metals smelted from ores dug out of holes in the ground and powered by petrol extracted from rather deeper holes in the ground.

All of these minerals have to be taken from where nature put them. The aggregates used in building houses are fairly widespread and therefore cheap because they do not have to be carried far. Others such as the ores from which various fairly common metals are extracted are not so widespread and the sources of the rare metals used in electrical and photographic work are even less common. Thus, the locations of the initial stages of extractive industries are inevitably decided by nature.

Intermediate and finishing industries however are governed by different factors. In the old days when transport depended on horse and cart, artisans had to use local materials. Nowadays transport has become relatively cheap and machines can do the work — especially the boring repetitive work — previously done by hand. The pattern of industry has therefore changed and will continue to change as techniques improve. The pattern of demand also changes in line with taste and the change in price of goods and services. Whilst the considerations which determine location are less restrictive, these are factors which must be taken into account to ensure success.

This does not mean that an industrialist can or should be able to set up just where he fancies. It does mean that the planning system must take account of economic imperatives — to the need for efficient factories and offices with good transport and communication facilities as well as attractive scenery. The considerations are not necessarily compatible and it must be remembered that much of the countryside which we consider 'natural' is the product of development — perhaps unpopular at the time — made by our ancestors.

The planning system calls for planning permission before any significant development can take place. Development is defined very widely and includes not only building and engineering operations but any significant change of use of buildings or land. Fortunately for the health of our economy, planning authorities are required to grant an applicant this planning permission 'unless there are sound and clear-cut reasons for refusal'.

Each generation has its own priorities. The creation of the wealth which our generation inherited was certainly associated in some places with a ruthless disregard for what would now be called its environmental effects. Today industry remains the essential creator of material wealth but is increasingly skilful at showing that it is not only an essential part of the community but aims to be a good neighbour. It should be welcomed accordingly.

CONTRASTING VIEWPOINTS
'Should industry be free to locate where it prefers?'

Rt Hon David Blunkett Labour MP Former leader of Sheffield City Council

For those who believe that industry or services exist for people and not people for them, economic choices have to be balanced by social constraints.

There will clearly be times when there is a clash between the immediate interests of a company — often a multinational company — and a community, or the nation as a whole. Financial gain for one might be at the economic, social or environmental expense of a larger number of people. For instance, purchasing and then closing down a competitor in the same industry may be profitable for a multinational company but disastrous for the community and work force affected, and even for the balance of payments of the nation. It may be cheaper to site a chemical works near to an accessible road and rail network, or mineral resource, but doing so could destroy an area of natural beauty or a unique ecological site.

For those who believe that 'free market forces' should always have full play, and that we should not use the democracy at local government or national government level to intervene, any restraint on private enterprise is considered to be interference. Democracy was developed and extended, however, to do just that. To ensure that those who do not have wealth and power have the opportunity to have their interests promoted and protected.

That is why we have planning regulations, environmental protection and the protection of people's health and well-being to prevent the location of some activities in a particular site; factories, for instance, with hazardous emissions being placed near housing.

That is also why we need regional and local economic policies and financial incentives to encourage companies to locate businesses particularly in areas of high unemployment or severe structural change. Only if industry or services are socially owned can they be directed to a particular geographic area, but persuasion and financial inducements can go a long way to promoting a balanced policy which is in the interests of the vast majority.

Rural manufacturing industry

One feature of new high-tech industry in Britain is that it is located away from the old industrial conurbations and inner-cities. It is usually sited in new spacious factory units, well-planned industrial estates, and sometimes in a countryside setting. Figure 15.9 shows examples from the Cambridge area. The lack of an industrial estate does not necessarily prevent industry being set up in rural areas, as Fig. 15.10 illustrates. In the south Cambridgeshire village in which this photograph was taken there are manufacturing businesses in two old school buildings and the old village bakery, in addition to the building shown.

This out-of-town location pattern favoured by new high-tech industry is just part of the most powerful trend in manufacturing location in Britain since the 1960s: the shift of manufacturing activity and employment away from the large towns to small towns and villages. Figure 15.11 shows that during the 1970s the only growth in manufacturing jobs was in rural counties, and that the more urban an area the greater was the decline in its employment.

Figure 15.9 Four kinds of industrial estates in Cambridge a) a traditional estate b) multiple-use of an historic building c) a purpose-built development of small factory units by the City Council d) a privately-developed business park

Figure 15.10 The Multiprint factory. Industry can be inconspicuous in rural locations

Transcript of an interview with Multiprint

Question	Answer
'When did Multiprint start?	1978, in Royston. We had very cramped premises – just a garage really.
So, when did you come to Litlington?	In 1980. There was just me and one employee. I've had twenty-six jobs altogether and started printing as a kind of extra. Now, there are ten employees, plus me and my brother.
Ten! What kind of workers are they? Do they all live locally?	Oh, they're all 'unskilled' I suppose – no real *qualifications*. In fact skilled workers would be hard to find around here. Now, let's see . . . four live in the village, two in Steeple Morden, two in Biggleswade, one in Saffron Walden and one in Sandy. There is also a woman in the village who does our typing and another woman who does some book-keeping – both in the village.
So, what kind of products do you make?	We make stickers, sales displays and stuff like front-panel displays on amplifiers. We print T-shirts and that kind of thing.
Who for?	Well we've done stuff for BR, Estée Lauder, Rothmans and even Encyclopaedia Britannica.
How do you make contact with firms like that?	Through agencies. We sell through agencies. We have no salespeople. Business has been increasing at about 25 per cent per year.
Right, now for the important questions. Why Litlington? Why did you move here?	Well, we both lived here and the rent on the old bakery building was cheap – very cheap, much cheaper than Royston. Also, we were able to *buy* the premises . . . we'd never have been able to afford a real factory in the town. It was also quite convenient because we had some space at the back to build an extension – a more spacious, purpose-built unit.
When did you do that?	1983.
Was that easy?	Yes – but we had to build to a high specification and there was trouble with planning permission at first. After two *objections* to our plans we were granted permission, but we had to double-glaze all the windows, give it a tiled roof, cavity-wall insulation and even a special chimney pot.

Fig. 15.11 shows an increase in manufacturing jobs in rural countries – notably Hampshire, Cambridgeshire and Northumberland, even (in small absolute numbers) in the north-west Highlands of Scotland. But, for Britain as a whole, there was a massive decline in this period, owing to massive losses from the traditional centres of industry. This has been stemmed but not regained. These traditional centres were mostly in the large conurbations.

The reasons for the shift from urban to rural manufacturing can best be obtained by speaking to the 'new rural manufacturers' themselves. Below is a transcript of an interview with a rural industrialist, the result of a piece of fieldwork undertaken in the village of Litlington in South Cambridgeshire in October 1984.

And that satisfied all the villagers did it?	All except one – the next door neighbour. She's a right old complainer and she gets the Environmental Health people out regularly.
What for?	Complaints about the noise (all the guys like to have the radio on) and 'fumes'. Absolutely stupid. They're moving now so perhaps we'll get some peace.
Do you think you *are* noisy?	Not really. And her attitude is really counterproductive; because she's made such a noise we don't feel too sympathetic to her anymore – like, you know, we've just painted the outside – well we haven't painted the wall facing her! Saved us about £80.00!
Anyway, what do you think are the advantages of locating in Litlington?	Difficult to know where to begin really. . . . 1. Flexible. If business falls off we can just contract, maybe let out the factory unit to someone else. 2. No problem about inaccessibility – 10 minutes from Royston Station, London in 40 minutes. Also the customers like the easy parking. 3. Customers like visiting a village – down the pub for lunch, no stress. 4. Cheap, low rates. 5. Supplies are no problem – most suppliers deliver once a day from London. In emergencies we can use the Red Star same day service at Royston Station. . . . and I reckon that's about it.
Any disadvantages?	Sometimes special orders are tricky – if we have to cut special shapes or have to use a special finish and so on, because it's not worth stocking *all* the equipment. In these cases we have to hire equipment – maybe from Cambridge or Letchworth. But it's not too bad. All in all we are happy here – and the business is doing very well.'

Plate 33 British Isles: relief

This map shows higher areas in a yellow tint. Note that it does not include any of the human geography of the British Isles.

1. Attempt a freehand drawing of the shape of the British Isles. After four or five attempts, you should try to complete a recognisable rough copy in about one minute.

2. Identify the five highest mountain ranges and the five longest rivers in the United Kingdom.

3. Identify the location of the following major cities:
London, Birmingham, Liverpool, Manchester, Newcastle, Glasgow, Edinburgh, Southampton, Bristol, Cardiff, Swansea, Belfast, and Aberdeen. Check with your atlas to see if you are right.

Plate 34 British Isles: rock types

Compare this map with the relief map (Plate 33) of the British Isles. Use the table on page 11 to give you more information.

1. What kind of rocks chiefly make up: the Pennines, the Cambrian Mountains (Wales), the Southern Uplands (Scotland), and the North West Highlands (Scotland)?

2. From the evidence of the answers to question 1 can you make any positive statement about the relationship of the hardness of rocks and their age?

3. In which part of England would you find granite tors?

4. Where is the hub of the chalk hills which are common in southern England?

Plate 35 British Isles: climate

1. Which areas of the British Isles are warmest in a) January? b) July?

2. Which areas of the British Isles are coldest in a) January? b) July?

3. In which general direction does the temperature change throughout the year? Suggest an explanation.

4. In what way does the change in pressure (shown in isobars on the maps) affect the weather?

5. Which area of the British Isles has a) most annual rainfall? b) least annual rainfall?

6. In which general direction does the rainfall amount change? Suggest an explanation.

7. Suggest reasons why areas of Devon, Wales and Derbyshire should have a lower than average number of warm months compared to the areas surrounding them.

Plate 36 British Isles: population

The information on these maps is by county (see the map at the front of book)

1. Which counties show the highest percentage increase over the period 1961–1981? Suggest a reason for this increase.

2. Which counties show the highest percentage decrease in the period 1961–1981? Suggest a reason for this decrease.

3. Which counties have reversed a 1961–1971 decline in the 1971–81 period? Suggest a reason for both the decline and the subsequent change.

4. Identify the counties in which urban population is over 92 per cent.

5. Identify the counties in which more than 20 per cent of the population is OAPs. Suggest reasons for this uneven distribution in Britain.

ORKNEY ISLANDS
Westray
Sanday
Stronsay
Mainland
Scapa Flow
Hoy
South Ronaldsay
Pentland Firth
SHETLAND ISLANDS
Herma Ness
Unst
Yell
Fetlar
Mainland
Whalsay
Foula
Bressay
Sumburgh Head
Fair Isle
ATLANTIC OCEAN
NORTH SEA
IRISH SEA
Cape Wrath
Pentland Firth
Duncansby Head
Butt of Lewis
Flannan Isles
Lewis
Clisham 799
St. Kilda
Sound of Harris
Harris
North Uist
South Uist
Barra
Barra Head
Outer Hebrides
The Little Minch
The Minch
Inner Hebrides
Skye
Cuillin Hills 1009
Rhum
Coll
Tiree
Mull
Ben More 966
Thurso
Loch Shin
Oykel
Dornoch Firth
Loch Broom
Loch Maree
Ben Wyvis 1045
Moray Firth
Kinnairds Head
North West Highlands
Beauly
Loch Ness
Moriston
Loch Morar
Findhorn
Spey
Deveron
Don
Cairngorms 1311
Ben Macdhui
Dee
Grampian Mountains
Ben Nevis 1343
South Esk
Ben Lawers 1214
Loch Tay
Tay
Earn
Firth of Tay
Loch Awe
Ochil Hills
Firth of Lorn
Loch Fyne
Loch Lomond
Firth of Forth
Forth
Jura
Islay
Goat Fell 874
Arran
Firth of Clyde
Clyde
Holy I.
Malin Head
Rathlin I.
Mull of Kintyre
North Channel
Ayr
Southern Uplands
Tweed
Teviot
The Cheviot Hills
Merrick 843
Nith
Annan
Dee
Irthing
Tyne
Solway Firth
Luce Bay
Mull of Galloway
Cross Fell 893
Eden
The Pennines
Wear
Tees
Derwent
Lake District
Scafell Pike 978
Cumbrian Mts.
St. Bees Head
Isle of Man
Cleveland Hills
North York Moors
Flamborough Head
Ouse
Derwent
Morecambe Bay
Ribble
Aire
Don
Spurn Head
Humber
High Peak 636
Mersey
Derwent
Witham
The Wash
Trent
Norfolk Broads
The Fens
Great Ouse
Welland
Nene
Waveney
Lough Foyle
752 Errigal Mtn.
Foyle
Bann
Mts. of Antrim
Donegal Bay
Lough Neagh
Lower Lough Erne
Mourne
Blackwater
Strangford Lough
Erris Head
Upper Lough Erne
Mourne Mts.
Slieve Donard 852
Lough Conn
Moy
Achill I.
Clew Bay
Dundalk Bay
Erne
Lough Mask
Lough Corrib
Lough Ree
Slyne Head
Suck
Boyne
Galway Bay
Aran Is.
Shannon
Lough Derg
Lugnaquillia Mtn. 926
Wicklow Mts.
Nore
Barrow
Slaney
Suir
Shannon
Galty Mts.
Dingle Bay
Blackwater
Carrauntoohil 1041
Lee
Carnsore Point
Bandon
Dursey Head
Cape Clear
Anglesey
Conwy
Caernarfon Bay
Snowdon 1085
Dee
Cardigan Bay
St. George's Channel
Cambrian Mountains
Severn
Teifi
Wye
Avon
St. David's Head
St. Brides Bay
Usk
Black Mts.
Brecon Beacons 886
Tywi
Severn
Cotswold Hills
Thames
Chiltern Hills
Chelmer
St. Govan's Head
Carmarthen Bay
Bristol Channel
Thames
Isle of Sheppey
North Downs
Leith Hill 294
Lundy
Hartland Pt.
Exmoor Forest
Avon
Mendip Hills
Salisbury Plain
Test
Parrett
Torridge
Exe
Stour
Avon
New Forest
Arun
Rother
Dungeness
South Downs
Beachy Head
Solent
Isle of Wight
Bodmin Moor
Tamar
Dartmoor Forest
Lyme Bay
Bill of Portland
English Channel
Start Point
Land's End
Lizard Pt.
Isles of Scilly
Scale 1:4 000 000
0 50 100 150 km
Conic Projection
© Collins ◇ Longman Atlases

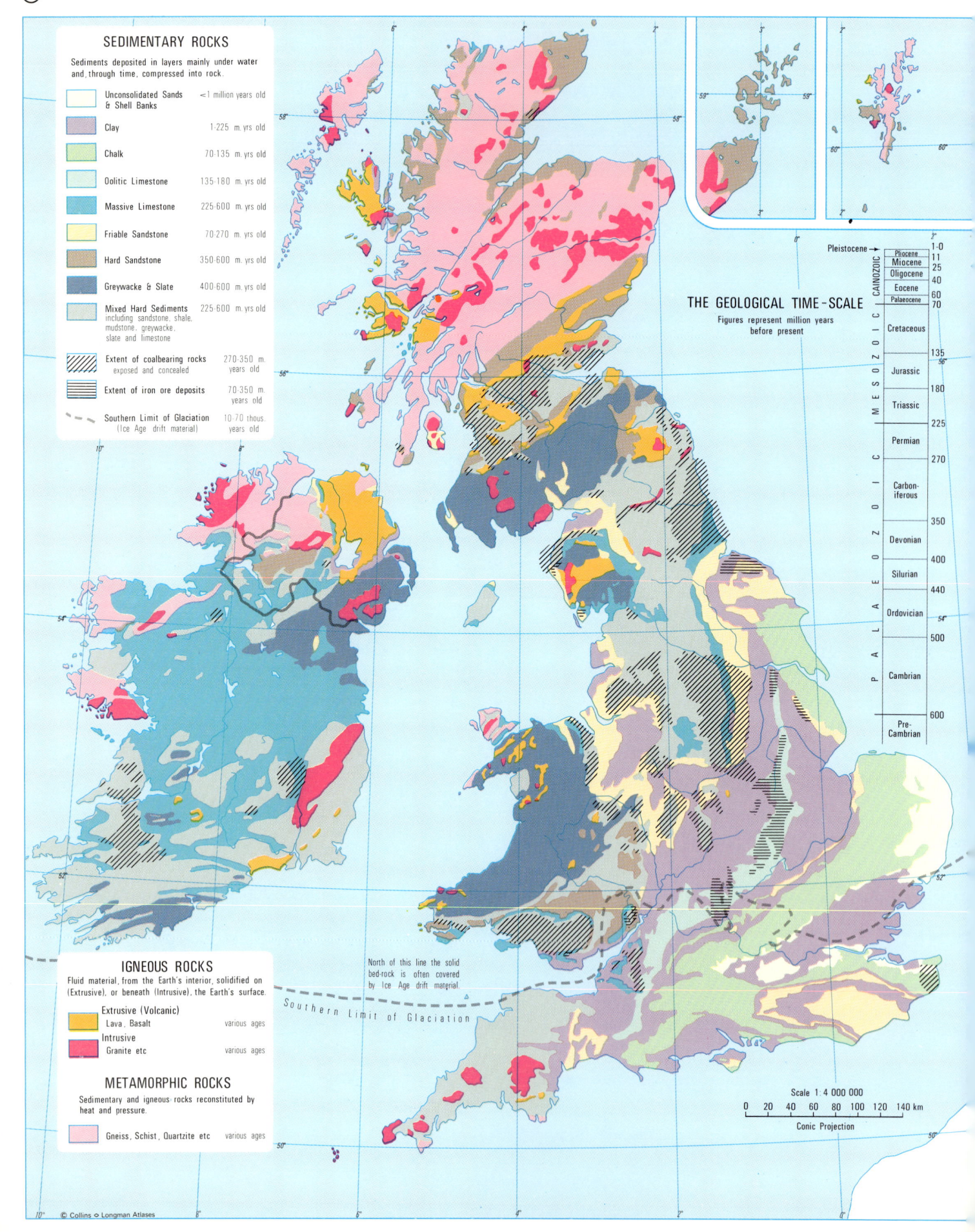

SEDIMENTARY ROCKS
Sediments deposited in layers mainly under water and, through time, compressed into rock.

	Unconsolidated Sands & Shell Banks	<1 million years old
	Clay	1-225 m. yrs old
	Chalk	70-135 m. yrs old
	Oolitic Limestone	135-180 m. yrs old
	Massive Limestone	225-600 m. yrs old
	Friable Sandstone	70-270 m. yrs old
	Hard Sandstone	350-600 m. yrs old
	Greywacke & Slate	400-600 m. yrs old
	Mixed Hard Sediments including sandstone, shale, mudstone, greywacke, slate and limestone	225-600 m. yrs old
	Extent of coalbearing rocks exposed and concealed	270-350 m. years old
	Extent of iron ore deposits	70-350 m. years old
	Southern Limit of Glaciation (Ice Age drift material)	10-70 thous. years old

IGNEOUS ROCKS
Fluid material, from the Earth's interior, solidified on (Extrusive), or beneath (Intrusive), the Earth's surface.

	Extrusive (Volcanic) Lava, Basalt	various ages
	Intrusive Granite etc	various ages

METAMORPHIC ROCKS
Sedimentary and igneous rocks reconstituted by heat and pressure.

	Gneiss, Schist, Quartzite etc	various ages

THE GEOLOGICAL TIME-SCALE
Figures represent million years before present

Era	Period	Million years
CAINOZOIC	Pleistocene	1-0
	Pliocene	11
	Miocene	25
	Oligocene	40
	Eocene	60
	Palaeocene	70
MESOZOIC	Cretaceous	135
	Jurassic	180
	Triassic	225
PALAEOZOIC	Permian	270
	Carboniferous	350
	Devonian	400
	Silurian	440
	Ordovician	500
	Cambrian	600
	Pre-Cambrian	

North of this line the solid bed-rock is often covered by Ice Age drift material.

Southern Limit of Glaciation

Scale 1:4 000 000
0 20 40 60 80 100 120 140 km
Conic Projection

© Collins ○ Longman Atlases

ACTUAL SURFACE TEMPERATURE & PRESSURE
January

°C
- 16
- 14
- 12
- 10
- 8
- 6
- 4
- 2
- 0

Isobars in millibars reduced to sea level

Scale 1:10 000 000
0 100 200 300km

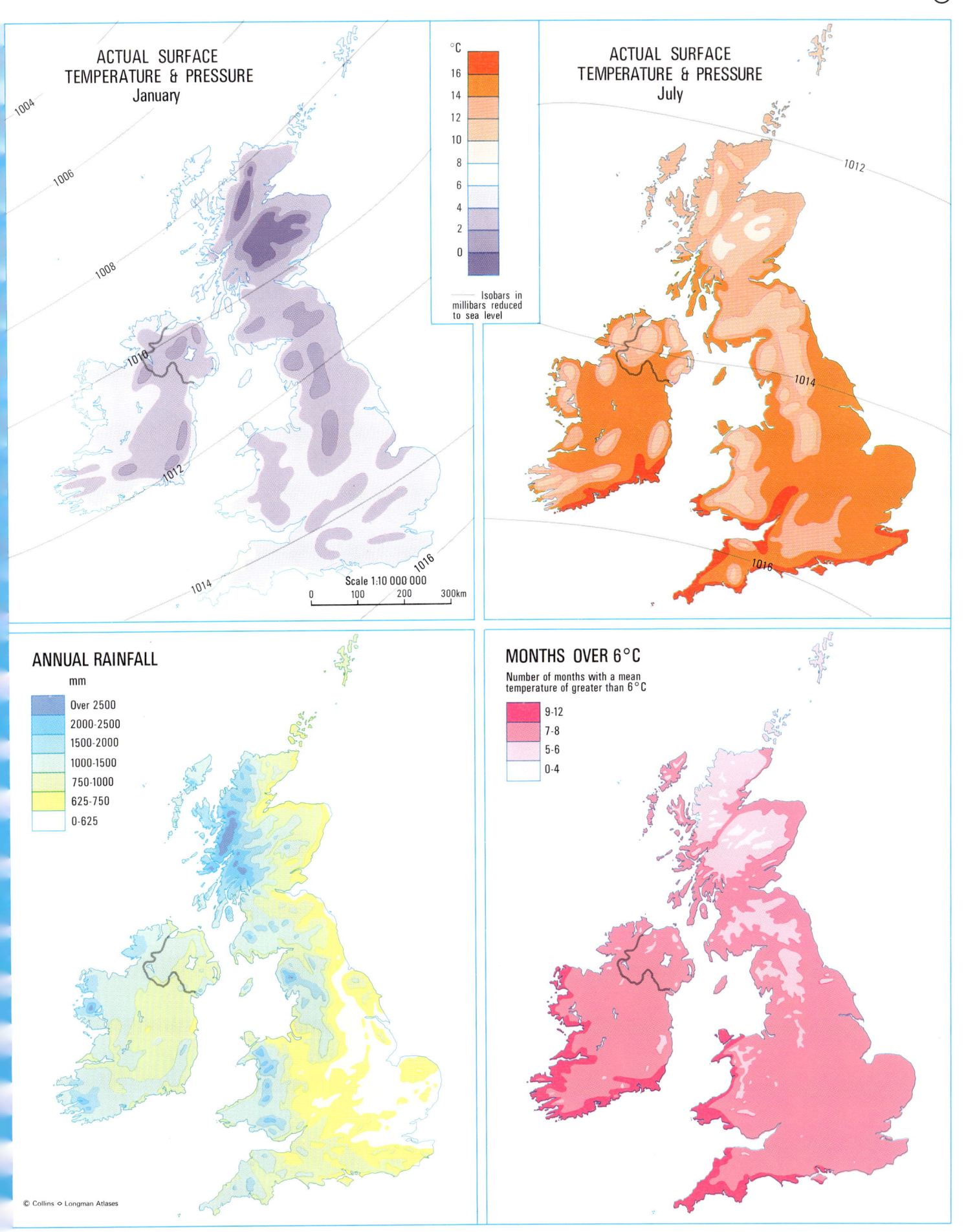

ACTUAL SURFACE TEMPERATURE & PRESSURE
July

ANNUAL RAINFALL

mm
- Over 2500
- 2000-2500
- 1500-2000
- 1000-1500
- 750-1000
- 625-750
- 0-625

MONTHS OVER 6°C

Number of months with a mean temperature of greater than 6°C
- 9-12
- 7-8
- 5-6
- 0-4

© Collins ◊ Longman Atlases

POPULATION CHANGE, 1961-1971

Percentage increase or decrease over decade

- 17·1–24·0
- 11·1–17·0
- 5·1–11·0
- 0·6–5·0
- −5·9–0·5
- −11·0–−6·0

Average: 5·1%

Note: Irish data has been mapped by province on this map

Sources: Censuses of Population

POPULATION CHANGE, 1971-1981

Percentage increase or decrease over decade

- 24·1–47·0
- 17·1–24·0
- 11·1–17·0
- 5·1–11·0
- 0·4–5·0
- −5·9–0·3
- −11·0–−6·0

Average: 0·3%

Sources: Censuses of Population

URBAN/RURAL POPULATION

Percentage of urban dwellers

- 98·1–100·0
- 92·1–98·0
- 89·6–92·0
- 75·1–89·5
- 49·1–75·0
- 27·0–49·0

Average: 89·6%

No comparable data available

Source: Census of Population, 1981

PENSION AGE POPULATION

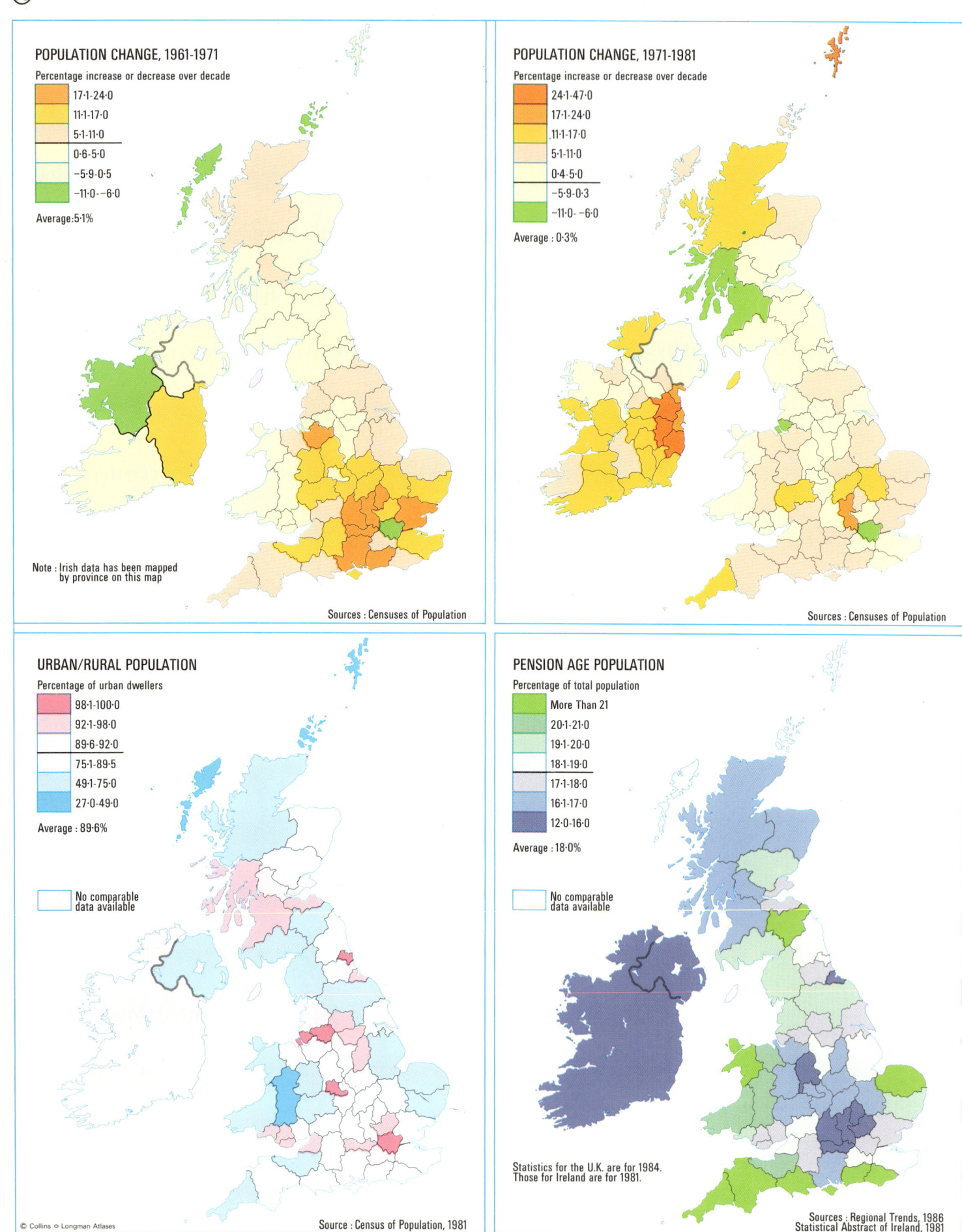

Percentage of total population

- More Than 21
- 20·1–21·0
- 19·1–20·0
- 18·1–19·0
- 17·1–18·0
- 16·1–17·0
- 12·0–16·0

Average: 18·0%

No comparable data available

Statistics for the U.K. are for 1984. Those for Ireland are for 1981.

Sources: Regional Trends, 1986
Statistical Abstract of Ireland, 1981

© Collins ○ Longman Atlases

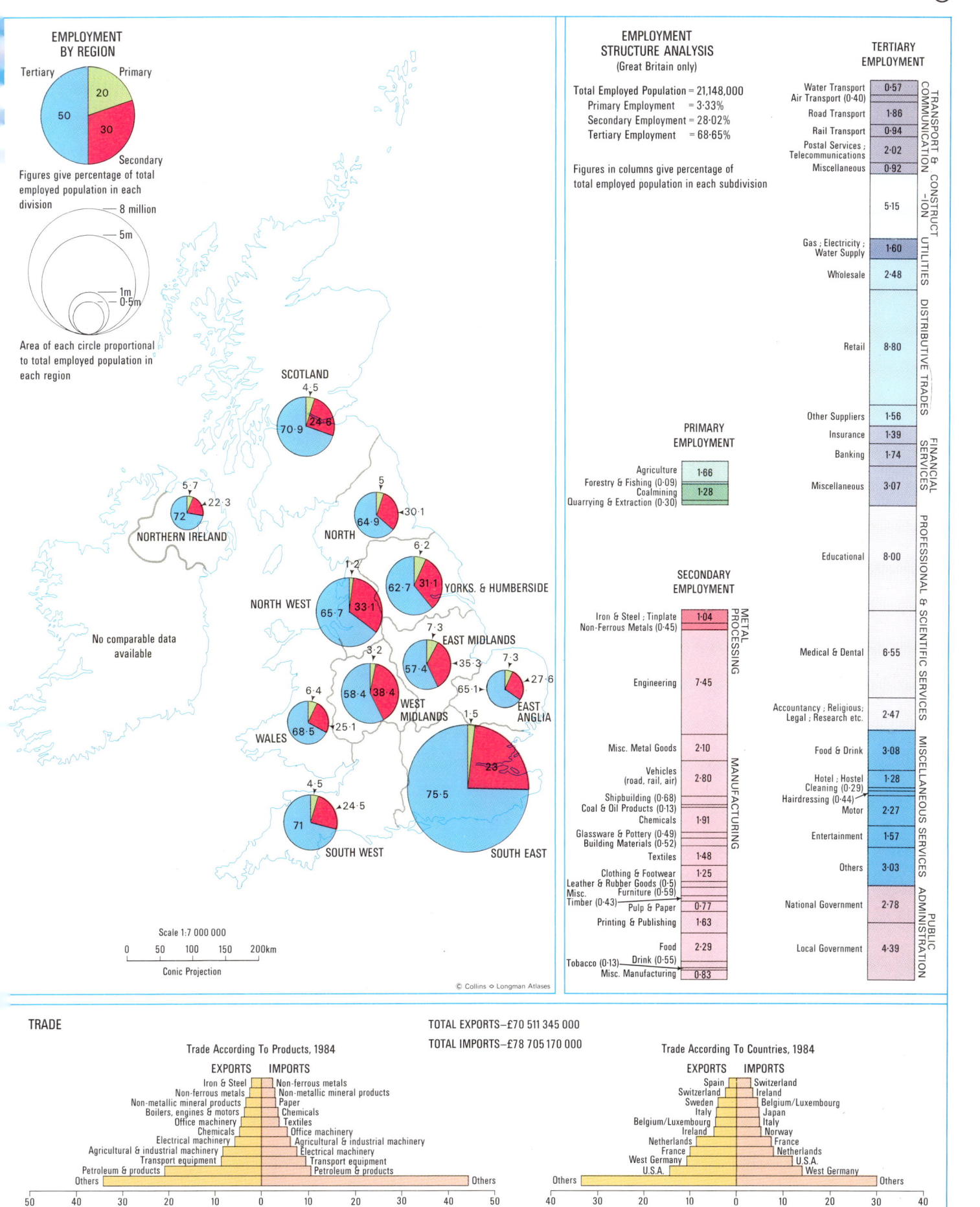

EMPLOYMENT BY REGION

Tertiary 50 | Primary 20 | Secondary 30

Figures give percentage of total employed population in each division

Circle sizes: 8 million, 5m, 1m, 0.5m
Area of each circle proportional to total employed population in each region

Regional pie chart figures (Primary / Secondary / Tertiary)

- **SCOTLAND**: 4.5 / 24.6 / 70.9
- **NORTHERN IRELAND**: 5.7 / 22.3 / 72 (No comparable data available)
- **NORTH**: 5 / 30.1 / 64.9
- **YORKS. & HUMBERSIDE**: 6.2 / 31.1 / 62.7
- **NORTH WEST**: 1.2 / 33.1 / 65.7
- **EAST MIDLANDS**: 7.3 / 35.3 / 57.4
- **WEST MIDLANDS**: 3.2 / 38.4 / 58.4
- **EAST ANGLIA**: 7.3 / 27.6 / 65.1
- **WALES**: 6.4 / 25.1 / 68.5
- **SOUTH WEST**: 4.5 / 24.5 / 71
- **SOUTH EAST**: 1.5 / 23 / 75.5

Scale 1:7 000 000 — 0 50 100 150 200km — Conic Projection

© Collins ○ Longman Atlases

EMPLOYMENT STRUCTURE ANALYSIS
(Great Britain only)

- Total Employed Population = 21,148,000
- Primary Employment = 3.33%
- Secondary Employment = 28.02%
- Tertiary Employment = 68.65%

Figures in columns give percentage of total employed population in each subdivision

PRIMARY EMPLOYMENT

	%
Agriculture	1.66
Forestry & Fishing	0.09
Coalmining	1.28
Quarrying & Extraction	0.30

SECONDARY EMPLOYMENT

METAL PROCESSING
	%
Iron & Steel ; Tinplate	1.04
Non-Ferrous Metals	0.45

MANUFACTURING
	%
Engineering	7.45
Misc. Metal Goods	2.10
Vehicles (road, rail, air)	2.80
Shipbuilding	0.68
Coal & Oil Products	0.13
Chemicals	1.91
Glassware & Pottery	0.49
Building Materials	0.52
Textiles	1.48
Clothing & Footwear	1.25
Leather & Rubber Goods	0.5
Misc. Furniture	0.59
Timber	0.43
Pulp & Paper	0.77
Printing & Publishing	1.63
Food	2.29
Tobacco	0.13
Drink	0.55
Misc. Manufacturing	0.83

TERTIARY EMPLOYMENT

TRANSPORT & COMMUNICATION
	%
Water Transport	0.57
Air Transport	0.40
Road Transport	1.86
Rail Transport	0.94
Postal Services ; Telecommunications	2.02
Miscellaneous	0.92

CONSTRUCTION: 5.15

UTILITIES
	%
Gas ; Electricity ; Water Supply	1.60

DISTRIBUTIVE TRADES
	%
Wholesale	2.48
Retail	8.80
Other Suppliers	1.56

FINANCIAL SERVICES
	%
Insurance	1.39
Banking	1.74
Miscellaneous	3.07

PROFESSIONAL & SCIENTIFIC SERVICES
	%
Educational	8.00
Medical & Dental	6.55
Accountancy ; Religious; Legal ; Research etc.	2.47

MISCELLANEOUS SERVICES
	%
Food & Drink	3.08
Hotel ; Hostel	1.28
Cleaning	0.29
Hairdressing	0.44
Motor	2.27
Entertainment	1.57
Others	3.03

PUBLIC ADMINISTRATION
	%
National Government	2.78
Local Government	4.39

TRADE

TOTAL EXPORTS — £70 511 345 000
TOTAL IMPORTS — £78 705 170 000

Trade According To Products, 1984

EXPORTS (top to bottom, ascending values):
Iron & Steel, Non-ferrous metals, Non-metallic mineral products, Boilers, engines & motors, Office machinery, Chemicals, Electrical machinery, Agricultural & industrial machinery, Transport equipment, Petroleum & products, Others

IMPORTS:
Non-ferrous metals, Non-metallic mineral products, Paper, Chemicals, Textiles, Office machinery, Agricultural & industrial machinery, Electrical machinery, Transport equipment, Petroleum & products, Others

Percentage of total exports/imports (scale 50 to 50)

Trade According To Countries, 1984

EXPORTS:
Spain, Switzerland, Sweden, Italy, Belgium/Luxembourg, Ireland, Netherlands, France, West Germany, U.S.A., Others

IMPORTS:
Switzerland, Ireland, Belgium/Luxembourg, Japan, Italy, Norway, France, Netherlands, U.S.A., West Germany, Others

Percentage of total exports/imports (scale 40 to 40)

AGRICULTURE

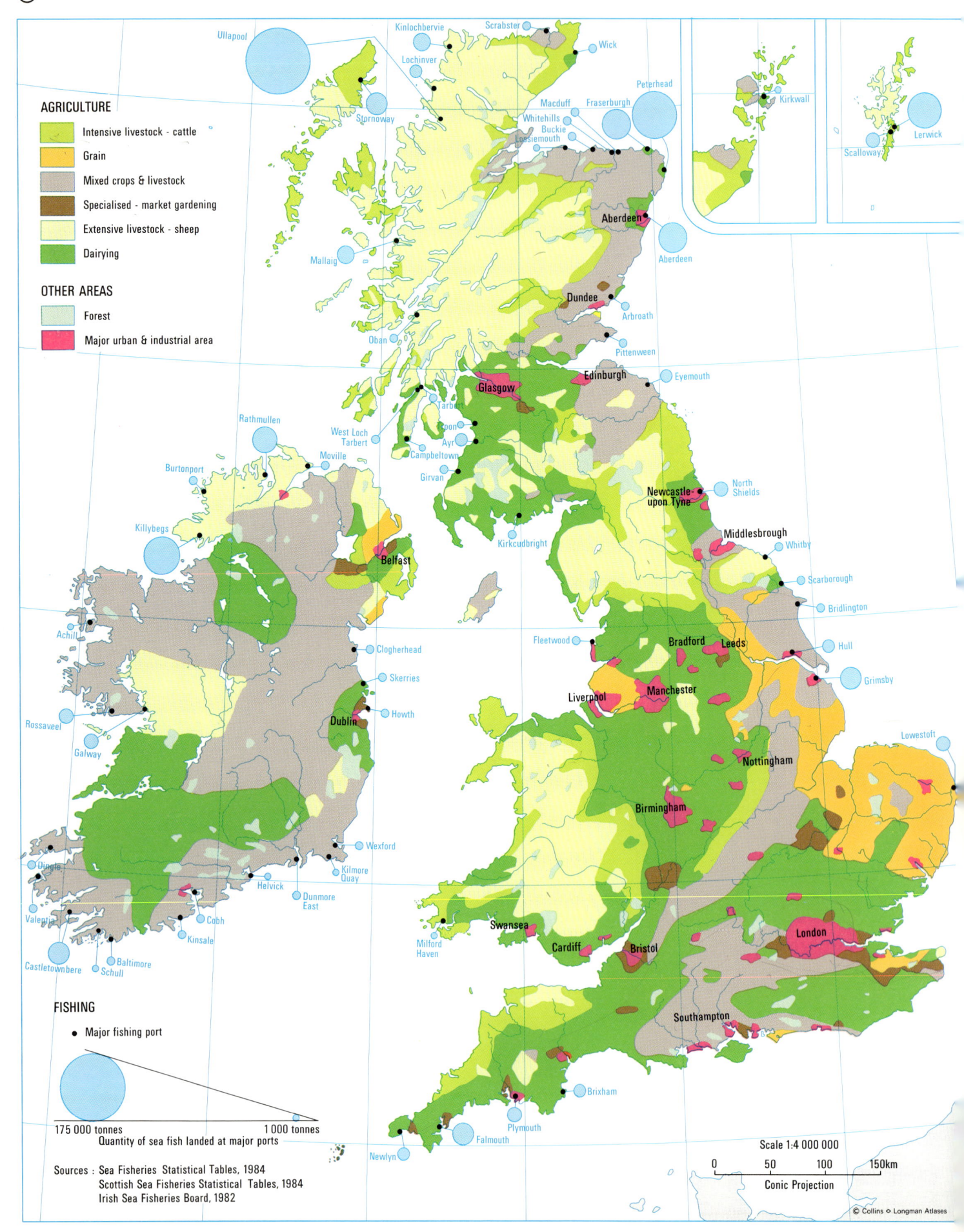

- Intensive livestock - cattle
- Grain
- Mixed crops & livestock
- Specialised - market gardening
- Extensive livestock - sheep
- Dairying

OTHER AREAS

- Forest
- Major urban & industrial area

FISHING

- Major fishing port

175 000 tonnes — 1 000 tonnes
Quantity of sea fish landed at major ports

Sources: Sea Fisheries Statistical Tables, 1984
Scottish Sea Fisheries Statistical Tables, 1984
Irish Sea Fisheries Board, 1982

Scale 1:4 000 000
0 50 100 150km
Conic Projection

© Collins ◇ Longman Atlases

Production of Oil, Coal and Natural Gas

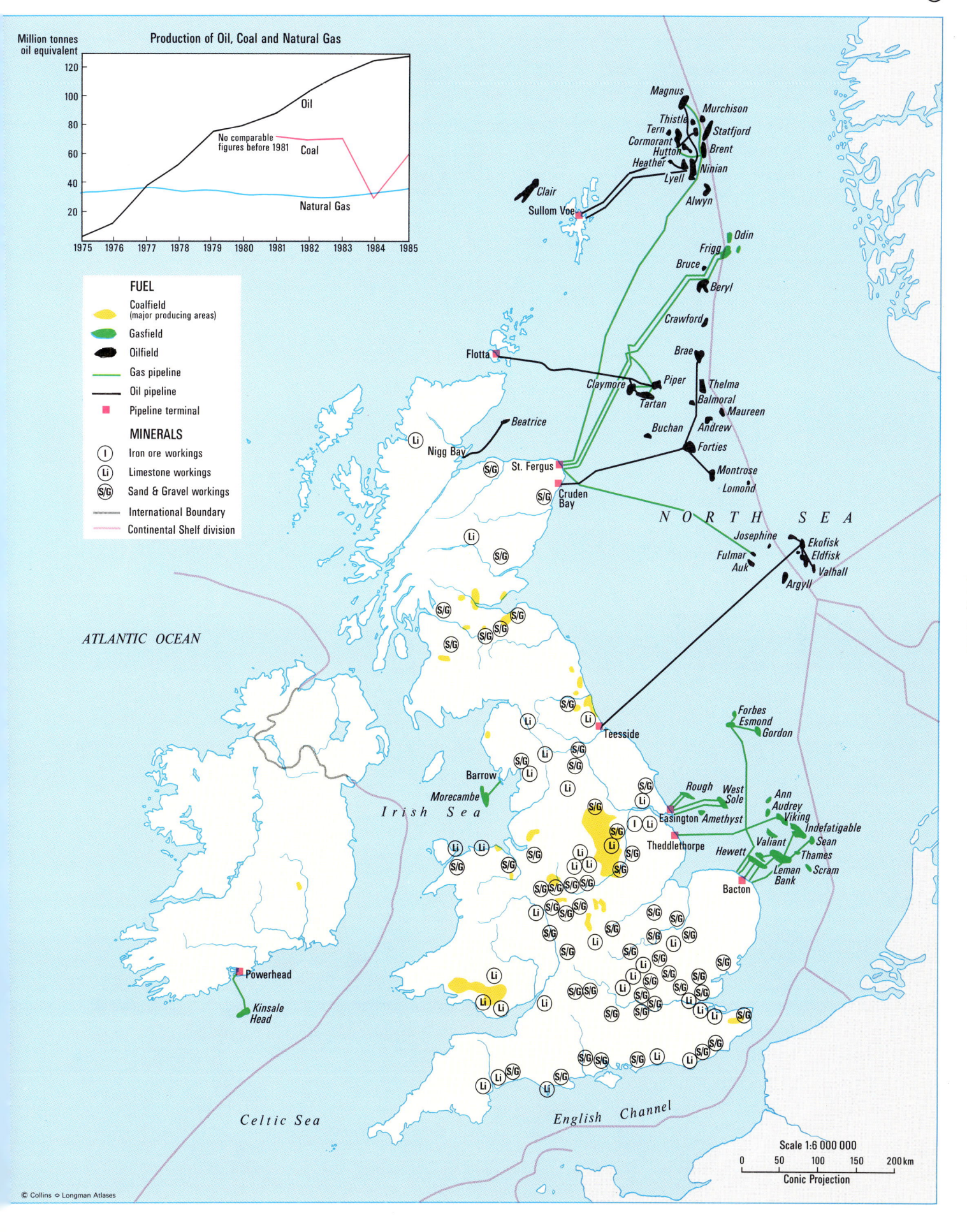

FUEL
- Coalfield (major producing areas)
- Gasfield
- Oilfield
- Gas pipeline
- Oil pipeline
- Pipeline terminal

MINERALS
- I Iron ore workings
- Li Limestone workings
- S/G Sand & Gravel workings
- International Boundary
- Continental Shelf division

Oilfields and gasfields (North Sea):
Magnus, Murchison, Thistle, Statfjord, Tern, Cormorant, Brent, Hutton, Heather, Ninian, Lyell, Alwyn, Clair, Sullom Voe, Odin, Frigg, Bruce, Beryl, Crawford, Brae, Thelma, Piper, Balmoral, Claymore, Tartan, Maureen, Buchan, Andrew, Forties, Montrose, Lomond, Josephine, Ekofisk, Eldfisk, Fulmar, Auk, Valhall, Argyll

Forbes, Esmond, Gordon, Rough, West Sole, Ann, Audrey, Viking, Indefatigable, Amethyst, Valiant, Sean, Hewett, Thames, Leman Bank, Scram

Terminals/locations: Flotta, Beatrice, Nigg Bay, St. Fergus, Cruden Bay, Teesside, Barrow, Morecambe, Easington, Theddlethorpe, Bacton, Powerhead, Kinsale Head

Seas: ATLANTIC OCEAN, NORTH SEA, Irish Sea, Celtic Sea, English Channel

Scale 1:6 000 000
0 50 100 150 200 km
Conic Projection

© Collins ◊ Longman Atlases

HOUSING STANDARDS

Percentage of households with no bath or shower

- 7·1–10·0
- 3·1–7·0
- 2·0–3·0
- 1·5–1·9
- 1·0–1·4
- 0–0·9

Average: 1·9%

No comparable data available

Source: Census of Population, 1981

CAR OWNERSHIP

Percentage of households with no car

- 52·1–60·0
- 46·1–52·0
- 39·6–46·0
- 32·1–39·5
- 28·1–32·0
- 20·0–28·0

Average: 39·5%

No comparable data available

Note: Irish data has been mapped on a regional basis

Source: Census of Population, 1981

HOUSE PRICES

Average price paid by Building Society borrowers

- £35 001–£40 000
- £30 001–£35 000
- £25 001–£30 000
- £24 001–£25 000
- £22 000–£24 000

Average: £30 000

No comparable data available

Source: Regional Trends, 1986

UNEMPLOYMENT

- 18·1–23·0%
- 16·1–18·0%
- 14·1–16·0%
- 12·1–14·0%
- 9·1–12·0%
- 5·0–9·0%

Average: 14%

No comparable data available

Note: Irish data has been mapped on a regional basis

Sources: U.K.–Employment Gazette, 1986
Ireland–Dept. of Social Welfare, 1983

© Collins ◇ Longman Atlases

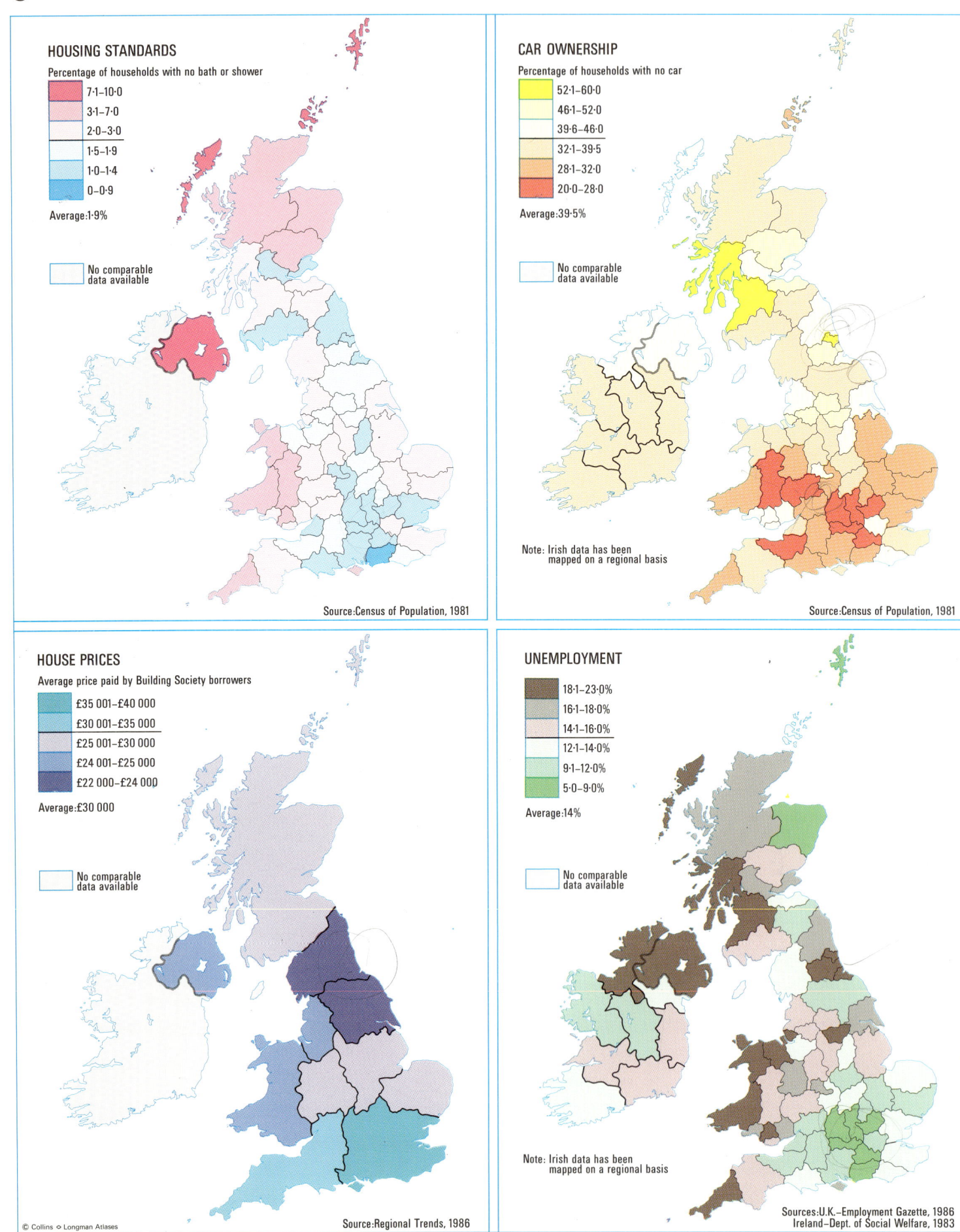

Plate 37 British Isles: employment and trade

1. In which areas of Britain would you find the greatest percentage of workers in a) primary industry? b) secondary industry? c) tertiary industry?

2. In which single area of Britain would you find the greatest *absolute number* of workers in these three industries?

3. Look at the employment structure analysis bar chart. Which industries are the leading employers in primary, secondary and tertiary sectors? Which industries would you expect to *grow* significantly in the future as employers?

4. Look at the trade pyramid graphs. In which industry do we export much more in value than we import? To which countries do we export much more than we import?

Plate 38 British Isles: agriculture and fishing

Compare this map with the maps of relief and climate (Plates 33 and 35).

1. Which are the major areas for a) sheep-farming? b) dairy-farming? c) grain farming? Do there appear to be any links between the major type of farming in an area and its climate? Or between farming and relief?

2. With which factor (shown clearly on the map) does market-gardening appear to be associated? Can you suggest a reason?

3. At which six fishing ports in the British Isles is the greatest quantity of sea fish landed? Why may these ports *not* necessarily be the biggest and busiest of the 'major fishing ports'?

Plate 39 British Isles: extractive industries

Compare this map with the map of rock types (Plate 34).

1. Does the location of mineral workings (iron ore, limestone, sand and gravel) bear any relationship to the pattern of rock types shown on Plate 34? What 'note' on the rock types map offers a clue to the distribution of sand and gravel workings?

2. What *other* minerals are mined in Britain, besides those shown on the map? (See Plate 12 for a clue.)

3. The discovery of natural gas has often preceded the discovery of oil. Where do you think future oil exploration may take place around the British Isles?

4. Which offshore oilfields appear to have the *cheapest* transportation costs? Why do you think that oil from the Ekofisk and Eldfisk fields on the Norwegian side of the international boundary, is piped to Britain and not back to Norway?

Plate 40 British Isles: social well being

1. Which areas of the United Kingdom have the greatest percentage of poor housing? Can you suggest a reason?

2. Compare the map of car ownership with the map of urban/rural population in Plate 37. Is there a link between high car ownership and living in the countryside? Which areas have over 52 per cent of households without a car?

3. Compare this map with Fig. 12.5 on page 119. Which are the most 'expensive' places to live in the United Kingdom if you are seeking to buy a house?

4. Which were the areas of greatest unemployment in 1986? Which were the areas of least unemployment? Can you explain the low figures for north-east Scotland?

Database: the second industrial revolution

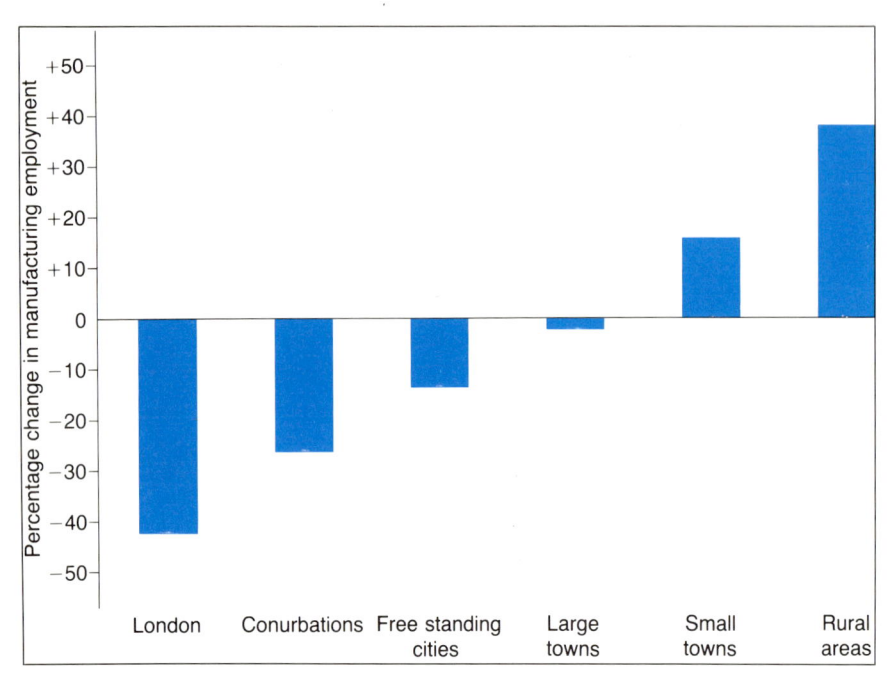

Figure 15.11 Manufacturing decline in areas of Britain 1960–78

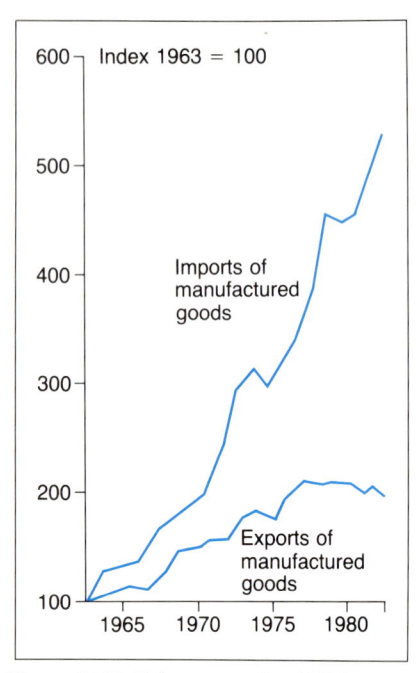

Figure 15.12 Volume growth of UK imports and exports of manufactured goods

Figure 15.13 Employment trends in major UK industries 1951–1981

Industry (thousands)	1951	1961	1971	1981	% change 1951–81
Agriculture, forestry and fishing	1,126	855	432	360	−68
Mining and quarrying	841	722	396	332	−61
Food, drink and tobacco	727	704	770	632	−13
Chemicals and allied trades	435	499	438	395	− 9
Metal manufacture	616	626	557	326	−47
Engineering and electrical goods	1,601	2,031	2,028	1,730	+ 8
Shipbuilding and marine engineering	277	237	193	144	−48
Vehicles	735	838	816	636	−13
Other metal goods	458	525	576	428	− 7
Textiles	986	790	622	363	−63
Leather, leather goods and fur	78	60	47	31	−60
Clothing and footwear	676	546	455	313	−54
Bricks, pottery and glass	314	321	307	216	−31
Timber, furniture	326	304	269	227	−30
Paper, printing and publishing	515	605	596	493	− 4
Other manufacturing industries	264	295	339	265	negligible
Total: Manufacturing	9,975	9,958	8,841	6,891	−31
Construction	1,388	1,600	1,262	1,132	−18
Gas, electricity and water	357	377	377	340	− 5
Transport and communications	1,704	1,673	1,568	1,440	−16
Distributive trades	2,689	3,189	2,610	2,635	− 2
Insurance, banking, finance	435	572	963	1,233	+183
Professional and scientific services	1,524	2,120	2,916	3,695	+142
Others, miscellaneous	3,485	3,519	3,379	3,993	+ 15
Total: Service sector	11,582	13,050	13,075	14,468	+25

Source: Central Statistical Office Annual Abstract of Statistics

Figure 15.14 UK Balance of Payments 1975 and 1985 (£m)

Exports	1975	1985
Food beverages & tobacco	1,388	4,931
Basic materials	556	2,161
Oil	734	16,050
Other mineral fuels & lubricants	93	662
Semi manufactured goods	5,851	20,043
Finished manufactured goods	9,987	32,237
Commodities & transactions not classified according to kind	731	1,968
Total	19,330	78,051

Imports		
Food, beverages & tobacco	4,089	8,523
Basic materials	1,967	4,795
Oil	3,791	7,887
Other mineral fuels & lubricants	121	2,200
Semi manufactured goods	5,355	19,958
Finished manufactured goods	6,746	35,339
Commodities & transactions not classified according to kind	594	1,461
Total	22,663	80,162
Visible Balance	−3,333	−2,111

Workbase

1. Consider the two maps in Fig. 15.2.
   a) Which regions had the highest and lowest unemployment percentages in 1979 and 1986?
   b) Which regions had the highest *total* of unemployed workers in 1979 and 1986?
   c) Which regions seem to have suffered least from increasing unemployment between 1979 and 1986?

2. Consider these four statements, and the other evidence in this book. Say which of these statements you believe to be true and *give the evidence for your answer*.

   - There is a division between the North and the South in the pattern of Britain's unemployment.
   - Britain increasingly has the same problems of unemployment in every region.
   - The biggest totals of unemployment are found in the regions which contain large cities or conurbations.
   - Unemployment is increasing in all regions in Britain.

3. Turn to Fig. 15.14 on page 158, which shows the changing balance of payments in the UK, and look at Fig. 15.12. Some people argue that we should 'protect' British industries from foreign competition by charging a tax on goods from other countries. This would make British-made goods appear cheaper and keep people in work, whilst providing the economy with more money. Can you see any *disadvantages* to such a policy?

4. Search for newspaper or magazine cuttings which describe firms being given new investment. Try to identify the kind of industry which is involved. A wall display to illustrate Britain's new industrial growth could be constructed.

5. How would you explain the location of the three growth areas of high-tech industries in Britain (the M-4 corridor, the Cambridge region, the central valley of Scotland)? See pages 149–155

6. Look at Fig. 15.13.
   a) List the five industries which have lost most workers in actual numbers between 1951 and 1981.
   b) List industries which have done well in the same period.
   c) Give two reasons for the decline in employment in manufacturing.
   d) List the five industries which have lost most workers in actual numbers between 1971 and 1981.
   e) Compare your list in d) with your list in a).
   f) What reasons can you find for any differences?
   g) What messages does the table give to school-leavers?

Chapter 16
The role of Government

The location of Britain's traditional industries was decided in the nineteenth century: the towns, cities and conurbations which lie on the coalfields are the evidence of this. But, today, the conditions that influence industrial location have changed, as have the nature of the industries themselves.

Nevertheless, we can write a list of factors which affect the location of industries, *though with different importance at different times in history*:

- **Raw materials** Are they bulky or difficult to transport?
- **Source of energy** Does the industry use a lot of energy?
- **Communications** Is the location well-served by transport links?
- **Land costs and availability** Is there room for vehicles to park, load and unload? Is there room for expansion?
- **Labour** Are workers easily available – especially *key* workers, who may have particular skills and expertise?
- **Environment** Is the location an attractive place to live and work in?

These are the kinds of questions that the board of a company might ask when it thinks about locating a new factory. But of course these factors do not affect all industries in the same way – just as they vary through time. In the nineteenth century Britain's industry was mostly influenced by raw materials and energy factors; in the twentieth century industry has become increasingly footloose. More recently, factors such as land availability and attractive environments have become important.

Thus, different parts of Britain have experienced dramatic changes in their fortunes. Boom-towns of the nineteenth century, such as Merthyr Tydfil on the South Wales coalfield and Consett in Durham, are now experiencing difficult times and needing to find a new industrial base; boom-towns of the mid 1900s, such as Coventry and Birmingham – the heart-land of engineering – now have some of the largest numbers of unemployed in Britain.

The health of industry is usually the key to the health of the community. Some parts of 'traditional Britain' are now 'depressed areas'. As far back as 1934 the Government of Britain began policies which tried to reduce the unfairness of this by encouraging firms to locate in these areas. For some firms, this action (**regional policy**) has been a more important factor in location than any of those listed above.

Regional policy

Regional policy, designed to influence industrial location (by the intervention of the Government), began in a fairly small way in the 1930s. It grew steadily, especially in the 1960s, and was at its greatest extent in the 1970s. The Governments of the 1980s have reduced it again – preferring to allow industrialists to make a 'free market decision'. Sometimes, if the company is a multinational, the decision is made by a company head office located beyond Britain's shores.

The policies are of three major kinds:

- **financial incentives** given to companies to encourage them to move to or expand in particular areas (known as **Assisted Areas** – see Fig. 16.1);
- **planning controls** which limit industrial development and building *outside* these areas;
- **direct intervention** by building up the infrastructure (e.g. roads, environmental improvements) within the Assisted Areas. This may not only make the region more attractive to industrialists but also create jobs in the construction industry.

Figure 16.1 Assisted areas and enterprise zones in Britain, 1984

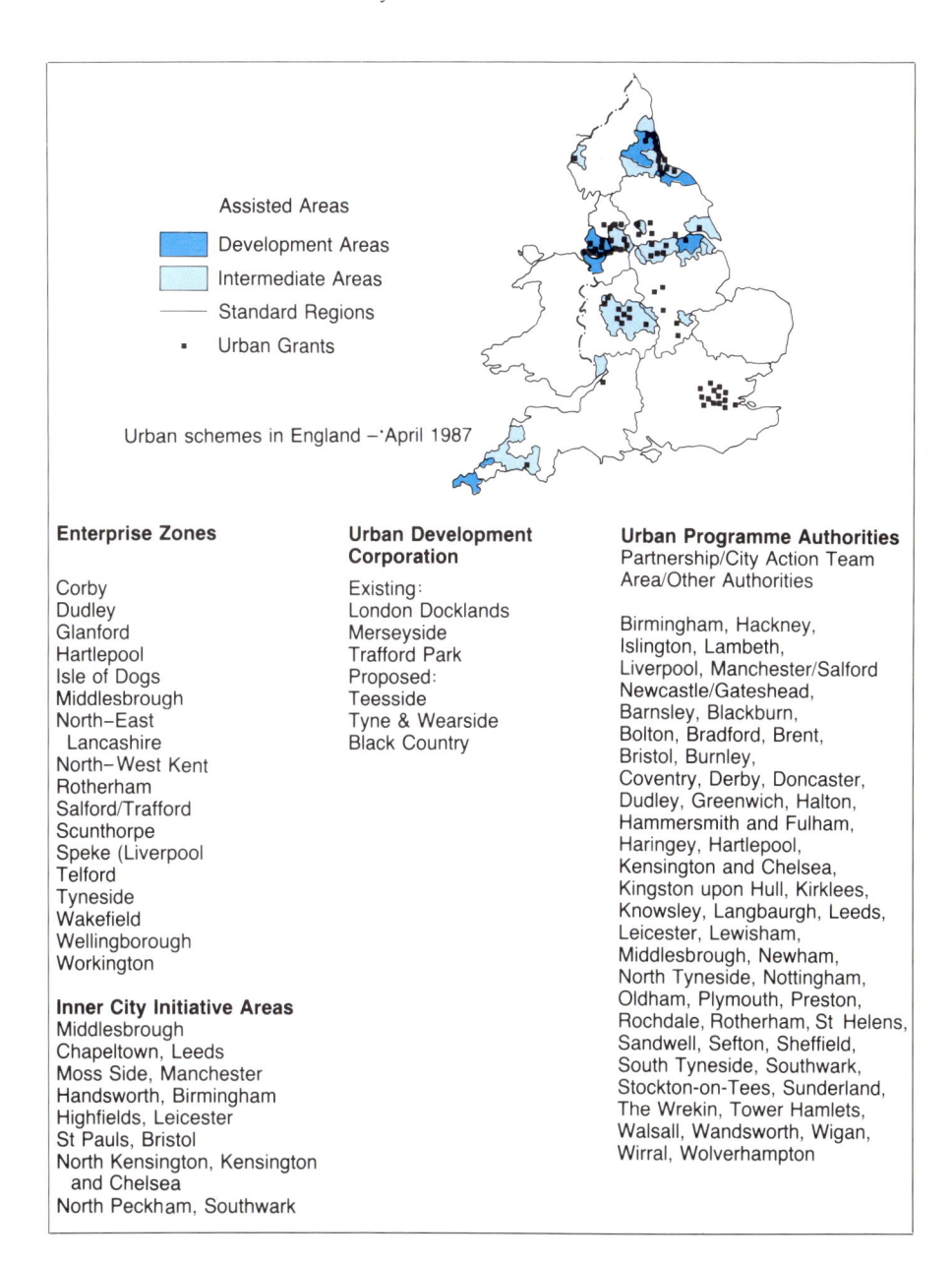

Assisted Areas
- Development Areas
- Intermediate Areas
- Standard Regions
- Urban Grants

Urban schemes in England – April 1987

Enterprise Zones

Corby
Dudley
Glanford
Hartlepool
Isle of Dogs
Middlesbrough
North-East Lancashire
North-West Kent
Rotherham
Salford/Trafford
Scunthorpe
Speke (Liverpool)
Telford
Tyneside
Wakefield
Wellingborough
Workington

Inner City Initiative Areas
Middlesbrough
Chapeltown, Leeds
Moss Side, Manchester
Handsworth, Birmingham
Highfields, Leicester
St Pauls, Bristol
North Kensington, Kensington and Chelsea
North Peckham, Southwark

Urban Development Corporation

Existing:
London Docklands
Merseyside
Trafford Park
Proposed:
Teesside
Tyne & Wearside
Black Country

Urban Programme Authorities
Partnership/City Action Team Area/Other Authorities

Birmingham, Hackney, Islington, Lambeth, Liverpool, Manchester/Salford Newcastle/Gateshead, Barnsley, Blackburn, Bolton, Bradford, Brent, Bristol, Burnley, Coventry, Derby, Doncaster, Dudley, Greenwich, Halton, Hammersmith and Fulham, Haringey, Hartlepool, Kensington and Chelsea, Kingston upon Hull, Kirklees, Knowsley, Langbaugh, Leeds, Leicester, Lewisham, Middlesbrough, Newham, North Tyneside, Nottingham, Oldham, Plymouth, Preston, Rochdale, Rotherham, St Helens, Sandwell, Sefton, Sheffield, South Tyneside, Southwark, Stockton-on-Tees, Sunderland, The Wrekin, Tower Hamlets, Walsall, Wandsworth, Wigan, Wirral, Wolverhampton

There are several types of Assisted Area. Those regions with rapidly declining coal and shipbuilding industries became **Special Development Areas** and had the most generous incentives because of the severity of their problems. Other regions of high unemployment were called **Development Areas and Intermediate Areas**.

Figure 16.5 shows a summary of the financial incentives available to industry. Figure 16.7 shows the total amount of money spent by the government since 1960.' This money is used as a kind of 'carrot' to industries; planning controls represent the 'stick' of Government policies. Together, carrot and stick seek to move industry to places where it might not otherwise have gone.

In the 1960s and 1970s the main form of planning control was the Industrial Development Certificate (IDC). A firm would have to get permission (and a certificate) in order to build any new factory over a certain size; permission was refused in areas of low unemployment. The idea was that firms should be encouraged to locate in an area of high unemployment. This particular policy ended in 1981, mainly because by that time *all* regions in Britain had high levels of unemployment and the Government did not wish to prevent firms from setting up – in whichever part of the United Kingdom they favoured!

Today, regional policy is less generous and less widespread than it used to be. Experts have calculated that between 1960 and 1975 it produced about half a million new jobs in the Assisted Areas. The Government argues, however, that with the high levels of unemployment *everywhere* it does not make sense to redirect industrial growth to certain regions of the United Kingdom only. For the Assisted Areas that remain, though, it is clearly seen as very important.

At the beginning of Part IV of this book we saw how Britain's employment structure has changed; fewer people have jobs in manufacturing industry and more people have jobs in services (see Fig. 15.13). The Government wants to try and attract service industries to areas like mid-Glamorgan (see the extract from *The Guardian* below), as well as manufacturing firms. Some experts think that these service industries will become increasingly important in the future as jobs in manufacturing decline still further. Regional policy therefore, which is concerned mostly with factories and machines, cannot produce many jobs: this is another reason why the Government has cut back its regional policy in recent years. Local people also understand this problem, as the following newspaper article makes clear; there are more jobs in the leisure, recreation and retail industries than in manufacturing, the locals argue.

Figure 16.2 *The Guardian,*

Rhondda hopes to mine a seam of history

People in the Rhondda Villey, South Wales, which has 30 per cent unemployment, are opposing plans to reclaim a former colliery for industry, providing new jobs.

Hundreds have signed petitions supporting Rhondda borough council's alternative proposal to convert the Lewis Merthyr Colliery into a museum to commemorate the valley's mining history.

'We need new industry but we also want to preserve our heritage,' said the mayor of Rhondda, Councillor Edward Hopkins.

'Mardy Colliery is now the only pit still operating in the valley, where there were once 66 collieries, and we must seize this opportunity to set up the museum.

'We are proud of our forefathers but we are also far-reaching in our thinking.

'The museum and ancillary craft shops would attract tourists and lay the foundations for creating far more jobs than five or six factories.'

But Mid-Glamorgan County Council is not convinced that a museum would be the best use even for part of the 10-acre site.

The two councils are seeking reclamation grants from the Welsh Development Agency, which is carrying out a study to determine the best use for a number of sites in the Rhondda, including Lewis Merthyr.

Previous efforts to attract new industry to the valley have had mixed results. Half the development agency's 35 factories are vacant but the borough council has created 338 jobs in small, auxiliary units in the past two-and-a-half years.

The incentives 'jungle'

Although the government's regional policy is less widespread than it used to be, the total amount of aid available in different parts of the country from sources other than the Government, is huge:

- One of the types of assistance offered by Mid Glamorgan-County Council is a 'Recruitment Grant Scheme', which is a cash grant of £780 for each job that is provided for young people. This is *not* part of the Government's regional policy. It is a **local authority grant** paid by the County Council – local authorities can offer incentives like this. In fact, many do, and some are better than others. For example, Durham County Council offers about £700 per new job, plus cash help with certain bills (such as the rates, or bank interest to be repaid on loans).
- There are other types of assistance available in some parts of the country. Certain small areas have been made into **Enterprise Zones** (see Fig. 16.1) which are areas where factories can be obtained free of rent and rates, for a time. These are also areas where planning controls are at an absolute minimum; there is no 'red tape' to slow things down. Enterprise Zones have been set up where there is particularly high unemployment. Notice from Fig. 16.1 that they are *not* necessarily located in the Development Areas – one of the more successful ones is the Isle of Dogs in London.
- Parts of the country which had suffered huge and tragic losses of jobs by the contraction of the steel industry in recent years could offer extra financial assistance to new industries in the form of special loans from the British Steel Corporation. Examples of such locations are Corby in

The closest development area to London on the M4

If London and the South East are where your customers are located, then you'll need to be near them.

We are the closest 'development area' to London on the M4 motorway, offering some of the best incentives for qualifying new and expanding businesses.

Compare Mid Glamorgan's prime location with other developing areas in the U.K. and you'll realise why more and more businesses are locating here.

We can help with new factory units, training and relocation grants, loans and other incentives you may qualify for. You'll be impressed with the company you'll be keeping. Other companies have been getting the best out of our position on the M4 for quite a while. Come and see for yourself.

Re-routing your business to Mid Glamorgan could put you on the road to success

For more information, contact the Industrial Development and Promotion Unit, Mid Glamorgan County Council, Greyfriars Road, Cardiff CF1 3LG or telephone 0222 820880.

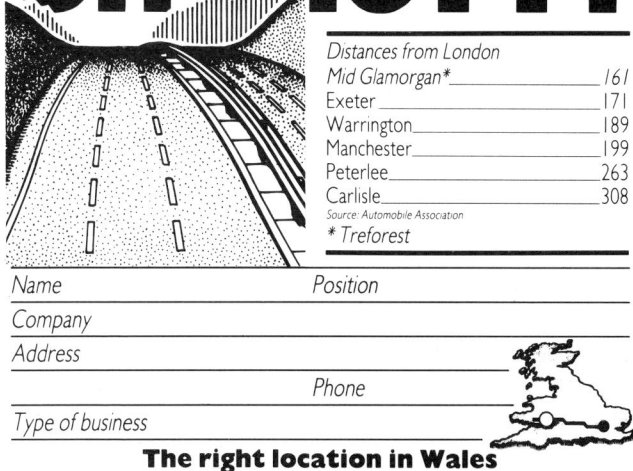

Distances from London
Mid Glamorgan*_____161
Exeter_____171
Warrington_____189
Manchester_____199
Peterlee_____263
Carlisle_____308
Source: Automobile Association
* Treforest

Name _____ Position _____
Company _____
Address _____
_____ Phone _____
Type of business _____

The right location in Wales
Mid Glamorgan

Figure 16.3

Northamptonshire and Consett in County Durham. These towns can obtain yet more aid through the European Community (EC).
- In addition, some rural parts of the country can obtain assistance from the Council for Small Industries in Rural Areas (CoSIRA), in the form of loans.

The list of incentives is complicated and difficult to understand. For a business wishing to find the most attractive financial location in Britain, it is an 'incentives jungle'. The attraction of certain locations is huge and the various financial incentives often outweigh the other factors of locations, so long as you know how to apply for them!

A problem that remains however, is that all of the incentives are only for short periods.

> # Question
> What do you think might happen to a firm when the free rent period, rate rebates, loans and grants run out?

The best way to ensure that local jobs are created – and that they *stay* – is for *local people* to be encouraged to form new businesses themselves. The area where this has been tried most successfully is not in 'traditional' Britain but in London, through the establishment of **worker co-operatives**. (You can remind yourself of the unemployment problem suffered in parts of London by looking at Fig. 15.2). The Greater London Enterprise Board sees a great future in worker co-operatives – which are firms owned and controlled by its workers. They are set up with the help of grants and loans from the Board and many have been very successful.

Image and infrastructure

No matter how generous the financial incentives offered by the various types of government departments, firms will not wish to locate in an area whose **image** is a negative one. The idea of coal tips, dirty buildings and derelict land is not attractive, especially to the 'new' industries. It is also true that firms may not risk choosing a location whose infrastructure is poor, inconvenient and possibly expensive to operate from. This is especially true if it is the road network which is inadequate in some way.

Responses to the unemployment crisis

The whole country faces high levels of unemployment. As we have learned, some localities have suffered more than their fair share of job losses and have already come face-to-face with an **unemployment crisis**.

The locality in the United Kingdom with the most generous package of incentives and Government-help to tackle such a crisis is probably N. Ireland. The attempts to re-industrialise after the loss of many heavy industries have been quite successful. However, few people think that unemployment in this area will diminish much further, and the mass of incentives will be judged to have been successful simply if unemployment can be stopped from rising again.

It is sometimes easy to forget what **long-term unemployment** really means.

An MP named Ellen Wilkinson wrote a book called *The Town that was Murdered* in 1939. It was about Jarrow, which suffered badly from the decline of the shipbuilding industry. She wrote:

> These unemployed middle-aged and elderly men who can be seen walking the streets of Jarrow during the hours when their more fortunate fellows are at work were efficient workmen, some of them highly skilled. The ships they built were amongst the best that sailed the seas. And, like all workmen, they are deeply conscious of the high tradition of good workmanship which they had established. Men with that record, and that ability, do not take easily to charity. They do not wish to answer a barrage of questions in order to obtain a new pair of blankets. They wish to live their lives as independent units. All they want is the chance to work.... These men have done nothing that they should go cap in hand to seek assistance ... [they] are paying the price of rationalisation.

Much has changed since the 1930s, but what Ellen Wilkinson wrote then has a meaning for parts of the United Kingdom in the 1980s.

Some experts believe that de-industrialisation and the resulting unemployment crisis is actually the start of what is now known as the **leisure society**. There will be less work and more time for hobbies, sports and other recreational activities. Many people hope that this itself will be the growth industry of the future. This leisure industry is a service industry – part of the sector in which jobs have been expanding.

But, at the end of this chapter on industrial changes in Britain, we should ask a number of questions:

1. Will the leisure industry produce the *right kind* of jobs? For example, will a leisure industry provide jobs for unemployed steelworkers?
2. Will new jobs in the leisure industry be in the right places? Will developments in leisure industries be in areas of low unemployment?
3. The people with the most leisure time are those people out of work. Will *they* be able to afford to make use of new leisure facilities?

Nationalisation has been an important feature of Britain's industry, especially since the Second World War. Since 1979, when the Conservative Party formed the Government under Mrs Thatcher, there have been fewer and fewer nationalised industries. The Government has **'privatised'** a number of industries, such as:

Britoil
Jaguar Cars
British Telecom
Sealink Ferries
British Gas
The Trustee Savings Bank
British Airways
British Steel

The intention is to enable as many nationalised industries as possible to pass into private, as opposed to public (Government) ownership.

This has proved to be a very popular policy for the Government, and it may prove to be one of the most dramatic changes of the 1980s. The Labour Party is against privatisation and might immediately 'buy back' several of the privatised industries. It is interesting to note that the Labour Party no longer calls this 'nationalisation'; it prefers now to say that such industries would be 'passing into **social ownership**'. The arguments that rage on this issue can be summarised like this:

CONTRASTING VIEWPOINTS

'Should Government be involved in running industry?'

Rt Hon Norman Tebbitt, MP, Former Chairman of the Conservative Party

Conservatives believe that Government should do what Governments must do - that is to defend the country, maintain law and order, and look after those unable to care for themselves. Tasks which cannot reasonably be performed by the individual citizen or private interest.

But Government should *not* attempt to become involved in areas where others know best. Britain's industry is just such a case in point: industrialists are better equipped to run businesses and win markets for Britain than politicians or civil servants in Whitehall.

Industry is successful, in the end, if it produces goods which you or I or customers abroad want to buy at a price which we can afford. And the best people to respond to our wishes are people who know about the goods, about how to produce them, and about how cheaply they can make them.

But just as government should not *interfere* in the running of industry, nor must it ignore it: for Government must create the conditions in which industry can flourish, for example low inflation and sensible trades union laws to promote harmony, not chaos, in industrial relations.

So Government should aim to create a climate for enterprise, wealth creation and growth. A climate of low taxation (to give people an incentive to work even harder), and low inflation and interest rates (to allow industry to compete effectively abroad). And once the climate has been created, Government must allow industrialists to get on with their job, to prosper or fail and make room for those who can succeed.

The social ownership supporters

- Privately-owned firms are often inefficient. The motor vehicle firm Rover (formerly British Leyland) was nationalised to stop it going bankrupt as a result of huge losses made as a privately owned firm.
- Bigger profits do not benefit all workers in the same way. Shareholders benefit, but not all workers are shareholders.
- Profits can be boosted quickly by private owners by rationalisation (see page 134), which makes many people jobless. This might not mean long-term success.
- The Government ought to keep control of public service industries like telephones, otherwise there is a danger that supplying telephones to remote (unprofitable) areas will not happen. A similar argument holds for British Rail, gas, water, electricity and other industries.

For privatisation

- Privately-owned firms are more efficient and successful.
- Everybody works harder for a privately-owned firm, because bigger profits mean larger salaries and wages. This is the incentive.
- More people own shares in the privatised industries. More people, therefore, have a part-ownership
- The Government does not have a potential loss-making industry hanging around its neck.

The nationalisation-privatisation debate is one of those issues where people often find themselves on one side or another. In other words, people often seem to have clear-cut views. Try to find out what people you know think

Rt Hon Bryan Gould, Labour MP

Governments are inevitably involved in industry. Even the least active government must buy the products of industry to equip its police and military. In practice, nearly all modern governments accept a much wider range of responsibility. As a minimum they set and enforce the industry standards for working conditions and pay, and make sure that the environment and the consumers are properly protected.

But beyond this, most governments understand the need to intervene to ensure that there is effective competition which industry itself would try to stifle. The Americans, usually regarded as non-interventionists, have among the oldest and most rigorous anti-trust legislation, and most governments find it necessary to act against monopolies.

Private companies, left to themselves, fail to adequately invest in the future - whether it is in training, scientific research or equipment. Governments of those countries with the best record on this, like Japan or Germany, have very active industrial policies. Britain has a poor record in these matters and as a result has a very uncompetitive industry.

Norman Tebbitt was himself an active Secretary of State for Industry. His problem is that he has to pretend not to believe in it. Socialists are pragmatic about state involvement in industry; we recognise that in the most successful countries, success is largely based on close co-operation between government and industry.

about the arguments; if you find they are clear-cut in their opinion, try to find out their *reasons*.

Figure 16.4 An extract from a speech in Parliament by the Minister of Energy

GOVERNMENT PROPOSALS FOR THE PRIVATISATION OF THE ELECTRICITY SUPPLY INDUSTRY IN ENGLAND & WALES

STATEMENT BY THE SECRETARY OF STATE FOR ENERGY, THE RT. HON. CECIL PARKINSON, MP, TO THE HOUSE OF COMMONS, 25 FEBRUARY, 1988.

With permission, Mr Speaker, I will make a statement about the future of the electricity supply industry in England and Wales.

In our manifesto, we promised to bring forward proposals to privatise the industry. Our purpose is to give the customer and the employees a better deal and a direct stake in the industry.

... I therefore propose to introduce legislation at the earliest opportunity to provide powers to restructure and privatise the industry. These powers will be used to reorganise the CEGB into three new companies.

The first will be a new generating company, owning some 30 per cent of the CEGB's existing capacity, all of it non-nuclear.

The second will comprise the remainder of the CEGB's generating capacity, both fossil-fuelled and nuclear.

The third will be a national grid company, whose ownership will be transferred to the twelve existing Area Boards.

The Area Boards will in turn be converted into twelve distribution companies, preserving their strong regional identity... Mr Speaker, in future the distribution companies will be able to look to private generators, Scotland, France, the two large generating companies or their own generation to meet demand.

The new structure will introduce competition, which will be the best guarantee of the customer's interests.

168 A Geography of Contemporary Britain

Database: the role of Government in industry

Figure 16.5 Aid for industry in the 1970s

Incentive	Special Development Area	Development Area	Intermediate Area
Building grant	22%	22%	20%
Machinery grant	22%	20%	0
Factories	Five years rent free	Up to two years rent free	
Loans	Special favourable rates to encourage new jobs		
Removal grant	Up to 80%		
Help with moving workers	Free fares. lodging allowances		
Training	Free at a Government Skill Centre		
Tax allowances	Tax reductions on buildings and machinery		
Contracts preference	Contracts from Government departments and nationalised industries		Nil

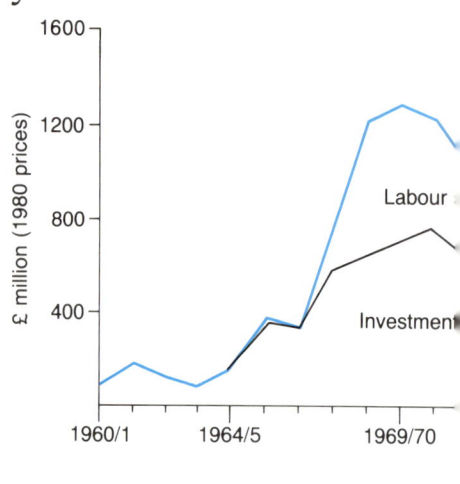

Figure 16.6 Who gets what, where? (average pay for adult men (Source: New Earnings Survey, 1986))

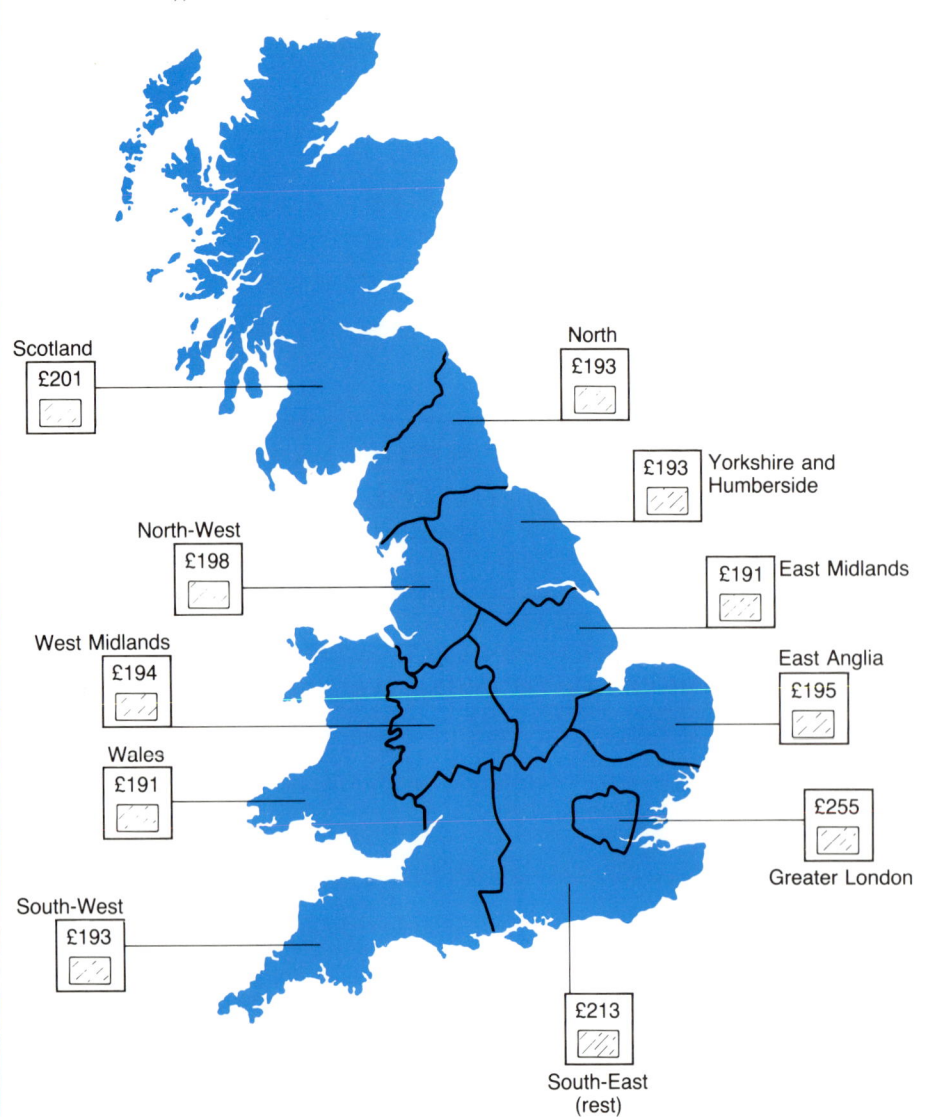

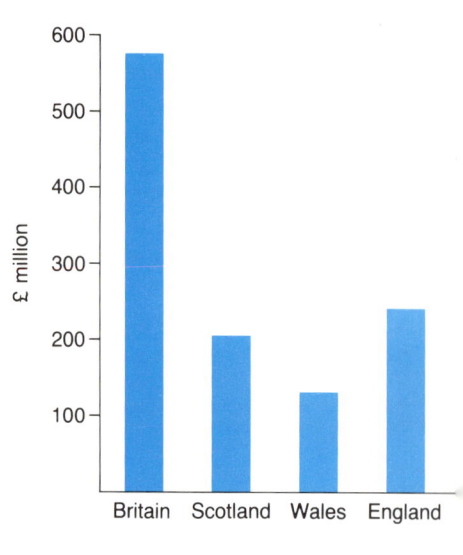

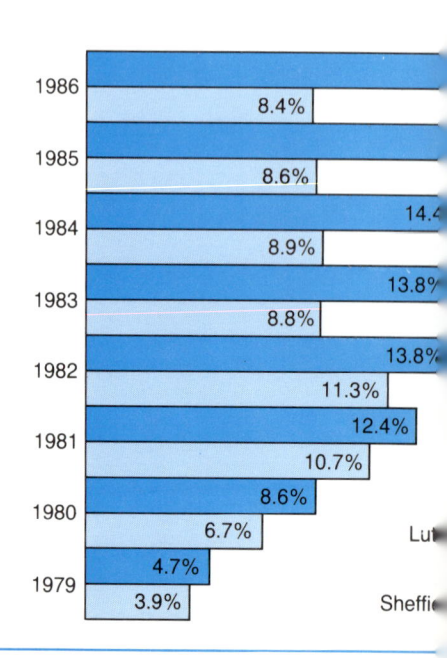

Scotland £201
North £193
Yorkshire and Humberside £193
North-West £198
East Midlands £191
West Midlands £194
East Anglia £195
Wales £191
Greater London £255
South-West £193
South-East (rest) £213

Figure 16.7 Government expenditure on regional policy

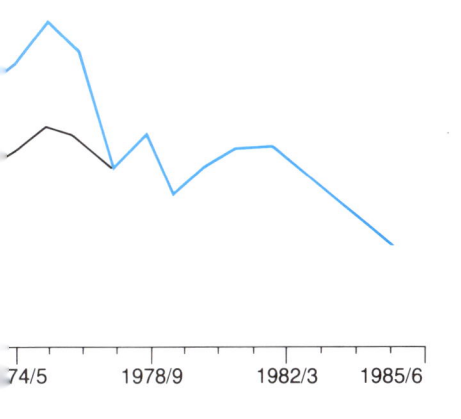

[Graph with x-axis labels: 74/5, 1978/9, 1982/3, 1985/6]

Figure 16.8 Regional assistance to industry: the amount of spending per head for regions of Britain in 1984

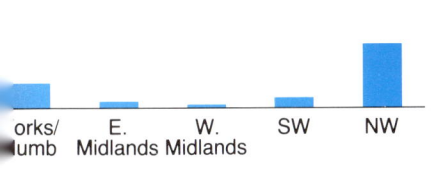

[Bar chart with labels: orks/Humb, E. Midlands, W. Midlands, SW, NW]

Figure 16.9 Unemployment rates and house prices in Luton and Sheffield, 1986 (Source: *Times Educational Supplement*, 13 February 1987)

Sheffield Three-bed semi (average) £27,000

Luton Three-bed semi (average) £50–60,000

Workbase

1. Look at the map of assisted areas (Fig. 16.1). With the aid of a wall-map or atlas, identify and list these areas, giving each of them an appropriate regional name. Name one major town in each of the regions.

2. Imagine a town in which a large steel-works closes down. Four thousand workers are made redundant and the unemployment rate of the area reaches 30 per cent. The workers are used to, and skilled in, heavy manual work. There is no chance of the works re-opening.
    a) Make a list of other types of firms or businesses which might also go out of business as the result of the closure of the steelworks
    b) If you were a school-leaver in this town what would your plan of action be to find a job?
    c) If the local MP came to address a town meeting, what questions would you want to put to him or her about the future of the town? How could the Government best help the town?
    d) An example of a town which had to face this problem in real-life was Corby in Northamptonshire. Try to find out how Corby has fared following the steel-works closure.

3. Look at the advertisement, Fig. 16.3. Look in the daily and weekly papers of your own region and see if you can find similar advertisements which try to show the advantages of a place to industry. Display these on your classroom walls. Which ones do you think make the most effective case and why?

4. Look at Fig. 16.7. Write a paragraph, describing the graph, which shows expenditure on regional policy. How far would a change of Government from Labour to Conservative be likely to affect such policies? A Conservative Government came to power in 1979; do you see any sign of this on the graph?

5. Look at Fig. 16.8. Which region of Britain receives the most assistance per head of the population? Which receives least?

6. Look at Figs 16.6 and 16.9. Make sure you know in which regions Luton and Sheffield would be on Fig. 16.6.
    a) Where in Britain is the average pay for males the highest? What is the average pay for men in the regions where Luton and Sheffield are situated?
    b) Ought the Government to do anything to help iron out regional differences? If so, what? If not, why not?

The role of Government

Part V
Britain's energy and communications

The life of any single British household links directly into a great web of wider systems of power and communications in the United Kingdom. The house in which Mr and Mrs Average live will use a certain amount of energy each day, summer or winter. Energy will be used for cooking, lighting, and (in winter) for heating rooms. The winter heating may be by central-heating from an individually operated source of power (an oil-fired boiler, perhaps) but even its starter-motor will depend on electricity coming into the house via the National Grid. Many houses use a mixture of energy sources – gas, electricity, oil, and perhaps 'solid fuel' (coal or wood).

The cost of each of these fuels has varied over recent years. For some time oil was a cheap energy source, but recent international decisions to cut back on production have pushed up its price again; gas has also been relatively cheap in Britain (largely because of the introduction of natural North Sea gas, to replace manufactured town gas) but the price has been rising recently. Sometimes the Government adjusts a surcharge to the production of oil, gas or coal, in order to keep the different sources generally competitive with each other.

It also takes energy to move Mr and Mrs Average, and their family, from place to place. The train which takes the parents to work may be powered by electricity; the bus which takes the Average children to school will be driven by diesel or petrol fuel; the car which the parents drive will also use oil as an energy source. The *amount* of energy that the family uses will depend on their location and the distances travelled each day. The distances have tended to increase considerably in Britain in the last thirty years, as personal mobility has grown and the number of cars, motor-cycles and bicycles has increased in each family.

Even the food which the Average family eats represents a considerable use of energy and communication. The breakfast cornflakes which they munch are made from maize which has travelled by ship from the USA to be processed in Britain. The cardboard packets which hold the cornflakes have been users of energy in their manufacture (from paper-pulp made in Scandinavia). It took power and energy (probably from a mechanical chain-saw) to chop the trees down and move them to the port; and to bring them to their British factory destination.

And you would need only to look in the living-room of Mr and Mrs Average to see their dependence on other forms of communication. The telephone is rented from British Telecom and links the house, not only to the local area, but, via cables and satellites, to the rest of the world. Several different kinds of energy source may be involved in keeping that network in action. The television set has similar links, and has used up much energy in its manufacture, even before it has been moved from its place of manufacture to the home.

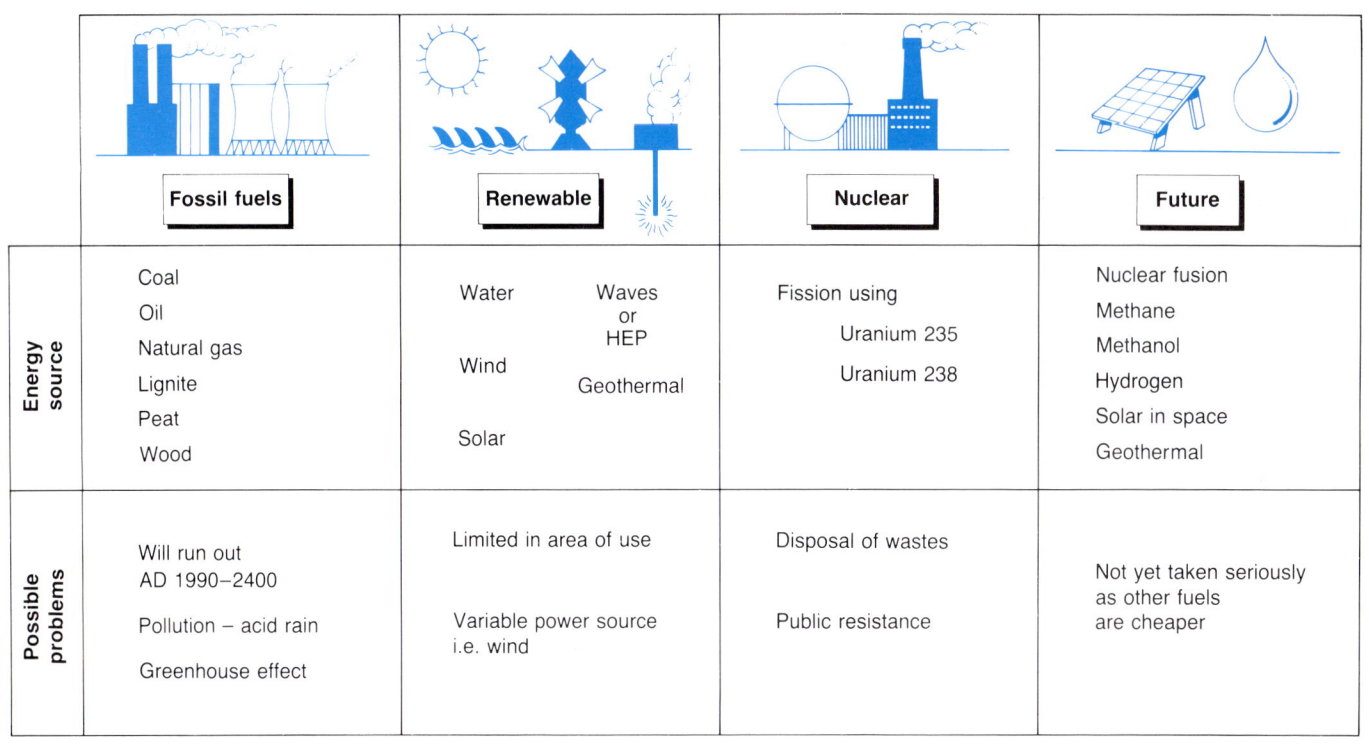

	Fossil fuels	Renewable	Nuclear	Future
Energy source	Coal Oil Natural gas Lignite Peat Wood	Water Waves or HEP Wind Geothermal Solar	Fission using Uranium 235 Uranium 238	Nuclear fusion Methane Methanol Hydrogen Solar in space Geothermal
Possible problems	Will run out AD 1990–2400 Pollution – acid rain Greenhouse effect	Limited in area of use Variable power source i.e. wind	Disposal of wastes Public resistance	Not yet taken seriously as other fuels are cheaper

Figure V.1 Energy — present and future

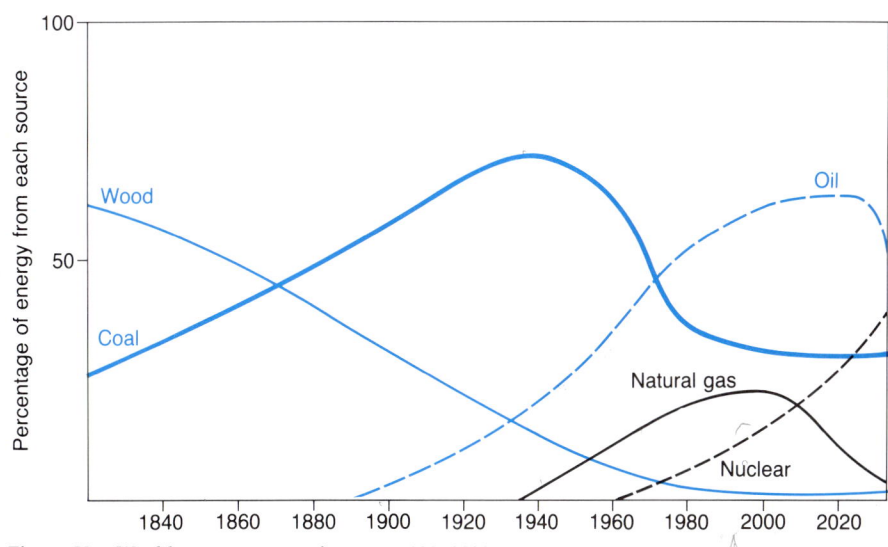

Figure V.2 World consumption of energy 1820–2020

Figure V.3 Inland energy consumption in the United Kingdom, 1983

	Million tonnes coal equivalent	Percentage
Coal	106.8	35.0
Oil	114.8	38.0
Natural gas	71.3	23.4
Nuclear	7.9	2.6
Hydro electric power	2.2	1.0
Total	303.0	100.0

Source: UK Digest Energy Statistics, 1986

So these ideas can be established;

- Households are units which create and use networks of transport and communications. Some are visible networks; others not. All these networks use energy to keep them going.
- The amount of energy used by each individual household varies with its lifestyle, and the household's view about energy costs as part of the family budget.
- The costs of energy include costs of installation of plant (such as boilers, or central-heating), running costs (the regular bills), and taxes which may be imposed by the Government.
- Most households probably do not realise just how dependent they are on the national provision of energy, nor how much energy they use in their everyday lives.

Chapter 17
The case for coal

Compared with many other countries, Britain has considerable reserves of coal. Experts estimate that these will serve us for the next 200 years at the present rate of consumption. But – as the miners' strike of 1985 showed – the country is not as dependent on coal energy as it once was. The mining of coal depends not on finding it, but on being able to mine it and sell it at an economic price in competition with other fuels.

In mining areas where seams are thin (less than one metre wide) or are badly broken by folding and faulting, costs of extraction are high. Older collieries may have to close because all the easily-mined coal has been extracted in years past. Thus newer coalfields are opening up and exploiting new and deeper seams of coal at a cheaper cost per unit. The Selby coalfield in Yorkshire is an example of a large-scale high-technology coalfield which is being developed for the 1990s; even the main London-Edinburgh railway line was shifted to take account of its workings.

Not all coal is of the same type; in the coalfields of the North-East it is most suitable for producing blast-furnace coke in the steelworks; the anthracites of South Wales are best for domestic boilers, because they give a high heat ratio to the amount of ash which they create; the Midlands coalfields produce coal suitable for the power stations of the Central Electricity Generating Board.

Coal was nationalised in 1946 and is now run through British Coal (the old National Coal Board, NCB). British Coal gives some subsidies to collieries, but the aid per tonne is not as high as in some other European countries (for instance, Belgium and West Germany).

In recent years there has been considerable tension between miners' unions and the NCB because management has sought to close collieries which it claims are no longer producing coal at an economic rate. The calculations have been disputed by miners' unions. There has also been great concern about the effects of closing a pit when the local community has depended on it for employment for many years. It is not easy to uproot families and whole neighbourhoods and move them on, just because the good coal seams have run out.

Case study: the Vale of Belvoir

The coalfield in West Leicestershire is an old-established one, coming to the end of its useful life. But in East Leicestershire new reserves were discovered in 1978 in a pleasant farming area, the Vale of Belvoir (see Figs 17.1 and 17.2). This was the sequence of events:

1978   The NCB discovered coal reserves estimated at 700 million tonnes in the Vale of Belvoir. A plan was produced indicating that the area affected covered 230 square kilometres. The development of mines, housing, roads etc. required 240 hectares of good farmland. Output was estimated at 7.4 million tonnes per annum.

Figure 17.1 Model of the Asfordby Mine, Vale of Belvoir, Leicestershire

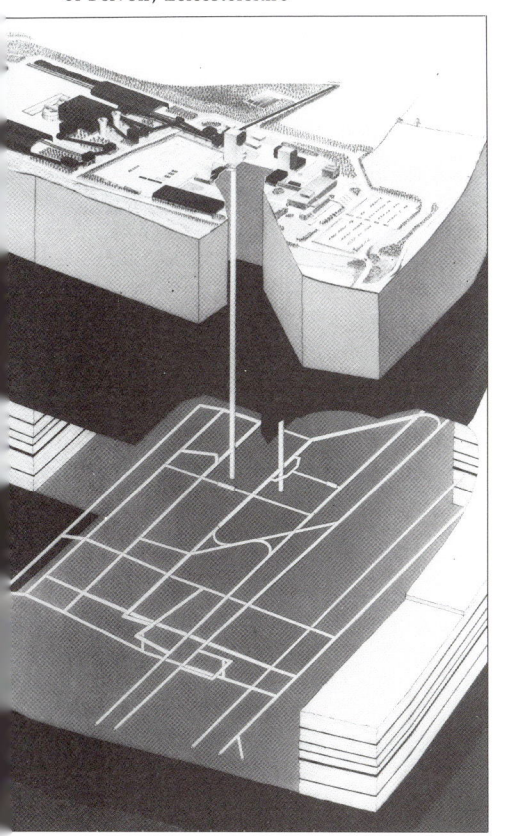

1979   The NCB plans were the subject of a public enquiry.
         Those supporting the NCB were local people who saw the promise of more jobs, and local traders who hoped for more trade and profit. The CEGB supported the plan because it would receive cheap coal for its Trent Valley power stations to the North-West.
         Opposing the plans were many landowners, including the farmers and the Duke of Rutland, who lives in a picturesque castle overlooking the Vale. Environmental protests came from those who saw the possibility of waste-tips and pit-head gear changing the rural landscape of the Vale.

1980   The enquiry ended. The inspector in charge decided that mining should go ahead, but that no waste should be tipped around two of the mines. He sent his recommendation to the Secretary of State.

1982   The Secretary of State decided that the proposals were not good enough and invited the NCB to submit revised proposals.

1982   The NCB resubmitted proposals, but for only one mine at Asfordby. To meet the criticisms of the environmental groups, much of the waste was destined to go underground to fill up old mine workings.

1983   The revised plans were submitted to the Leicestershire County Council and were approved.

1984   Final Government approval was given. Annual production was planned at 2.2 million tonnes. 500 new jobs were to be created in the first phase of development and in total new employment was estimated to rise to 1,100 by 1989. The cost of the new mine would be £400 million.

1987   The Asfordby Mine is under construction and the next step will be the preparation for new proposals for mines at the other two sites.

NW Leicestershire coalfield

Long established mining area

Old mines approaching exhaustion

Old established mines were here prior to the environmental movement

★ 1   Desford – drift mine closed 1984

★ 2   Snibson – near Coalville. Exhausted (no coal left), closed 1983

       Four other mines to close over the next ten years

NE Leicestershire coalfield

New discovery

New mines to be opened

New mines to be located at Asfordby (3), Hose (4) and Saltby (5)

Environmentally sensitive area

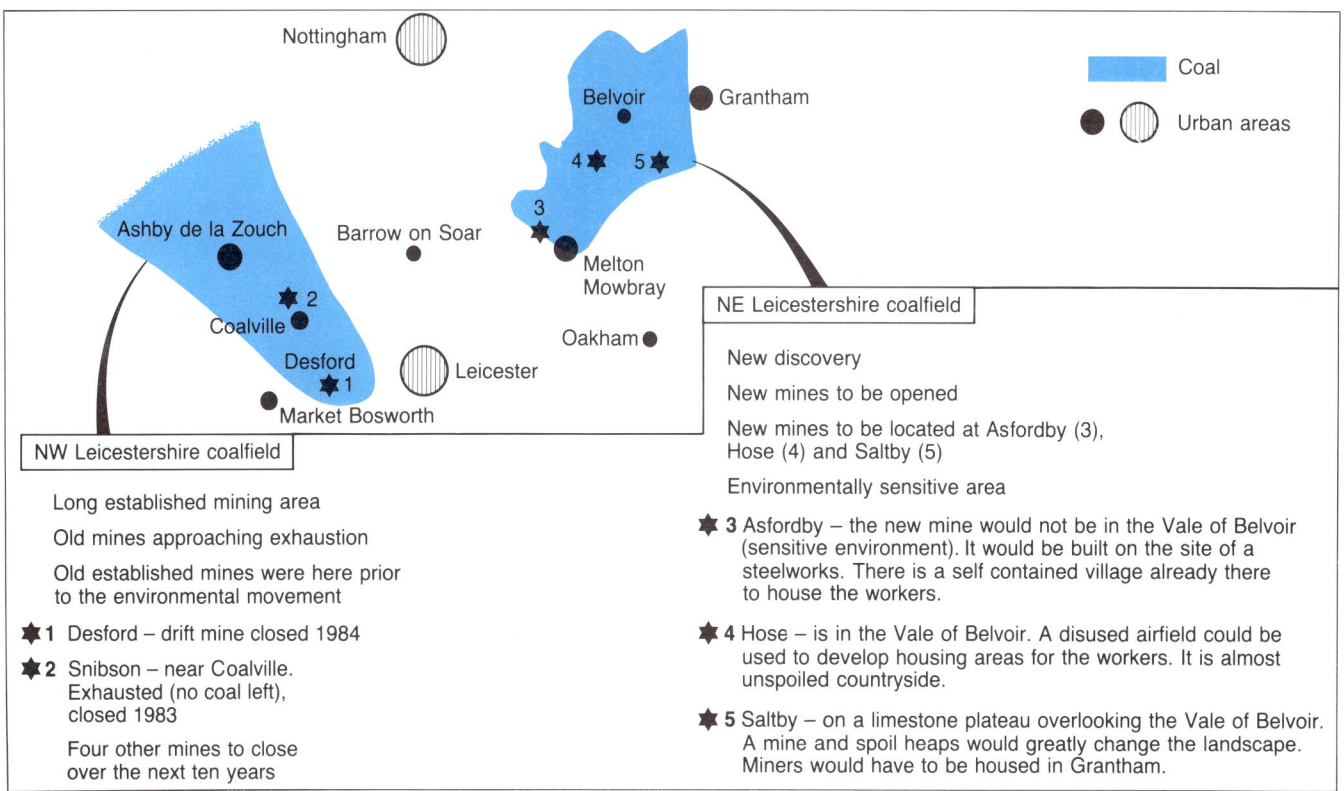

★ 3   Asfordby – the new mine would not be in the Vale of Belvoir (sensitive environment). It would be built on the site of a steelworks. There is a self contained village already there to house the workers.

★ 4   Hose – is in the Vale of Belvoir. A disused airfield could be used to develop housing areas for the workers. It is almost unspoiled countryside.

★ 5   Saltby – on a limestone plateau overlooking the Vale of Belvoir. A mine and spoil heaps would greatly change the landscape. Miners would have to be housed in Grantham.

Figure 17.2 The Leicestershire Coalfield

Database: coal

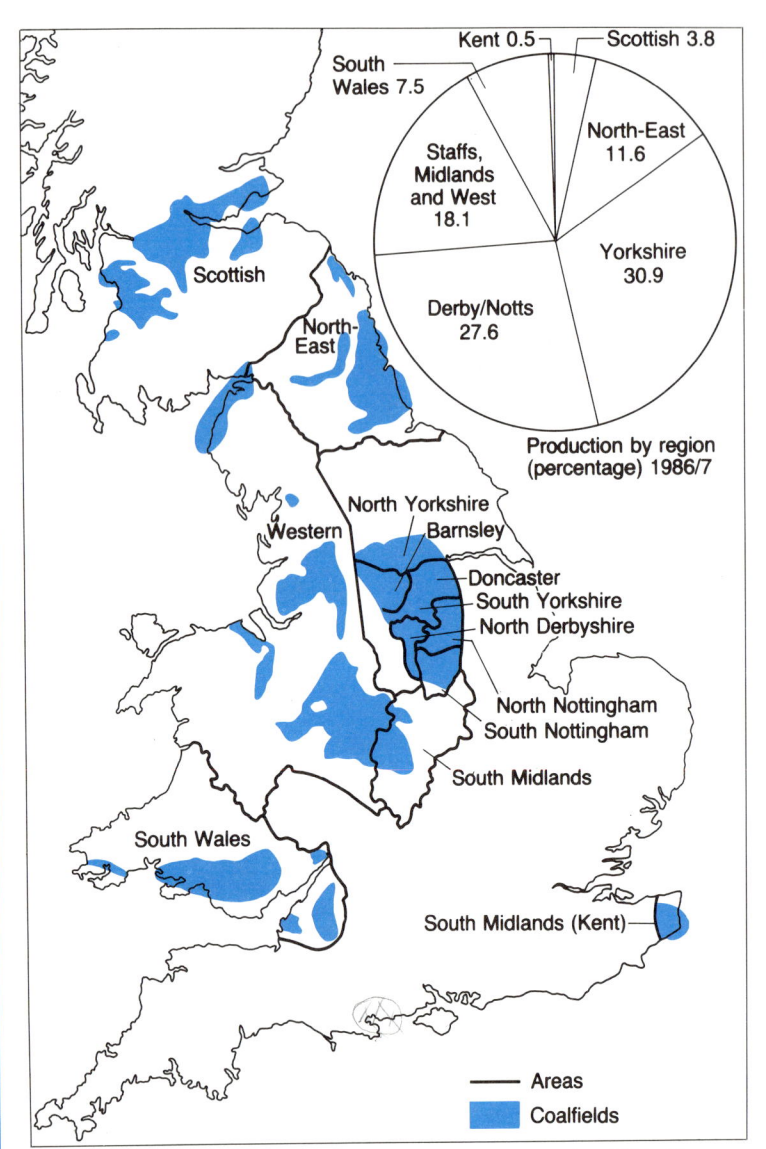

Figure 17.3 British coal areas and percentage output by region 1986–87

Figure 17.5 Trends in mining in the UK (Source: *NCB Annual Report* 1982–83)

Figure 17.4 Production in British coalfield areas

Coalfield	Output (mill. tonnes) 1963/4	% of all coalfields	Output (mill. tonnes) 1980/1	% of all coalfields	Output (mill. tonnes) 1987	% of all coalfields	
Scottish	16.4	8.7	7.8	7.0	3.4	3.8	
N.E. England	32.2	17.0	14.2	13.0	10.2	11.6	
Yorkshire	43.9	23.4	31.6	28.5	27.0	30.9	New Selby coalfield
Derby/Notts	39.3	20.9	29.3	26.5	24.1	27.6	New Belvoir coalfield, Asfordby
Staffs, S. Midlands and West	34.7	18.5	19.7	18.0	15.8	18.1	
S. Wales & Bristol	19.4	10.3	7.7	7.0	6.5	7.5	
Kent	1.6	—	*	*	0.5	0.5	
	187.5	100	110.3	100	87.2	100.0	

* included in S. Midlands

Source: *British Coal Corporation Annual Report 1986/7*

Figure 17.6 Sources of coal consumption in the UK

	1981/2	1986/7
Power stations	82.0	82.7
Coke ovens & fuel plants	8.4	13.2
Domestic	8.0	8.6
Industry	8.7	8.1
Other inland markets	3.7	1.8
Exports	9.4	2.5
Total	120.6	116.9

Source: UK Digest of Energy Statistics, 1985.

Figure 17.7 Output per face in UK mines

Output per face in tonnes	1974/5	610
	1977/8	620
	1979/80	680
	1981/2	718
	1982/3	784
	1986/7	1,044

Source: NCB and British Coal Corporation Annual Report 1986/7

Workbase

1. Read the case study of the proposed Vale of Belvoir coalfield. Write a speech which might be made at a public meeting called to discuss the development of the coalfield by *one* of these three speakers:
   a) a miner from the West Leicestershire coalfield;
   b) a farmer in the Vale of Belvoir;
   c) a planner from British Coal in London.

2. Look at Fig. 17.3
   a) Which area do you think is now the 'heartland of British coalmining'? Give two reasons for your choice.
   b) Compare the map with the geological map, Plate 34. How many coalfields are mining coal concealed *beneath* the surface rocks?

3. Look at Fig. 17.4 which shows coalfield production over a period of twenty-five years.
   a) Which coalfields look in most danger of closure?
   b) In which coalfields has production increased?

4. Consider Figs 17.4 and 17.5. Suppose you were asked, as a consultant to British Coal, to assess the health of the coal industry over the last twenty-five years. What major points would you make in your report?

5. Write an essay on the topic 'The problems of closing a pit'.

6. Draw appropriate diagrams to represent the figures shown in the tables, Figs 17.6 and 17.7.

Chapter 18
Oil and gas

Oil: Britain's black gold?

Oil is a very valuable and versatile fossil fuel. Britain has estimated reserves of 13 million barrels – most of which are thought to be under the North Sea. Oil produced from British oilfields already makes us self-sufficient, but this may be true only until about the year 2020. World reserves may last until about 2050 on present calculations (but the discovery of new fields, the changes in fuel use, and the improvement of fuel-saving devices on engines may push this date further onwards).

In the 1980s oil has accounted for 40 per cent of all the energy used in Britain. It is used in various forms – diesel fuel, petrol and high-octane aviation fuel, as well as paraffin and thinner forms of oil. Our transport systems and our domestic heating systems mostly depend on oil; so does our food supply, because most agriculture is highly mechanised. Present-day farming requires high inputs of fertilisers and pesticides, and many of these are oil-based.

Oil consumption grew steadily throughout the 1970s as more people became car owners, installed central-heating in their homes, and used more electricity (some of which was produced from oil-burning power stations). But in 1973–4 a political crisis in the main production area, the Middle East, halted exports of oil to Europe for a time and caused a dramatic price-rise. This showed the increasing dependence of countries on oil exports. In Britain there were two major effects:

- The Central Electricity Generating Board reconsidered plans to 'phase out' coal-fired power stations. It also increased its interest in nuclear-powered stations.
- There was a greater demand for fuel conservation in cars and lorries; and homes were built with better insulation, so that they did not need so much powered heat.

Some developing countries, such as India, found themselves in great difficulty, since they used almost all their valuable foreign currency reserves to buy the now-expensive oil, leaving hardly any money to buy other manufactured goods.

Oil consumption slumped – falling by 35 per cent between 1974 and 1984. The Middle Eastern countries within OPEC (the Organisation of Petroleum Exporting Countries) then *deliberately* sought to restrict production, and so maintain the price of oil at a reasonable level. So there are now cyclical changes in price and amounts available as the oil producers seek to avoid having *too much* oil available on the market and as the oil consumers look for their own supplies of oil and alternative ways of finding fuel. This explains why there are sometimes 'petrol price wars' between the large producers such as Esso and Shell and smaller distributors of oil who step in to buy surplus stocks (when the price is right) and who then sell it to outlets not linked to the major oil companies. At other times these small filling-stations may have to pay more than their 'tied' big brothers, if there is an oil shortage.

Oil and the British Government

The British Government actively encouraged the search for oil in the North Sea in the 1970s, and controlled it by being the authority to grant licences for exploration in various 'sections' of the sea-bed. Private enterprise exploration companies bear all the costs of the search for oil and its movement to shore (by tanker or pipeline). If they strike oil, they are likely to make profits, but they also have to pay a tax to the Government on each barrel of oil brought ashore. (See Plate 39.)

The more oil obtained from oilfields in British waters, the less Britain needs to spend on importing oil from other countries. But, even so, the Government has been anxious to control the amount of oil used from the fields around the British coast. In the meantime it has encouraged further searches in the Irish Sea and the English Channel. There have also been some explorations on land, at Eakring (Notts), Wytch Farm (Dorset), Humbly Grove (Hants) and Pumpherstone (Scotland). The Wytch Farm site has proved to be a fully-economic proposition. It is hoped that production will increase from 6000 barrels per day in 1985 to 40,000 barrels per day in 1990. But the site – near the Dorset 'Heritage' Coast – poses a clear conflict between the needs of the economy and the views of conservationists, who fear that attractive Dorset heathland may be destroyed.

Figure 18.1

	Total indigenous petroleum production (thousand tonnes)
1975	1,567
1976	12,171
1977	38,265
1978	54,006
1979	77,854
1980	80,468
1981	89,480
1982	103,219
1983	114,917
1984	125,924
1985	127,527

Source: Department of Energy Annual Abstract of Statistics 1987

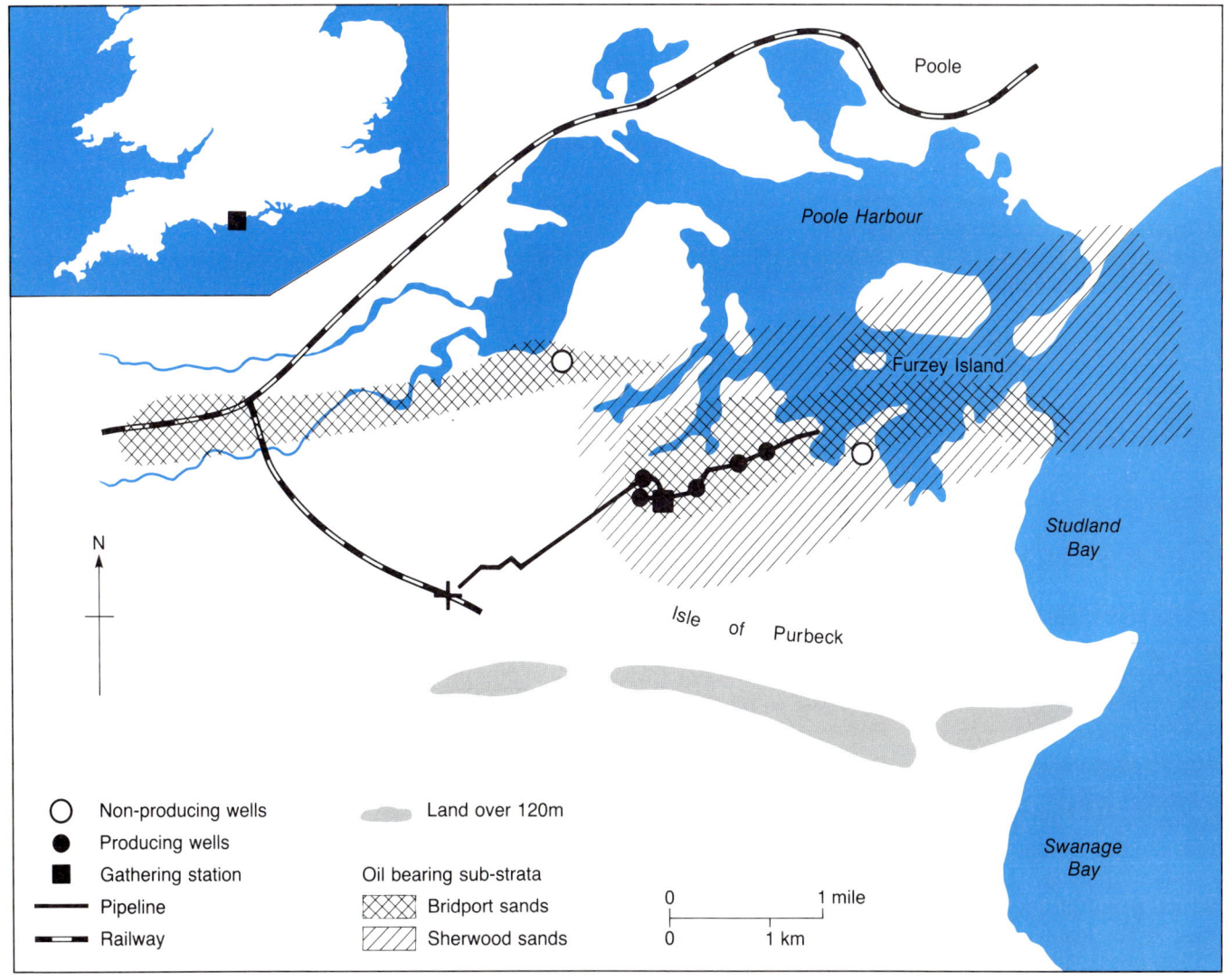

Figure 18.2 The Wytch Farm oilfield

Even if further large reserves are discovered, it is unlikely that their exploration would be encouraged quickly. Given the 'scare' of 1973, and the knowledge that oil reserves may eventually be used up, there is always likely to be restraint on production. The price of petrol may fluctuate from time to time, because producers worldwide adjust to demand and try to make sure that they stay in business and make a profit in return for the investment which they have made and the risks that they have taken in financing oil exploration.

The costs and benefits

Oil is easily transportable and usable and so it has many benefits as a source of energy compared with other fuels, if it sells at a reasonable price. But there are also costs – and not only in financial terms.

- The use of land for oil refineries, storage areas and oil tanker ports is considerable. Some environmental and conservation groups oppose particular developments because of the disturbance to the countryside and the habitat of birds and plants.
- The lead in petrol is a source of air pollution. Though it helps to improve the performance of modern high-compression engines, it is also a hazard to health when pushed out into the atmosphere through vehicle exhausts. Some countries have already banned the addition of lead and EC laws may make it illegal in Britain by 1990.
- If oil is spilt by tanker-ships – either in unloading, through an accident, or through the illegal flushing-out of tanks whilst at sea – it creates oil-slick hazards which affect bathing beaches and other areas of coastline.
- The burning of heavy fuel oils with a high sulphur content creates 'acid rain'. This increased acidity in rainfall has already been noticed in Scandinavia. It is claimed that Britain has caused the death of hundreds of animals, plants and fish in Norway and Sweden because it has allowed high levels of sulphur emission from power-station chimneys. The prevailing winds have carried these emissions eastwards. Britain has recently promised to control this.

Case study: Sullom Voe

If you had visited the Shetland Islands in 1960, you would have found a quiet group of islands off the north Scottish coast, suffering from population decline. Lerwick, the main town and harbour, was the base for a small fishing fleet, and the main link for ferries to the Scottish mainland. To the north of Lerwick lay a natural, deep-water harbour called Sullom Voe (see Fig. 18.4), quite unused.

Exploration for oil in the mid-1960s revealed oil reserves in the North Sea, to the east of Shetland, in the area now known as the Brent oil field. This was the first of many discoveries in the same area in the 1970s. The oil exploration firms needed a major deep-sea oil terminal for the pipelines which would pump the oil ashore. Sullom Voe was an obvious choice, despite the fears and protests of some of the islanders.

The first oil came ashore in 1978 from two giant under-sea pipelines which had been laid from the Brent/Beryl field and the Ninian field. By 1981 Sullom

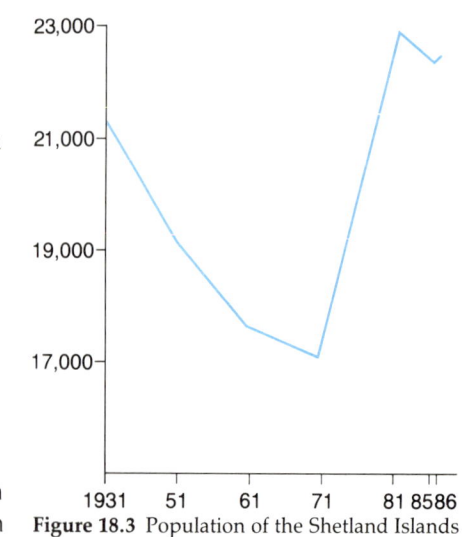

Figure 18.3 Population of the Shetland Islands

Voe was in full operation. On 24 October 1982 a record 1,345,635 barrels of oil came into the terminal on *one day*.

The development of the terminal has had a massive impact on the low heather-covered hills which surround the harbour. But it has also deeply affected the lives and the economies of the Shetland Islanders. The Shetland Island Council and the Highlands and Islands Development Board have sought to guide profit from the development into helping other industries on the islands and in improving the quality of life for those who live there. But the Shetlands can never go back to being the quiet, deserted islands which they once were.

Figure 18.4 Sullom Voe, plan of the terminal

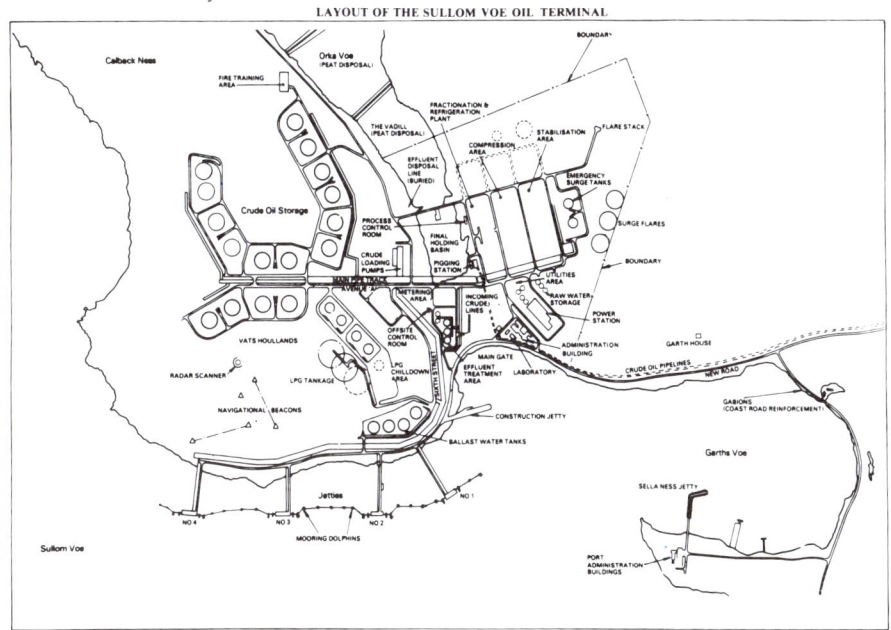

Figure 18.5 Sullom Voe, before the terminal was built

Figure 18.6 Sullom Voe, after development

The growth of the gas industry

Gas produced from coal was first used to light a room in a house in Redruth, Cornwall, in 1792. The widespread use of gas for lighting houses and streets dates from 1812 when parts of Westminster, London, were first illuminated with gas lamps. The invention of the gas mantle increased the popularity of gas lighting. The use of gas for heating and cooking grew rapidly from the end of the nineteenth century. Today it is rare to see a gas lamp, but central-heating systems are often gas fired and gas cookers are very popular.

The production of gas in the United Kingdom until the mid 1970s was achieved by heating coal in a closed container. After 1830 private companies had been established in most towns and cities to manufacture and sell gas, as well as to pipe it into houses and factories through gas-mains laid under the streets. The manufacture of gas depended on a constant supply of coal, usually from the local railway company. Gas-works were easier to locate in a town as the gas had to be stored in large gas-holders at least 15 metres high. But this manufactured, **'town gas'** had its disadvantages besides the danger of explosions, the 15 per cent carbon monoxide content made it toxic – inhaling it was a common form of suicide.

By 1945 other fuels, such as oil and electricity, were competitors in the energy market. The gas industry developed more efficient methods of gas production and searched for new markets for the by-products. In 1961 **natural gas** was discovered at Gröningen, in the Netherlands, raising hopes that similar gas finds might be possible in the southern North Sea. And soon afterwards commercial quantities of gas were discovered off the coast of Norfolk. The reserves were so large that plans were made to convert all gas-burning appliances in homes and factories in the United Kingdom to burn the new North Sea gas.

Government involvement

The Government has been involved in the gas industry since 1948; before this date the production and distribution of gas was in the hands of private companies. In some areas the competition of private enterprise led to rival gas companies laying gas-mains on opposite sides of the same street.

One of the growing needs of the gas industry, once it was under one management, was to create a single connected gas-distribution network, similar to the electricity supply super-grid. The advantage of such unified grids is that a shortage in one area can be made good using the surplus from another. The gas grid has now been established. It has been completed since the discovery and use of North Sea gas.

Environmental considerations

North Sea gas is a particularly clean and efficient fuel. The process of extraction and cleaning produces little pollution. Transportation is by pipeline under sea or land and the gas itself is non-toxic. Modern pipeline networks do create some disruption whilst they are being installed across the country, but within a year it is difficult to see where the pipes were laid. Even the maintainance and supervision are hidden, as most routine work is undertaken by 'pigs' within the pipes which are pushed along by the gas pressure. A 'pig' is a plastic ball containing sensors and radio transmitters: when a fault is discovered it is pinpointed by the 'pig' and the position is relayed by short-wave radio to the surface. Helicopter surveys of the pipeline network each fortnight constantly look for problems such as landslides and other damage to the pipes.

Will gas soon be a fuel of the past?

North Sea gas, will not last for ever; by AD 2040 very little gas will remain commercially exploitable, unless consumption falls or massive new gas fields are discovered. At some time prior to this date it is likely that we will be using synthetic natural gas (SNG) which is obtained from either coal or oil. The Westfield pilot plant in Fife can already produce SNG from coal.

Case study: the Frigg field

Between 1969 and 1972 there was a great burst of exploration for oil and gas in the North Sea. The drilling ships and rigs gradually worked their way northwards, searching for the rich deposits which geologists had predicted.

In 1971 a trial drilling struck gas off the coast of Scotland, and subsequent exploration confirmed that the gas was in sufficient quantity to make it worthwhile to bring it ashore by pipeline. The area was 60 per cent in Norwegian territorial waters and 40 per cent in British waters, so several companies became interested in exploiting the area. See Plate 39.

British Gas – supplying many homes in Britain – calculated that natural gas would be cheaper to supply in some areas than gas manufactured by chemical processes (town gas) and so signed a contract with the Total Oil Company and bought the gas which was produced in part of the Frigg field.

The development of a field in such deep and difficult waters needs a great deal of money and huge amounts of equipment. The plan devised for the Frigg field was to build five platforms over the area where the gas reserves were located, in waters over 100 metres deep. One of the drilling platforms was an eight-legged steel frame weighing 8,000 tonnes. On top of this was placed an 800 tonne deck, with another 2,500 tonnes of drilling equipment. A second drilling platform was made of concrete and was even heavier. Each of the two drilling platforms would drill twenty-four wells to produce gas. Two other platforms of smaller size processed the gas before feeding it into pipelines. A fifth platform had 'hotel' accommodation it for the rig workers.

The first season of work was in 1975 and the first gas came ashore in 1977. Two pipelines were laid from Frigg to the mainland terminal at St Fergus on the Scottish east coast. Altogether there were 60,000 lengths of pipe – each 12 metres long – with each pipe 19 mm thick and 800 mm in diameter. A total of 275,000 tonnes of steel was used in building the pipelines.

To protect the pipes from the sea, it was necessary to cover them with a coating of bitumen and concrete before they were towed out to be laid. The pipes were placed in a trench in the sea-bed. The trench was carved out by powerful jets of water from special hoses on board pipe-laying vessels.

The capital investment was great, the technology relatively new and untried, and the weather conditions often very harsh. Many wells which were drilled turned out to have little gas to supply them after all. Financial risks were high. But in the end some wells were rich in fuel and the gas will flow until at least the year 2000. The gamble of exploration has paid off.

182 A Geography of Contemporary Britain

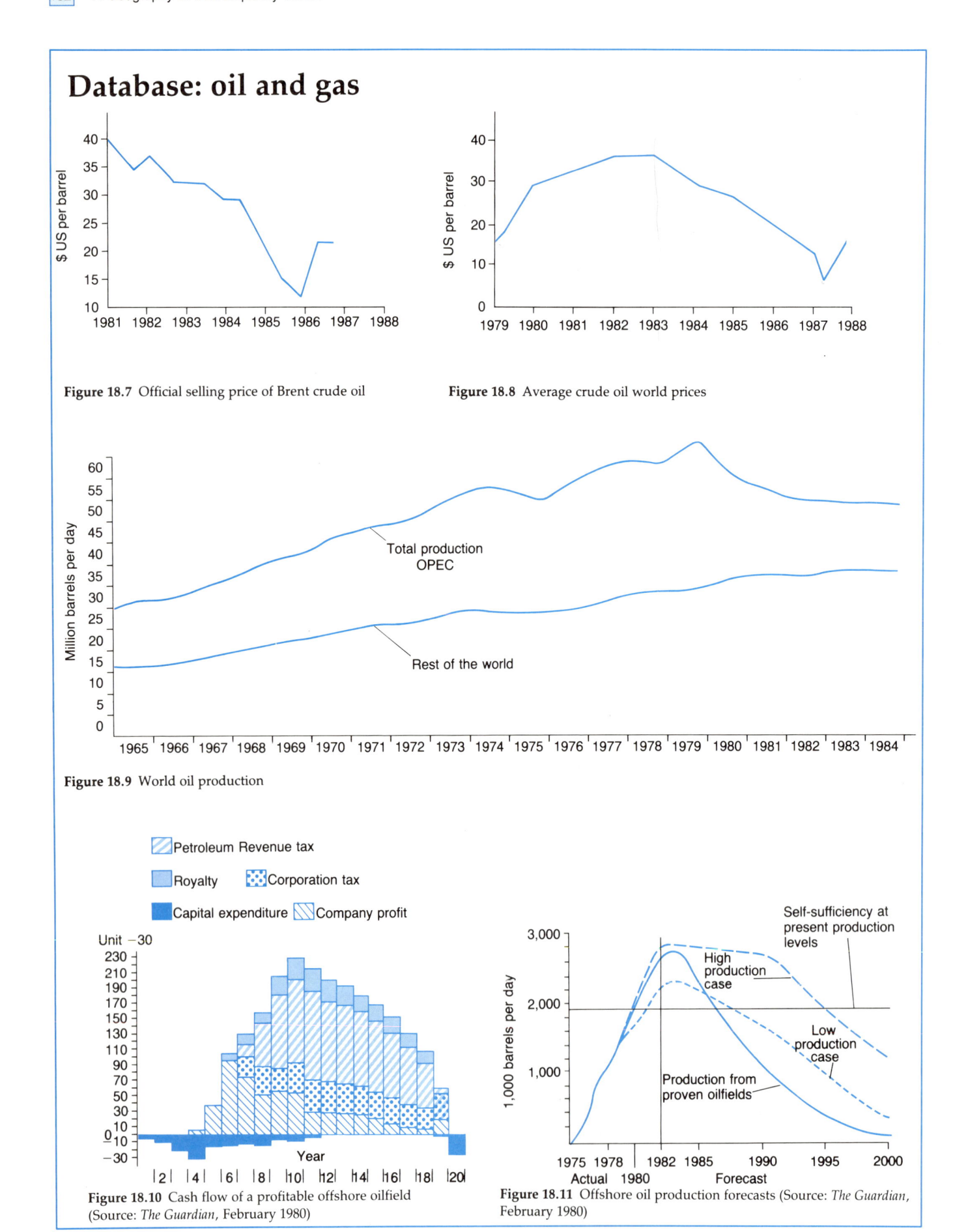

Database: oil and gas

Figure 18.7 Official selling price of Brent crude oil

Figure 18.8 Average crude oil world prices

Figure 18.9 World oil production

Figure 18.10 Cash flow of a profitable offshore oilfield (Source: *The Guardian*, February 1980)

Figure 18.11 Offshore oil production forecasts (Source: *The Guardian*, February 1980)

Workbase

1. Look at Plate 39.
   a) Identify the major pipeline terminals in Britain and the fields which are sending oil by pipeline to them.
   b) Why do you think fields on the Norwegian side of the international boundary send their oil to Britain?
   c) Why do you think British North Sea gas is more expensive than Dutch gas?

2. Read the case study of Sullom Voe in Shetland (pages 178–79).
   a) If you were Chairman of the Shetland District Council what industries would you be seeking to develop, knowing that the oil will not last for ever?
   b) Write a press release which you might give to a Scottish daily newspaper on this topic.

3. See if you can discover (by reading newspapers or watching television news) where *else* in Britain exploration is going on for oil and gas.

4. Look at Figs. 18.8 and 18.9.
   a) Why do you think that oil prices have *fallen* in recent years?
   b) Look at Fig.18.9. What action have the OPEC countries taken to try and stop the fall in prices, and why? Do you think they can be successful?
   c) Name six other major oil-producing areas besides Britain.

5. Find out the difference in price between electricity and gas per btu (British thermal unit) in your area. Your regular fuel bills or local shops should be able to give you the information.

6. Compare the popularity of gas, electricity, oil and solid fuels for heating and cooking by the households of your class. Compile the information into a graph, for display. Discuss the findings.

7. Compare offshore and onshore drilling for oil in respect of:
   a) technical;
   b) economic; and
   c) environmental advantages and disadvantages.

8. Evaluate the hazards and dangers in the exploitation of oil, gas, coal and nuclear power. Which do you think is the safest fuel industry and why?

Chapter 19
Electricity, nuclear power, and the future

Electricity

Unlike coal, gas and oil, electricity is a **secondary energy source**; it is produced by using one of the primary fuels to heat up water, which is then turned into steam and passed through a turbine to generate electric current. The electricity used in Britain is produced at power stations which feed into the National Electricity Grid. The power-stations use a variety of fuels – coal, oil, nuclear and hydro-electric energy, with coal presently the most widely used. Whether the Central Electricity Generating Board should continue to develop new nuclear-powered stations is a matter of much present interest and concern.

Electricity is widely used for lighting, heating and as a source of power for machinery in many factories. Its main advantages are that it is easily accessible in most parts of the country (more so than gas or oil), is easy to transport and is clean.

In the nineteenth century each town had its own small power-generation company with small power stations built independently. These used coal as a primary fuel, brought in by rail (itself using coal to power the steam engines which pulled the wagons).

As demand for electricity grew rapidly in the 1920s and 1930s, power lines between areas were gradually linked up into a National Grid. Power stations were rebuilt on larger and more efficient lines, though still mainly dependent on coal. Only in the period since 1945 have oil-fired and nuclear-powered stations become significant contributors to the grid.

The easy transportability of electricity has always been a great point in its favour as a source of power. A small, easily buried cable can deliver energy to every home and factory. If the power supply is being 'over-loaded' in one region, the grid can bring in power supplies from elsewhere, since there is usually excess capacity of production in the system.

The use of electricity speeded the development of 'footloose' industries (see page 150) away from the coalfields. Many high-technology industries are highly dependent on electricity.

The Government nationalised private electricity companies in 1947 and now has powers, through the CEGB, to influence decisions about investment in power stations and to maintain control of price levels in relation to other competing fuels.

The recent explosion and subsequent radiation leak at the Chernobyl nuclear power station in Russia highlighted the concern which has been growing over the safety of nuclear power stations. Safety standards in Britain are high, but opponents of nuclear power argue that the possibility of a leak can never be totally discounted. The Government's view is that we should rely on a variety of different fuels for our power supply and not be completely dependent on any single fuel source.

CONTRASTING VIEWPOINTS

'Should Britain be developing nuclear energy?'

Rt Hon Peter Walker MBE MP, as Secretary of State for Energy

Nuclear power is the safest form of energy yet known to man. Death and injuries in other energy industries dwarf the figures for the nuclear industry. No other industry has had applied to it the incredibly strict safety standards that have been applied in Britain to the nuclear industry.

There has never been a nuclear emergency at any of this country's civil nuclear installations in over a quarter of a century of operating experience. The movement of spent nuclear fuel has never caused a hazard to the public. The average amount of radiation received by the public from the nuclear industry is one-tenth of one percent of the radiation we all receive from natural resources.

It is time that Britain recognised the contribution to our commercial success that the nuclear industry can provide. French industry has a £1 billion advantage over British industry because France obtains 65% of its electricity from nuclear generation. Belgium obtains 55%, West Germany and Japan obtain a quarter, but Britain as yet only 20%. Even in Britain, the South of Scotland Electricity Board is able to charge its consumers 10% less for their electricity than the price in England because of the larger proportion of nuclear electricity it generates.

In recent months much nonsense has been spoken and written about the nuclear industry; the smallest incident, causing no form of injury to anybody, has been exaggerated as a great national threat. It is time people realised that there is 370 times more radiation from the bricks and stones of our houses than from the nuclear industry; we even get 170 times more radiation from what we eat.

Our electricity, gas and coal industries have remarkable records of safety, but just imagine the opposition to all these forms of energy if they were to be introduced today for the first time. Imagine the possibility of persuading certain journalists and environmental groups to accept electricity, where faulty wires could burn down buildings, accidents could kill children and dogs could be electrocuted. Imagine the outbursts against gas pipes under our streets and in our homes with the possibility that there could be explosions.

With skilled and dynamic leadership, Britain's nuclear industry is providing one hundred thousand jobs, making a considerable contribution to our balance of trade, reducing the nation's energy costs and providing a display of the scientific and engineering skills of the British people.

Arthur Scargill, President, National Union of Mineworkers

Nuclear power is unsafe, uneconomic and absolutely unnecessary. Three terrible disasters (at Britain's Windscale in 1957, the USA's Three Mile Island in 1979 and the Soviet Union's Chernobyl in 1986) have demonstrated the dangers we face.

In Britain, we have evidence of cancers among children and adults born near and working in nuclear plants. Sections of our coast and seas have been poisoned for thousands of years to come by radioactive waste from those plants.

Electricity authorities have now admitted that nuclear-generated electricity costs between 20 and 30 per cent *more* than electricity from coal! Coal, together with wind, wave, tidal, geothermal barrage and - above all - solar power can meet our energy needs indefinitely.

Why, then, have a nuclear programme at all? The answer is that British Governments have continued to use it to produce plutonium for making atomic weapons of death and total destruction.

I have four questions to put to those who argue for nuclear power: Can they guarantee:

1. That workers in the nuclear industry will not continue to show increased rates of cancer because of radioactivity?
2. That there will not be another terrible accident such as Windscale, Three Mile Island or Chernobyl?
3. That our environment will not become more and more contaminated with radioactivity and plutonium?
4. That plutonium will not fall into the hands of criminals or political terrorists?

If the answer to just one of these is 'no guarantee', that's enough to stop *all* nuclear programmes. If the answer is 'no guarantee' to all four, then nobody can challenge the case against nuclear power. *Every nuclear expert, in fact, does agree that there can be no guarantees.*

Case study: Sizewell B

It was agreed that the whole question of Britain's future needs for energy should be considered during a public enquiry into a proposal for another nuclear-power station at Sizewell, on the eastern coast of Suffolk (Sizewell B).

The Central Electricity Generating Board put in plans for a new kind of station based on pressurised-water cooling of the central core of the reactor (PWR), rather than the existing advanced-gas cooled type (AGR).

The enquiry lasted over a year and the report, eventually published in January 1987, took many months to prepare. But the inspector conducting the enquiry upheld the CEGB's case in the face of much opposition from environmental and anti-nuclear groups. He decided that the new kind of reactor would be safe, and that the country's energy needs would be best served by another nuclear-powered station, rather than one using oil or coal to drive its turbines. He agreed that the Sizewell B station would cause some damage to the local environment but felt that national needs were more important than local ones.

Figure 19.1 Sizewell 'A' Nuclear Power Station, Suffolk, opened in 1966

Figure 19.2 Pressurised water reactor

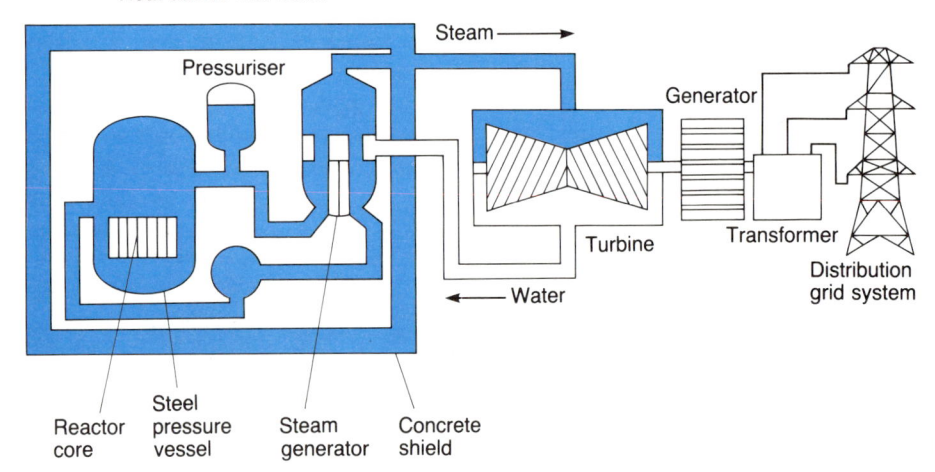

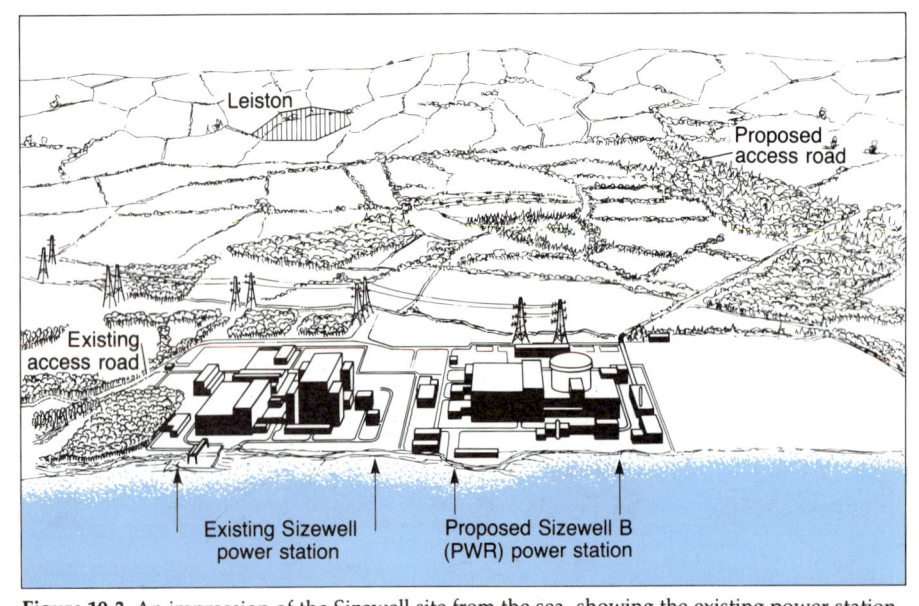

Figure 19.3 An impression of the Sizewell site from the sea, showing the existing power station and the proposed B station

Electricity, nuclear power, and the future 187

Few people knew of Sizewell, a quiet coastal hamlet, before its designation as the site of a nuclear power station (Sizewell A) which began operations in 1966. The reasons for the choice of this location by the CEGB were:
- The area around the site was very sparsely populated (a factor affecting safety and possible environmental intrusion).
- It was a coastal location and this would allow the use of sea water for cooling the reactor and dispersing heat (Sizewell A uses 123,000,000 litres an hour).
- There were firm ground foundations – necessary because of the heavy weight of the reactor vessels and other components and also an advantage in the construction of the extensive concrete shields which were built around the central part of the station.
- It was near to areas of high-demand for electricity (the south-east) and would reduce the need for power transfers from Midland power stations.
- A railway was nearby – the safest way of transporting spent fuel-rods away is by rail.

The Sizewell A reactor had operated satisfactorily and there was space for a second power station alongside, so there was good reason for the CEGB's choice of site. Local engineering industry and farming had declined in recent years and over 500 jobs were provided at Sizewell A, so it was not surprising that there was considerable local *support* for the building of another station, despite the fears of national enviromental groups.

There was as much concern about the disruption which the building of Sizewell B would cause as about safety of the station when in operation. The CEGB promised to improve road access and build a by-pass to satisfy local demands; they also agreed to use sea-dredged and transported 'aggregate' (for cement) and bring in major components for the power station by sea. They also promised landscaping and tree plantations to screen the new station. 'Although a power station is too big to hide, we'll do what we can' said the CEGB.

The building of Sizewell B has gone ahead and it is planned to be operating by 1994. It will cost £1,500 million to build, but will produce enough electricity to meet the needs of the whole of East Anglia. Hopefully this will be in complete safety, but can we ever be sure?

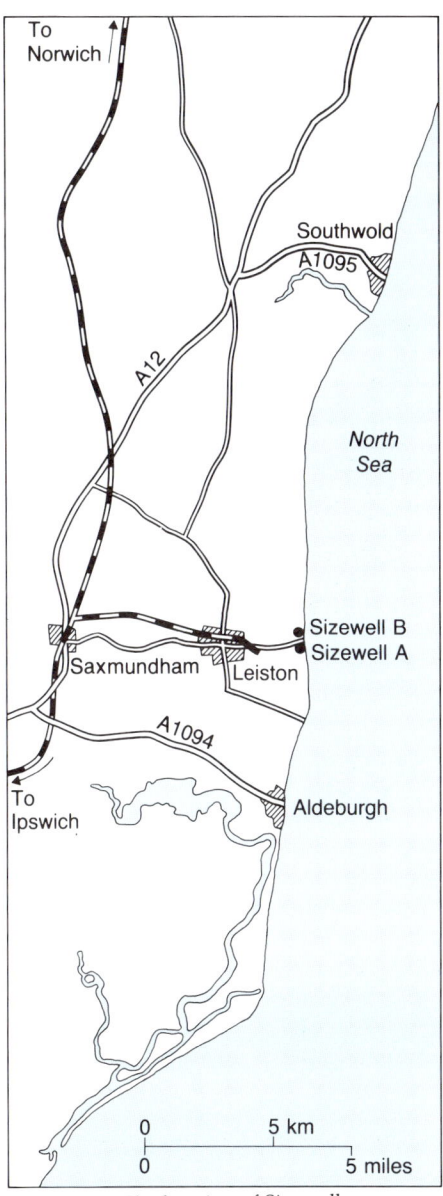

Figure 19.4 The location of Sizewell

Figure 19.5 The size of a nuclear power station in comparison with other familiar buildings. Do you recognise any of them?

Plate 41 A modern coal-cutting 'shearer' in action at Bagworth Colliery, Leicestershire. The use of machinery like this considerably increases the amount of coal that can be mined per shift. Why are some older mines unable to benefit from such equipment?

Plate 42 The Brent 'D' oil production platform in the North Sea. It not only drills for oil but also stores, meters and pumps it ashore. Note the 'accommodation vessel' whose legs can be seen *behind* the platform. What factors might affect the decision to develop a production platform over a borehole which finds oil or gas?

Plate 43 The Wylfa nuclear power station, Anglesey, opened in 1972. The Central Electricity Generating Board built artificial hills, over 100 feet high, to blend the station into the surrounding countryside. Why might the CEGB also be the owners of the sheep grazing in the foreground of this picture?

Plate 44 A Gas pipeline. Work in progress, sinking a pipeline beneath the River Tweed on the borders of England and Scotland.

Plate 45 A Gas pipeline. The same scene, two years later. Can the environment be 'the same' once the pipeline has been built?

Plate 46 A 'steam special' crossing the famous Ribblehead Viaduct in the Pennines, on the railway line from Settle to Carlisle. Can the use of such lines for tourism replace their former importance as freight?

Plate 47 An aerial view of Heathrow Airport, London. Can you identify a) the runways b) the four major terminal buildings?

Plate 48 The growing telecommunications industry has recently been privatised and there is now competition in telephone provision. This is one of the areas of expanding employment for both men and women in Britain; Britain's prosperity in the future will probably depend on the success of industries such as these. Can you name other industries in which job prospects should be bright in the year 2000?

⑪

42

43

44

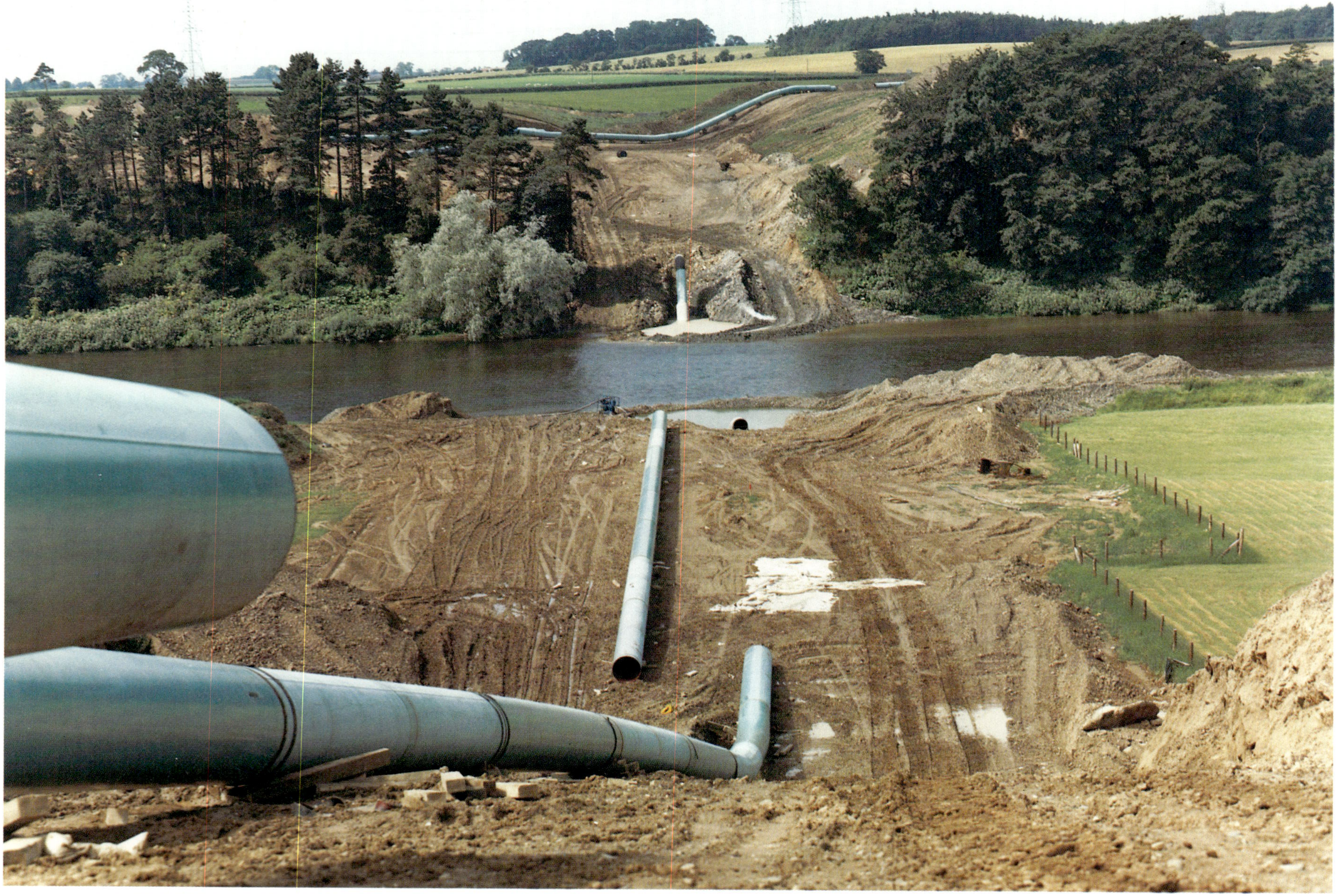

45

46

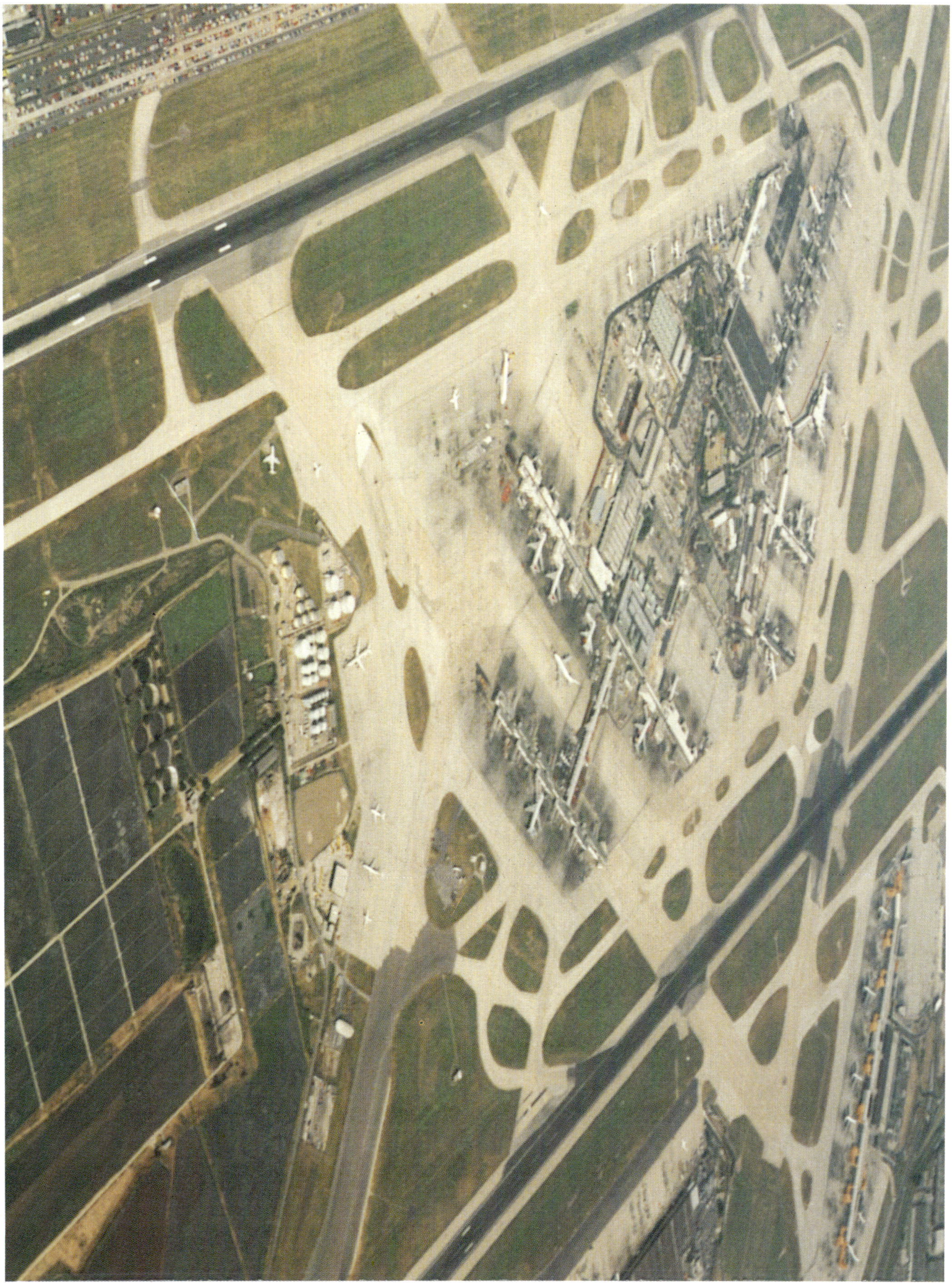

47

(48)

Electricity, nuclear power, and the future

Energy Futures

Biomass

Energy from the sun is trapped by plants. Each year the total net primary production of all the vegetation in the world is ten times the world's annual energy consumption. Trees and plants 'fix' carbon by photosynthesis using the sun's energy and this energy is can be re-released on burning or as the material decomposes as garbage or dung. In Brazil sugar-cane is used to make ethanol which is added to petrol (in a proportion of 20 per cent ethanol, 80 per cent petrol). Over 100,000 barrels are produced each day – four million tonnes per annum. At the petrol pumps the mixture of ethanol and petrol is called Gasohol.

Both soft and hardwoods can be grown as fuel for burning. Water weeds, such as the water hyacinth and seaweed, can be anaerobically fermented (without oxygen) to produce methane gas.

The countries most likely to take advantage of biomass energy are those where plants grow fastest – tropical countries, where rainfall is high. But even in the United Kingdom we use biomass energy from peat, bio-gas from animal wastes and gas extracted from garbage landfill sites. There are a number of sewage disposal works which generate sufficient methane gas from effluent not only to power generators, providing electricity for the sewage works, but also to supply power to the National Grid.

Figure 19.6 Alternative energy supplies

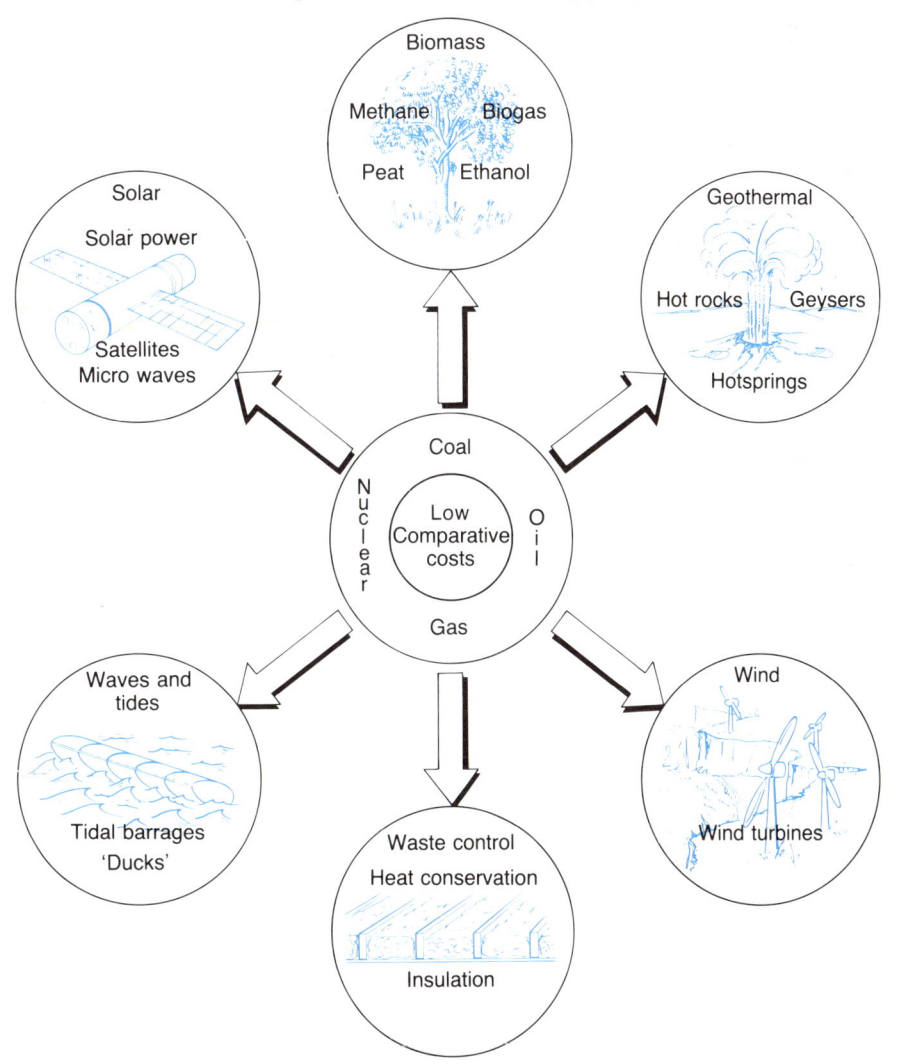

Hot Rocks (Geothermal Energy)

In Iceland, New Zealand and other countries hot water and steam emerge as geysers and hot springs which can be harnessed for electricity production and direct space-heating. Below the earth's surface there are 'hot spots', for example 5 kilometres below Rosemanowes in Cornwall ... the rock temperature is approximately 200°C. Trials are taking place to extract this energy by drilling deep bore-holes; the rocks will then be fractured using explosive charges, creating cracks into which water can then be pumped and raised to the surface. The water emerges at a temperature of 65–75°C and it can be used for direct input into central-heating systems.

Research indicates that energy equivalent to four million tonnes of coal a year could be produced by this method in the United Kingdom. The most likely areas are Cornwall, Durham, the Inner Hebrides, Bath and Bristol, the Hampshire Basin and the Midland Valley of Scotland.

Wind power

Wind power has long been a source of energy in many countries, including the Netherlands, Greece and the United Kingdom. The wind is not an ideal energy source as it is unreliable, – in additon, to produce electricity very large numbers of wind generators would be required.

In 1982 a wind-turbine owned and operated by the CEGB started to feed electricity into the National Grid. Its maximum power output is 200 kilowatts (1 kilowatt powers a one-bar electric fire for one hour). The turbine is situated north of Carmarthen Bay in Wales and is experimental at present. To be really effective, wind-turbines will have to be much larger and there will have to be many more, perhaps on wind farms with hundreds of rotors.

In 1984 the Government gave a grant of £12 million for wind-turbine research. Two sites have been chosen: one at Burgar Hill, Orkney, the other at the Carmarthen Bay site. The Orkney wind-turbine will produce sufficient power for a thousand homes: it has massive twin-blades on a tower 45 metres high and will deliver 3 megawatts when wind speeds are over 17 metres per second. A third turbine may be built at Richborough in Kent.

What will be the environmental impact of hundreds of wind turbines? To provide a similar output to that of a large power station (1 million kilowatts) would require a thousand wind turbines spread out over 800 km^3.

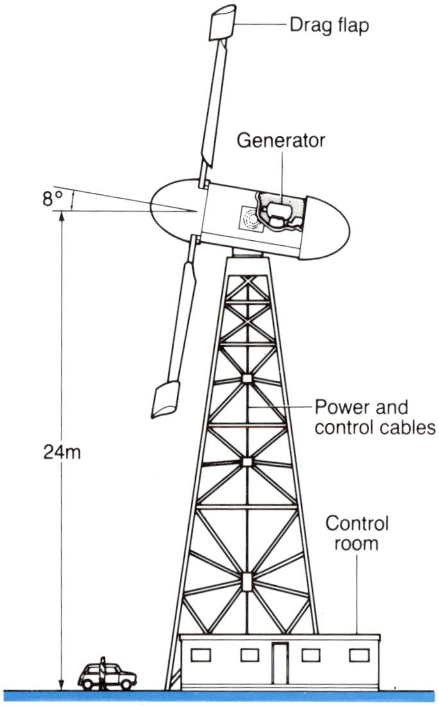

Figure 19.7 The CEGB'S 200 kw wind turbine at Carmarthen Bay

Solar power

19,000 solar systems are at work in the United Kingdom heating homes and offices. Heat is collected using black, heat-absorbent panels enclosed in glass. The heat trapped is transferred into the buildings using water or ducted air, via heat exchangers. Solar collection is usually combined with high levels of thermal insulation, using double-glazing as well as wall and roof insulation. Houses designed to take advantage of the sun's heat are also sited so that the living areas and solar collectors face south.

Solar heating is designed to supplement other forms of heating, whether produced by electricity, gas or oil. In future, solar heating may contribute up to 60 per cent of the energy input of an average house in the United Kingdom.

Scientists are dreaming of solar collectors in space. Photovoltaic cells mounted on satellites could be operational by the end of the century, with power being transmitted to earth using microwave beams. One such satellite would weigh 10,000 tonnes. Forty satellites could supply 40 per cent of Europe's power needs by AD 2030.

Figure 19.8 Energy flows in the United Kingdom, 1986

Iron and steel industry	3%
Other industry	16%
Transport	41%
Domestic users	27%
Other	13%

Waves and tides

Electricity produced by tidal rise and fall is produced at La Rance in western France. To generate power in this way both a particular shape of coastline and a large tidal range each day are necessary. As the tide comes in, it passes through holes in a dam wall to an upper river estuary, where it is trapped. As the tide ebbs, it passes back to the open sea, via the turbines, and so generates power. The most suitable location in the United Kingdom for a similar project would be the Severn Estuary (see the article from *The Guardian*, Fig. 19.9). Studies completed in 1980 showed that tidal-power projects could be built at one of two locations in the estuary. The northern site will probably be chosen as it will be cheaper to build, costing £4.5 million. It would provide 6 per cent of United Kingdom energy needs and would create 21,000 jobs for ten years. Salt-water flooding would be reduced to the north of the dam. Disadvantages of the scheme include the impact on wildlife habitats, especially the thousands of wading birds, as well as the increased amount of silt that would accumulate. At present power generated in this way would be more expensive than that from oil or coal-fired stations.

Figure 19.9 *The Guardian*

Severn barrage to generate electricity is feasible says Energy Department scientist

A tidal barrage to generate electricity from the Severn estuary has been declared technically feasible by an investigating committee under the chairmanship of the Department of Energy's chief scientist, Sir Hermann Bondi.

The Under-Secretary for Energy, Mr John Moore, said yesterday that the economics of the scheme were still uncertain, but that output from the barrage's turbines would be more than had previously been calculated. If the costs of coal and oil-fired power stations continued to rise, tidal electricity might soon be competitive.

The Bondi committee has selected two possible lines for the barrage. The westerly of the two, which would harness nearly all the estuary's potential energy, would run from Aberthaw on the Welsh coast to a point just west of Minehead.

But probably more economical, in the committee's view would be a less ambitious barrier running from Sand Point, just east of Weston-Super-Mare to Lavernock Point, roughly half way between Barry and Cardiff. The flood tide would be allowed through sluices into the upper estuary and then forced to blow back through power-generating turbines on the ebb.

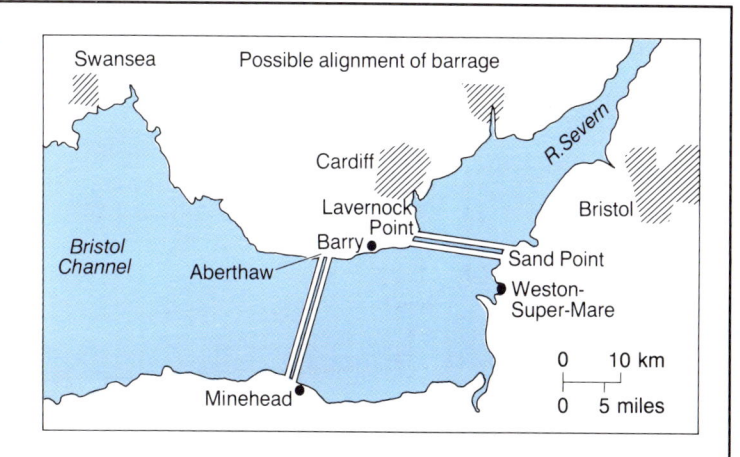

The barrage would make use of the estuary's exceptionally large tidal range that produces the Severn bore. It would be one of the biggest civil engineering projects ever undertaken and its cost has been estimated at anything from £3 billion to £9 billion.

If, however it can generate electricity at between 2p and 3p per kilowatt/hour, as the latest reports suggest, it is on the brink of being economically competitive without the physical hazards of nuclear power or the political problems of oil and coal supply. Its vast output could satisfy 5 or 10 per cent of Britain's total electricity demand.

But before its feasibility can finally be established, a lot more work has to be done on its environmental implications, including the effect on tides elsewhere on the coast.

Dennis Johnson adds: One of the leading advocates of a Severn barrage over the past 10 years, Dr Tom Shaw, of Bristol, said last night that it could be started towards the end of the present decade.

Dr Shaw, formerly senior lecturer in civil engineering at Bristol University and now a consultant design engineer with a national civil engineering group, said the Government's report confirmed what he had believed for many years.

'The Department of Energy is now saying that a barrage would produce electricity only a little more expensively than nuclear generation and more cheaply than by other methods,' he said 'That means the prospect for tidal power can only get better as costs increase.

'This project will attract world wide attention as the first of its kind. I think there should now be an attempt to begin involving the public so that the idea of a project on this scale is accepted. It is no longer just talk.'

Case study: Milton Keynes – solar city?

Figure 19.10 A house, mainly heated by solar panels, Milton Keynes, Buckinghamshire

Britain's newest city, Milton Keynes, has invested money in a number of experimental schemes to see if houses can be heated more efficiently. Firms were allowed to build a special housing estate in which futuristic house designs could be tried out, with an emphasis on methods of heat conservation.

The Homeworld Estate, in the Bradwell Common area, has thirty-seven houses built in various styles. Ninety-five per cent of the houses had higher standards of insulation than was required by the building regulations of the time. Most used partial heating by solar panels.

In Futurehome 2000 all the major rooms faced south and a glass conservatory trapped warm air for distribution around the house. The Ideal Home had a massive array of solar panels (see Fig. 19.10). The Bradville House, built in 1975, had its heat and cost budget carefully monitored by experts. Over a five-year period it was estimated that 56 per cent of all heating needs could be provided by solar powered panels – which cost no more than their capital cost and installation.

The Milton Keynes Development Council was also energy-conscious in other ways. It offered householders grants to insulate their houses, and closely monitored the heat losses in its own offices and remedied them. It also sought to encourage housing layouts in the city which maximised the use of the sun to heat living areas.

Electricity, nuclear power, and the future 193

ENERGY WORLD INDIVIDUAL PLOTS

The Round House

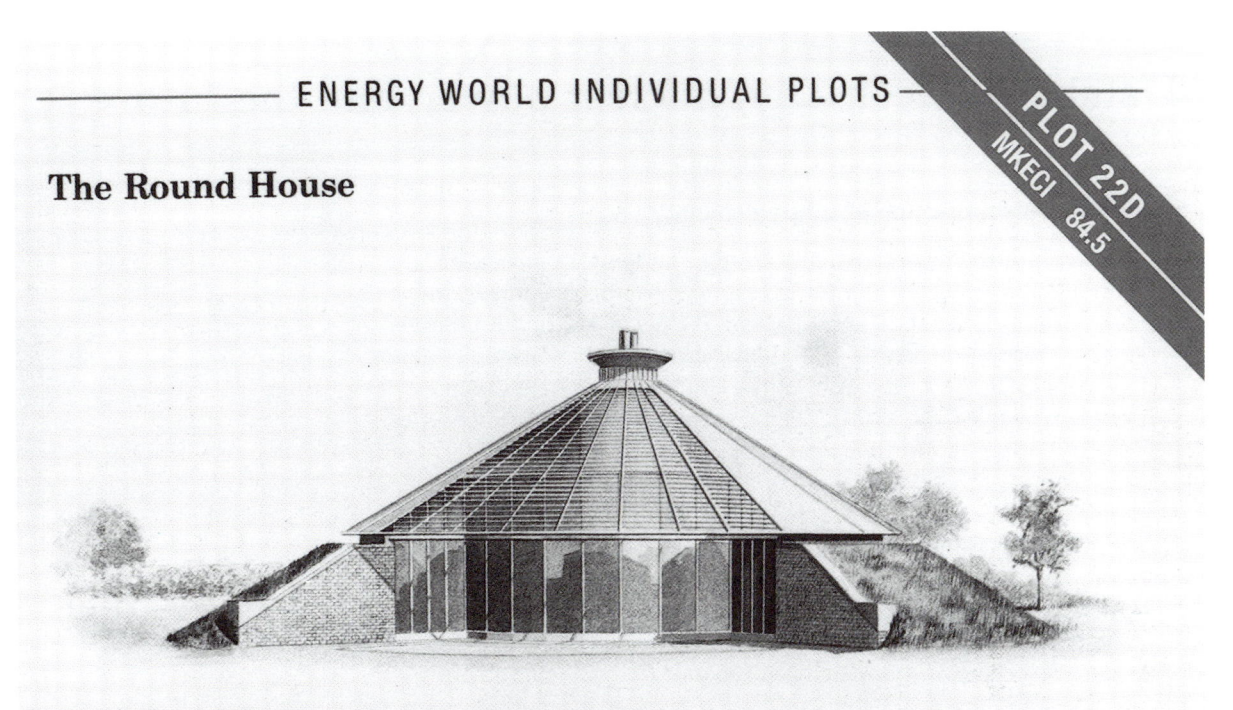

PLOT 22D
MKECI 84.5

DESIGNED AND BUILT BY: Keith Horn Dip Arch (Hons) RIBA K C Developments
ESTIMATED MARKET VALUE: £180,000

ACCOMMODATION
- Floor area 200m^2
- 4 bedrooms
- 2 bathrooms
- Living area
- Study
- Snug
- Dining/recreation area
- Kitchen
- Utility room
- Conservatory
- Double garage
- Swimming pool

ENERGY HIGHLIGHTS
- Two storey integral conservatory providing pre-heat ventilation
- South facing living spaces
- High levels of insulation to ground floor, walls and roof
- Double glazing using low emissivity glass
- Protective earth berms
- External adjustable sun shade louvres
- Mechanical heat recovery system
- Thermal heat store in conservatory

The Round House is designed to be energy efficient by means of its shape, plan form, thermal capacity, and efficiency of the heating and ventilation systems.

The circular plan and conical shape minimise external surfaces. The sloping earth berms protect and insulate the external walls. The berm slope combines with the roof profile to minimise wind impact and associated heat loss.

The construction materials of concrete and brick provide a large thermal mass which is heated principally passively through the southern glazing. The conservatory floor and south facing central core wall act as primary heat stores. High levels of insulation in the floor and walls help maintain the solar energy gain.

The south facing conservatory is a major design element which provides increased solar heat gain to adjoining living spaces, preheats the ventilation air for distribution to the spaces and heats the heat stores. It also acts as a draught excluding vestibule in winter and additional living space in spring, summer and autumn. The conservatory is double glazed throughout, and is protected from overheating by adjustable external louvres.

A mechanical ventilation and heat recovery system distributes pre-heated air, extracts waste heat from kitchen and bathrooms and offsets condensation.

A low temperature water filled underfloor heating system provides the main source of low cost heat. A high efficiency solid fuel fire provides supplementary seasonal heating.

The south facing pool is designed to be both pleasing and functional by reflected light to the interior in winter and providing cooling summer air.

FOR FURTHER INFORMATION:
Keith Horn Dip Arch (Hons) RIBA
K C Developments
18 St Pauls Place
Canonbury
London
N1 2QF
Telephone 01-359 8008

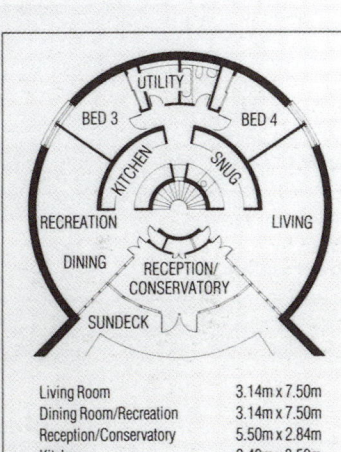

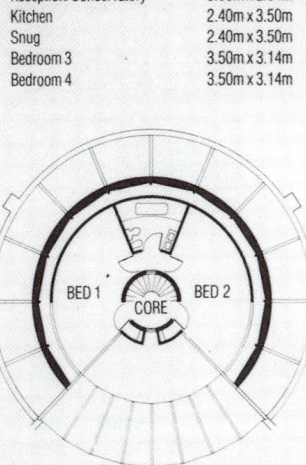

Living Room	3.14m x 7.50m
Dining Room/Recreation	3.14m x 7.50m
Reception/Conservatory	5.50m x 2.84m
Kitchen	2.40m x 3.50m
Snug	2.40m x 3.50m
Bedroom 3	3.50m x 3.14m
Bedroom 4	3.50m x 3.14m

Bedroom 1	3.55m x 6.50m
Bedroom 2	3.55m x 6.50m

MILTON KEYNES ENERGY WORLD

Figure 19.11 A description of one of Milton Keynes' experimental houses

Database: Electricity, nuclear power, and the future

The CEGB's projection of future demands

At one extreme, if there were to be high and energy-intensive economic growth and no new investment in nuclear power, our coal-burn in the year 2000 could be in excess of 130 million tonnes, against a background of a total demand for coal of some 200 million tonnes. However, in the light of the country's recent economic performance, assumptions like this seem optimistic.

At the other end of the scale, if there was to be the largest programme of nuclear construction consistent with a declining economy between now and the year 2000, the CEGB's coal burn would be *lower* than today's.

Taking a pragmatic view, an annual coal-burn of about 70 million tonnes in the year 2000 seems probable.... In all circumstances – even taking our nuclear plans into account – our coal-burn is likely to rise. So whatever happens, our reliance on coal will remain considerable ...

Source: CEGB brochure

Figure 19.12 Present and future sources of UK electricity generation

1984 (February) Fuel burn in UK power stations		2090	
Coal	75%	Coal	
Nuclear fusion	14%	Nuclear fusion	
Oil	8%	Wind	Electricity generation
Hydro	3%	Hydro	
		Waves/tides	
		Geothermal	
		Bio-gas	

Source: The Guardian, 20 September 1984

Figure 19.13 UK nuclear generation

Type	Magnox	AGR	PWR	Others
Date first commissioned	1956	1962	1965*	1967**
Number in operation	11	6	1	1
Fuel	Uranium in magnesium alloy rods	Enriched uranium oxide	Enriched uranium	Enriched uranium
Heat transfer by	Gas	Gas under pressure	Water under pressure	Heavy water

* Prototype Dounreay 1975
** Windfrith; no more of this type to be built

Figure 19.14 Electricity generation in the UK

Electricity, nuclear power, and the future 195

Workbase

1. Identify the area of Suffolk in which Sizewell is situated in your atlas. Find the approximate locations of other nuclear stations listed below:

Hinkley Point (Somerset)	Dounreay (North coast of Scotland)
Bradwell (Essex)	Hunterston (Ayrshire, Scotland)
Dungeness (Kent)	Chapelcross (north of Solway Firth)
Hartlepool (Cleveland)	Heysham (Lancashire)
Sellafield (Cumbria)	Berkeley and Oldbury (Severn Estuary)
Winfrith (Dorset)	Torness (East Lothian, Scotland)
Wylfa (Anglesey, Wales)	Trawsfynydd (near Harlech, Wales)

   What do they appear to have in common in terms of location?

2. Study Fig. 19.14 and answer these questions:
   a) What reasons can you put forward for the cluster of power stations along the Rivers Trent, Ouse and Don?
   b) What do you notice about the location of the oil-powered stations?
   c) What determines the location of a 'pumped-water station' and how do you think it operates?
   d) What do you notice about the locations of nuclear-powered stations? Can you suggest a reason for this, *different* to the reason in b)?

3. Scandinavian countries have recently accused the Central Electricity Generating Board of killing fish, animal and plant life in their countries.
   a) How could the CEGB possibly do this?
   b) What is the name given to the central 'agent' in this controversy?
   c) How could the problem be solved?

4. Look at Fig. 19.12.
   a) Which of the energy sources do you think will be *most* important in the year 2090?
   b) What will decide *your* choice of energy sources when you move into a house of your own?

5. These three stories were in *The Times* on 14 July 1988:
   a) Britain is to become the first country in the world to dismantle a nuclear power station. Berkeley, Gloucestershire, built in 1962 is to be taken out of operation after completing its expected life-span of 30 years. The area is expected to be a safe 'greenfield site' after another 100 years.
   b) Thousands of highly radioactive fuel rods will be taken from Berkeley inside heavily shielded metal flasks. They will go to Sellafield, Cumbria, for reprocessing.
   c) The Sellafield nuclear reprocessing complex is likely to become a package-holiday centre. The recently opened £5 million visitors centre will be the main attraction.

   Compare and comment on these news items.

6. Write a paragraph of comment about 'The Round House' (Fig 19.11) from the point of view of a prospective owner.

Chapter 20
Transport and communications

Transport

Consider the following problems (first work out the answers on your own and write them down; then compare them with the answers of another person considering why you agree or disagree):

1. You are the manager of a coal-mine in north Nottinghamshire and supply the Ratcliffe-on-Soar power station with regular, daily supplies of coal. Your options are either to use fifty lorries or one train. Which form of transport would you use and why?
2. You have a new job and have to commute to the city each day. Do you use a train or car? The railway station is 5 minutes from your house and the city terminus is 4 minutes from your new office; total travel time 30 minutes. Your car will get you there in 50 minutes, if there are no traffic jams; you will have to park in a public car park. Costs for rail and car are almost identical. Which do you choose and why? If you join a car-sharing scheme, would that make any difference to your decision?
3. Your factory makes carpets. They go all over the United Kingdom in small lots, never sufficient to fill one single container. You do not own a fleet of lorries. A local road-haulage firm guarantees door-to-door delivery, and so does British Rail. The local man is slightly cheaper than BR, unless you can fill a container. What is your decision?
4. You are a baker. You have to deliver bread and cakes to five different shops and one large supermarket by 10 a.m. each morning. Do you use road, rail, or . . . ?
5. You are a Glasgow-based businesswoman and have to attend a meeting in London, which will start with coffee at 10.30 a.m. Your options: rail, using the Inter-City 125; air, using the British Airways shuttle. What are the advantages and disadvantages of each method of travel?
6. You have to travel from Manchester to Paris once each month. Cost is no problem. How will you travel and why?

Some of the factors you will have considered when thinking about the six problems may have included:

- The cost per kilometre of the transport you chose.
- The time taken to complete your journey.
- The amount of goods you intended to carry.
- How many passengers were making the journey.
- The convenience and pleasure of any journey.

All these factors *consciously* affected some of your decisions, but probably the most important were **cost** and **convenience**.

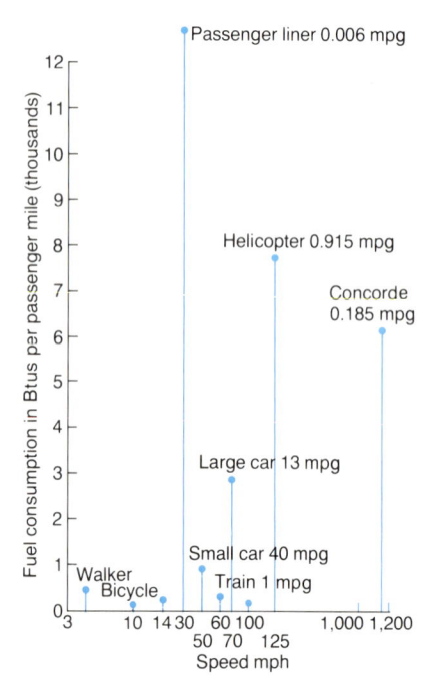

Figure 20.1 Energy versus speed

The next three factors will affect those already listed, but they are usually hidden:

- Whether the network you are using – road, rail, air, canal – is expanding or contracting. Roads are still expanding their networks, as more and more motorways are built each year. Railways have been contracting, as each year more stretches of railway track fall into disuse. Even some parts of the road-user network, for example the country bus services, are less used as more of the population own cars.
- Does the network you are using receive subsidies from local or central government, as do the uneconomic railway lines of rural Scotland?
- Is the transport you are using publicly or privately owned?

Each of the above factors has an effect on:

- The location of factories, businesses, leisure and shopping facilities.
- The quality of life in town and country, especially for those who do not own cars.

The sections which follow consider in more detail, motorways and cars, ports and airports, railways and telecommunications; all of the factors will be connected with these forms of transport in one way or another.

Road men in reverse?
Change your methods, Motorway planners are told; but they still have secrecy on their side

Figure 20.2 A view of the planning process

The mighty motorways

Figure 20.4 and 20.7 clearly show that during the last twenty years great changes have taken place in the patterns of transport in the United Kingdom. The most dramatic change is that road transport is now vitally important for both goods and passengers: in the 1980s 90 per cent of all passengers travelled by road and nearly 80 per cent of all freight went by road.

The first few kilometres of motorway were opened in 1953. The Government realised that the United Kingdom road system required modernisation and that the real need was for fast, straight roads that avoided main towns and linked the major centres of population and commerce Now there are nearly 3000 kilometres of motorway and many kilometres of dual-carriageway that have been upgraded to motorway standards. The main motorways link:

- the South with the North (M5/M6 and M1);
- the East with the West (M4 and M62);
- some isolated areas with main M routes (M2, M50 etc.);
- M routes to the London ring motorway (M25).

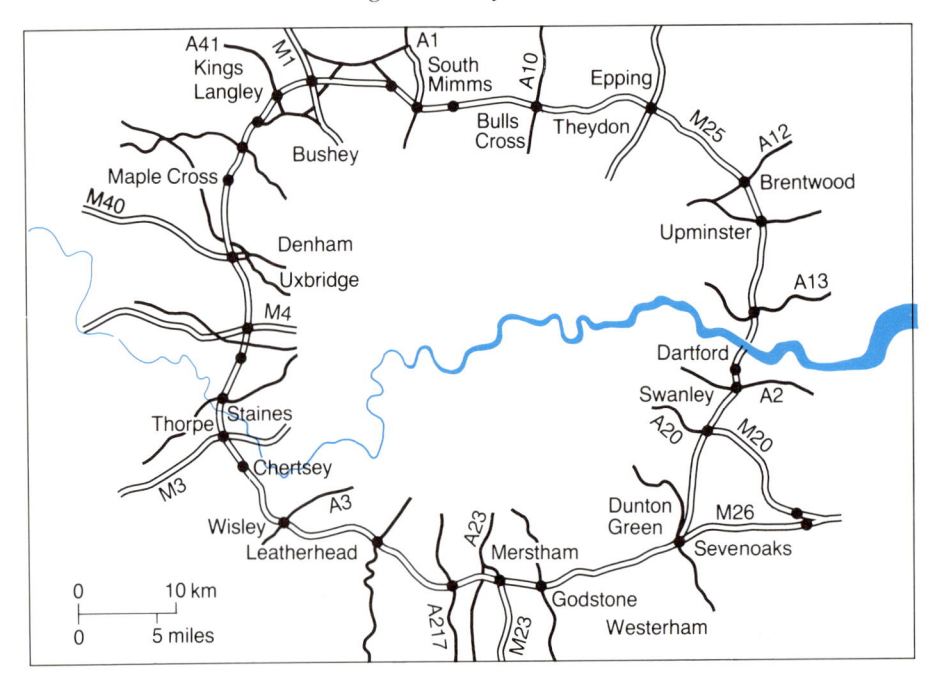

Figure 20.3 The M25 around London

Why did this sudden spurt of motorway building take place? Some of the possible reasons are:

- petrol was much cheaper in the 1960s (see page 182–183);
- the economy was in good shape and many more people were becoming car-owners for the first time. Car-ownership increased from 1 million in 1930 to 10 million in 1962, 15 million in 1980, with a projected 21–28 million cars by the year 2000;
- an increasing amount of freight was moving by road.

With this massive demand, the Government invested heavily in a road-building programme particularly from 1970 to 1976. Since that time road construction has slowed as a result of:

- the increase in oil prices;
- the difficulties in the United Kingdom economy, part of a world economic recession;
- the fact that the motorway network is almost complete.

Roads form patterns called **networks**. The efficiency of any network can be measured in a number of ways, including times to travel from one part of the network to another. One way to increase network efficiency is to build new connections within it, as is the case when new river crossings are built. The increased efficiency can then be calculated as time-saving, comparing old journey times with new ones using the new bridge connection. This sort of exercise can be undertaken using the Severn Bridge on the M4, or the Humber Bridge linking the M180 with the M62; both bridges have resulted in great journey time savings.

Notice on Fig. 20.4 that time is shown as more important than distance. If you had to travel in the time of stage-coach Britain, the country would have felt much larger than it does to-day in modern motorway Britain.

New roads have other effects, one of which is to attract traffic from other routes. The M25 is already attracting increased volumes of traffic (see Fig. 20.3) as it links many motorways, London's major airports and also creates a fast ring road for the capital. Even in its first months of operation there were traffic jams at peak times at the Dartford Tunnel, where the M25 crosses the Thames; a second tunnel is now planned.

Figure 20.4 'Shrinking Britain': hours from London by the fastest mode of transport

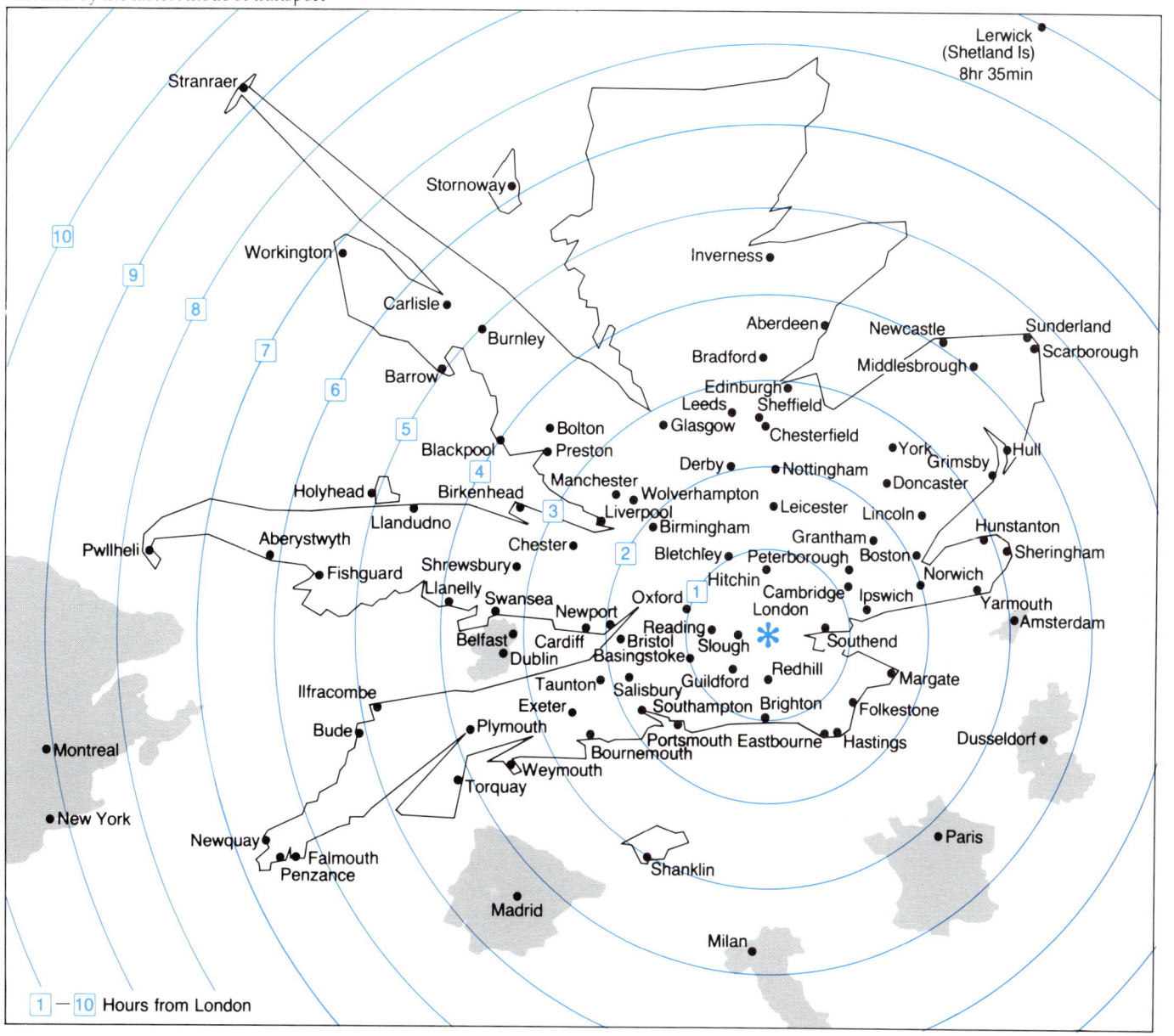

Case study: the Humber Bridge

The new Humber Bridge was opened on 17 July 1981. It was the longest single-span suspension bridge in the world (1,410 metres). It reduced the distance between Scunthorpe and Hull by 55 kilometres, creating a link between the two banks of the Humber. It cost £100 million to build, not the estimated £13 million (1965). Nor did it live up to the estimates of its use. At the planning stage 24,000 vehicles a day were projected to cross the bridge, yet by 1981 only 4,000 vehicles a day were making the journey. The tolls collected do not even pay the interest on the money borrowed to build the bridge. This makes it a very expensive piece of civil engineering. Many economists think that the bridge is an expensive mistake, as industrial and commercial growth does not seem to have been attracted to the area. Others believe that it is a good investment and that eventually it will be an area which will be attractive to EC industrialists. The question remains, was the bridge worth building? Couldn't the money have been better spent on another estuary bridge over the Thames, the Clyde, the Mersey, or on the English Channel Tunnel?

Railways – transport of the past?

Study the two maps of the railway network (Figs 20.5 and 20.6) for 1950 and 1982. In only thirty-two years the total railway system has shrunk from 32,000 kilometres to approximately 14,000 kilometres, a reduction of more than 50 per cent. Why has the railway declined so much as a form of transport? What improvements have taken place over the last thirty years and what might any future system be like?

We can understand some of the reasons for the decline of the railways by considering the past:

- By 1900 the railways were very popular; they had been developed and were owned by private companies. Each company competed for trade and sometimes parallel routes were built. This duplication of routeways was wasteful.
- Some routes were built to serve areas and industries that never became as important as predicted. After nationalisation these lines were not profitable.
- Some lines were built to serve industrial areas which have since declined, as in shipbuilding, coal-mining and steel. As the industries became smaller profits fell and lines became uneconomic.
- By 1950 much of the rail network was in need of repair after seventy years of use.

The Beeching (1962) and Benson (1963) Reports suggested that to save money the network should be drastically reduced, concentrating on those lines that were profitable. Lines retained should be making money, or serve special social needs (for instance, some lines in rural Scotland and Wales).

At the same time that the cuts in the railways were being proposed, road transport was attracting more passengers and freight; pipelines were being built for fuel transport, and increasing numbers of passengers were travelling from city to city via the air shuttle services. These factors further reduced demand for rail transport.

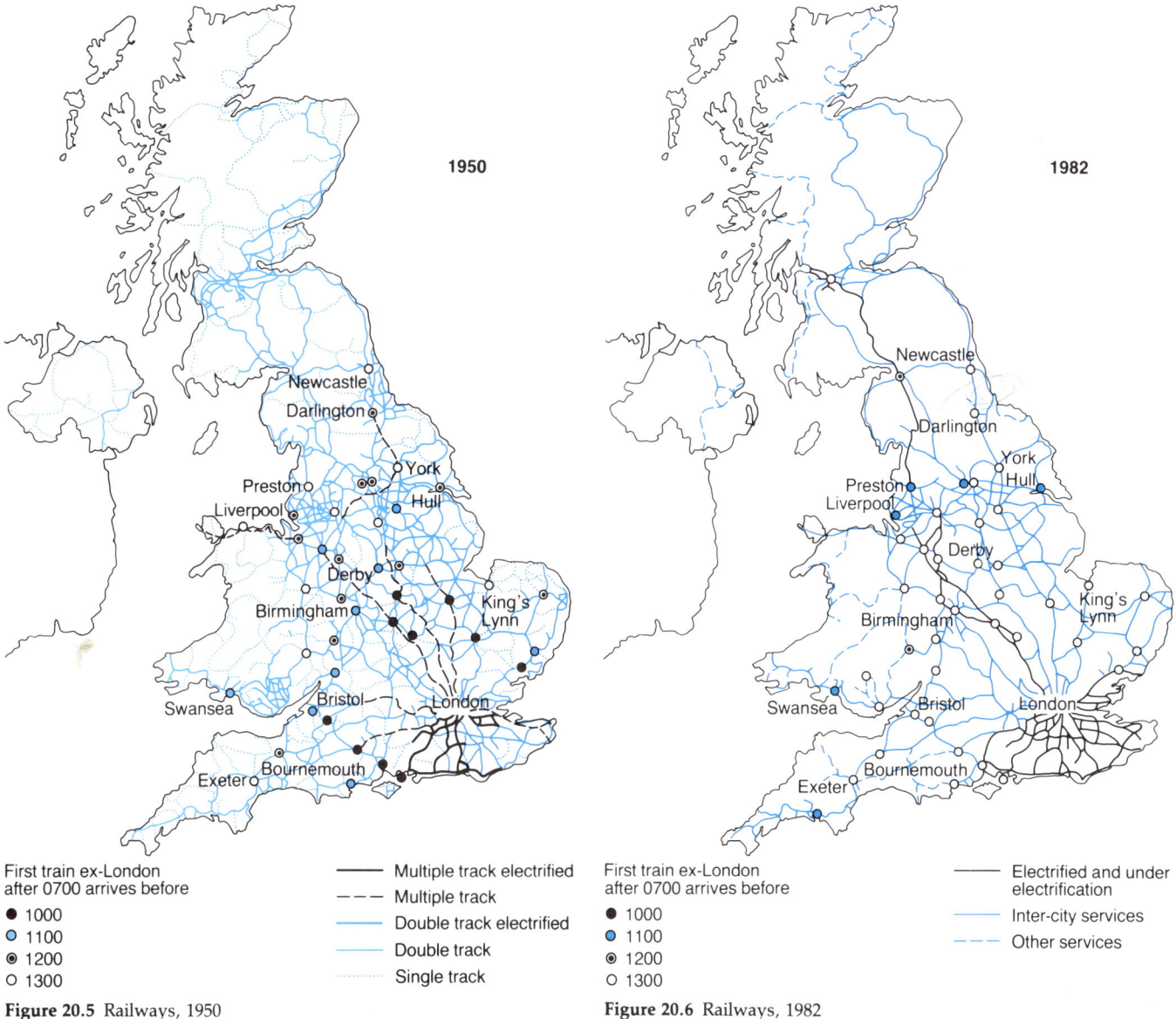

Figure 20.5 Railways, 1950

Figure 20.6 Railways, 1982

Figure 20.7 Encouraging tourists to use rail travel while in Britain

The replanning of the much reduced rail network had to include:

- a fast, efficient passenger service between the large metropolitan and urban centres;
- a reliable service for freight between the most important industrial and commercial regions;
- improved commuter services within major metropolitan centres;
- some socially necessary services in isolated rural areas.

This led to:

- the development of the InterCity 125 passenger service, using new high-speed trains between such centres as Leeds and Edinburgh, London and Bristol etc.;
- the Freightliner goods and Red Star parcels services, as well as improved freight services for customers such as British Steel, British Coal and the CEGB;
- the development of better commuter services into cities like Manchester, Newcastle and London;
- some rural lines in Scotland, Wales and East Anglia remaining to serve seasonal needs or isolated rural communities.

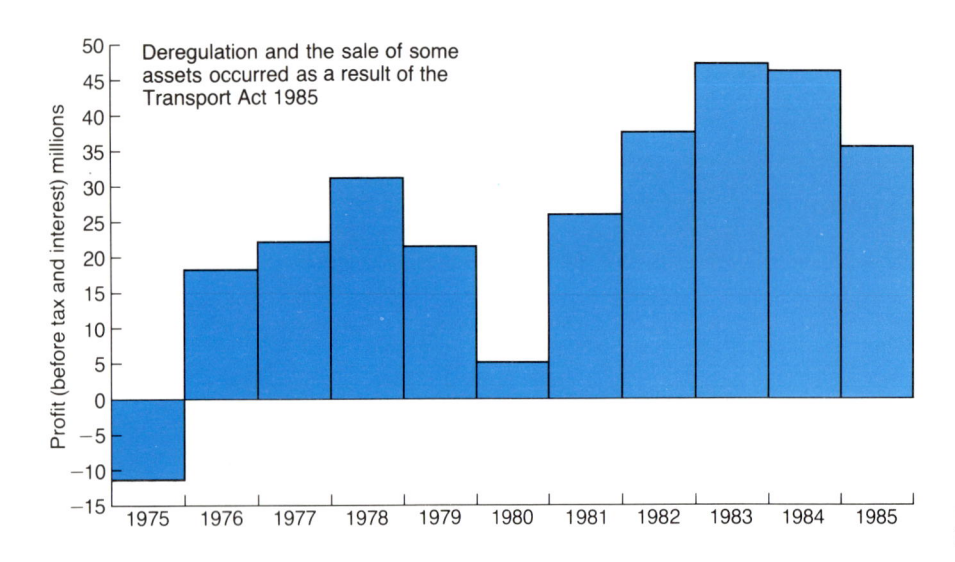

Figure 20.8 Operating profits of the National Bus Company

(Chart note: Deregulation and the sale of some assets occurred as a result of the Transport Act 1985)

After all this reorganisation, the reduction of the size of the network and the improvements introduced in services, did the plan work? Did freight and passenger traffic increase? Yes and no!

- Yes, it has worked for the InterCity 125 which attracted increasing numbers of passengers from its inauguration. However, new competitive fares offered by the National Bus Company and airlines seemed to have halted the growth in 125 passengers at present.
- Yes, modernisation has reduced travel times between cities. Improved track, better signalling, electrification and more 125 trains have made the system more efficient.
- No; it has not worked for freight. Since 1950 the total volume of freight has decreased by more than 45 per cent. The best customers remain the coal, steel, oil and other mining industries.

The future of the railway network depends on how attractive it is to its potential customers in the prices it charges or the services it offers, as well as the amount of financial help it receives from the Government. In Europe subsidies to the railways are at least double those in the United Kingdom. France, by spending a great deal of Government money, has developed a railway system with superb, fast, long-distance routes and cheap commuter lines.

The future in the United Kingdom may well include new, thermally efficient steam trains as well as new standards of comfort and service that will attract passengers back to the railways. Projects like the Channel Tunnel will attract rising volumes of freight traffic to and from Europe.

The Channel Tunnel

Tunnels and bridges have been proposed to cross the Channel since the times of the Emperor Napoleon – they have never been built. In 1970 trial tunnels were started on both sides of the channel; by 1974 all work had stopped. In 1979 a single track railway tunnel was proposed at a cost of £700 million, this was shelved. In 1984 either a twin railway tunnel or a multi-purpose bridge were proposed. The bridge would cost £90 billion, the twin tunnel £8 billion. The tunnel would carry cars and passengers by rail, the more expensive bridge would have an all-weather roadway for cars and lorries as well as a railway.

Finally, in 1986 plans for a tunnel were approved by France and the United Kingdom and construction is now underway.

Ports – sea versus air, bulk versus speed

In the modern world passengers and freight are continually on the move, both within and between countries. Activity connected with this movement is concentrated at sea and airports. Both sea and air transport have their advantages and disadvantages: ships can carry large bulk cargoes (thousands of tonnes), but they are slow and carry passengers expensively (except for cruises and ferry crossings). Aeroplanes are very fast and in comparison with ships carry small cargoes but millions of passengers; air freight is often 'perishable' (because it need only be carried for a short time), but freight costs kilo for kilo are usually much higher by air.

Each type of transport requires quite different terminal and cargo handling facilities. Modern seaports have deep water, coastal berthing, and equipment that can handle bulk cargoes of oil, liquid gas and mineral ores. Some seaports specialise in handling container traffic, as well as roll-on, roll-off ferries. Airports are built on very large level sites to accommodate runways, repair workshops, passenger and freight terminals; they are usually built near large concentrations of population. Both transport modes carry passengers and freight, domestic and international. Fig. 20.9 shows that the balance of these activities is different for sea and air transport.

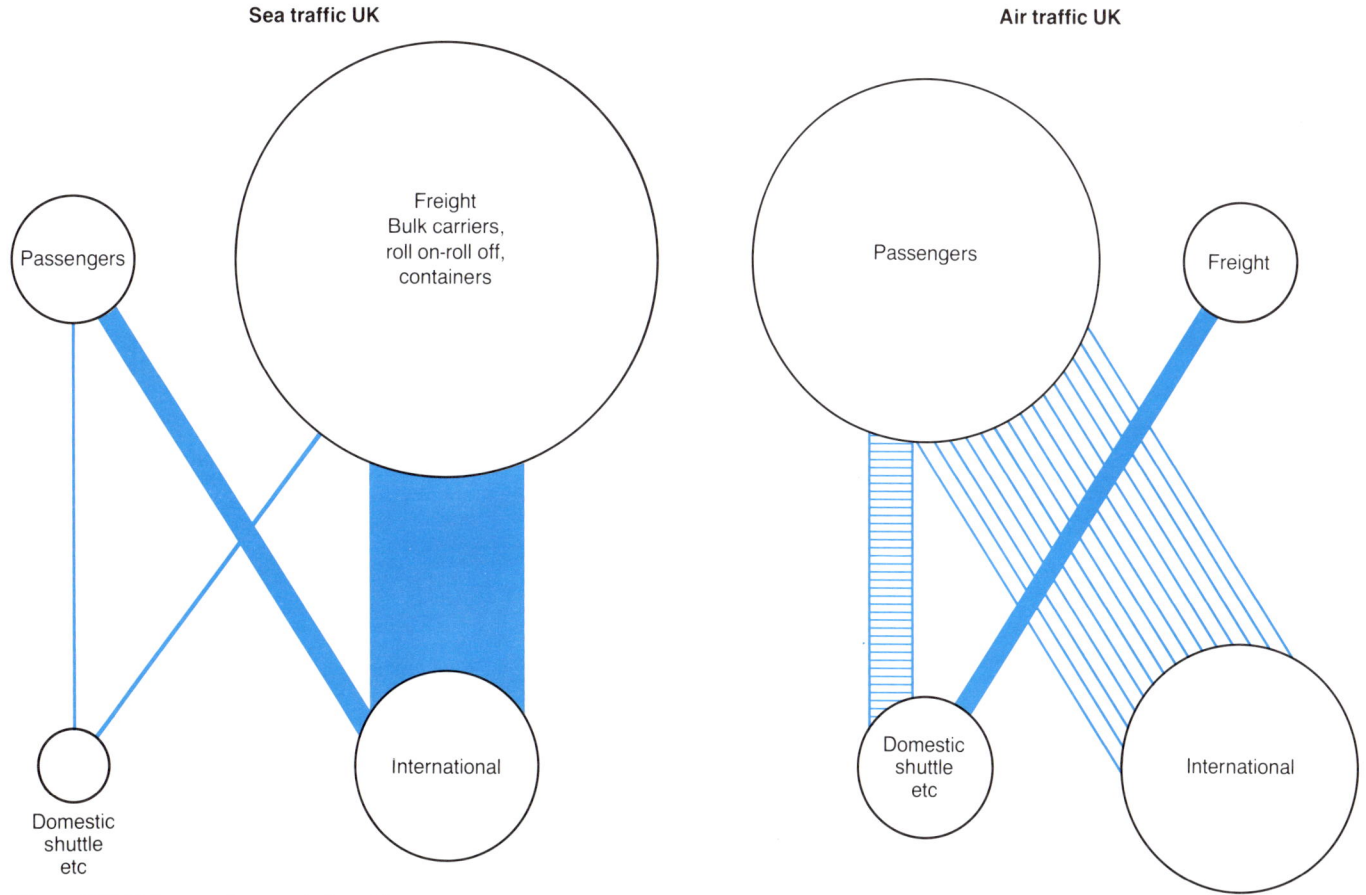

Figure 20.9 Volumes of sea and air traffic

Airports

Due to the global position of the United Kingdom in relation to other major centres of world commerce, trade and industry, 65 per cent of all passenger movements (58 million in 1980) are to or from other countries. The two

204 A Geography of Contemporary Britain

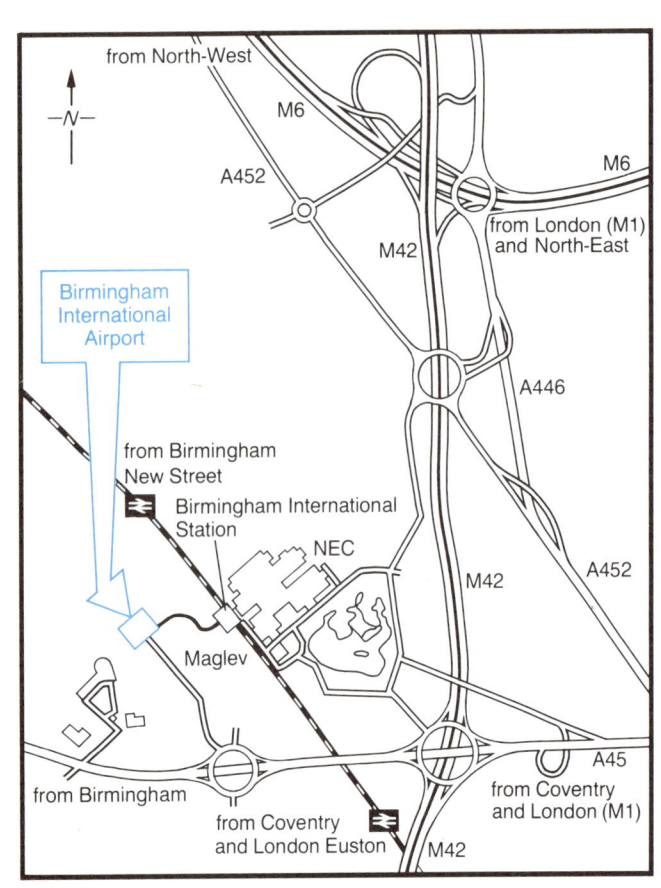

Figure 20.10 Birmingham Airport and its transport links

Figure 20.11 Gatwick, near Crawley, Sussex, is London's second airport. It is well-served by road and rail, but working to capacity

London airports, Gatwick and Heathrow, handle the greatest number of passengers each day; but many other regional airports also derive more than 50 per cent of their business from foreign passenger movements. Air freight traffic has increased by a factor of seventy since 1946, from 0.1 million tonne kilometres to 7.1 million tonne kilometres in 1980.

The demand for air transport continues to grow, encouraging plans for the expansion of regional airports, as well as the building of a third London airport.

One regional airport, Birmingham International Airport, is growing because:

- it is able to attract short-haul European flights;
- it is at the centre of Britain's motorway network (see Fig. 20.10);
- it has a rapid transit system, the MAGLEV shuttle, which can transfer passengers to Birmingham International Railway Station in 90 seconds;
- Birmingham is the site of the National Exhibition Centre.

London's third airport

Since the early 1960s a third airport for London has been proposed, the problem has been where to build it. A Government enquiry decided in 1967 that a site at Stansted in Essex was the best site. But in 1968 the President of the Board of Trade announced that he would set up an enquiry to decide where the new airport should be built, as the earlier Stansted decision was felt to have been too hasty. The report of this commission (Roskill) was published in 1971; after considering seventy-eight possible sites, and when four sites had been investigated in detail: Cublington (Buckinghamshire), Nuthamstead (Hertfordshire), Stansted (Essex) and Foulness (Essex). Cublington was chosen as the best site.

The Government rejected this advice and decided that the new airport should be built at Foulness and be called Maplin. However, the site was very expensive to develop, and was environmentally sensitive; in the end no development took place.

In 1984 the Government announced plans for the expansion of Stansted with projected passenger numbers rising from 500,000 (1984) to 15 million (1990) and eventually to 25 million. So after thirty years of argument and enquiry Stansted became the favourite again, a decision which discouraged expansion plans at Birmingham and other regional airports.

Seaports

Most seaports have seen both an increase in the total bulk and value of trade over the last ten years. They have had to modernise to keep pace with the changes in ship size and cargo type.

The size of ships has grown from an average 20,000 deadweight tonnes in 1950 to 100,000 deadweight tonnes in 1960, and to ships of over 200,000 deadweight tonnes in the 1970s. These large ships are usually international bulk-cargo carriers of oil, gas and mineral ores. They require specialised docking and cargo-handling facilities. Other developments have included the widespread use of containers; these are usually standard-sized metal boxes 2.5m × 2.5m × 6–12m. These can be carried on lorries or railway trucks and are easy to stack in ships' holds. These too require specialised dock handling facilities.

Ports which specialise in container-handling are both international, such as Tilbury and Heysham, and more local, such as Felixstowe which specialises in container-traffic to the continent. Specialised facilities are also needed for the roll-on, roll-off ferries, such as those at Dover and Harwich, which also specialise in trade with the EC.

Figure 20.12 A GEC equipped Maglev vehicle at Birmingham Airport

Telecommunications

Communication not only includes modes of transport such as ships, aeroplanes, trains and cars, it must also cover the fastest form of transport, the electronic message as it speeds through cables, via laser beams or communication satellites. At the moment there is a world wide revolution taking place in communication technology, involving new techniques, new machines and new ideas which are already affecting patterns of employment both in their type and location. Work that involves data handling, data searches, data manipulation or transformation can now be carried out at home using a telephone link, television monitor, a computer and some fairly simple instructions.

Some of the areas already affected by these developments are:

- banking;
- shopping;
- data access;
- business and finance;
- news;
- electronic mail;
- citizen data bases.

Each of these eight areas is being affected by the revolution which is gaining pace as new computer systems and new forms of communication links are developed. Each stage of development creates the opportunity for spatial changes in the distribution of business, commerce, shopping etc.

Intelsat 1 (1965) Capacity 240 circuits

Intelsat V (1979) Capacity 12,000 circuits

Intelsat VI (1986) Capacity 33,000 circuits

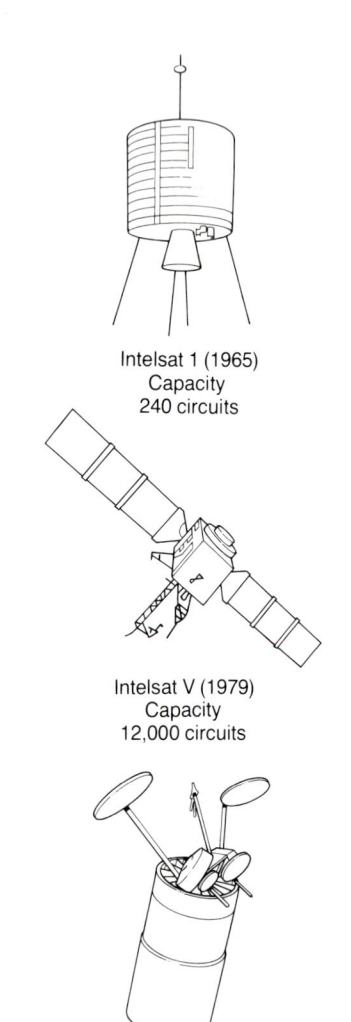

Figure 20.14 The development of communications satellite capacity

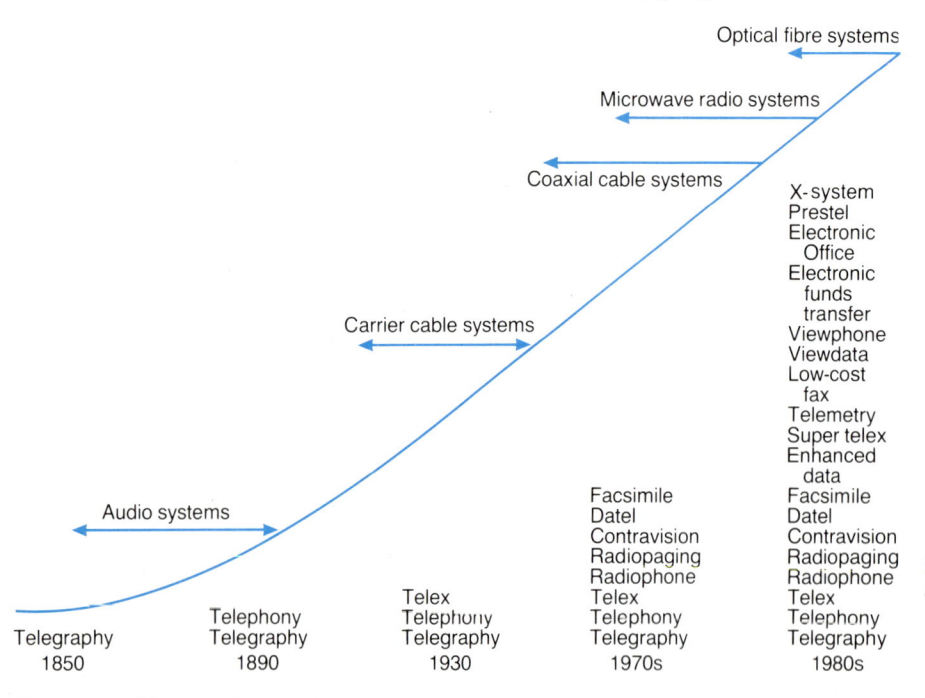

Figure 20.13 The growth in services

Banking

The high streets of most towns in the United Kingdom now have at least one bank with a cash-card dispenser. A piece of plastic with a coded magnetic strip can be inserted into the machine at any time of day or night and will produce cash, a balance statement, or order a new cheque book. This is all accomplished without a personal transaction with a bank employee and without paper.

Shopping

It is no longer necessary to make a journey to the shops to buy goods; using a home computer or one of the more specialised terminals it is possible to choose, order and pay for goods in the comfort of your own home and then wait for them to be delivered.

In some shops a light-pen is passed across computer coded strips on the goods this totals the bill, naming individual items, and your personal account is debited. At the same time the stock-control lists for the store are updated from the information coming from the till.

Data access

PRESTEL and CEEFAX give access to large data banks of regularly updated information. Imagine that you were able to call up a range of information which related directly to your school geography or history syllabus for GCSE examinations. As these two subjects involve new factual inputs, perhaps you would do better working at home at your own computer terminal; you would then only need to go to school for three days each week, or less, depending on how much study could be rearranged on the computer. It would mean you could plan your own working time, you could study at night and go out during the day. Some of the business world is already moving in this direction. In California some small firms are made up of a series of individuals all working at home; the firm's employees meet once a month socially, but during working hours they are in contact with each other via video and computer links.

Figure 20.15 The back-garden satellite-dish is likely to be a common sight of the future, for wider TV reception

Business and finance

> The financial institutions have been taken by storm. Electronic wizardry has radically altered working practices and a totally paperless City is a real possibility in the not too distant future.
>
> Information has become virtually instantaneous and voluminous, money can be merely push-buttoned around the world ... computers can be drawn into the decision making process ... the human element can be easily eliminated.
>
> John Huxley, *Sunday Times* 7 October 1984

The new touch-screens (see Fig. 20.16), which are part of British Telecom's new City Business System, give instant access to financial information across the world, as well as providing multi-line telephone factilities with one touch of a finger. The system stores its own information, up to 10,000 pages,

Figure 20.16 Touch screens in the City.

as well as providing 10,000 exchange lines for up to 1,000 financial dealers. Again, these developments have implications for the future location of business, as well as saving forests of paper.

News

Using the new technology it is now possible to produce an edition of the *New York Herald Tribune* newspaper in the USA and then send the whole paper electronically to Hong Kong. Local news can be inserted and a Hong Kong print run set up. The paper will be on sale in Hong Kong long before the New York edition comes in by plane across the Pacific Ocean.

Electronic mail

The same features are true of the new electronic mailbox systems. Within and between companies it is possible to send messages to specific individuals. If an executive in the Coca Cola Corporation, USA, wishes to send instructions to a colleague opposite number in Tokyo, it can be done at the touch of a button. When Tokyo opens for business, the electronic mail is flashed onto the screen, acted upon, and replied to. No dispatch or carrier service is necessary, no paper need change hands, no trains, planes or boats are involved.

Citizen data bases

Information about you is held in the files of the Department of Health and Social Security (DHSS). Absolutely identical information is held in at least five different files, in five different locations, some on computer, some on paper; if it were on one computer, which was accessible by each of the five departments, it might make life easier for the civil servants at the DHSS. Other information about your parents is held on the computer files of the banks, insurance companies, the Gas and Electricity Boards, the Driver Vehicle Licensing Centre in Swansea, British Telecom (if you have a telephone), the Inland Revenue and others. In fact there are about 200 data bases held by the British Government, in addition to the many private ones. Perhaps it would be a good idea to store more of this information in one central computer; it would give the doctor a better idea about your problems, it would give the police a good idea about your bank account, it would give the DHSS access to health records.

Data storage, retrieval, manipulation and control have great possibilities and dangers. The revolution in data access and the changes in working practices have all sorts of implications including location, function and paper reduction.

Technology

Without great progress in technology none of these developments would have been possible. There are now a number of brand new communication networks in the United Kingdom whose capacity is massive. First, the efficiency of the telephone system has been improved with the introduction of X-System, with its digital switching, there is also the growing glass-fibre-optic network (Fig. 20.13), as well as laser and satellite systems (Fig. 20.14).

Database: Transport and communications

Figure 20.17 United Kingdom passenger traffic estimates (in 000,000,000 passenger kms)

	1960	1986
Road (private)	56%	85%
Road (public)	28%	7%
Rail	16%	7%
Air	–	–

Total for 1986: 506,000,000,000
Air is too small to count as it is less than 1%

Source: Department of Transport, 1986

Figure 20.18 United Kingdom goods traffic estimates (in 000,000,000 tonne kms)

	1960	1986
Road	60%	83%
Rail	38%	9%
Air	–	–
Pipelines	–	8%

Source: Department of Transport, 1986

Figure 20.19 Major bulk cargoes 1985/6. Ports in Rank order of in/out traffic

	Millions of tonnes	Oil over 50% of cargoes	Ore and Scrap more than 50% UK imports
Sullom Voe	59.40	*	
London	51.70	*	
Tees	30.56	*	
Milford Haven	32.46	*	
Grimsby/Immingham	29.12	*	*
Forth	29.05	*	
Southampton	25.16	*	*
Orkney	16.11	*	
Medway	10.94		
Liverpool	10.36		
Felixstowe	10.07		
Clyde	9.91	*	
Manchester	9.51	*	
Dover	9.27		
Port Talbot	6.79		*

Source: UK Digest of Transport Statistics 1986

Figure 20.20 Container and roll on-roll off traffic at leading ports in the UK 1985 (in millions of tonnes)

Felixstowe	9.13
Dover	8.77
London	4.26
Hull	3.82
Grimsby/Immingham	3.23
Southampton	1.93
Liverpool	1.86
Manchester	0.61

Workbase

1. Study Fig. 20.6. Consider where each of the following factors might be introduced on a British Rail route most effectively, in order to attract custom. Give one route for each factor, and a reason.

Better track	Electrification	A more frequent
Better rolling stock	Luxury meals	service
More comfortable seats	Guaranteed seats	Lower fares
Lower Freight costs	Faster parcel delivery	Larger windows on existing carriages

2. Collect a brochure for ferries to Europe from your local travel agent. How many different ports are used, and what are their European destinations? Identify the ports from an atlas, and draw an outline map of Britain's south-eastern coast, showing their location.

3. Here are some factors which have to be taken into account when a new major airport is located. How important do you consider each of them? Give a weighting to them (10=very important, 0=of no significance) and then consider your answers against those of someone else in your class who has done the same exercise.

Factor	Weighting
Nearness to a major motorway	
Within 30 kilometres of a major city centre	
A firm geological foundation for runways	
Landing and take-off paths not over housing	
Nearness to a railway line	
No other airport within 30 kilometres radius	
Land used of little other importance	
Close to major hotels	
Large numbers of potential workforce nearby	
Away from existing commercial air routes	

   Apply your final scale to a) Stansted, Essex (which is being developed as London's third major airport); b) Hyde Park in central London; c) Foulness, near Southend (once considered as a possibility for London's Third Airport). All these three places have areas of land large enough for a major airport.

4. What are the dangers and disadvantages of a single computer base for information about British citizens?

5. What effect do you think the communications revolution will have (by the year 2000) on:
   a) business and industry location?
   b) road networks?
   c) rail networks?
   d) air networks?

6. Given the tremendous increase in 'instant communication' around the world through telephones, fax machines, television, etc, consider the possible *dis*advantages which may occur.

Part VI
Conclusion
Chapter 21
Beyond Britain's borders

Britain and the world

Heathrow Airport is the busiest international airport in the world – an indication that today, as for centuries past, Britain's life is linked with other countries beyond her island boundaries.

These links have been strong since the days of the early invaders (see Chapter 3), through the Tudor and Elizabethan ages of exploration, and the Victorian days of Empire, until the present day. This partially explains why geography has always been an important subject in British schools.

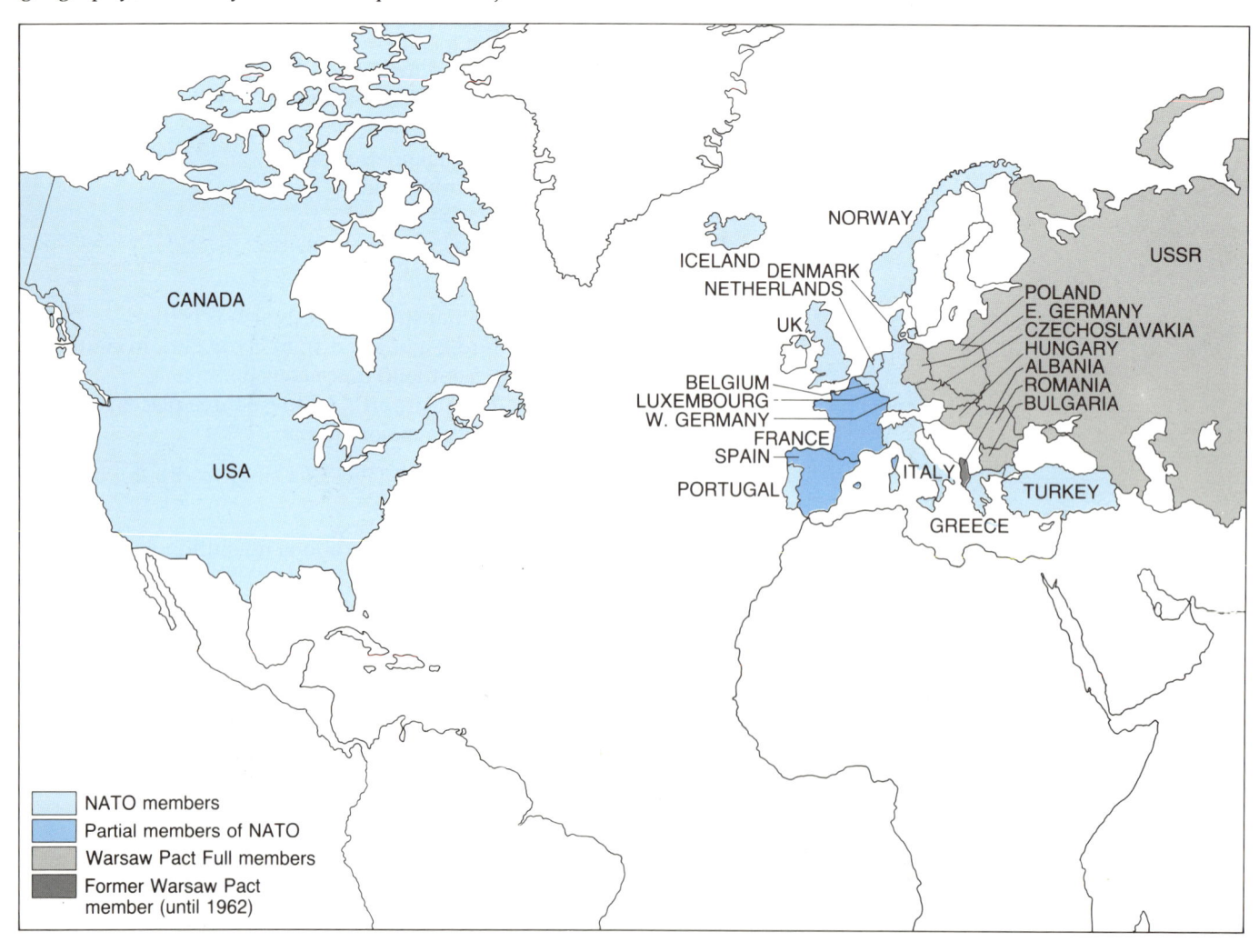

- NATO members
- Partial members of NATO
- Warsaw Pact Full members
- Former Warsaw Pact member (until 1962)

Today, the days of Empire are past, but Britain depends heavily on many other countries around the world for trade. We are not **self-sufficient** in what we produce and so have to import many foodstuffs and raw materials. In return we export a small amount of minerals (notably oil and china-clay), some manufactured goods and an increasing number of **invisible exports** (banking services and financial help from the City of London are an important part of these). We also earn an increasing amount from **tourism**.

Despite the useful – but temporary – bonus of selling North Sea oil and gas, we have struggled to have an equal **balance of payments** in recent years. Our previous supply of cheap imports from the Empire (for example sugar from Trinidad, cocoa from Ghana) has declined as countries have gained independence and sought instead to diversify and sell their goods to the highest bidder.

At the same time, our exports have declined in key manufacturing industries – partly because our older industries have not proved so efficient or competitive as those of other countries. Some blame this on restrictive union practices, or inefficient management, or both. It is also true that in parts of the Third World labour costs are very much lower than in the United Kingdom. Without the protection of 'imperial tariffs' we have very much felt the draught of competition since the Second World War.

Britain, the UN, and NATO

Britain, like most other countries in the world, belongs to the United Nations, a 'talking-shop' of nations which has its headquarters in New York. The UN has many debates about major world issues, but much of its most effective work is done by specialist agencies such as the Food and Agriculture Organisation (FAO), the World Health Organisation (WHO) and the United Nations Childrens Fund (UNICEF).

Figure 21.2 Greenham Common, Berkshire, was the focus of much protest when NATO Cruise missiles were stored there

Only a few countries do not belong to the UN; Switzerland – which tries to keep itself free from *all* groupings in order to act as an 'honest broker' – is the most notable. The Swiss have a very small army and air force and successfully avoided involvement in both world wars.

Britain, however, has traditionally had a strong defence force on land, sea and air, partly caused by its long period of responsibility as a colonial power. Since 1945 it has been one of the nations in possession of nuclear weapons, which it holds as a deterrent to the use of force by other nations. But holding nuclear weapons for any purpose makes some people uneasy and there is a continuing debate about whether or not we should continue to do so. The focus of this debate in recent years has been the placing of (nuclear) Cruise Missiles at the airbases at Greenham Common (Berkshire and Molesworth (Cambridgeshire). Concern has spilled over into protests and sit-ins. The missiles were withdrawn in 1988.

Britain is a member of NATO (the North Atlantic Treaty Organisation) along with America, Canada, and other Western European nations. NATO is a military alliance which seeks to balance its forces against those of the Warsaw Pact (the USSR and Eastern European nations). NATO believes that it is safer to keep peace by mutual strength than by any other means. Opponents of this view argue that unilateral disarmament (by one country or one side without waiting for the other) is the only way in which the deadlock can be broken – otherwise we face an indefinite time spending large amounts of money on defence, when it could be spent on other more pressing needs.

Figure 21.3 250,000 people joined this CND demonstration in Hyde Park, London in 1982

Britain and the EC

The European Community (EC) was established by six nations in 1957, after moves towards economic union in the post-war period. Britain, after an initial period of indifference, sought to join in 1963, but was blocked by France. It eventually joined in 1973 after a referendum, but there has been a substantial body of opinion which has continuing reservations about the need or benefit of joining.

The European Parliament of the EC meets in Strasbourg, and the headquarters of the Community is in Brussels. Each of the twelve nation members pays money into a joint budget and this is later re-distributed. Britain's share of the costs is quite high, and it has had some reservations about the way the Community's money is spent:

- One regular controversy has been over the Common Agricultural Policy (CAP) which provides subsidies to farmers and buys surplus food which may be produced in order to maintain prices. It is felt that some inefficient farmers, notably in France, are kept in business by this system and that the 'butter and grain mountains' and the 'wine lakes' should not be allowed to accumulate as they do. The British farmers feel that the CAP is largely unhelpful in many ways and would like it changed; but other countries seek to protect their own agricultural systems.
- There has been a long-standing dispute about fishing in the North Sea and English Channel. As a major fishing nation, Britain has been concerned that the boats of other nations have 'over-fished' the traditional breeding grounds within our own territorial waters. A 1983 agreement gave the United Kingdom only 37 per cent of the catch of the seven most important species of fish in Community waters – far less than the 60 per cent which we had claimed on past activity. As a result of the EC fishing policies the size of British fishing fleets has diminished greatly in many major ports such as Hull, Grimsby and Newlyn.

Figure 21.4 The EC heads of Government meet

- One reason given for going into the EC was the increase of possible customers – but of course the same applies to other nations too. Though we have increased the proportion of our trade with Europe in recent years, our position on the geographical 'rim' of the Community increases transport costs. Our industries – already 'sick' for other reasons – have found it difficult to survive. However, EC aid to under-developed and decaying regions has helped some areas and created new jobs.

Britain and the Commonwealth

The Commonwealth is a grouping of nations which grew from the former British Empire. Most countries from the Empire, on reaching their independence, have chosen to stay associated with Britain and to remain in free association in a worldwide association which has the Queen of England as its symbolic head. The English language is a common link between all Commonwealth countries; almost all also share a heritage of British parliamentary institutions and are democracies.

There are forty-nine countries within the Commonwealth, spread over the major continents and oceans; one of its strengths is that it includes both developed and less-developed nations and so represents a wide variety of viewpoints in its regular informal discussions. The Commonwealth Prime Ministers, who represent a quarter of all the world's population, meet every two years for an informal conference.

There is not nearly as much visible organisation in the Commonwealth as the United Nations or the European Community, but this probably works to its advantage. Sir 'Sonny' Ramphal of Guyana is the present Secretary-General and he encourages a wide range of informal contacts and discussions.

Figure 21.5 The Queen amongst the Commonwealth President and Prime Ministers

Database: beyond Britain's borders

The countries of the Commonwealth and their populations listed in order of gaining independence

UK   55,780,000
Canada   25,600,000
Australia   15,450,000
New Zealand   3,300,000
India   748,000,000
Pakistan   87,125,000
Sri Lanka   15,800,000
Ghana   13,040,000
Malaysia   16,100,000
Cyprus   665,200
Sierra Leone   3,520,000
Tanzania   21,730,000
Western Samoa   163,000
Jamaica   2,300,000
Trinidad and Tobago   1,200,000
Uganda   13,990,000
Kenya   20,330,000
Malawi   7,100,000
Malta   345,418
Zambia   6,650,000
The Gambia   687,817
Maldives   200,000
Singapore   2,560,000
Guyana   950,000
Botswana   1,050,000
Lesotho   1,470,000
Barbados   253,055
Naura   8,042
Mauritius   1,000,432
Swaziland   676,049
Tonga   104,000
Bangladesh   101,700,000
Bahamas   235,000
Grenada   88,000
Papua New Guinea   3,420,000
Seychelles   65,244
Solomon Islands   270,000
Tuvalu   8,229
Dominica   74,851
Saint Lucia   136,952
Kiribati   62,000
St Vincent and
   the Grenadines   127,883
Zimbabwe   8,420,000
Vanuatu   135,000
Belize   166,200
Antigua and Barbuda   81,500
St Christopher and
   Nevis   43,309
Brunei   221,900

The present members of the European Community and their populations

Belgium   9,860,000
Netherlands   14,530,000
Luxembourg   367,200
France   55,500,000
FDR   61,000,000
Italy   57,200,000
Denmark   5,120,000
Ireland   3,540,000
United Kingdom   55,780,000
Greece   9,970,000
Spain   39,300,000
Portugal   10,190,000

Workbase

1. Identify the twelve largest (by population) countries of the Commonwealth on a world map. How many continents do they cover? If the Commonwealth remains a lively 'grouping of friends' what implications may that have for future world relationships?

2. Can you suggest why a) Switzerland b) Norway, Sweden and Finland c) Czechoslovakia and Poland have not applied for membership of the EC?

3. Consider the benefits of EC membership for a) Cambridge; b) Consett; and c) northern Scotland, and write paragraphs on each. Are the similarities greater than the differences?

4. Write an essay on 'Britain's position in the world in the year 2000', using evidence from other chapters in this book.

Britain and the future

At the start of this book, we asked the question; might Britain be part of the new 'Fourth World'? A declining traditional industrial base poses many problems, especially for those who live in particular towns like Consett or Workington, but also for the nation as a whole. The loss of such a base may present opportunities as well as problems. Is our future as an 'industrial' nation at all?

We also have to consider our future role in the world community. Can we afford to continue as a world nuclear power, or would Europe be a safer place if NATO ceased to match the power of the Warsaw Pact nations? Can disarmament be successfully negotiated while each side is suspicious of the other? The coming of 'perestroika' and more open relations between East and West, is a hopeful sign.

And – perhaps less publicised, but no less important – will our environment survive into the twenty-first century? Will we be able to preserve it from the hazards of pollution, unthinking vandalism and short-term policies of all kinds? This is a question for all future citizens and one which should be serious enough to spur them – *you* – to action.

Index

Index of places in the British Isles referred to in this book

Aberdeen 119
Asfordby 173
Ayr 64

Bath 64, 76, 190
Bellnoe Farm (case-study) 34
Belvoir, Vale of 172
Berkshire 53, 213
Bilston 138
Birmingham 56, 57, 61, 90, 116–7, 130, 205
Black Country 127
Blackpool 64
Bourneville (Birmingham) 130
Bracknell 108
Bradford 18, 128, 130
Brent (oilfield) 178
Brentford 135
Brighton 64, 115
Bristol 19, 104, 151, 190, 201
Buckinghamshire 205
Burnt Oak 86, 88–9

Caistron (case-study) 53
Cambridge 19, 111–2, 151, 153
Cambridgeshire 119, 153, 155, 214
Cardiff 115, 138, 191
Carmarthen Bay 190
Carsington 56
Channel Islands 38
Cleveland 67
Clyde 200
Clydebridge 138
Clydeside 151
Clywedog 56
Coalbrookdale 125
Cockfosters 86
Coniston Water 45
Consett 113–4, 137, 138, 146, 160, 164
Coquet, River 53
Corby 138, 163
Cornwall 49, 190
Coventry 7, 61
Cricklewood 83, 86
Cublington 205
Cumbernauld 109
Cumbria 7, 12, 13

Dales (see Yorkshire Dales)
Dart, River 13
Dartford Tunnel 199
Dee Estuary 61
Derby 56
Derwent, reservoir 58
Docklands (London) 96–7

Dorset 177
Dover 205
Dundee 7
Durham 113, 146, 160, 164, 190

Eakring 177
East Anglia 22, 128, 151, 188
East Ham 90
East Midlands (see Midlands)
Ebbw Vale 138
Edgware 83, 86, 87
Edinburgh 115, 151, 201
Eire (see Ireland, Republic of)
Elan, reservoir 56, 61
Ellesmere Port 141
England 2, 22, 60, 61
English Channel 13, 177, 200, 214
Epping 86
Essex 205
Exe, River 6
Exeter 100

Fal, River 13
Felixstowe 205
Fens, The 53
Fife 181
Forest of Dean 127
Foulness 205
Frigg (oilfield) 181

Gateshead 104
Gatwick Aiport 205
Glamorgan 162, 163
Glasgow 22, 76, 115, 123, 141, 151, 196
Goathland 69
Golders Green 86, 89
Greenham Common 213
Greenock 151
Grimsby 214
Grizedale (case-study) 45
Guernsey 39
Guildford 103

Halewood 141
Halifax 128
Hampshire 53, 105, 155, 177 (basin), 190
Harlow 101
Hartlepool 138
Harwich 205
Hay's Wharf (London) 96
Hebrides 190
Helmsley 69
Hemel Hempstead 109
Hendon 88–9
Heathrow Airport 205, 212
Heysham 205

Highlands 34, 155, 178
Hounslow 86
Huddersfield 128
Hull 200, 214
Humber, River (bridge) 199, 200
Humberside 140
Hutton-le-Hole 69

Ilford 76
Ireland, Republic of 2, 3, 4, 22, 32, 44
Irish sea 177
Irlam 138
Isle of Dogs 96, 163
Isle of Wight 13

Jarrow 165

Kilburn 83–4

Lake District 45, 64
Lancashire 128
Lee Valley 38
Leeds 18, 128, 201
Leicester 61
Leicestershire 172–3
Lerwick 178
Letchworth 108, 133
Limehouse 96
Linwood 141, 143
Litlington 155
Liverpool 22, 115, 141
Llanberis 117
Llanwern 138
London 19, 38, 79, 90, 141, 146, 163, 164, 196, 199, 201, 205

Manchester 18, 19, 115, 123, 196, 201
Maplin 205
Melton Mowbray 102
Mersey, River 200
Merseyside 19, 141
Merthyr Tydfil 160
Middlesex 88
Midlands, West, East 19, 22, 55, 56, 57, 61, 116–7, 127, 137, 138, 140, 141, 143, 187
Milton Keynes 103, 110, 192–3
Morecambe Bay 61

Newcastle-on-Tyne (see also Tyneside) 7, 19, 90, 119, 201
Newlyn 214
Ninian (oilfield) 178
Norfolk 18, 27, 77, 180
North sea 181–2, 214

Northampton *110*
North-East (see also Tyneside) *172*
Northern Ireland *2, 3, 4, 5, 140, 146*
Northumberland *53, 155*
North-West (see also Lancashire) *173*
Nottingham *115*
Nottinghamshire *177, 196*
Nuthampstead *205*

Orkney *190*
Oxford *111*
Oxfordshire *53*

Pennines *49*
Peterborough *110*
Port Talbot *138*
Pumpherstone *177*

Queens Park (London) *93*

Radcliffe-on-Soar *196*
Ramsgate *115*
Ravenscraig *138*
Reading *151*
Redcar *138*
Redditch *110*
Rhondda *119, 162*
Robin Hood's Bay *69, 71*
Rosemanowes *190*
Runcorn *109, 110*
Ruislip *86, 88*

St Fergus *183*
Salford *76*

Scarborough *64, 70*
Scilly Isles *38*
Scotland *2, 7, 15, 19, 34, 119, 141, 146, 151, 190*
Scunthorpe *138, 200*
Severn, River *56, 60, 61, 191,* (bridge) *199*
Sheffield *18, 90, 115*
Shetland Isles *178–9*
Shotton *138*
Sizewell *186–8*
Snowdon *66*
Solway Firth *61*
South Wales (see Wales)
Southampton *105*
South-East *53, 55, 137, 141, 143, 146*
Southend *64*
South-West *64, 128*
Speke *141, 143*
Stansted *111–112, 205*
Stevenage *108*
Stonehenge *66*
Suffolk *18, 186*
Sullom Voe (case-study) *178–9*
Sunderland *104*
Sussex *127*
Sutton Bank *69*
Swansea *7, 119, 209*
Swindon *151*

Tees, River *6*
Thames, River *79, 200*
Tilbury *205*
Totteridge *108*
Trent Valley *173*

Trimpley *56*
Tyne, River *58*
Tyneside *58, 123*

Ulster (see Northern Ireland)
United Kingdom *2, 4, 44, 45*

Wales *2, 15, 19, 44, 56, 60–1, 127, 138, 146, 160, 162, 172, 190*
Wapping *96*
Wash, The *61*
Washington (County Durham) *7, 109, 110, 114*
Watling Street *83*
Weald, The (see Sussex)
Wearside *58*
Welwyn *109*
West Country (see South-West)
West Midlands (see Midlands)
Westminster *79, 80, 180*
Weston-super-mare *64, 191*
Whitby *69*
Windermere, Lake *45*
Wolverhampton *91*
Workington *7*
Wytch Farm (oilfield) *177*

York, Plain of *53*
Yorkshire *18, 19, 50, 51, 52, 67, 128, 138–9, 140*
Yorkshire Dales *50, 118*

Index of topics

Agglomeration *126, 135, 151*
Agribusiness (see agriculture)
Agriculture *27–41, 68*
Agricultural revolution *18*
Airports *203–5*
Alluvium *11*
Aquifer *55, 56*
Assisted Areas *161*

Balance of payments *21.3*
Barrows *15*
Basalt *3*
Biomass *189*
Bronze Age *15*
Butter *32*

CAP (see Common Agricultural Policy)
Carboniferous rocks *11*
CBD (see Central Business District)
Celts *15*
Central Business District *78, 101–4*
Chalk *49, 55*
Channel Tunnel *200, 202*
Coal *172–3*

Coal Measures *11*
Coalfields *7*
Coasts *71*
Common Agricultural Policy (of EC) *32*
Commuter-villages *116–7*
Concrete *49*
Conifers *43, 44*
Conurbations *79–99, 126*
Country Parks *65, 66*

Deciduous trees *43, 44*
De-industrialisation *123, 146–7*
Development Areas *161*

Economies of scale *134–5*
Electricity *184–9*
Enclosures *18*
Enterprise Zones *163*

Factory-farming *29*
Farming (see agriculture)
Footloose-industry *135, 150, 184*
Forestry *34, 42–47, 69*

Garden-cities *108*
Gas (see oil and gas)
Geothermal power *190*
Glass *52*
Granite *49*
Green belts *76, 91, 108–9*
Gross National Product *1*

Heavy industry *125*
Hedgerows *27*
HEP (see Hydro-electric power)
Hill-farm (case-study) *34–7*
Hill-forts *15*
Hinterlands *101*
Hi-tech industries *111, 149*
Hydro-electric power *34*
Hypermarket (see superstores)

Ice Age *10*
Igneous rocks *11*
Industrial inertia *135–6*
Industrial revolution *7, 11, 125–6*
Industry *122–169*
Industrial revolution *7, 11, 125–6*

Index

Invisible exports 213
Iron and steel 127, 136–7

Leisure 64–75
Leisure-society 165
Limestone 49, 52, 55, 70
Luddites 129

Market-gardening (case-study) 38–9
Metamorphic rocks 11
Mining and quarrying 48–53
Moorlands 44, 67–8
Motor-vehicle industry (case-study) 141

National grid 184, 189, 190
National Parks 65
Nationalisation 137, 165
Neolithic Age 15
New Towns 91, 108–9
Nuclear-power stations 184, 186–8

Oil and gas 49, 176–183
Open-fields 18

Paper 43, 45, 52
Peak land-value intersection 101
Pedestrianisation 102–3
Pedestrian precincts 103
Physical environment 10–14
Pollution 59

Population 15–25
Population pyramid 21
Ports 203–5
Potash 49, 70
Precipitation 55
Primary activity (see agriculture, mining and quarrying)
Privatisation 165–7

Railways 80, 200–2
Rationalisation of industry 134
Regional policy 160
Resort-towns 21, 22, 64
Roads 49
Rural areas 19, 26
Rural-urban shift 19

Sand and gravel 49, 52, 70
Sandstone 55
Secondary activity (see industry)
Second-homes 117
Sedimentary rocks 11
Settlement, types of 76–8
Shopping 100–7
Soil 45, 55
Soil erosion 27
Solar power 190
Special Development Areas 161
Steel-making 52
Stone Age 12

Subsidies 32
Substitute costs 134
Suburbs 86–8
Sunrise industries (see hi-tech industries)
Superstores 104–5

Tarns 45
Telecommunication 206–9
Terrace-ribbing 86
Tidal power 191
Timber (see forestry)
Tourism 213
Tower-blocks 89–90, 93
Transport 133, 196–211
Trees (see forestry)

Unemployment 164–5
Urban development 49, 79–121
Urban models 78

Villa-studding 86–88

Water-supply 54–63
Wave-power 191
Wind-power 190
Woollen-industry 18